1977

MUSIC IN BALI

Da Capo Press Music Reprint Series

GENERAL EDITOR
FRANK D'ACCONE
University of California at Los Angeles

MUSIC IN BALI

*A Study in Form and Instrumental Organization
in Balinese Orchestral Music*

by

COLIN McPHEE

with photographs by the author

DA CAPO PRESS · NEW YORK · 1976

Library of Congress Cataloging in Publication Data

McPhee, Colin, 1901-1964.
  Music in Bali.

  (Da Capo Press music reprint series)
  Reprint of the ed. published by Yale University Press,
New Haven.
  Bibliography: p.
  Discography: p.
  1. Music—Bali (Island) 2. Gamelan. 3. Musical
instruments—Bali (Island) I. Title.
[ML345.B3M25 1976]   781.7'598'6   76-4979
ISBN 0-306-70778-0

MUSIC IN BALI

MUSIC IN BALI

A Study in Form and Instrumental Organization

in Balinese Orchestral Music

by COLIN McPHEE

with photographs by the author

New Haven and London, Yale University Press, 1966

Foreword

COLIN MCPHEE has given us a long-needed comprehensive survey of Balinese music, accurately detailed in its descriptive treatment and analysis of music and musical forms and complete in its presentation of different orchestral methods employed by the Balinese gamelan. For those who have come to know and love the island of Bali—a paradise in the world of the arts, where the creative genius of countless musicians, dancers, and artists has made beauty a way of life—McPhee has long been recognized as the most qualified and sensitive spokesman. The rich and ancient heritage of Hinduism has persisted in modern Bali as a robust panoply of religious festivals and holidays, practiced by a truly communal society in which the cultivation of the arts is as important as the cultivation of rice. Perhaps no other society in the world today knows such a complete integration of religion and social living. Studies by the anthropologist and ethnologist, by the historian and the social scientist, have shown us that it is indeed difficult to achieve an accurate statement of the configuration of Balinese society. The abstract nature and symbolism of music and dance and their inseparable relationship to the expression of religious faith represent one of the least accessible and most significant areas of study. This contribution by Colin McPhee, therefore, stands not only as an invaluable document among the few reliable treatises of the diverse musical cultures of the world but also as a warm testimonial to a creative people unique in the field of human relations.

The achievement of such a magnum opus did not come about casually. This work represents more than thirty years of experience, love of subject, and devotion to detailed observations and study. During the decade of the 1930s, when Colin McPhee as a young composer built his *House in Bali*, this island was virtually untouched by the tarnishing hand of tourism. Through the troubled years of World War II, the revolutionary period, the aftermath of reconstruction, and up to the present economic crises of guided democracy, the artistic vigor of Bali has continued to flourish. However, growth, evolution, and change are the order of an artistic world; and in the 1930s McPhee, realizing that some of the older forms of gamelan were dying out, meticulously described these traditions, transcribed the music, and even, through his own enthusiasm, rekindled the interest of the Balinese themselves.

In the fall of 1961, he joined the faculty of the Department of Music and the Institute of Ethnomusicology at UCLA. That same fall Tjokorda Mas, from Ubud, and Wajan Gandera, from Pliatan, began a two-year period of residence at the Institute in order to train American and foreign students in the performance of the Balinese gamelan. During that time McPhee worked frequently with the two Balinese and, to their delight, was able to reconstruct musical styles of gamelans which are no longer extant in Bali today. They in turn were able to demonstrate the latest developments in gamelan style. During that time McPhee was teaching, among other things, a course on the music of Indonesia and several times held a special seminar on the compositional techniques of Balinese music. In this sustained period of interest and activity from the early thirties, McPhee remained, for the Balinese musician, one tangible link with the Western world. In 1958, when I was privileged to purchase a fine gamelan for UCLA, I was assured by several musicians whose opinion had been sought that this was an excellent set of instruments because its tuning system was the very one which McPhee liked.

During the fall semester of 1963 Colin McPhee resigned from the University to devote the few remaining weeks of his life to the completion of this book. Continuing under great difficulty to give attention to every detail, he completed the work, but died before seeing the final page proof.

This is a book which could have been written by only one man—a sensitive composer with a deep musicological interest, a man whose musical ear and musical integrity could not be content with a superficial examination. How very few composers in the Western world have afforded themselves the considerable time and profound experience of learning to comprehend another musical language! For the Western composer, performer, and teacher of music, Balinese music is here described in its own terms and clearly evaluated and explained. For the humanist, the social scientist, and the anthropologist, McPhee has placed Balinese music within the proper context of society. For present and future generations of Balinese musicians *Music in Bali* will stand as a record of their most sacred heritage—as it has been in the recent past, as it is in the present, and as it probably will be in the future.

MANTLE HOOD

Los Angeles, California
January 1964

Acknowledgments

FOR THE PREPARATION of this book I am grateful to the J. S. Guggenheim Foundation for a Fellowship, the Bollingen Foundation for a publication grant, Columbia University for an Alice H. Ditson grant, to the Institute for Intercultural Studies for Benedict and Quain grants, and to Yaddo, where writing was first begun in 1942. It is impossible to name and thank sufficiently the many Balinese friends—musicians, dancers, actors and scholars—who so generously contributed their time and enthusiasm to my work in Bali, and without whose cooperation the present book could not have been written. For further collaboration in the field I have to thank Gregory Bateson, Jane Belo, Raoul Goris, R. Morzer-Bruyns, the late Walter Spies, and the late William Stutterheim. For continued support and encouragement in preparing this book I am deeply indebted to the late Ruth Benedict, Aaron Copland, Sidney and Henry Cowell, at whose house at Shady, N. Y., many pages were written, Marian Eames, who gave much time and thought to editing my study, "Dance in Bali," for the last issue of *Dance Index* (1948), George Herzog, Mantle Hood, Jaap Kunst, who urged me to undertake this work, Minna Lederman, who in 1935 published my first article on Balinese music in *Modern Music*, Carleton Sprague Smith, and Virgil Thomson. Thanks are due Carl A. Rosenthal, whose copying of the music examples was accomplished with skill and intelligence, and to Shirley J. Hawkins for her patient work in the final stages of the enterprise. C. Arthur Smith, of Westcott & Thomson, Inc., guided the book through the complex production process with resourcefulness and diligence. And finally, I am forever indebted to Margaret Mead, both for help in the field and for her sympathy and special interest in the present book, patiently reading and advising on the manuscript over a long period of time.

Thanks are also due The John Day Company for permission to include certain pictures from *A House in Bali* and *A Club of Small Men*.

C. McP.

Contents

Note on Orthography and Pronunciation

Modern Indonesian spelling is used in place of the former Dutch system. Thus oe is replaced by u, j by y, dj by j, and tj by ch.

Pronunciation:

a as in *bath*	final i as *ee*
final a as in *America*	o as in *dog*
e as in *the*	ō and final o as in *so*
é as ay in *bay*	u as in *boot*
è as in *bet*	èr as *air*
i as in *bin*	ge as in *gun*

The plural of Balinese nouns is generally indicated by an additional *s*, but for sake of euphony the *s* is dropped in compound names; e.g., gamelans, but *gamelan gong*, which may mean one or more gamelans of the type known as *gong*.

When the word *gong* is italicized in the text it refers to a special form of gong known by that name in Bali. Otherwise it is used in the accepted Western sense, and indicates any Balinese instrument belonging to the gong family. Balinese terms are italicized throughout the text, except in the musical examples.

Introduction

THE PRESENT BOOK is a composer's account of music in Bali, the small island of the Indonesian Republic to the east of Java, as it was practiced in the decade preceding World War II. It is primarily an account of instrumental music and the many different forms of instrumental ensembles, ancient and modern, to be found in Bali at the time. Most of these survive today, despite the changing Indonesian scene, furnishing music throughout the year for the many religious rites and popular celebrations that crowd the Hindu-Balinese calendar of festivals. The present study is based on notes and musical material collected in the years I lived on the island, off and on, from 1931 to 1939.

At that time little was known about Bali. I had been drawn to Indonesia by the chance hearing of some recordings which a friend had brought back from the East. Some of these were popular songs and stylized episodes from traditional plays, sung or declaimed to the soft rhythmic accompaniment of unfamiliar percussion instruments. Most enchanting, however, to a young composer in search of new sounds were the recordings of the gamelan, the Indonesian orchestra composed primarily of tuned bronze gongs of many sizes and shapes, various forms of metallophones, little cymbals, and hand-beaten drums. The Balinese recordings in particular had a polyrhythmic complexity, an animation and metallic shimmer, like nothing I had ever heard. Nothing would satisfy me but to hear this music at its source.

I originally planned to spend a few months in Java and Bali, and then go on to Southeast Asia where, in Burma, Thailand, Cambodia and Laos, instrumentally related but considerably smaller orchestras were to be found. But the Balinese field turned out to be so rich and varied that I found I could not leave, and what started out as a simple exploration trip ended in the building of a house on the island, and a more or less continuous residence there until the end of 1938.

The musical situation at that time was unbelievable. With a population of approximately one million, for the most part crowded into the central part of this small island of 2,905 square miles, there were literally thousands of active music clubs and dramatic societies. Here, miraculously coexisting in time, was a wealth of ancient and recently developed orchestras, from archaic and rarely played sacred ensembles to the large and highly perfected modern gamelan created primarily for diversion. A few of the remaining palaces still maintained large orchestras for ceremonial occasions, and a village was poor indeed that did not possess at least one gamelan to play for temple festivals. I soon found that the word gamelan could mean an orchestra of some forty players or a small ensemble of four or five. Some fifteen different types of ensemble were in use at the time. In addition to the large gamelan of gongs and metallophones heard everywhere there were little orchestras of xylophones, ensembles of flutes and antique percussion instruments, ensembles composed entirely of great iron-keyed metallophones, and ensembles in which the different timbres of bamboo, wood, and bronze were combined. Here was a rich storehouse of new resonances and instrumental methods waiting to be explored. Each ensemble had its own particular scale form and musical repertory and its special place in supplying music for ritual, dance, or drama.

The 1930's were marked by unusual musical activity throughout the island, and represented a period of transition in Balinese musical history. Much new music was being created by young Balinese composers who showed a bold disregard for the confining restrictions of traditional musical form. Striking new orchestral effects, impossible to obtain in the older gamelans, were a feature of the newer music, further distinguished by its restless exuberance and sudden and dramatic changes of mood. At the same time the classical repertories, of unknown age and authorship, impressive in their architecture, melodic breadth, restraint, and formal unity, were rapidly disappearing. Older gamelans constructed with a seven-tone scale were being abandoned altogether in favor of the popular ensemble of five or even four tones. With no adequate system of notation to preserve them, many of the older repertories had survived through oral tradition alone. These could be lost overnight with the death of a leading musician or the disbanding of a group. By the end of the thirties the ensemble known as the *gamelan Semar Pegulingan*, dedicated to Semar, god of Love, and once the elegant recreational orchestra of the courts, had all but vanished. The imposing *gamelan gong gedé*, the great ceremonial orchestra of the palace and temple, was to be found only in far-off hill villages where the old style of music was still preferred, and was replaced everywhere else by the more modern gamelan known as the *gong kebyar*.

To try to preserve in some form of record this period in Balinese music, while older styles and methods survived, became my one desire. At that time there was no adequate field equipment to be had for recording such elaborate music as that of the Balinese gamelan, and I realized I must rely on staff and cypher notation alone. There were still available a small number of recordings made in Bali in the late 1920's by the German companies, Odeon and Beka, but these were for the most part no more than three-minute excerpts, priceless for their documentary value, but unable to give any true idea of the wider continuity of the music.[1] Prior to this, in 1925, the Dutch musicologist Jaap Kunst, who was later to publish many intensive studies of Indonesian music, had written his book dealing with Balinese music, *De Toonkunst van Bali*. This richly documented but purely introductory work has yet to be translated into English. It offers a valuable outline of Balinese music at the time, but is largely devoted to a musicological discussion of Javano-Balinese instrumental scales, their origin and evolution. The theory that these, along with a large number of related Eastern scales, derive in structure from the same source as the scales of ancient China, which is based on the famous theory of blown fifths developed by von Hornbostel, is maintained by many musicologists. Others are inclined to reject it. Whatever their ancient origin, there is no final standard in Bali today for instrumental scale formation. The two leading scale systems of Java, *pélog* and *sléndro*, prevail in Bali, although not generally distinguished by these names. They are, however, interpreted with great leeway. No two gamelans are tuned exactly alike, and deviation can be great. Each gamelan creates its own individual tonal world. Some seem

---

[1] The masters to these have long since been lost. Many were destroyed under the Hitler regime. A few were reissued at one time by Decca but even these are now unavailable. Eighty-four titles from my collection of records obtained in importing firms and small shops of Bali and Java have been copied on tape and deposited in the Record Archives of the Institute of Ethnomusicology at the University of California, Los Angeles (see Appendix 6).

to approach the Western tempered system in their tuning, but others veer away in fascinating, exotic intervals.

In spite of this lack of standardization, and in spite of the basic differences of intonation between Western and Eastern scales, I resolved to write the present book, documented by musical examples in Western notation, in hopes that an account based on actual musical practices might contribute to the record begun by Kunst. The problem of scales and tuning should not be allowed to stand in the way of a report on the music itself and the unusually active part it plays in Balinese life.

There is a sufficiently accurate way of defining the intonation and interval structure of any scale. The tones of the scale may be expressed in figures which give the number of their vibrations per second, while the distances between these tones are measured in terms of *Cents*. The *Cent* is equal to a one-hundredth part of the equal-tempered semitone. 50 *Cents* thus describes a quarter-tone; 100 *C.* a semitone; 150 *C.* a three-quarter tone; 200 *C.* a whole tone; 700 *C.* a fifth; 1200 *C.* the octave. This method makes possible the immediate comparison of the intervals of exotic scales, both with each other and in relation to Western tempered tuning. It is thus possible to compare different gamelan tunings of any form of Balinese scale.[2]

The vibration figures of the different scales were obtained through the use of the monochord.[3] Various tunings of each are given, not in support of any theory, but as evidence of the considerable changes in interval structure of what is considered to be the same scale which can occur with different gamelans. Placed side by side for comparison, they demonstrate, not the final structure of any scale type, but rather the freedom with which it is interpreted in actual practice. Thus the musical illustrations in the following chapters should always be considered with the respective tunings given in Chapter 7 in mind. For the Westerner used to the security of standardization it is startling to learn that in Bali, as in Java, the same compositions can be played in what we should consider quite different scales, but which turn out to be, in actual practice, no more than modified tunings.

The musical illustrations have been selected from material I obtained during performances, at rehearsals, or through private instrumental dictation. Structurally, Balinese musical forms are based on repetition. The longer, more elaborately planned compositions in classical form consist of a series of melodic sections of different length, each of which is repeated a number of times—generally three or four for the longer and more for the shorter. Many compositions are based on the ostinato form, in which a brief motif or short melodic unit is repeated indefinitely, forming a simple background for constantly changing drum continuity. Thus it was possible to transcribe material during actual performance, correcting and filling in notations with each repeat. Most Balinese orchestral music is an instrumental

---

[2] Distances in terms of *Cents* can be computed from the vibration numbers of any two tones by means of a logarithm table—a simple but time-consuming process. The system was developed by the English pioneer in ethnomusicology, Alexander J. Ellis (1814-90), and completed with the publication of Erich von Hornbostel's logarithmic table in 1921. The operation is described in Grove's *Dictionary of Music and Musicians*, 2, 718 (see "Interval"), and also in "Comparative Musicology and its Methods," in Curt Sachs' *The Rise of Music in the Ancient World, East and West* (New York, Norton, 1943). The most complete exposition of the system can be found in Jaap Kunst's brochure, *Ethnomusicology* (The Hague, Martinus Nijhoff, 1959).

[3] A simple instrument for pitch measurement still considered satisfactory in field work. It is described in Kunst's *Ethnomusicology*.

development of simple nuclear melody, slow in tempo and regular in beat, which is performed in unison by one section of the gamelan. This could be noted as fast as it was played and was of great value for future reference. Many complete compositions were later constructed, with or without Balinese aid, from nuclear melodies obtained this way.

Much was learned, especially regarding modern stylistic methods, through repeated attendance at the rehearsals of a young and eager group intent on technical perfection, where difficult passages would be repeated again and again. During rest periods we would discuss some technical detail, and the musicians were always happy to demonstrate, with charming patience, the complexities of a particularly complex passage.

I also obtained material from musicians who came to my house in Sayan, a small village in the hills of Gianyar district. Here I had a Steinway grand piano, a musical wonder on which small boys from the village delighted to improvise polyrhythmic duets, their surprisingly keen ears quickly leading them to approximated Balinese scales. Musicians from near and far left their instruments at the house, which became a kind of musical conservatory. In spite of sometimes harsh differences in tuning, my early experiments in transcribing directly from gamelan instruments to piano developed into an abstract and useful method of recording. Dictating musicians soon adjusted their ears and were quick to point out errors in passages played back. The system worked two ways, for it was also possible for me to note and point out changes, intentional or accidental, in passages replayed by the dictating musicians.

The older style music was obtained principally in remote villages where some ancient form of gamelan was still in use. For a small sum I could engage the musicians to go through and repeat their traditional repertories of ceremonial music. Exclamations of pleased surprise would be heard from the men when, after noting some nuclear melody the first time it was played, I sat down at an instrument to play it along with them on the repeat. Work was always a pleasure. Even in the most isolated villages information was given willingly, and rare musical manuscripts of palmleaf were generously offered for my inspection and sometimes even copied at my request.

I owe much to the musicians of three different gamelans I organized in Sayan, both for observation and for pleasure. They practiced nightly at my house, learning music of different styles from teachers I called from all parts of the island. The first gamelan, a xylophone ensemble known as the *gamelan gandrung* or *jogèd* was formed to accompany the dance lessons and practice periods of I Sampih, a small boy living at my house, who was learning the popular street dance known as *gandrung*.[4] Later, the old and beautiful instruments of a *gamelan Semar Pegulingan* were loaned to me by Anak Agung Mandera of Pliatan, and a second group of musicians was organized for the specific purpose of reviving forgotten recreational music of the courts. The last, a special four-tone ensemble known as the *gamelan angklung*, heard at all village festivals, was made up entirely of small boys aged five to nine, something unheard of in Bali at the time. Only two of these children had any previous musical experience. Various teachers were engaged, in order that the group might learn

---

4 Twenty years later, a star dancer, Sampih accompanied the gamelan of Pliatan village which toured Europe and America during the season 1952–53 under the direction of Anak Agung Gedé Ngurah Mandera. He was brutally murdered shortly after his return to Bali.

both old and new style music. Alert and enthusiastic, the youngsters practiced nightly with devotion; within a year they had mastered a difficult repertory and had become a functioning orchestra in village and temple ceremonies.[5]

I owe even more to the many Balinese friends made through a common interest in music. Foremost of these was I Lotring from the little fishing village of Kuta, a composer and dance teacher who was known throughout the island for his many-sided musicianship and original musical style. I owe much of my acquaintance with forgotten court music to I Lunyuh, an old man with an amazing memory who thirty years before had been a leading musician at the court of Payangan, a few miles north of Sayan. For over a year he trudged twice a week to my house, to play for me on the *trompong* the old ceremonial music of the *gamelan gong* and to teach the members of the *Semar Pegulingan* gamelan the lovely melodies and elegant style of an orchestra they had never heard. There was the Anak Agung of Saba, an impetuous young noble with an enthusiasm for both cockfighting and the arts, who painted his own dramatic murals, trained his own dancers, and led the musicians of his gamelan at breakneck speed with his tense, dynamic drumming. There were the countless youths and small boys from gamelans all over the island, always ready to sit down and play some melodic fragment or ornamental passage. And there was Madé Lebah from the Pliatan gamelan, a young man famed for his drumming and *gendèr* playing, who drove my car, helped train and sometimes composed music for the three Sayan gamelans, and who introduced me to out-of-the-way villages whose music I should otherwise never have discovered.

I have often been asked if, with no musical notation before them, Balinese musicians ever play a piece the same way twice. Is their performance not essentially improvised? This shows a complete misunderstanding of gamelan organization. Other than in solo parts there can be no place for spontaneous improvisation where all component parts are doubled by two, four, six, or more instruments. Unison in the different parts must prevail or utter confusion results. While different gamelans may play the same composition differently, each must always play its own version as learned at rehearsal. This, of course, does not mean that all performances are note perfect. Individual mistakes occur from time to time, but the main line is firmly held by the ensemble as a whole.

In considering the musical examples, a distinction should be made between solo and unison passages. The solo is never the final melodic version, for here the performer is free to take certain liberties in the way of embellishing tones or retarding a melodic tone. The unison passage, on the other hand, has concrete finality. It is something worked out. It exists in the minds of the musicians as clearly as though it were read from a printed page. Like the composition itself, it can only be changed at rehearsal, when some other pattern may be substituted.

Metric signatures and bar lines have been used arbitrarily to break the material into visual units of convenient size. For the sake of visual clarity, the sixteenth-notes of a 4/4 unit are usually divided into groups of four, using tied notes where needed to express syncopations,

---

[5] For a detailed account of what turned out to be a most amusing project, see "Children and Music in Bali" by the author in Mead and Wolfenstein, *Childhood in Contemporary Cultures* (Chicago, 1955).

although in many cases it would have perhaps been better to express the patterns in terms of 3 plus 5, or 3 plus 3 plus 2, etc., after the Indian system of counting *tala*, to which they often seem rhythmically related. In some cases this has been done, to call attention to some pronounced counter-rhythmic pattern. Balinese, however, feel a basic quadruple beat too strongly, as shown by the various and periodically regular forms of gong punctuation, to justify the consistent breaking down of secondary patterns into continuously irregular units.

To indicate the single repeat of a melodic section or period and the far more frequent multiple repeat, the following two symbols have been employed:

‖: :‖   single repeat

‖: :‖   multiple repeat

Unless otherwise stated in the example, the *fermata* symbol, ⌢ , does not indicate a tone held beyond its normal length but is used to mark the final or closing tone of a melodic section or complete composition.

This volume is by no means a complete record of musical activity in Bali during the thirties. Devoted primarily to instrumental music, it does not take into account various performances such as *jangèr*, a form of revue made up of Balinese popular songs, acrobatic skits, and scenes from *arja* plays, or the *kèchak* male chorus, today an entertainment mainly for tourists but formerly used to accompany ritualistic trance dances known as *sanghyang*. The various styles of chanting classical poetry have also been passed over, forming as they do material for a separate study.

For a Westerner, the special musical gift of the Balinese is most tellingly expressed instrumentally. With their growing interest in complex orchestral interplay and love for lavish, percussive sound, Balinese musicians have kept a restricted musical style intensely alive and glowing. One has only to listen to the many hybrid forms of music prevalent throughout the East today to wonder at the continuation of a purely Balinese music which, like the dance, still remains free of outside influence. This was evident as late as 1957, when the *gamelan gong* and dancers from Tabanan made their appearance in the United States. While we may lament the complete and unrecorded disappearance of the gamelans of the former courts, still we value indeed the musical creativity carried on in the villages. Narrow as the tonal frame of five- and four-tone scales may seem, for imaginative Balinese musicians the resources of their traditional scale systems still seem to be inexhaustible.

Part One: Music in Balinese Life

Chapter 1

The Balinese Scene

FROM A MUSICIAN'S viewpoint Bali is the ultimate happy island where music, dance, and drama are not only loved by all but play a most important part in daily life. In ceremonies of the temple and the village music is as necessary as incense, flowers, and offerings. The festive note may often sound confused, since it is not unusual for several gamelans to assemble within the temple courts for different events. From time to time they mingle in a lavish splendor of clashing tonalities, resounding simultaneously in different keys and at different speeds. The final aim of any celebration is that there be *ramé*, exuberant noise and festive crowds.

In the years I lived on the island the air was constantly stirred by musical sounds. At night hills and valleys faintly echoed with the vibrant tones of great bronze gongs. By day drums thundered along the roads to the clash of cymbals as chanting processions of men and women carried offerings to the far-off sea or followed tall cremation towers to the village cremation grounds. From rocky streams rushing down from the mountains rose the languid, nasal singing of bathers; while in terraced rice fields birds were frightened off by the rhythmic clacking of little windmills or the moaning hum from tall bamboos, converted into Aeolus flutes by every breeze. During the month of winds great kites, each furnished with a vibrant strip of bamboo, throbbed in wiry chorus. Small bells were attached to oxen yokes, weavers' shuttles, pony carts, and to the necks of domestic pigeons, along with tiny whistles, which made shrill music as the flocks wheeled above the trees. And in the few palaces that still maintained some degree of former splendor, firecrackers at sunrise accompanied the golden outburst of ceremonial music by the palace gamelan, heralding a day of celebration.

Today villages continue to ring with music through the night as absorbed audiences follow the performance of some dance drama or shadowplay, while in the musicians' club-houses men meet four or five evenings a week to practice newly learned compositions or rehearse some standard piece with youthful dancers still in training. Past and present merge in this small island where a way of life survives which is long since departed elsewhere in Indonesia. The explanation can be found in Bali's past.

Once part of the great Hindu-Javanese Empire that dissolved in the late fifteenth century with the spreading of Islam, Bali has since remained in cultural isolation, the one island of Indonesia practically immune even now to either Islamic or Christian conversion. The Balinese still prefer to hold firmly to their Hinduist religion and rich cultural heritage in which music, dance, and drama have always played a leading part.

The introduction of Hinduism to Bali was gradual, as it was in Java and other islands of the archipelago. Trade relations between India and Indonesia had been established as early as the first century A.D. During the next few centuries Hindu traders, followed by priests and scholars, and by princes with their retinues of craftsmen, architects, musicians, and dancers, came in increasing numbers and introduced Hindu culture to a civilization already highly developed. The following centuries saw the rise of an increasingly distinctive Indonesian-Hindu civilization which finally flourished under the Majapahit Empire of east Java in the thirteenth and fourteenth centuries. This was the golden age of Indonesian artistic achievement. Hinduism had been well assimilated and a highly individual culture had reached its peak.

During the Majapahit Empire, Bali was sometimes a vassal state, sometimes free. Hindu-Javanese culture had been introduced in previous centuries, and as Islam spread in Java more and more of the Javanese nobility, wishing to retain their Hindu religion and long-established way of life, migrated to Bali, bringing, as their Hindu ancestors had done before, their retinues of priests, warriors, and craftsmen. Most Balinese nobles and high-caste families of today are descendants of refugees from Java who arrived sometime before the final collapse of the Majapahit Empire in 1478.

Bali, however, is no mere replica of medieval Java, as is sometimes claimed. It is true that many traditions remain unchanged. Newly built temples preserve the classic Hindu-Javanese architectural style. Ancient musical instruments, long since forgotten in Java, have been retained along with their equally ancient ceremonial music. Historical romances from ancient Java, and Hindu epics, condensed and given new imagery by medieval Javanese court poets, continue to supply the plots for most plays and dances. Even the lyrics for popular songs are still composed in stanza patterns of Majapahit origin.

But in both music and dance Balinese creativity has been constantly at work. Generations of dance teachers, while retaining the stylized gestures and movements, have gradually transformed the slow-moving, formal dramas of the traditional theater into swift-paced, dramatic choreographies. Music has undergone a similar transformation. One has only to compare the archaic style of the old ceremonial ensembles, the baroque elegance of the few court orchestras that survived in the thirties, with the orchestration and virtuoso performances of modern gamelans to realize the creative changes that have produced the Balinese music of today.

The difference between the music of Java and Bali is striking. With essentially the same instruments, scale systems, basic musical forms, and orchestral methods, each island produces its own style of music differing from the other in mood and color as night from day. A mystic, perfumed atmosphere surrounds the Javanese gamelan, whose soft, shockless resonance has been refined to the ultimate degree of perfection. In strong contrast the Balinese gamelan stands out dramatically in its hard, metallic vitality and the almost feverish intensity with which the newer music is performed. In spite of prolonged isolation the Balinese have produced a music as contemporary as jazz.

The changes that took place in Bali in the early years of the present century have undoubtedly influenced the development of the modern musical style. Until the beginning of Dutch rule in 1906 Bali was divided into a number of small kingdoms across whose borders there was intermittent petty warfare. In each kingdom, the royal courts and smaller palaces of the leading nobility were cultural centers, maintaining large gamelans for ceremonies and for recreation, and frequently supporting dancers and companies of actors, along with crafts-

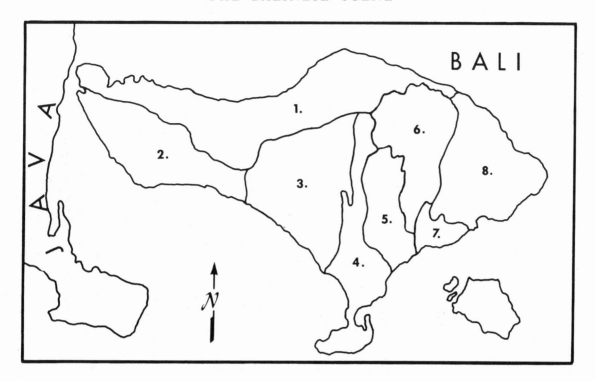

The Districts of Bali

1. Bulelèng	5. Gianyar
2. Jembrana	6. Bangli
3. Tabanan	7. Kulungkung
4. Badung	8. Karangasem

North Bali: 1. West Bali: 2, 3.   South Bali: 4, 5, 6, 7. East Bali: 8.

men who specialized in masks, puppet figures, theatrical costumes, and stone carvings. The surrounding villages, following suit according to their means, had their own less imposing orchestras and theatricals for festivals and temple ceremonies. Under Dutch rule the island was at last consolidated, and divided into eight districts, each under the guided administration of some former regional ruler. A deep cultural change now began to take place. One by one the leading palaces relinquished their traditional formality and display. Court theaters were discontinued and gamelans sold to neighboring villages or given as payment for what were once feudal services. A few lesser nobles continued to keep their gamelans and maintain dancers, but in the thirties nearly all court gamelans had become the property of village music clubs or reposed in government-run pawnshops.

Today in Bali music is above all a popular art. In most villages music clubs are lively recreational centers where training dancers and practicing music form an absorbing pastime. Standards remain high, for the basic aim of music remains unchanged—that of providing festive music and entertainment for all occasions, especially during the periodic three-day temple festivals, when the program of dances, plays, and music should be as long and varied as possible.

Chapter 2

The Village Music Clubs

THE SMALL Balinese village of the mountains and regions far off from central Bali is ordinarily a casteless community under the direction of a board of elders who meet at regular intervals to decide on village matters. The people lead quiet lives, engaged for the most part in raising rice, cassava, sweet potatoes, and maize. The village gamelan is seldom heard except during the temple festivals that take place every seven months at the time of full moon. Its chief task is to perform the traditional program of ceremonial music and accompany the simple ritual dances in the temple. For the rest of the year the instruments are stored away, the valuable bronze gongs and metallophone keys dismounted and locked up in the temple storehouse. Rehearsals are almost unknown, for the orchestral style is plain. The music itself is easy to perform and requires little technical skill.

The thickly populated lowlands of central Bali present a very different picture. The larger villages and towns are divided into *banjars*, or wards, each with its own administration, temples, gamelans, and dancers. In most villages there is at least one *puri* or nobleman's residence. In the larger towns these residences may assume the dimensions of a royal palace, but few retain their former feudal powers or cultural influence. Occasionally a well-rehearsed gamelan is still maintained for recreation and household ceremonies. Most gamelans, however, are either village or *banjar* property, or belong to organized clubs.

To be a musician or dancer and not belong to a *seka*, or club, is unthinkable. The club system sets the pattern for all village activities, from road-mending to making music. Within each *banjar* are innumerable organizations and societies, ranging from the groups for the irrigation of the rice fields or repair of the temples to the carefree Kite-Flyers' Club or *Tuak* (palm-wine) Drinkers' Association.

Along with these are the various music, dance, and theatrical organizations, some established in the unknown past, others formed in recent years. No village could possibly employ all the different types of gamelan on the island or present all the different forms of dances and plays. Some villages are noted for their traditional mask plays or their *lègong* dances, performed by three small girls. Others may be known for their preservation of the ancient *gambuh* theater or for their modernized and celebrated *gamelan gong*. But in every village will be found at least one *gamelan gong*, traditional or renovated, to perform the stately ceremonial music without which no public celebration, religious or otherwise, is complete. In addition will be found the small *gamelan bōnang*, composed entirely of gongs, which is carried in ceremonial processions, and the sweet-toned *gamelan angklung* which may also be included in processions but whose main place is in the temple. These are usually found in every *banjar* of the village, playing for *banjar* festivals and occasionally convening for some great event.

6

THE VILLAGE MUSIC CLUBS

While these three gamelans are sufficient for basic needs, most villages include various other ensembles—an orchestra of bamboo xylophones to accompany the popular *jogèd* or *gandrung* dance, the little ensemble of metallophones known as the *gendèr wayang* to furnish music for the shadowplay, the orchestra of one or two flutes and percussion to accompany the romantic operettas known as *arja*, and, if the village or *banjar* is sufficiently prosperous, a large gamelan to accompany the *lègong* dance, contribute music to the temple, and play for other forms of theatrical entertainment. In addition, here and there, a village will include an ancient and sacred ensemble such as the *gambang*, to play special music during the rites preceding cremation. These supply ritual music not only for their own villages but also for other villages in the district.

The club is largely a male organization. Musicians of the gamelan are all male, and range from the alert small boy of nine to the withdrawn elder in his fifties. The traditional plays are performed by men alone, with youths taking the few feminine roles. Modern plays include teen-age boys and girls for the romantic parts and a few older men for heavier roles.

Modern music and theatrical clubs that depend on frequent rehearsal to bring their performances to the desired perfection are well organized, with a clubhouse and a system of graded fines for absence from practice or failure to show up at a performance. Repeated absence may bring about expulsion. The club includes not only the active musicians of the gamelan but an almost equal number of followers to carry and look after the instruments, repair the quickly worn-down mallets used for striking the metallophone keys, and arrange the mats at a performance. Dramatic clubs consist not only of actors, dancers, and musicians but also include a leading coach, costume makers, and make-up specialists.

Few clubs make any profit, except from tourists. Services to village festivals are given free. Engagements outside the village are generally paid in food and refreshments, small gifts for all, and a token sum of money. Most of the club members earn their living as farmers, fishermen, or craftsmen. In the larger towns they may work as chauffeurs, bus drivers, or perhaps as clerks in civil service. Money received by the club from engagements, together with membership dues, is reserved for the upkeep of the gamelan, new costumes, and perhaps for engaging some renowned teacher to create a new composition or choreography for the club. Any money remaining at *galungan* time, the ten-day festival that recurs every seven months, is used up in the club's periodic barbecue feast.

The more professional and better paid clubs invest their money in coconut or rice plantations and divide the profits at regular intervals. Star dancer and minor musicians share alike; attendant members receive dividends on a calculated smaller scale. But whether they are financially well off or not, most clubs spend lavishly on the upkeep of their instruments and costumes. Club members whose normal daily fare is rice accompanied by greens and a bit of dried fish still manage to raise funds for lacquer and goldleaf imported from China to regild the gamelan, the towering headdresses of the dancers, and their richly ornamental costumes. Mallet handles and the poles that support the larger gongs are often decorated with bands of thinly beaten silver, while the elaborate and fragile crowns of the small *lègong* dancers are sometimes fashioned from sheets of beaten gold. All this, however, is in the best court tradition of the past. For the Balinese audience theatrical glitter is as necessary to the finished performance as the perfected dance and music.

The thatched rehearsal pavilion of the gamelan club engaged in training new dancers or practicing its repertory is always open to the passerby who may pause to watch a dance lesson in progress or listen to the musicians as they rehearse. The young dancers are generally trained during the day, with only a few essential instruments to accompany them. Most clubs meet in the evening after the day's work, to practice or learn new music, or to rehearse with the dancers when they have finally mastered some choreography. Not all clubs have dancers, however. Many devote themselves to music alone, partly for pleasure, partly to keep their repertory of compositions to be played on festive occasions or at some great gamelan competition. But for most clubs music, especially the recently composed music, is somehow incomplete when played without dance to give meaning and glamor to the performance.

It is in watching these nightly rehearsals of the gamelan, when different sections are practiced separately and individual passages singled out to be gone through alone, that the real secret of gamelan organization is revealed. The music is often intricately polyphonic; the methods of even the smallest ensemble are complex. The full range of the larger gamelans can extend over seven octaves, from the lowest gong to the top note of the smallest metallophone, and the orchestral effect of the modern gamelans is lavishly elaborate. Yet no separate part in itself represents real technical problems. The gamelan is broken down into separate instrumental groups, each with its own particular function which remains the same from one composition to the next. Once learned, any instrumental technique becomes automatic. The complex structure of the entire ensemble is thus composed of various interdependent units, each incomplete in itself but all integral to the last note in creating the total orchestral effect. As in all other Balinese group activities, each man has his own assignment on which he can concentrate, with no one assignment exacting enough to fatigue, thus maintaining the final effect of undying vitality.

This basic principle for gamelan organization is realized in many different ways, according to the type of ensemble. In the older gamelans the orchestral style is so simple that rehearsals are barely needed. In modern ensembles the component parts are elaborated, partly through wider instrumental range, partly through more intricate rhythmic interplay between the instruments. Yet, in spite of the increasingly higher speed at which much of the music is performed today, technical difficulties do not increase proportionately. The main problem is still one of good ensemble playing, attained through constant practice.

The club of long standing is kept vigorous by the addition from time to time of youthful new members, eager to learn the more animated, complicated parts, and the gradual dropping out of older members. Newcomers already have some conception of instrumental technique, for they have been in and out of the clubhouse since early childhood and have been allowed to try out the instruments by themselves. Children have seen dances and heard music since before they could walk. No audience is complete without its front row of youngsters who line the edges of the stage clearing like birds along a telegraph wire. They sit among the musicians during a performance and even in the middle of a phrase a father will often pass the hammer with which he was playing to the small boy in his lap.

New compositions are learned from a teacher through melodic dictation, phrase by phrase, with each phrase repeated until a complete melodic section has been memorized. The ornamental parts are patiently worked out in the same way. Learning a new composition may take the group a month. Only after another month of practice will the music really begin to flow. The ease and rhythmic precision desired by all before playing the piece in public may not be reached before several months have passed. Music to accompany dramatic choreographies such as *lègong* presents further problems and may take even longer before the perfect coordination of phrase, accents, and tempo changes with the gestures and movements of the dancers has been attained.

Yet learning is a pleasure from the start. Without the drudgery of having to learn a notation, a musical satisfaction is experienced from the very beginning. From the outset musicians can concentrate on complex rhythms, changes of dynamics and precision of ensemble. While one club plays with brilliant intensity, allowing the swiftly moving music to rise and fall with dramatic turbulence, a club two villages away will perform the same music with cold precision or even indifference. Much depends on local or regional styles, on the enthusiasm of two or three leading spirits of the club, and above all the two drummers who animate the entire orchestra.

Clubs everywhere go through phases of enthusiasm and boredom. They may continue to give fine performances for years. They may disband overnight through a sudden quarrel among members or through a voted decision that they have "had enough." When this happens the instruments may be stored away, sold to some other club, or placed in the district pawnshop. With a final meeting the proceeds are divided and the *seka* is formally terminated.

Chapter 3

Music and the Temple

No BALINESE village, however small, is complete without its Temple of Origins, erected for the honoring of the village ancestral gods, and the Temple of the Dead, consecrated to Kali Durga, goddess of death and the dark forces of the underworld. In rice fields and on hilltops, in the mountains and by the sea stand innumerable temples and shrines, plain or richly carved, dedicated to Hindu gods and countless divinities of forest, lake, and stream.

For months the temples stand empty and silent, except for the occasional visit of one who would ask some favor of the gods. But once every seven months, at the time of *ōdalan*, the feast celebrating its founding, each temple suddenly blossoms with floral offerings, towers of fruits and sweets, banners, and tall white parasols. In the outer courtyard the *gamelan gong*, placed in a special pavilion, the *balé gong*, opens the three-day feast with an early morning program of ceremonial music. There is a confusion of musical sounds and those of pigs and fowl being slaughtered in the temple kitchens in preparation for the coming feast. By the time the women arrive with their household offerings the men are already engaged in preparing the various feast dishes to be eaten at noon that day.

Late that night the gods of the temple are invoked. They are invited to descend and occupy the shrines prepared for them, to share the feast and be entertained with music, dances, and plays which have been rehearsed for their special pleasure. On the last night favors will be asked for in return, after which the gods will be informed that the feast is over and politely requested to depart.

Although no two temples conduct their *ōdalan* festivals in the same way, nor will any one temple conduct its ceremonies quite the same way a second time, one basic objective forms the core of the event. Contact with the unseen gods is sought. Mediums, generally women or young girls, are brought into trance by incense smoke and chanting, to become mouthpieces for the gods, from whom advice and favors are asked. As the priest addresses the medium he is answered with words of sound counsel, of warning, or with words which may convey no meaning whatever. Complaints are sometimes heard regarding the run-down condition of the temple, the insufficient number of ritual dancers, or the need for retuning the gamelan.

In smaller villages the *gamelan gong* is sufficient to supply the main music for the festival. Most of the time it remains in the outer court of the temple where, off and on during the feast, throughout the day and late into the night, the musicians play the familiar program of ceremonial compositions. If there is no special *lègong* orchestra in the village the gamelan will be carried into the inner temple to accompany the ritual dances that mark the ceremonial opening and termination of the festival.

The slow-moving dances are beautiful in their formality and simplicity. Unlike the dance forms of the theater, these require little technical training beyond uniformity of

10

movement. They consist mainly of stylized processionals around the shrines and offerings, performed by the older women or by the unmarried girls of the village. In some villages certain dances may be performed by men or unmarried youths. Two distinct types of dance may be noted. In one the dance itself is a form of offering, a ritualistic beginning and termination of ceremonies. In the other the dancers present symbolic offerings of incense, holy water, oil, and wine, each bearing in the upheld palm of the right hand a smoking brazier, cup, or small bottle.

The theatrical events which form the entertainment part of the festival take place in the outer court or in the clearing before the temple gates. Here the people can see enacted in the form of dance or drama, mask-play or shadowplay, their favorite episodes from the ancient Hindu epics and Javano-Balinese historical romances known to all. These legends, in which gods, heroic kings, and holy men are forever engaged in the destruction of evil forces, both entertain and edify. The plays are built on episodes in which brave deeds and noble acts set an example of ideal conduct and manners, while interludes of comedy offer earthy contrast as they burlesque the ways of ordinary mortals.

While smaller villages may have to engage performers from outside, most larger communities have their own organizations to supply at least the essential entertainment. This consists, before anything else, of *baris*, a ceremonial dance by trained male dancers, which may or not include a story, and *wayang kulit*, the beloved shadowplay with stories from the *Mahabharata* and *Ramayana* which takes place at night. *Baris* and *wayang kulit* form the nucleus of the festival program that can be extended by the inclusion of many other performances— *tōpèng*, the historical mask-play dealing with the exploits of purely Balinese kings, *lègong*, with romantic or mythological choreographies, and *arja*, the popular modern singing-play.

Occasionally in place of the customary *gamelan gong* for the *ōdalan* festival some sacred ensemble of ancient instruments no longer in general use is found, such as the *gamelan gong luang* or the *gamelan selundèng*, each having its own particular form of ritualistic music. Each is proudly honored in its village as the *gamelan pusaka*, heirloom gamelan, or *gamelan peturun*, of ancient descent. Stipulated offerings, decreed at some unknown date, must be made before the instruments may be taken out, and further ones made before they may be played. How widespread these ancient ensembles may once have been no Balinese today can say. Their sacred role in earlier ritual is perhaps nowhere more clearly seen than in the mountain village of Bayung Gedé, once the possessor of a *gamelan selundèng*. Here the instruments have long ago fallen apart; no one knows what has happened to the metallophone keys, of which only two remain, still guarded along with other inherited ceremonial objects of the village temple. At the time of the *ōdalan* the keys are unlocked and formally laid among the offerings. At the appointed time the keys are held up and struck in token of the lost gamelan.

Whether they belong to some sacred heirloom ensemble or to a popular, newly assembled orchestra, all gamelan instruments, along with masks, puppets, and dancers' headdresses, are periodically purified once in thirty weeks on the day of *tumpek wayang*, dedicated to musical and theatrical paraphernalia, and blessed anew by the village priest. Musicians will not begin to play at any public performance before the customary stick of burning incense and salver of floral offerings have been laid beside the gamelan. Even at rehearsal a little offering of blossoms and incense can generally be found lying somewhere near the instruments. No

11

dancer, theatrical club, or newly formed orchestra would think of making a public debut without a preliminary *melaspasin* or consecration ceremony in the temple, accompanied by prayers for a successful performance. Music, dance, and drama retain much of their serious nature as a form of offering, and as such have an aura of holiness. The dedication of a new temple or clubhouse, weddings, or the first three birthdays of a child, are all occasions for plays and music. A community or an individual will sometimes promise to some special divinity a theatrical or musical performance in return for a granted favor.[1] The prolonged *ngaben* or rites of cremation, private or communal, are an elaborate combination of requiem ceremonies and festival program celebrating the final release of the soul. The religious rites of Balinese daily life thus continue to play a major role in keeping alive a traditional need for dance and music.

---

[1] Thus a boy in my household made a vow in the temple, which he later kept, to give an *arja* performance in the village, with a famous all-star company, if he recovered his stolen bicycle. The bicycle was recovered and the performance given. The cost of the entertainment was probably greater than the value of the lost property.

Chapter 4

Decline of the Palace

WHILE retaining certain restrictions, the Hindu caste system of subdividing the population is increasingly lightly felt in Bali. Three aristocratic classes, composing the *triwangsa* or nobility, are recognized—Brahman, Kesatrya, and Vesya. The bulk of the population, however, are commoners, sometimes referred to as Sudras or Kaulas, but more generally spoken of as *wong jaba*, "outsiders." From the Brahman class come the high priests, or *pedandas*, who officiate at great ceremonies. Far more numerous are the village priests or *pemangkus*, who come from the *jaba* class. From the Kesatryas once came the former rulers or rajas, while the Vesya class is made up chiefly of persons of princely descent. Even in the thirties the informality of the system in Bali was evident in the organization of the gamelan, where musicians from all four classes could be found united in the occupation of making music.

The greater courts of Bali once boasted of at least five different orchestras to supply ceremonial and recreational music. In the outer courtyard stood the great *gamelan gong gedé*, whose forty-odd musicians played each morning for an hour or so. Handsomely carved with dragons or baroque foliage, the instruments gleamed with lacquer and goldleaf; the resonant orchestra rang out majestically, filling the air with vibrant sound. Within the palace, in the courtyard known as the *Semarabawa*, place of Semar, the Love God, the chiming, soft-toned gamelan known as the *Semar Pegulingan*, named after Semar of the Sleeping Apartments, played in the afternoons and evenings.

Two smaller ensembles were maintained for special dramatic presentations. The *gamelan gambuh*, composed of flutes and percussion instruments, was reserved for the formal performances of the *gambuh* plays, which were given only on state occasions. The quartet of metallophones known as the *gendèr wayang* could be heard almost nightly as it played for the epic dramas of the shadowplay. For all processions of state and warring expeditions there was the *gamelan bebōnangan*, composed of gongs, cymbals, and drums. Each orchestra required specially trained musicians. Only a few were expert in all styles.

The *gamelan gong*, in addition to playing ceremonial music, was used to accompany certain performances such as *baris* and *tōpèng*. A few courts enlarged their *gendèr wayang* ensemble to accompany the *nandir* dance, performed by two trained youths and said to be the forerunner of the more recent *lègong* dance. In some courts the *Semar Pegulingan* accompanied informal performances of *léko* or *guderug*, a recreational dance in which members of the court could perform in turn with a trained girl dancer as partner.

Public performances were given in the outer court or, on more festive occasions, on the *alun-alun*, the open square before the palace. Here even the plainest farmer could watch and enjoy plays and dance-dramas performed by actors and dancers long schooled in the traditional art of stylized movement and gesture. He could admire the magnificent costumes and finely carved masks and at the same time listen to music equally glamorous in sound, performed with all the authority of traditional court style. These inspiring performances furnished the models in both method and style for the surrounding region, to be copied and adapted with varying degrees of success as court dancers and musicians found employment teaching village clubs. The best trained dancers and finest gamelans are still to be found in those villages which once came close to palace influence.

The elegant standards of court performances were partly a feudal tradition but also owed much to the direct interest and active part which Balinese princes and nobles took in dramatic and musical matters. Many appeared in plays and dances, carved their own dance masks, trained their own dancers and musicians, and directed their own gamelans with the intricate drumming that controlled all changes in tempo and dynamics. Dancing, acting, and musicianship had always formed part of the accomplishments of a noble, along with scholarship and technical skill in various crafts. To quote a passage from the *Raja Kapa-kapa*, an old Javanese treatise on the conduct of a prince:

> A man of condition should be well versed in the history of former times and the literature of his country, and know the correct mode in which each poem is chanted, as well as the way of striking the gamelan. He must know how to count the years, months, and days, and understand the *kawi* language (ancient literary Javanese). He must be clever in painting, wood-carving, gold- and iron-work, needle-work, and the making of shadow-puppets and musical instruments. He must be skilled in horsemanship and the management of an elephant, and have the courage to destroy all evil men and drive away all women of loose character.[1]

During the thirties a few princes and lesser nobles continued to appear in stage presentations, giving vivid performances in both traditional and modern style. A few still trained their own dancers, insisting on a perfection of movement, gesture, and coordination with music that held audiences literally spellbound. Others continued to carve theatrical masks of great beauty and purity of style, or painted on cloth, in the stylized and florid manner of the past, episodes from the Hindu epics presented in the shadowplay. Some continued to hold quiet evenings of reading aloud from the classics, declaiming for a few listeners the ancient Javanese texts in the formal oratorical style of the classic theater.

The large court gamelans however were a thing of the past. Only a few of the leading district palaces continued to maintain their *gamelan gong* for ceremonial occasions. Two *Semar Pegulingan* orchestras could still be heard, one at the court of Gianyar, the other at the court of Karangasem; while the court of Tabanan alone still held together its large company of *gambuh* actors and musicians. The other few remaining *gambuh* companies were kept alive in certain villages, to be engaged at the courts on occasions such as weddings and cremation rites, when their appearance still formed an important part of the program.

With changing times it was inevitable that the *gamelan Semar Pegulingan* should disappear. It was a luxury orchestra, and had not the functional importance of the *gamelan gong* which, if no longer maintained by the palace, could always be requisitioned, as it is today, from the village.

---

[1] The above slightly abridged passage is given in full in Thomas Stamford Raffles, *History of Java*, 2 vols., 1817.

DECLINE OF THE PALACE

The district palace, however, continues to celebrate important court events, along with national holidays held throughout Indonesia, with elaborate programs of music, dance, and theater. Like the temple at the time of its *ōdalan*, the palace is transformed into a festival center. Crowds gather in the square before the palace where the leading gamelans, the best dancers, and the foremost dramatic companies from nearby and distant villages have been summoned, sometimes to appear again and again in a program that may continue for days.

Chapter 5

Plays and Dances

BALINESE plays and dance-dramas are before all a stylized synthesis of formal gesture and choreography, closely coordinated with music. They are performed either as pantomime or with words which, according to the type of presentation, are either sung or formally declaimed against a musical background. The lines of all the leading characters are in *kawi*, and are given a line-by-line translation or free paraphrase in colloquial Balinese by the ever-present attendants. Classical stage conventions prevail. Even in modern plays and dances, actors and dancers still retain with remarkable fidelity the stylized postures and hand positions characteristic of the dancing figures in the stone reliefs of ancient Hindu-Javanese monuments such as the ninth century Borobudur.

In all Balinese dramatic presentations dancing and acting are so closely interwoven that it is impossible to define where one ends and the other begins. In all plays and scenes within plays which are performed with music, gestures and movements, both abstract and pictorial, are rhythmically integrated with the music, controlled and modeled by its metric form and inner phrase structure. The players have their set positions on the stage, and move or intermingle in elaborate patterns of progression. Even the recited lines, declaimed in an artificially theatrical style, are delivered in rhythmical adjustment to the musical phrase. The formalized dialogue and movements of the players combine with the music to create a remote and romantic atmosphere of legend and unreality.

While in the classical plays musical accompaniment continues throughout, modern popular versions tend to have increasingly long interludes of comedy, in which the orchestra is silent. These are the contrasting episodes of reality, wherein the characters are for the most part ordinary mortals who talk in plain everyday speech. In these plays within plays that often overshadow the main plot, one may see caricatured the village priest, the pompous official, a woman in pangs of childbirth, or the ludicrous foreigner, Arab, Chinese, Dutch, or American. The dialogue is lively and often improvised; movements are natural and realistic, often amusingly exaggerated. Formal dances may be introduced, but they are usually artful parodies. While the dancers and actors of the main episodes are clothed in glittering costumes, the characters of the comic interludes generally look as though they had stepped out of the surrounding audience.

More important performances generally take place within the *taring*, an open pavilion erected over a long rectangle that forms the stage, around which sits and stands the audience. In fine weather most performances are given in the open, with the stage boundaries marked by bamboo railings and poles festooned with flowers. At one end sit the musicians, and at the other is the stage entrance, framed by a pair of ceremonial parasols and usually concealed by a pair of closed curtains. No stage scenery is used beyond a papaya tree, which may be

16

planted in the center of the stage to represent a forest or burial ground. Plays and dances take place in the late afternoon or evening and often continue through the night.

The plays are not preserved in written dramatic form and consist of loosely connected episodes presenting the main events of the story, which can be extended or contracted at will. The tales and legends are completely familiar to all members of the audience, who know in advance the denouement to every plot. The interest and pleasure of the audience lies elsewhere—in the legendary world evoked, the style and technical finish of the performers, their physical beauty, their fine costumes, the appealing timbre of their voices when singing, and the colorful music which bathes the whole performance in sound. No one seriously minds when, in the middle of a performance that has taken two hours to get under way, rain begins to fall and the play is suddenly brought to a swift ending.

Although the well-known myths and chronicles are presented with improvisational liberty in dramatic form, they remain permanently fixed in the written literature, preserved in a wealth of classical literary forms whose poetic stanzas and epic prose are never-ending sources for actors' lines. The same legends are presented over and over again as drama or as stylized dance, or on the luminous screen of the shadowplay.

The characters of the plays are recognizable as types rather than individuals. So stylized is the formal beginning of the play, with its many danced entrances of leading characters, that it is sometimes more than an hour before the audience will have any clue as to what story is to be presented. Each character is projected through set conventions of movement, gesture, facial expression, and voice production, combined to create a special unity of personality that must be consistently preserved throughout the play. While the basic conventions allow for subtle variation in character portrayal, two basic and significant contrasting styles of dance movement and dramatic projection are distinguished—the *alus*, meaning fine, polished, and the *kras*, meaning strong, vigorous, rough. Dancers and actors specialize in one style or another, filling roles most suitable to their physical appearance. Youths and girls alike who are of delicate feature, fine-boned and naturally supple, are chosen for the *alus* parts. A more robust physique and deeper voice are needed for *kras* portrayals.[1]

The *alus* style is reserved for the gods, the heroic kings and princes who epitomize all noble qualities, and for the heroines, divine or mortal. The *alus* hero resembles Chaucer's "gentil knight" in his fine bearing, restraint, and fearlessness. On the stage he presents an ambiguous figure in the feminine grace of his movement, the delicacy of his gestures, and the stylized falsetto of his diction. His facial expression is one of fixed and smiling serenity. In mask-plays the *alus* mask is distinguished by its smallness, the narrow eyes half closed like a grain of rice, the mouth carved in a faint smile. Unmasked actors preserve this expression at all times except at moments of dramatic tension, when a sudden raised eyebrow or narrowing of the eyes to a menacing slit indicates a mounting anger.

The vigorous *kras* style is used in projecting a far wider range of characters, extending from the heroic warrior prince to demonic kings, demons, and monsters. Dance movement is

---

[1] The Middle English word "gentil" approaches the meaning of *alus* when applied to character. *Alus* describes one who is of aristocratic appearance, by nature gentle, generous, reserved, but at the same time capable of supreme heroism. The *kras* type is inferior. If a hero he is essentially impetuous and brusque. If an evil character in the theater he may be a formidable foe, or merely slow thinking and easily outwitted.

free and strong; gestures are proud or threatening, and lack the soft fluidity of the *alus* manner. The *kras* mask, which serves as model for facial expression, is marked by round bulging eyes and an arrogant mouth. With demonic characters, when it is always needed to project a supernatural role, the mask assumes a bestial expression, with long fangs carved at the corners of the now purely animal mouth. While the *kras* style can have, with heroic characters, both nobility and dramatic power, in the descending hierarchy of evil kings, sorcerers, and demons it grows increasingly brutish and fantastic.

All plays depend in essential plot on conflict between the opposing forces of good and evil—as irreconcilable on the Balinese stage as those of *Paradise Lost*. Large or small, the cast is composed of two balancing sets of kings, princes, court officials, and attendants. The dichotomy of right against left, light against darkness, lies at the heart of all these dramas. Performances presenting episodes from the *Mahabharata* are based on the continuous strife between gods and demons and the prolonged wars between the two royal houses, the rightful Pandawas and the opposing Kurawas. Plays from the *Ramayana* center around the abduction of Sita, Rama's young and virtuous wife, by the demon-king Rawana, and the battles between Rama's allies, the apes, and the demon hordes, which end in Sita's recovery. The romantic *arja* plays take as their basic theme the Cinderella or Frog-Prince motif,[2] or deal with rivalry between two brothers, *kras* Grantang and *alus* Chupak, who are in competition for the princess of Daha.[3] In the grim but beautifully presented dance-play, *Chalonarang*, the powerful sorceress by that name, protégée of Durga who rules the underworld, is finally destroyed by the more powerful magic of the great saint, Mpu Bharada.[4]

In all performances music plays an important and integrating role, thematically announcing the entrances and accompanying the entrance dances, supporting dialogue, giving background to romantic scenes, and adding rhythmic excitement to scenes of conflict. The basic repertory common to all theatrical performances is so well known that even the smallest child can tell from the music who will next emerge into view, herald or prince, lady-in-waiting or princess, comic attendant, sorceress, dragon, or magic bird.

The opening of any play is a long formality in which each of the leading characters in turn makes an entrance dance, ushered in by personal attendants. Prince is preceded by court official, who in turn must be preceded by heralds. Lady-in-waiting prepares the way for princess or heroine. Acolyte precedes saint, and apprentices of the sorceress prepare for the entrance of the witch herself in a series of preliminary dances. Thus, before two opposing characters can first confront each other, a long dance prologue in contrasting styles and varied costumes has introduced the main cast in correct order of precedence.

These entrance dances, in which the rank and nature of the character portrayed is expressed in appropriate movement and gesture, are beautiful in their long delay and stylized elegance. Each dancer entering the stage gives the impression of approaching from a long distance. For a long time the dancer remains framed in the entrance way, moving but not advancing. Only after this two-dimensional image has been established does the dancer begin a slow advance downstage, gradually emerging as a plastic figure whose movement

---

[2] As in the stories, *Chilinaya* (Pretty Naya) and *Katak Hiju* (Green Frog).
[3] See Appendix 1, the Chupak story, p. 357.
[4] See Appendix 1, the Chalonarang story, p. 358.

18

must be interesting at all angles in order to project to a surrounding audience. From time to time the main course downstage is broken by detours to right or left which trace an arc or spiral on the stage. When through, the dancer may either remain on the stage awaiting his or her superior, or retire as a new set of characters begin their series of entrances.

The closest unity exists between performer and orchestra. Movement and gesture are bound to the music through the drumming, the vital link connecting dancers with musicians. Two drums, a leader and a follower, create between them an intricate continuity of hand and finger strokes that controls the tempo of both dancers and musicians and defines the phrase structure of the melody with syncopated accents and sudden breaks. The drummers must rehearse many times with the dancers, who rely entirely on the drum continuity for direction.

While the specific drum patterns for each different form of dance are fairly stable, different districts, and even neighboring villages, have their own preferences in tempo, dynamics, and accentuation, so that no two dancers, performing the same role to the same music, move exactly alike. Star performers, engaged to appear with different companies, prefer to bring their own leading drummer and cymbal players. The musicians of the gamelan are quick to adapt and in performances such as *arja*, where the orchestra is small, no preliminary rehearsal is necessary. But in performances such as *lègong*, where the orchestra is large and the choreographies elaborate and individualized, the dancers, who depend on their own drummers, cannot move with a strange orchestra without at least one detailed rehearsal.

The motifs, melodies, and compositions identified with special characters and character types in the theater also recur again and again in musical repertories that do not accompany any stage performance. The standard repertory of the *Semar Pegulingan* gamelan consisted largely of music from the *gambuh* theater, now transferred from a small ensemble of flutes and percussion to a large gamelan of metallophones and gongs. In the repertory of the modern *gamelan gong* are many new compositions based on motifs and melodies from classical repertories, which are performed as purely instrumental music. The same melodies are frequently incorporated in short instrumental pieces for the *lègong* gamelan, which may be played as preludes before the performance begins.

The intensity and rhythmic animation with which the Balinese perform much of their music is closely related to the drama. The instrumental performance, with its sudden changes in tempo and dynamics, can be fully appreciated only through some understanding of the Balinese theater and the endless nuances of character—bright or dark, *alus* or *kras*—interpreted through the medium of gesture, movement, and music. Indeed, in listening to the performance of some modern instrumental composition one has often the impression that the musicians must have constantly in mind some imagined cast, some elaborately planned choreography with a scenario based on the conflict of left and right.

To give a complete list and description of the different dance and dramatic forms to be found in Bali during the thirties is far beyond the scope of the present work.[5]

The present study, however, with its frequent references to the Balinese stage, would be incomplete without some outline of the principal dance and dramatic forms, a summary of which will be found in Appendix 1.

---

[5] A vivid account of these is given in the book by Beryl de Zoete and Walter Spies, *Dance and Drama in Bali*, with a Preface by Arthur Waley, New York, 1958.

Part Two: The Practice of Music

Chapter 6

Musical Instruments

THROUGH the continued use in Bali today of archaic instruments and orchestras of unknown antiquity, along with their all but forgotten technical methods, a fascinating history of a musical development can be traced, ranging from the primitive ensemble of bamboo stamping-tubes (*bumbung*) to the modern gamelan of gongs and metallophones whose orchestral style is still in the process of development.

Nothing could be simpler to make or operate than the *bumbung*, still used in parts of Bali to accompany the dance sometimes performed at harvest festivals which is known as *jogèd bumbung*. The instrument consists of a bamboo tube, open at one end, closed at the other. The tube is held upright, closed end down, and pounded against a stone or plank. Used generally in a set of four of different lengths and pitch, each tube is held by a separate operator and pounded in turn to create rhythmic hocket patterns to which the dancers move (Fig. 104). By changing the order in which the tubes are pounded, variation in pitch patterns can be obtained.

In dramatic contrast to this simple rhythm ensemble stands the gamelan, composed of various types of instruments developed to exploit in different ways the resonance of bronze. The gamelan is essentially a percussion orchestra, and great care is taken in mounting the resonant material of the different instruments so that nothing may interfere with the vibration and natural duration of their tones. The larger gongs hang vertically in upright standards. The smaller, horizontally mounted gongs and gong-chimes lie on stretched cords, while all metallophone keys rest loosely upon various forms of shock absorbers or hang freely over their resonators. Depending on their size and structure, the different instruments are struck with hard or thickly padded mallets, to produce incisive or softly vibrant tones. The final result in the large gamelan is a complex blend of metallic and aerial sounds, some of which hardly seem to be of percussive origin.

In speaking of their different orchestras, Balinese make a general distinction between the "*gamelan krawang*," the gamelan in which *krawang*, bronze, forms the resonant material for the main body of instruments, and other ensembles, each of distinctive tonal color, in which iron, wood, and bamboo are used, combined or separately. Most of the musical instruments found in the various ensembles do not differ greatly in general principle from those employed in Java, though few bear the same names. Most, however, have acquired a distinctive Balinese form, while some, once known in pre-Islamic Java but long ago forgotten, have been preserved intact for special occasions in Hindu-Balinese ritual. Those instruments of bamboo that are known in Bali stem from the large and varied family of bamboo instruments found throughout the Archipelago.[1] These are the true folk instruments of Indonesia,

---

[1] For a fascinating catalogue of such instruments see W. Kaudern, *Musical Instruments of Celebes*, Ethnographical Studies in Celebes, *3* (1927) (6 vols. M. Nijhoff, The Hague, 1925-44). Many are described in the various publications of Jaap Kunst.

as opposed to the costly gongs and other instruments requiring the casting of bronze which were later developed, presumably for orchestral use in palaces and temples.

As in Southeast Asia, the actual time when bronze was first used in Indonesia in the making of musical instruments is not known. A few examples of bronze drum-gongs from the pre-Hindu era have been found in Sumatra and Java. One of enormous size is preserved in Bali at the main temple of Pèjèng, where it is guarded as a sacred relic that once fell from the moon. There is reason to believe such drums were introduced from Southeast Asia and used in connection with rain magic. Modern forms are still found today in the island of Alor, where they are used primarily as currency in the ceremonial paying off of debts and the purchase of wives.[2]

Although a considerable variety of musical instruments are to be found in Hindu-Javanese stone reliefs dating from around the eighth century A.D., there is barely a trace of those bronze instruments which compose the Balinese *gamelan krawang* of today. The greatest assortment of instruments is contained in the reliefs of the Buddhist monument, Borobudur (c. A.D. 750–850), of central Java. Here, in finely carved panels and walls depicting the life of Buddha, are many charming scenes in which musical instruments are shown in great detail. Musicians with drums, shell horns, and cymbals walk in crowded processions. Seated on the ground to accompany some dance, musicians are seen assembled in little bands in which lutes, bow harps, flutes, reed mouth organs, cymbals, and drums are combined in many ways. Bells appear in different forms—elephant bells, temple bells, jingle bells. In one panel they hang like blossoms in a tree beneath which a group of men sit conversing. One great gong may be seen suspended in a frame, as large gongs are hung in Bali today. An archaic form of xylophone is shown together with what may be a small gong, placed flat on the ground as gongs are sometimes placed in Bali. A metallophone resembling the Balinese *saron* appears elsewhere. But if ensembles of gongs and metallophones were known at the time, they were ignored in these reliefs by the recording stone carvers.

From the eleventh century on, there are occasional references in Javano-Balinese literature to musical instruments, many of which can be found in Bali today. Mention is made of various bamboo instruments which are still in use—the *kulkul*, slit drum; *chalung*, tube xylophone; *guntang*, tube zither; and *sundari*, a form of Aeolus flute. There are some references to bronze instruments. Most of the names are of Indonesian origin, although a few derive from Sanskrit. Significant as indicating the gradual instrumental conversion to bronze at that time is the use of the Sanskrit derived name, *bhèri*, originally a form of kettle drum (*bhairi*, Skt.), but now indicating a special form of gong which today, more commonly known as *bendé*, still an important instrument in the Balinese gamelan. Finally, the word gamelan, from the Javanese word, *gamel*, to handle (*gambel*, Bal.), appears in the fourteenth century historical work, *Nagara Kṛtagama*, but in a context which seems to refer to a single instrument with keys of either wood or metal.[3]

In the sixteenth century narrative, *Chalonarang*, musical instruments are referred to by the collective noun, *tabeh-tabehan*, derived from *tabeh*, to strike, thus indicating the percussive

<hr/>

[2] *The People of Alor*, Cora Dubois (Harvard University Press, Cambridge, 1960).
[3] "Kṛtawardhana (the king's father) began as an amateur to play the *gamelan*," Jaap Kunst, *Music in Java* (2 vols. The Hague, 1949) *1*, 112.

character of the instruments. A variant of this word, *tabuh-tabuhan*, a striking mallet or stick, is used in Bali today to indicate not only percussion instruments in general but also gamelan compositions, metric forms, and drum patterns collectively. *Menabuh* means to play any percussion instrument. *Menabuh gamelan* means both playing of and music by the gamelan. "*Tabuhin*," the word for "Start playing," means literally, "Strike up!"

For any further pictorial evidence of past musical activity in Indonesia we must look to the stone reliefs of the late Majapahit temples of the fourteenth and fifteenth centuries in east Java. Here, in the few glimpses offered, stringed instruments have all but vanished. Instead, gongs of various kinds appear, for the most part isolated and carried in processions, often by demons. Most interesting of these reliefs are those of Chandi Panataron, especially for their documentary representations of instruments long obsolete in Java, but found in identical form in Bali today. The strange dumbbell-shaped *réong*, long mistaken by archeologists for a kind of drum but actually a pair of small gongs mounted at the ends of a connecting crosspiece, appears four times in one panel. Four musicians are seated on the ground, the *réongs* lying across their laps. From the positions of the striking sticks in relation to the gongs we know that the men are engaged in performing interlocking polyrhythmic parts, as Balinese *réong* players continue to do today (Figs. 70, 71).

In another panel a pair of xylophones struck with forked sticks are shown twice. In their curiously irregular key arrangement and the large Y-shaped sticks used in striking the keys these unusual xylophones can at once be identified with the bamboo *bambang* that has been retained in Bali for the performance of special music played during the rites of cremation. But for any other traces of organized instrumental ensembles we may search the reliefs in vain.

In the report of his visit to the "Eylandt van Baelle" during the first Dutch expedition to the Indonesian Archipelago under Cornelius de Houtman, 1595–97, Aernoudt Lintgensz relates: "Then they held a great feast with drums, cymbals and many other instruments never seen or heard in our land." *D'Eerste Boeck* ('s-Gravenhage, 1915), another eyewitness account of the same expedition by Willem Lodewijckz, contains an illustration which shows a Javanese ensemble including four large suspended gongs (naively inaccurate however, since they resemble the Chinese flat gong), and two sets of gong-chimes. Another illustration shows two lines of dancing women, and a metallophone with bamboo resonators clearly indicated. From these accounts it is evident that by that time the gamelan had been organized in some form not too different from today, and was in use in both Java and Bali.

Excavations in central Java have yielded gongs, bells, and sets of metallophone keys of unknown age, possibly dating from the eleventh and twelfth centuries. Of later date, but still belonging to the Hindu-Javanese period are the rich finds in east Java, where gongs of all sizes, single and in tuned series, have been unearthed. It is clear that, as early Hinduism was absorbed, along with the evolution of a truly Indonesian art and culture a great change in orchestral methods took place in the centuries intervening between the building of the Borobudur and the arrival of the first Dutch expedition. By that time important instrumental development was probably at an end, although, if we may judge from Balinese activities in the thirties, modification and changes in instrumental combinations continued to be made. In the valuable descriptions, illustrations, and nomenclature of musical instruments contained in the nineteenth century accounts of Indonesia, Raffles' *History of Java* and John Crawfurd's *History of the Indian Archipelago* (3 vols. Edinburgh, 1820), most of the instruments found in the Javano-Balinese gamelan of today can be identified.

The Balinese continue to make their own musical instruments, with the exception of the large gongs, which have always been made in Java. Few if any of these large gongs are imported today. The innumerable old gongs, accumulated through the centuries and often superb in tone, are made to do. These gongs have had a long and romantic history, changing hands frequently in the past through the fortunes of regional wars, and in later days often finding their way into government-run pawnshops, to be redeemed perhaps by some newly organized village gamelan.

Instruments made from bamboo or wood such as flutes, xylophones and drums offer few problems of manufacture or availability of material. Any boy can cut for himself a jew's harp from the rib of a sugarpalm frond or make a shawm or whistle from a rice straw. But the forging of gongs and metallophone keys requires a special skill, and is the traditional craft of the *pandé krawang*, bronze smiths. These specialists are members of the time honored *pandé* guild, whose inherited occupation has always been to forge the weapons of war, work in gold, silver, or iron, and make all musical instruments in which *krawang* is used.

Krawang[4] is an alloy similar to Western bell metal, and is widely known in Indonesia. Its composition varies somewhat with the locale, but it is generally said to consist primarily of ten parts copper to three of tin. In Bali the alloy may also contain small amounts of iron, silver, and/or gold, and sometimes arsenic. The actual formulas remain the secrets of the *pandès*. *Besi*, iron, is used only for the large heavy keys of the archaic metallophones that compose the *gamelan selundèng*, an ancient ensemble mentioned in Balinese records as early as A.D. 1181, and now found only in one or two villages in east Bali. *Kunigan*, brass, is used in the manufacture of cymbals and the rack of small bells occasionally included in the gamelan.

Tiying, bamboo, as necessary a material as bronze in the making of most Balinese instruments, is used for flutes of different sizes, for slit drums, tuned rattles, xylophones, and the tube zither. Bamboo tubes furnish resonators for both xylophones and metallophones.

Kayu, wood, either teak or some equally hard wood, is sometimes used instead of bamboo for making xylophone keys. *Nangka* (jackfruit) wood is generally sought in the making of drums because of its hardness, fine grain, resilience, and durability. The large slit drums that hang in every market square are hewn from the trunks of forest trees. Wooden cowbells, such as those once seen in America, are furnished with one, two, or three clappers, and are made in all sizes, from six inches across to the cumbrous, booming thirty-inch size seen at plowing festivals.

Kulit kerbo, the hide of the *kerbo* or water buffalo, is used for drumheads and drum lacing strings, while the dried bladder (*babad*) supplies the cover to the soundbox of the *rebab* or bowed lute.

A deep earthenware jar supplies the resonator for the one-keyed xylophone that substitutes in the *gamelan jogèd*, an orchestra of xylophones, for the large gong known as the

---

[4] Known also as *gangsa*, and in Java as *gongso* or *prunggu*.

kempur. In a few remote villages coconut shells sawed open at the top have been found serving as resonators for xylophone keys (Fig. 75).

Before turning to the actual instruments and their particular use in the different game-lans, a brief outline of Balinese methods of orchestral organization is needed. The smallest instrumental combination found in Bali, known simply as the *charuk*, reduces ensemble music to the barest of essentials. Two instruments only are employed—a one-octave metallophone to sound the melody and a xylophone of similar range on which simple ornamental accompaniment is performed (Fig. 76). An expanded ensemble is found in the *gamelan arja*, a small but complete ensemble of six or seven instruments used in *arja*. Here the sung melodies are doubled or embellished by one or two flutes. The melodic line is punctuated at regular intervals by two percussion instruments of bamboo. The instrumental ensemble, along with the singers and dancers, is under the direction of a pair of drums, whose interlocking rhythmic patterns control both tempo and dynamics. Small cymbals underline the drums throughout, reinforcing them on important accents. Here in a nutshell are found the three basic elements of Balinese gamelan organization—melody, punctuation, and animation by drumming.

But in its fullest form, the large Balinese gamelan of from thirty to forty musicians is organized to sound, at different pitch levels:

a. the nuclear melody, limited to a one-octave range
b. the stressing at regular intervals of the nuclear melody, generally one tone in four
c. expansion of the nuclear melody into full melody with a range of two to three octaves
d. doubling and paraphrasing of *c*) in the octave above
e. ornamental figuration of the melody
f. the colotomy or punctuation of the melody
g. the drumming which conducts the gamelan

Because of the many types of Balinese ensembles and their different technical methods, the following account is devoted to the more prevalent instrumental forms. Special instruments and their role in the ensemble in which they are found will be described in their proper place.

According to the manner in which their sound is produced, Balinese instruments fall into four main categories:

a. idiophones; primarily self-sounding and percussive, including gongs, metallophones, cymbals, bells, xylophones, rattles, slit drums, stamping tubes
b. membranophones; drums with a membrane stretched over an opening
c. aerophones; now limited to the family of end-blown flutes but formerly including a form of oboe
d. chordophones; here consisting of the bowed lute and the tube zither.[5]

---

[5] The above system of instrumental classification, begun in 1888 by V. C. Mahillon, founder of the Brussels Musée Instrumental, and later developed by von Hornbostel and Sachs, is followed by Kunst in *Music in Java*. See also the chapter, "Terminology," Curt Sachs, *The History of Musical Instruments* (Norton, New York, 1940).

Foremost among the bronze instruments is the large family of gongs, employed in the gamelan as punctuating instruments or, arranged in tuned sets, used to perform both melody and ornamental figuration. Only the largest form of gong is known in Bali by the term, "*gong*."⁶ The other forms have each their individual name.

Like those of Java, Balinese gongs differ basically from gongs with a flat or convex surface, such as those found in India and China. Instead, the rim (*bibih*, lip) is bent down, giving varying degrees of depth. The surface (*awak*, body) is tiered, with a boss (*monchol* or *penchu*) rising in the center.

The larger gongs are hung vertically, and sounded by striking the boss with a thickly padded mallet (*tabuh* or *panggul*) (Fig. 47). The smaller, horizontally mounted gongs are generally struck with a string-wound stick (Fig. 23). Large or small, all gongs produce tones of definite pitch and great musical beauty. The sound of the great *gong ageng* is deep and vibrant, and will carry for miles on a quiet night. In the medium-sized gongs the tone becomes hollow and sweet, and as the gongs continue to diminish in size their tones grow increasingly clear and ringing.

Most important in the group of punctuating gongs is the *gong ageng*, used only in the *gamelan gong* and the processional *gamelan bebōnangan* (Fig. 7). Two such gongs, different in pitch, are employed. The slightly smaller, higher pitched of the pair is the male *gong* (*gong lanang*); the larger, lower pitched is the female (*gong wadon*). Suspended vertically within a framework of poles (*chanang*), the two *gongs* hang side by side, their surfaces facing each other so that one man, seated between the two, may strike first one and then the other. These two *gongs* are interdependent; their main function is to mark, in alternation, the end of each melodic section within the composition.

Considerably smaller in size and higher in pitch is the *kempur*, the third of the vertical gongs (Fig. 21). When used together with the great *gongs* the *kempur* plays a secondary punctuating role. In ensembles that do not include the two large *gongs* the *kempur* plays the leading punctuating role.

The (*be*)*bendé* completes the set of vertical gongs found in the *gamelan gong*. It differs from the others in that the boss is sunk to surface level, a process which mutes and shortens the tone.

Struck with a wooden mallet (Fig. 2), the *bendé* gives out a brassy clang. Its function is not colotomic. Instead, the *bendé* plays an individual role, and is really allied with the cymbals. A

⁶ Or *gong ageng*, *gong gedé*, meaning great gong.

smaller form of *bendé*, the *kajar*, is employed in some ensembles where, instead of being hung vertically it is held horizontally in the lap (Fig. 42).

In the *lègong* gamelan a small vertical gong, the *kemong* (or *kentong*) (Fig. 44) produces a prolonged and penetrating tone of remarkable beauty and purity, which contributes to the metric accentuation of the melodic period.

Two small isolated gongs, the *kempli* and the *kelenang*, mounted horizontally on separate frames (Figs. 17, 31, 41), are included in most ensembles for secondary punctuation. They are held in the lap or set on the ground, resting on a fold of cloth. All but obsolete today is the *pōnggang*, composed of two small gongs of different pitch mounted horizontally in a frame (Fig. 16). It is usually struck by one man, but the two gongs are sometimes set in separate frames and assigned to different players. Acting as a rhythmically filling-in instrument, the two gongs sound in regular or irregular alternation throughout the composition.

A simple form of gong-chime or set of tuned gongs is found in the curious *réong angklung* or *klèntèng(an)* still used in the Balinese *gamelan angklung* of today. This small orchestra is employed for processions, and the instrument was probably developed in order that the gongs could be easily played while carried. At each end of a transverse, dumbbell-shaped piece of wood a small gong is strung in vertical position. When carried, the *réong* is suspended horizontally before the player by means of a cord passed round the neck. The player strikes sideways on the gongs with a light stick held in each hand, as though striking the ends of a transverse drum. Two instruments are employed, thus forming a set of four differently tuned gongs. The two *réongs* are essentially interdependent instruments, and the players perform separate rhythmic patterns which interlock in continuous figuration. When the orchestra is set out on the ground, the *réong* is simply laid across the lap of the seated player (Figs. 70, 71). The four *réong* gongs may also be dismounted and carried separately, distributed among four players (Fig. 4). Or they may be set horizontally in a frame (Figs. 15, 72), in which form they are never carried.

Of recent development but deriving from the ancient *réong* is the modern *réong* or *réong gong* found in the modernized form of *gamelan gong*. Here the number of gongs is increased to twelve, which are mounted horizontally in a long framework. Four players are required, who combine to produce complex interlocking patterns, creating a continuous rippling figuration that captivates modern audiences.

Similar in appearance to the modern *réong*, but always used as a solo instrument, is the older form of gong-chime known as the *trompong*, whose gradual elimination from the modern gamelan cannot be sufficiently deplored. In classical compositions the *trompong* is the melodic leader of the gamelan. With a range of two octaves or more it can, at the hands of an accomplished player, transform the nuclear tones into spacious, ringing melody (Figs. 12, 23). Until recently the *trompong* was considered essential even in those gamelans including the modern *réong* (Fig. 90). Today its place is being taken over by metallophones, whose ornate expansion of the nuclear melody lacks the simplicity of the classic *trompong* style.

Our survey of gongs and gong-chimes ends with the *bōnang*, a set of four unmounted gongs of different pitch, somewhat larger than those of the *réong*. Like the unmounted *réong*, these are assigned to individual players and are carried in the processional ensemble known as the *gamelan bebōnangan* (Fig. 3). By sounding separate repeating rhythmic patterns the four players together create a short polyrhythmic ostinato which substitutes for melody in this marching orchestra of gongs, drums, and cymbals.

The large family of metallophones can be divided into two main categories according to their basic structure: *a*) the *gendèr* group, with keys hanging (*gantung*) over bamboo resonators (Fig. 10), and *b*) the *saron* or *gangsa* group, with keys resting (*jongkok*) on a low wooden base. The *saron* group is limited in range to a single octave. The *gendèr* family includes both single octave instruments and instruments that extend in range from two to three octaves.

The *saron* is probably the older form of metallophone, from which the *gendèr* was later developed. In its heavy, solid base (*plawah*) is cut a shallow trough which serves as resonator for the overlying keys. Or the base may contain a row of shallow round holes, increasing in depth from perhaps one to about four inches, which act as individual resonators to the keys above. The keys (*don*, leaf or leaves) do not come in contact with the base but rest on some form of cushion. They are held in place by means of metal pins that pass through holes bored at one or both ends of the key (Figs. 11, 13). The supporting cushions may consist of two lengths of rope nailed along each side of the base, or the keys may rest on individual cushions of cork or rattan wound around the base of each pin.

A hammer-shaped mallet (*panggul*) with a head of wood or horn is used to strike the keys. It is held in the right hand, leaving the left free to silence the key when desired. In slow tempo this is not necessary; the dying ring of each tone is completely covered by the loud percussive attack of the next. But in quicker tempo, to prevent an overlapping of tones, the left hand silences the vibrating key by grasping its end as the right hand strikes the next.

The *saron* is made in four sizes, pitched an octave apart. The function of the two larger forms is to sound in octaves the nuclear melody. Those in the upper register fill in with repeated tones or play some form of ornamental figuration. Today, however, all four sizes are rarely found in the same gamelan. The tone of the larger *sarons* is heavily metallic but of relatively short duration; that of the smaller forms is ringing and of anvil-like clarity.

The keys are tuned with a file and a scraper. Filing the end of a key raises its pitch; scraping the under side lowers it. Like all the metallophones of the gamelan, the *sarons* are constructed in differently tuned pairs so that when a pair sounds in unison a more pulsating tone is produced, resulting from the created beats or waves, *ombak(an)*. The lower pitched of the pair is called the *pengumbang*,[7] or hummer; the higher is the *pengisep*,[8] or sucker. While the larger *sarons* are tuned perhaps a quarter-tone apart, the difference in tuning decreases as the instruments diminish in size, so that the smallest pair are practically in unison.

The more fragile and complexly constructed instruments of the *gendèr* family are remarkable for their beauty of sound. The larger instruments produce mysteriously humming, throbbing tones, while the smaller ones are almost flutelike in quality. Especially in the larger instruments, tones are sustained for a surprising length of time because of the bamboo resonators. These play so large a part in developing the sound that the whole *gendèr* family might be more accurately defined as idio-aerophonic.

---

[7] From *kumbang*, a mason bee.
[8] From *ngisep*, to draw up, inhale, absorb.

The *gendèr* keys are strung on two leather cords and suspended over individual bamboo resonators (*tiying* or *bumbung*) arranged upright within a wooden frame, the *plawah*. The keys have holes drilled at each end, through which the cords are looped from above and held by means of rattan pins passed through the loops. The two cords are supported at regular intervals by metal props which stand between each key of the larger instruments (Fig. 10), and between every two keys in the others (Fig. 36). Each key thus hangs free above its resonator— a length of bamboo open at the top and closed at the bottom by a nodal wall. As the keys rise in pitch the depth of the resonator diminishes, so that in those instruments where the bamboos are not concealed by a decorative panel the nodes may be seen ascending in a diagonal line (Figs. 10, 69). Great attention is paid to trimming each resonator to the exact length at which it will produce an air column vibrating in unison with the key above. Tones of great purity and fine resonance result, and in the larger instruments the resonators prolong the tones to an astonishing extent. Long after the key has stopped vibrating, the tone continues to hum softly within the tube.[9]

As already mentioned, the *gendèr* group includes both one-octave instruments and instruments with a range of from two to three octaves. Like the *sarons*, the one-octave instruments are made in four sizes, pitched an octave apart. All four are normally included in the gamelan which accompanies the *lègong* performance, and in most other orchestras the two larger forms at least are indispensable. These one-octave instruments have individual names. In diminishing order of size they are known as the *jegogan* (Figs. 10, 37), *jublag* or *chalung* (Fig. 38), *penyachah* (Fig. 39), and *kantil(an)*. The nuclear tones are sounded by the *jublags*, and stressed at regular intervals by the *jegogans*. The two smaller instruments, doubling each other in octaves, are assigned various forms of ornamental passage work. The *jegogan* is struck with a padded stick similar to that used in striking the gong. For the others a hard mallet similar to the *saron* mallet is used.

Only the instruments with a wider range are actually distinguished by the name, *gendèr*. Two sizes are made, pitched an octave apart, the *gendèr gedé*, large *gendèr*, and the *gendèr barangan*, following *gendèr*. The *gendèrs* are further distinguished by the number of their keys; the *gendèr dasa* (ten), *gendèr telulas* (thirteen), and the *gendèr limolas* (fifteen) being the forms most generally known.

The *gendèr* is used mainly in the *lègong* gamelan, which does not include the *trompong*, and where it becomes the leading melodic instrument. The *gendèr* is played with both hands; a light mallet with a thin wooden disc for a head is held in each hand, between the second and third fingers. Silencing the keys becomes a problem, since both hands are in constant motion. Each key is muted by the last two fingers of each hand as the next key is struck (Fig. 97). The technique is difficult, requiring great flexibility of wrist. A detailed account of *gendèr* playing will be found on page 155.

The practice of making all metallophones in differéntly tuned pairs increases the special vibrancy of the whole *gendèr* family to an unbelievable degree. A far greater difference exists here than in the tuning of the *sarons*. The *jegogan* pair may be found tuned as much as 150 *Cents* (a three-quarter tone) apart, with the result that the pulsating beats greatly intensify

---

[9] Timed with a stop watch on one occasion, sound was still faintly audible within the resonator of a large *gendèr* three minutes after the key had been struck.

the natural vibrancy of the pair. Like the *sarons*, there is less difference in pitch as the instruments diminish in size. The two large *gendèrs* start, in their lowest register, with an approximate semitone difference in pitch, and end in their highest about a quarter-tone apart.

It is the presence of these metallophones with hanging keys and the elaborate system of their tuning which give the gamelan its unusual and beautiful resonance. The *gendèrs* are the truly lyrical instruments of the orchestra, softening the percussive sound of the *sarons* and penetrating the whole ensemble with their singing tones.

The two smaller sized one-octave members of the *gendèr* family are often referred to as *gangsa gantung*, with keys suspended, as opposed to the *gangsa jongkok* with keys resting, a name often applied to the *sarons*. For modern gamelans an extended form of *gangsa gantung*, actually a *gendèr* with a two-octave range, is now made in three sizes. Played with a single mallet, the new instrument combines the metallic brilliance of the *saron* or *gangsa* with the sustained tone of the *gendèr*. The single hand technique is easy to master. It also allows for great force and speed, and for the display of virtuosity characteristic of modern Balinese music. In those ensembles seeking still greater brilliance the keys of these instruments are mounted in traditional *saron* fashion, but rest over resonators like the keys of the *gendèr* family (Fig. 97).

Our list of metallophones concludes with the ancient *selundèng*, whose great iron keys are suspended over a wooden trough resonator (Fig. 84). A detailed description of this instrument is reserved for Chapter 16.

Two basically different types of xylophones are in use, one with long flat keys suspended over a shallow wooden trough, such as the *charuk* (Fig. 76) and the *gambang* (Fig. 78); the other with normal sized keys hanging over bamboo resonators and bearing the general name, *rindik*. Of these three, the *charuk* and *gambang* are ancient instrumental forms which have been retained for religious rites. Their special construction and instrumental methods are described in Chapter 16. The various forms of *rindik* are simply adaptations of the *gendèr*, employed in the village xylophone orchestras that accompany the *jogèd* dance. The *chungklik*, with wooden keys lying across a deep soundbox, is still occasionally seen in the gamelan, but is mainly a recreational instrument, sometimes found in the Balinese home. Almost obsolete now is the *grantang*, an ancient instrument of little resonance, whose keys consist of a series of tuned bamboo tubes, open at one end, and hung horizontally within a frame (Fig. 73).

Almost as archaic as the *grantang* is the *angklung*, a form of musical rattle, in which three or four bamboo tubes tuned in octaves are hung vertically within a harplike frame in such a way as to produce a single, clear-pitched tone when the frame is shaken (Figs. 62, 63). Once widely known in Indonesia, and still found in certain parts of Java, the *angklung* is rarely seen in Bali outside the district of Karangasem. A full account of this unusual instrument and the way it is employed in the gamelan will be found in Chapter 15.

Cymbals are made in many sizes and in two different forms—the large *chèngchèng* which may be carried in the hand, and the small *rinchik* of the theater which is mounted on a wooden base.

Some six or seven pairs of *chèngchèng* may be used in the special processional ensemble known as the *gamelan bebōnang* (Fig. 6) and in the traditional *gamelan gong* (Fig. 20). Each pair is of different diameter and thickness and differs recognizably in pitch from the others. Each player sounds his own assigned rhythmic pattern which can be clearly distinguished from the rest, and which forms an integral part in the polyrhythmic interplay of the group. When carried, the cymbals are held by means of a cord passed through a central hole from the concave side. When used with the gamelan, one of each pair of cymbals is placed upturned on the ground and struck with the other which is held in the hand. Some players operate two pairs in this way, holding a striking cymbal in each hand (Fig. 20).

The small *rinchik*, used in the theater and for dances, has a more delicate and ringing sound. In the *gambuh* orchestra the *rinchik* consists of an upturned pair of cymbals which are loosely attached to a base and a striking pair which are held in the hands (Fig. 29). Two or three players may be employed, but there is no polyrhythmic interplay. Instead, a single rhythmic pattern is sounded in unison. For the *lègong* and other dancers a single player is sufficient. Here the lower *rinchiks* are mounted in two sets of three, each set arranged so that the cymbals overlap slightly. The two sets are struck near the center by the upper cymbals.

The *gentorak*, a rack of small bells, is still found occasionally in certain gamelans. The bells hang from a series of hoops fastened one above the other around a central stick. The stick rests upright on the ground, held by the hand at the upper end. The rack is gently shaken back and forth to produce a continuous jingle (Fig. 47).

Three antique percussion instruments of curious form and delicate sound, the *gumanak*, *kangsi*, and *kenyir* (Figs. 33, 34, 31), remain to be described. Since they are found only in the orchestra which accompanies the *gambuh* plays, and since their use is so closely related to their individual sounds, an account of their special form and function is reserved for Chapter 10.

The form of drum or *kendang* employed in Bali is similar to the cylindrical drums in the Borobudur reliefs, where in several places they may be seen carried in a pair and struck with sticks (Fig. 49). The Balinese *kendang* tapers slightly, so that one end is smaller than the other and noticeably higher in pitch. Both ends are closed with a *kerbo* skin drumhead stretched across the opening and held down by a hoop. The two hoops are interconnected by leather or rattan lacing strings stretched back and forth in an N pattern. In the larger drums the strings are tightened by means of sliding rings that bind each pair in a Y pattern (Figs. 19, 50). The pitch of the drum can thus be raised or lowered by tightening or loosening the strings.

The drum is held in horizontal position, the smaller end to the left. When carried it is suspended from the neck by a cord (Fig. 3). Otherwise it rests across the knees of the seated player (Fig. 19). Two complementary drums, male, *lanang*, and female, *wadon*, are essential for most forms of music. Pitch differences between the two vary from a recognizable second to an approximate fifth.

For processions and in the ceremonial music of the *gamelan gong* the drum is struck both by hand and by a single drumstick held in the right hand. The drum used in the theater and for most dances is beaten by the hands alone. Here a wide variety of sounds is produced by different parts of the hand and fingers. Tones may also be open or muted by resting one hand

33

on a drumhead as the other is struck. Of the pair, the larger, deeper voiced *kendang wadon* is usually assigned the lead, but at all times the two drums are engaged in a complex interplay that supplies the rhythmic impulse for the orchestra.

A bowl-shaped form of drum hollowed from the bulging base of the coconut palm, known as the *terbang* or *terbana*, probably owes its origin to the Arabian *rebana* (Fig. 99). Of booming but inferior resonance, it is used only in the small ensemble of flutes and percussion that accompanies the popular entertainment known as *jangèr*.

Probably the favorite musical instrument in Bali is the *suling*, the end-blown flute of bamboo. Two separate types are to be distinguished, the large *suling gambuh*, a form of bass flute used in the *gambuh* orchestra (Fig. 25), and the various smaller *sulings* which are heard everywhere, both as recreational instruments and as the leading melodic instruments of the *arja* and *jangèr* ensembles (Figs. 86, 87).

The *suling* is open at the bottom and closed at the blowing end by a node. The embouchure is similar to that of the Javanese *suling*. On the underside of the instrument a small chip is cut away from the node and adjacent part. Immediately below the node a square hole is made. A flat narrow ring of bamboo or palmleaf is placed around the node, and the slit formed by the partly cut node and the ring itself acts as air duct, guiding the player's breath into the hole. The fingerholes (*song*) are found on the upper side of the *suling* and, according to the scale system of the instrument, may be four, five, or six in number.

The *rebab*, the two-stringed bowed lute which is also found in the Javanese gamelan, is probably of Arabo-Persian origin. The former practice of including it in the large Balinese gamelan has almost died out. Today it is found chiefly in the *gambuh* orchestra, where it is employed in unison with the *sulings* (Fig. 30). The only other form of chordophone found in the Balinese orchestra is the *guntang*, a one-string zither, described on page 294, which is treated as a percussion instrument, the string being tapped lightly with a stick (Fig. 88). It functions as time-beater and punctuating instrument in the *arja* and *jangèr* ensembles.

Outside the orchestral department are found various functional and recreational instruments which are seen throughout the island. Foremost of these is the *kulkul*, the slit drum of wood or bamboo used for sending signals, without which no village, temple, or household is complete.

The wooden *kulkul* is a hollowed tree trunk, closed at both ends, with a longitudinal slit. It is usually hung perpendicularly, and struck near the edge of the slit with a heavy stick or mallet. Found sometimes singly, but more often in a differently pitched pair, and occasionally in sets of three or four, these drums are usually hung in a high open tower beneath a protecting roof of thatch (Fig. 1). Some are of enormous size and may be heard for miles. Special signals exist for meetings, temple services, fire, and other emergencies. Many villages strike the hours of sunrise, noon, sundown, and midnight. The most commonly heard *kulkulan*, *kulkul* beating, is sounded on a differently pitched pair, which are struck in regular or irregular alternation.

The small bamboo *kulkul* consists of a single joint of bamboo, closed at each end by a node and also having a longitudinal slit. It is a familiar household instrument, hung in a convenient tree to summon home family members or send out emergency alarms.

At festival time a great wooden *kulkul* may be made and mounted horizontally in a scaffold (Fig. 105). For entertainment two youths beat out lively rhythms, improvising a simple dance (Fig. 107). As accompaniment, a line of boys beat out different rhythms on the *kōprak*, a bamboo slit drum extended to include a number of joints. Each joint has a slit, forming a separate *kulkul* in itself (Fig. 106). An account of this entertainment is given in Appendix 1, page 363.

The popular *sawangan layangan*, a bow-shaped one-string harp, is hung from kites (*layangan*), and produces a throbbing hum when the kite is in the air. The vibrating string is horsehair or rattan fiber tautly stretched across a bamboo bow which hangs from a crosspiece in the kite. In the monsoon season the sky is filled with pulsating sound as the bannerlike kites stream in the wind.

Another instrument played by the wind is the *sundari*, a form of Aeolus flute. In a node near the top of a thirty-foot bamboo reed a round hole is cut, and the bamboo set up in the open fields, giving out a faint or vibrant hum, according to the force of the wind. In addition there is the *sawangan dara*, a miniature bamboo whistle or pipe tied among the feathers or fastened to the necks of domestic pigeons. These create shrill tremulous sounds when the birds are sent up in flight. Small pellet bells, *gongsèng*, are often attached at the same time to the tail and feet of each bird; the sound of a flock thus equipped circling in the sky is strange and charming to the ear. In the home, snail shells are furnished with little clappers and hung in a light bamboo frame, to be suspended from some house beam where they may catch the breeze.

In concluding this survey, mention should be made of certain ritualistic instruments employed by the priest. During the chanting of *mantras* or prayer verses, the *genta* (*ghanta*, Skt.), a bronze handbell, is rung to mark the end of each stanza. At the beginning and at the end of the special purification rites known as *mecharu* the shell horn or *sangkah* (*çangka*, Skt.) is blown, first to summon and later to dispel the neighborhood demons. The *ketipluk*, a small clapper drum set horizontally on a handle, is still seen as part of the *pedanda's* ceremonial accessories. Two small balls are attached to the end of the handles by means of cords. These are made to strike the two drumheads alternately when the handle is given a quick half-turn, and can produce a brief or prolonged tremolo.

Chapter 7

Scale Systems, Scales, and Tunings

BALINESE gamelans follow various scale systems. According to the type of ensemble in which they are employed, instruments are constructed to sound, within the octave, a scale or *saih* (row, series) of four, five, or seven tones. Each scale form is complete in itself, a wide or narrow tonal world with its own particular music. No two gamelans are tuned exactly alike, and deviation in what is considered to be essentially the same scale can be great, so that one might with reason state that there are as many scales as there are gamelans. Some tunings (*patutan*[1]) approach the Western tempered system, others veer off in intervals impossible to define except in terms of *Cents*.[2] Moreover, the scale of any gamelan can be altered at will on retuning, modified both in pitch and interval relation.

For the purpose of more precisely describing their formation, Balinese scales are considered here as they are found in instruments with fixed pitch, rather than as interpreted by the voice, or by the *suling* or *rebab*. Singers are not normally included in the tuned gamelan, and when present are heard only during intervals when the gamelan is silent. Both *suling* and *rebab* are rarely found in ensembles of tuned instruments, and when included are played with great freedom of intonation. However, two examples of the seven-tone scale as found in the *suling gambuh* are included, since the *gambuh* scale system was considered a main source for gamelan tunings in the past. The rest of the scales and tunings presented in the following pages have been taken from bronze ensembles. They demonstrate in concrete form the Balinese conception of their inherited scale systems, and how these can be endlessly modified in instrumental practice.

If there were any uniformity of pitch or final standard for interval structure in the tuning of the different gamelan types, the problem of defining the various scale forms would be relatively simple. But no theoretical treatise on scale formation or instrumental tuning is known.[3] The distance between two tones may be described as "greater" or "smaller," but Balinese terminology contains no word for any actual interval other than the octave, *penangkep*. While the *pandé krawang* may own an inherited set of bronze or even wooden keys which preserve the scale from some vanished gamelan of the past, many gamelan clubs have their own tuners, who take their tunings from each other, copying or altering to suit themselves.

---

[1] From *patut*, right, correct.

[2] See page xiii, foot-note 2.

[3] A Balinese manuscript in the Kirtya Liefrinck-v.d. Tuuk collection at Singaraja, catalogued as No. IIIc, 1001, and entitled *Pepatutan gong gedé—Tuning of the gamelan gong gedé*—proved on examination to contain merely directions for the arrangement of keys on the different instruments, but gave no information on either the pitch or the tuning of the gamelan.

Despite their variability in tuning, all Balinese instrumental scales may be considered as belonging to either one or the other of two different tonal systems which in Java are known as *pélog* and *sléndro*. These names are not familiar to most Balinese, who have their own terminology. They are used in these pages for sake of reference to the two systems as found in Java.

Pélog may be defined as a seven-tone quasi-diatonic scale which is less of an actual scale than an instrumental system for the forming of different five-tone modal scales within the seven-tone scale. These five-tone *pélog* scales are characterized by their intervals of unequal size, and change in interval relation with each transposition of the five-tone series. *Sléndro* is an entirely different system, a completely different tonality, perhaps the result of a more sophisticated idea of instrumental tuning. It is essentially a pentatonic scale, with intervals tending toward a uniformity of size. Whereas in *pélog* distinguishable seconds and thirds occur, in *sléndro* the octave is divided more equidistantly. *Pélog* is believed by Western scholars to be the older scale form, introduced into Indonesia at some unknown pre-Hindu period. *Sléndro* appears to have been a later development.[4] In Bali, both *pélog*- and *sléndro*-type scales are also found in four-tone form.

Balinese musicians generally refer to seven-tone *pélog* as the *saih pitu*, series or scale of seven. In five-tone form, *pélog* is usually referred to as the *saih lima*, series of five, although each five-tone scale of the *saih 7* has its distinguishing modal name. *Sléndro* is simply known as the *saih gendèr wayang*, scale of the special *gendèr* used for the *wayang* or shadowplay. In the *pélog* system the Balinese also distinguish a six-tone series, the *saih nem*. This, however, is no true scale at all, but simply an instrumental system, no longer used but formerly occasionally employed in the *gamelan Semar Pegulingan* for the purpose of performing two separate repertories of music, one requiring the *trompong*, the other the *gendèr*, each having its own form of pentatonic scale.

While both *pélog* and *sléndro* systems as found in Bali are closely related to those of Java, they differ sufficiently in actual practice as to be considered here in their own purely Balinese context. Generally simpler than the intricate systems of Java today, they not only serve as the basis for a music which has become distinctly Balinese, but throw light, especially in the more archaic ensembles, on musical methods once known in Java but now completely forgotten.

In spite of its wider range, the seven-tone *pélog* gamelan has never been popular in Bali. Unlike Java, where such gamelans are widespread, the vast majority of Balinese gamelans have always been five- or four-tone. For most Balinese musicians, the *saih 7* is a revered mystery, a system reserved for ancient forms of court and sacred music. The essentially pentatonic character of Balinese scale formation is shown in the Balinese solfeggio system as found in

---

[4] "There cannot be any doubt about the fact that *sléndro* came to Java and Bali a good many centuries after *pélog*. *Pélog* was perhaps already imported by Malay-Polynesian peoples who came to Java many centuries before our Christian era. *Sléndro* seems to have entered Java simultaneously with a later culture in the eighth century A.D., when the dynasty of the Çailéndras ruled the central parts of the island, and to have derived its name from that same royal family; *gamelan sléndro* = *gamelan Çailéndra*." J. Kunst, from a lecture, "The Music of Java," delivered at the Netherlands Legation in London on Oct. 22, 1934.

the *saih 7*. Of the seven tones, five are named, *ding, dong, dèng, dung, dang.*[5] The two remaining tones, which lie, respectively, between *dèng* and *dung*, and *dang* and the following *ding alit*, small *ding*, are simply known as the *penyorog* or inserted tone and the *pemèro* or false tone. Thus, in ascending order, the tones of any scale in the *saih 7* system are found in the following sequence of five main and two secondary tones, the main tones indicated here by their respective vowels:

I   O   È   p   U   A   p   Ia

The two secondary tones occasionally may serve as accessory or substituting tones. Their special use will be discussed in later chapters. *Pélog* in its five-tone form, however, is complete in itself, and holds no suggestion of missing tones. Occasionally a composition from some seven-tone repertory which may employ six or all seven tones is adapted to a five-tone ensemble by simply omitting the secondary tones.

The Balinese themselves consider all five-tone *pélog* scales as originating in the *saih 7* of the *suling gambuh* (Fig. 25). In this form the scale is commonly known as the "*saih gambuh*," to distinguish it from the "*saih gambang*," the seven-tone system of the *gambang* and other sacred ensembles. The *saih gambang* has its own terminology, which will be discussed in the following chapter. The methods by which the different five-tone scales are formed within the seven-tone series can be more clearly demonstrated in the *gambuh* system.

In the *saih gambuh*, as found in the *suling gambuh*, four different scales are generally known, *Tembung, Selisir, Baro* and *Lebeng*. These are obtained by transposing the tonal series, *i o è u a*, from one position to another in the basic scale. The solfeggio shifts with each transposition. There is said to be a fifth scale, *Sunarèn*, but it is no longer used, and the method of locating it has been forgotten. To indicate playing in any given scale the word *tekep*, close or cover, is used, referring to the act of covering or closing the fingerholes of the *suling*. The terms *ambah* (take the way of), *jalan* (go), and *marga* (way), are also used, but more especially in the *gambang* ensemble. In referring to a particular scale one does not say *saih Tembung* (*Tembung* scale) but *tekep Tembung*, *Tembung* fingering, or *ambah Tembung*, take the way of *Tembung*.

The relation of these scales to each other within the seven-tone series is not entirely fixed, although fairly stabilized in the *suling*. But when the *saih gambuh* is transposed to the *gamelan Semar Pegulingan*, the relationship is found to change, as shown in the following table. The system now includes the fifth scale, *Sunarèn*, as well. It should be noted here that on an instrument with an extended range, each scale can retain its natural tonal sequence with transposition. On the one octave *saron*, only the scale *Tembung* can be produced without inversion.

It will be seen in the table on page 39 that both systems agree in the location of the first scale, *Tembung*, whose first tone, *ding*, is found on the first tone of the *saih 7*. On the *suling gambuh* the *Selisir* scale begins on *penyorog Tembung*, the fourth tone of the *saih 7*, although

[5] In Balinese mystic writings and in religious ritual these five tones are correlated to the five ceremonial directions (the four cardinal points and center or up), the five sacred syllables, the five pitches on which *mantras* are chanted, and the five ceremonial colors.

ding	Shiva	center	five-colored
dong	Iswara	east	white
dèng	Mahadéwa	west	yellow
dung	Brahma	south	red
dang	Vishnu	north	black

Saih 7 pegambuhan; suling gambuh

saih 7	1	2	3	4	5	6	7	upper register or pengelik						
								1	2	3	4	5	6	7
Tembung	i	o	è	(p)	u	a	(p)							
Selisir				i	o	è	(p)	u	a	(p)				
Baro					i	o	è	(p)	u	a				
Lebeng						i	o	è	(p)	u	a	(p)		
Sunarèn				?										

Saih 7 Semar Pegulingan; trompong[6]

saih 7	1	2	3	4	5	6	7	upper register or pengelik						
								1	2	3	4	5	6	7
Tembung	i	o	è	(p)	u	a	(p)							
Lebeng		i	o	è	(p)	u	a	(p)						
Baro				i	o	è	(p)	u	a	(p)				
Selisir					i	o	è	(p)	u	a	(p)			
Sunarèn							i	o	è	(p)	u	a	(p)	

Scale inversions in the one-octave saron[6]

saih 7	1	2	3	4	5	6	7
Tembung	i	o	è	(p)	u	a	(p)
Lebeng	(p)	i	o	è	(p)	u	a
Baro	u	a	(p)	i	o	è	(p)
Selisir	(p)	u	a	(p)	i	o	è
Sunarèn	o	è	(p)	u	a	(p)	i

the *Semar Pegulingan* versions of the first tone coincide with *dung Tembung*, the fifth tone of the *saih 7*. In all *gambuh* ensembles examined, the *Tembung-Selisir* relation remained as shown above in the *suling gambuh* system. In the *Semar Pegulingan* gamelans, the *Tembung-Selisir* relation remained as found in the *trompong* version shown above, while the location of the other scales sometimes changed.

Each of the five main tones of each scale can become the tonal center or tonic—the tone on which the composition opens and closes. A composition may also shift its tonal center at some time, starting on one tone and ending on another.

While the different scales all follow the same basic pattern of structure, their actual interval formation may undergo considerable change as the structure pattern is transposed. Yet it is not this change in intervals that distinguishes the scale so much as its change in register and timbre. The expressive character associated with each scale is best shown in the *gambuh* play, where the scale is changed with the entrance of each new character type.

---

[6] As found in the gamelan Semar Pegulingan of *banjar* Tampak Gangsal, Badung, whose scale tuning is given in Chart 2, (no. 4). In Klungkung (Chart 2, no. 3), the scale Baro began on the 4th tone, Sunarèn on the 6th, while Lebeng was unknown.

Tembung, lowest in register and dark in color, is used for characters of the vigorous (*kras*) type. *Selisir*, contrastingly high in pitch and of a brighter color, is reserved for characters of the gentle (*alus*) type, the high-born heroes and heroines. *Lebeng* is kept for secondary characters and scenes of conflict; while *Baro* is used for attendants and buffoons. Of all the scales, *Selisir* is considered the most expressive for music of a lyrical, *alus* character. It is precisely this scale, as found in the *suling gambuh* (see Chart 3), that is employed, though considerably modified through tuning, by the great majority of five-tone gamelans in Bali.

The scales and tunings presented in the charts given in this chapter are arranged in the following order:

> seven-tone *pélog* or *saih 7*, *gambuh* and *gambang* systems
> five-tone *pélog* or *saih lima*, *Selisir* form
> deviant examples of five-tone *pélog*
> four-tone *pélog*
> *sléndro*
> four-tone *sléndro* or *saih angklung*
> unusual tunings of *saih angklung*

The different tunings were chosen to show both basic conformity and unusual deviation in the tuning of each scale type. All are taken from outstanding ensembles which were active in Bali in the thirties. Each tuning is expressed primarily in figures giving the pitch vibrations of the different scale tone, as measured with a monochord tuned to International Pitch (A—435v.). The distances between the successive tones are expressed in terms of *Cents*.

While vibration numbers and *Cents* figures are sufficient to describe any scale, alone they convey little to the mind unaccustomed to thinking in these terms. For this reason, and for purposes of identification with the musical examples found in later chapters, the scale tones in the following charts are shown in reference to neighboring tones in the Western tempered system, International Pitch. Their proximity to, and their distance from any Western series of scale steps, and the deviation in each compared scale of the same type, can thus be estimated at a glance. As a further visual aid, the charts have been prepared on squared graph paper, each square representing a quarter-tone, or 50 *Cents*.

In Chart 1, which serves as introduction to the system, a seven-tone *pélog* scale is shown, together with its vibration numbers, in ascending diagonal alignment, to give a sense of the ascent of the scale. In a column to the left are given, for quick reference, the vibration numbers of the equal-tempered twelve-tone scale as it ascends from approximately the same degree of pitch. Below, in horizontal alignment, the intervals of the Balinese scale shown above are measured in *Cents*, and at the same time shown against the Western equigrade system. The relative pitch of each scale-tone and the actual distances between tones are thus immediately apparent.

A condensed graph, shown below, retains all the essential information, but reduces the chart to a single horizontal line. It illustrates the method employed in the succeeding charts.

Chart 2 contains six examples of seven-tone *pélog* or *saih 7*. The first two are versions of the *saih gambang*, and are taken from two different types of sacred ensemble, each with its own special form of music. The following examples, however, are all variants of the *saih gambuh*

40

Chart 1. Balinese *saih 7* scale; Krōbōkan village

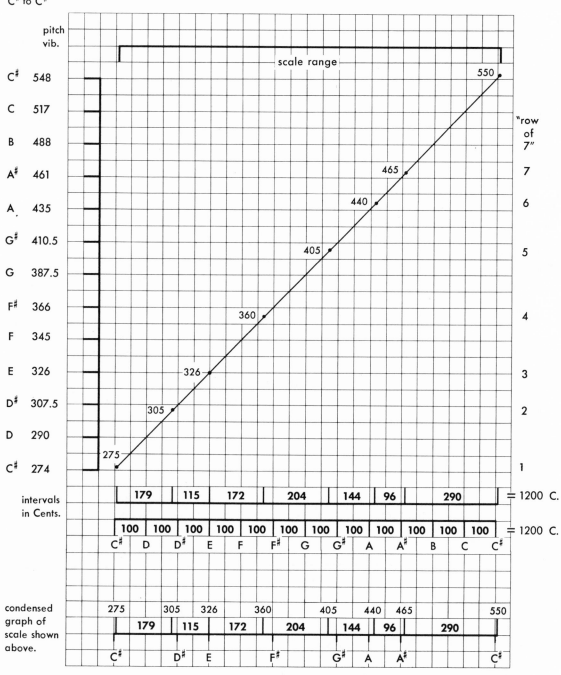

Chart 2. Six saih pitu scales compared

a) krawang ensembles

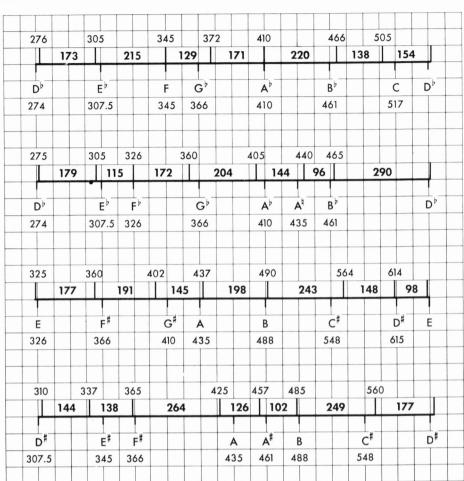

1.
gamelan
luang

banjar
Sèséh

2.
gamelan
gambang

Krōbōkan
village

3.
gamelan
Semar
Pegulingan

Klungkung

4.
gamelan
Semar
Pegulingan

Tampak
Gangsal

b) suling pegambuhan

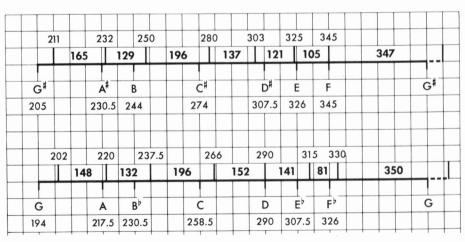

5.
suling
gambuh

Tabanan

6.
suling
gambuh

Batuan
village

system as found in the *Semar Pegulingan* and *gambuh* orchestras. Despite their differences in pitch and interval structure they represent a single scale system. Because of the fixed specifications for the making of the *suling gambuh*, its scale remains fairly standardized. But as found in the few *Semar Pegulingan* gamelans surviving in the thirties, the *saih gambuh* was interpreted with great freedom. In each case the original seven-tone series was transposed to begin approximately a fourth or fifth higher. The lowest five-tone scale, *Tembung*, was now raised to the *Baro* or *Lebeng* register of the *suling*, and the other scales transposed correspondingly higher, possibly to suit the requirement of the *trompong* which replaced the *suling* as leading melodic instrument. In addition, each of the five-tone scales showed little resemblance in interval structure to the corresponding scales of the *suling*. Yet in spite of these differences, the same repertory of music was performed by *gambuh* and *Semar Pegulingan* ensembles alike.

In the following chart, the two *suling gambuh* scales complement each other. While neither can be considered as final, they establish between them a general standard in pitch and interval formation. The Tabanan *suling*, starting a near semitone (84 *C.*) higher than that of Batuan, shown below it, remains consistently higher throughout, although a slight relative flattening of the fifth, sixth and seventh tones produces somewhat different intervals, at most, however, in the case of the sixth interval, a difference of 24 *Cents*—a barely perceptible eighth-tone.

Today the *Semar Pegulingan* has vanished, but the *gambuh* ensemble continues to preserve its traditional scale system of the past. Whether this system dates, as the Balinese believe, to an ancient pre-bronze period in Indonesian music remains an open question. For the Balinese, however, the *saih gambuh* does preserve a certain standard, perhaps the only one, for the formation of *pélog* scales. Most five-tone *pélog* gamelans today still conform very closely, both in general pitch and in interval formation, to the *Selisir* scale of the *suling gambuh*, the scale most suitable for *alus* music, whose lowest tone, *ding*, is located on the fourth step of the seven-tone series. In Chart 3, this scale, as found on the *suling gambuh*, is shown in its basic five-tone form in relation to the full seven-tone *saih gambuh*, Tabanan version (Chart 2, no. 5), which is given above it. The distance covered by the five main tones, or from *ding* to *dang*, is seen to be 875 *C.* (the sum of the five intervals), or a major sixth minus 25 *C.* The remaining

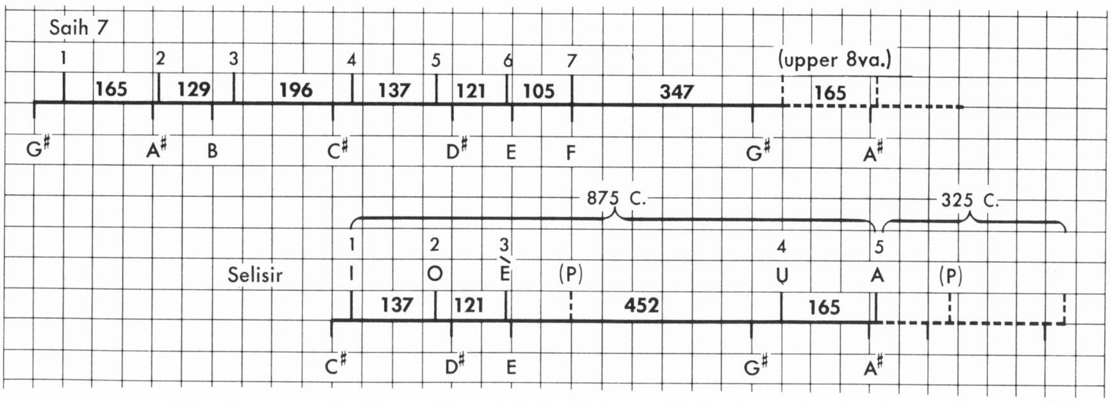

Chart 3. The saih 7 pegambuhan of the Tabanan suling, showing the location of the scale, Selisir

interval completing the octave, lying between *dang*, last of the five-tone series, and the adjacent *ding* which is the starting point for the series in the octave above, is a complementary 325 *C.*, or a minor third plus 25 *C.* Attention is called to these two distances since they undergo considerable modification when the scale is transferred to a bronze ensemble. Since the only interval that remains fixed in the Balinese scale system is that of the octave, it will be

Chart 4. Four Selisir scales compared

Selisir pegambuhan
and
Selisir gong

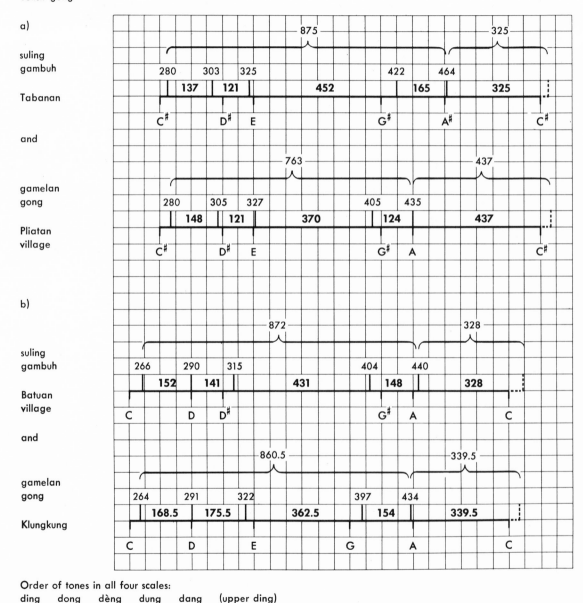

Order of tones in all four scales:
ding   dong   dèng   dung   dang   (upper ding)

seen that the size of the interval between *dang* and upper *ding* is conditioned by the sum of the intervals lying between the five basic tones, in other words the interval which frames these tones. Just how these two structural intervals can vary in relation to each other is shown in subsequent charts.

When the *Selisir* scale of the *suling gambuh* is transferred to the *gamelan gong*, it is commonly known as "*Selisir gong.*" In Chart 4, two examples of *Selisir gong* are compared with two examples of *Selisir gambuh*, as found in the *sulings* of Tabanan and Batuan.

In the first pair of scales, the *Selisir* scale of the Tabanan *suling* is given above that of the *gamelan gong* of Pliatan, a modern ensemble which is always kept well in tune.[7] The two villages lie some twenty miles apart but are in close musical communication. The Pliatan scale is given here because of the pitch coincidence of its lowest tone (280 v.) with that of the Tabanan scale. The interval modification which occurs is common enough in the tuned gamelan to establish the Pliatan scale as a perfectly normal interpretation by gamelan of *Selisir gambuh*.

What happens in this transference?

The three lower tones are seen to coincide closely with those of the *suling* scale shown above it. The two upper tones, however, are found to be relatively lower in pitch, reducing the distance between the two *suling* tones *ding* and *dang* a near semitone of 112 *C.*, and at the same time augmenting the distance between *dang* and upper *ding* by 112 *C.* This reduction of the distance between the two outer tones of the basic scale to an interval of less than 800 *C.*, a tempered minor sixth, is so prevalent in Balinese five-tone *pélog* gamelans that tunings showing distances of 800 *C.* or more become increasingly exceptional as the distance widens.

In the second pair of scales included in the same chart the *Selisir* scale of the Batuan *suling* is compared with that of the *gamelan gong* of Klungkung, an old-style court orchestra heard only on state occasions. Both scales are seen to begin at almost the same pitch, an approximate semitone below the two scales shown above. The Klungkung scale differs, however, from that of Pliatan by closely matching the *suling* in its unusually large distance of 860.5 *C.* between the two outer tones of the basic scale and the correspondingly reduced distance between *dang* and upper *ding*. The scale is given here as an unusual tuning of *Selisir gong*. To the Western ear at least it creates a very different tonal atmosphere from that of the *Selisir* scale as found in the Pliatan gamelan.

Chart 4 thus offers two markedly contrasting examples of *Selisir* as found in the *gamelan gong*. That of Klungkung seems to follow the *suling gambuh;* while that of Pliatan clearly modifies the *suling* scale. Their greatest difference is seen by comparing the distances which in each scale lie between *ding* and *dang* and between *dang* and upper *ding*.

Klungkung:	860.5	339.5 *C.*
Pliatan:	763	437 *C.*

In Chart 5, four more examples of *Selisir gong* scales are given for comparison, without further reference to the *suling gambuh* and with the Pliatan tuning serving as point of departure. The first three show approximately the same distances between *ding* and *dang*,

---

[7] This orchestra toured Europe and the United States in 1952–53.

averaging 750 *C.*, and with a complementary interval between *dang* and upper *ding* of 450 *C.* The more unusual fourth example, given here for contrast, contains the two distances of 800 *C.* and 400 *C.* All four scales are found to be at about the same pitch, with the fifth tone, *dang*, in three instances (Nos. 1, 2, and 4) coinciding exactly in pitch at 435 v. This coincidence recurs so frequently in *Selisir*-tuned gamelans that in many cases this tone alone was checked with a tuning fork pitched at A—435 v.

Chart 5. Toward standardization?

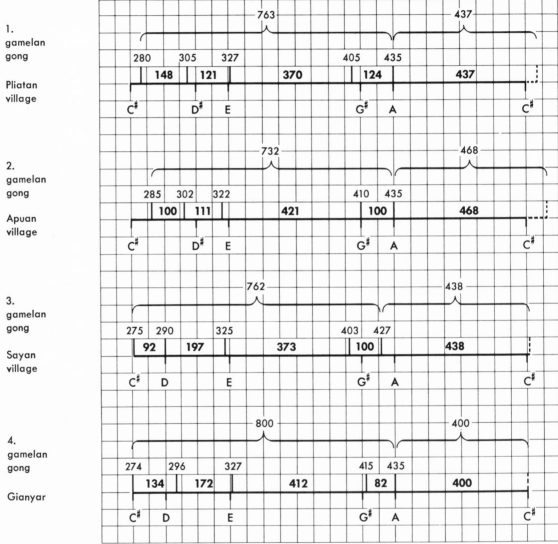

As for the actual scale tones, as found in the above Chart 5, they will be seen to shift in relation to each other with each tuning, modifying the interval structure so that each scale has a tonality quite its own. A glance downward on the chart will give some idea of the

46

change which can occur in each interval. In Scale No. 2 for example, the second interval, a near semitone of 111 C., becomes augmented in Scale No. 3 to a near major second of 197 C. Further examination will reveal other changes in interval relation, changes sufficient to cause each scale to be considered significantly different, by Western standards in its melodic implications. Yet, as previously stated, the different tunings are no more than variants of a single scale whose norm remains undetermined. In the last analysis, the tones *ding, dong, dèng, dung* and *dang* are not fixed tones at all, but tonal zones which allow for endless modification of pitch when it comes to tuning the gamelan.

Despite the differences in their intervals, the four scales just compared show a basic similarity in their sequences of seconds and thirds. Nos. 3 and 4, particularly the latter, approach so closely to Western tempered tuning that, for the purposes of the present book, the scale *Selisir gong* can be represented in Western notation, closely enough, by the tone symbols:

The *Selisir* scale is so commonly employed by the gamelans in Bali that it may be considered the most representative form of Balinese five-tone *pélog*. It is the one scale of the *gambuh* system which appears to be known everywhere, both instrumentally and vocally.

Far more irregular in formation than the *Selisir gong* scales of Chart 5 are the four examples of five-tone *pélog* found in Chart 6. Each was selected to show some unusual interpretation of the *pélog* scale. While the scales given in Chart 5 were all taken from the *gamelan gong*, the following scales are from three different gamelan types, the *Semar Pegulingan* in its five-tone form, *gamelan pelègongan*, and *gamelan barong*. It should be noted here that in spite of the pronounced differences in their scales, these three ensembles shared a common basic repertory of compositions deriving from the wider repertory of the *gambuh* theater.

Each scale has its special name, but with the exception of *Selisir pelègongan* (*lègong Selisir*), the other names were unusual in their particular applications, and could not be satisfactorily accounted for by the musicians themselves. They cannot be considered as final, or as part of a standardized system to distinguish different scale forms.

The first scale was described to me by Gusti Putuh, the leader of the gamelan from which it was taken, as "*Tembung chenik*," small (high-pitched) *Tembung*, perhaps because it is in the general register of *Selisir gong*. It is a scale of indescribable tonal beauty, remarkable for the unusual minor third occurring between *dèng* and *dung*, and the resulting near-major second found between *dung* and *dang*. My informant considered this tuning as exceptionally "sweet" (*manis*), partly because of the relatively lower pitch of the tone *dung*, a modification which produced a subtle but profound change in the tonal color of the gamelan. This unusual scale (or tuning) occasionally heard in older Balinese gamelans, is preserved in three Beka recordings of the gamelan in which it was found.[8]

The second scale in the following chart was taken from my five-tone *Semar Pegulingan* in Sayan. The tuning was copied at my request from a rarely heard *gamelan pelègongan* I discovered in the fishing village of Sanur. This gamelan had an unusual tonality of great appeal,

---

[8] See Appendix 6, Recordings, *gamelan Semar Pegulingan*.

partly because of its relatively high pitch, but (for me) chiefly because of the near-major second lying between the first and second tones of its scale. While the Sanur men considered this scale to be *Selisir*, the *pandé krawang* who tuned my instruments pronounced it as *Sunarèn*. But on comparing it with the *Sunarèn* scale as found in the seven-tone *Semar Pegulingan* I could discover no similarity in either pitch or interval structure. Once again, Balinese musicians described this tuning as remarkably "sweet," though few could say exactly why. Most

Chart 6. Away from standardization?

Four deviant five-tone pélog scales

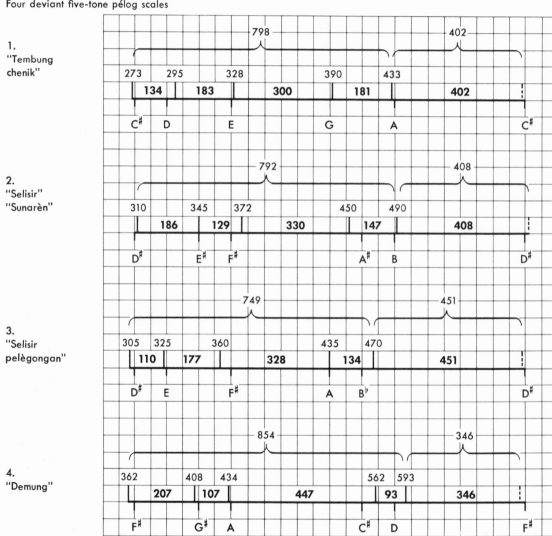

Order of tones: *ding   dong   dèng   dung   dang*

1. gamelan Semar Pegulingan; banjar Titih, Badung.
2. gamelan Semar Pegulingan; Sayan village.
3. gamelan pelègongan; Anggabaya village.
4. gamelan barong; banjar Taman, Sanur village.

attributed it to the relatively high pitch of the scale, of which they were immediately aware. Finally a few musicians agreed with me that the special charm of the scale was also due to the relatively higher (smaller) "voice" (*swara*) of the second tone, *dong*. But whether this was a characteristic of the *Sunarèn* scale none could say.

The third scale, *Selisir pelègongan*, a name in common use, is included here for sake of comparison with *Selisir gong*. It is higher in pitch throughout—a characteristic of the *gamelan pelègongan*. The version given here resembles the "*Selisir*" or "*Sunarèn*" scale found immediately above it except for the more normal position of its second tone, *dong*.

The last scale was unaccountably called "*Demung*" by the members of the gamelan from which it was taken, the name of a modal scale in the quite unrelated *gambang* system. This was probably an old confusion with the name, *Tembung*. It is in an unusually high register, starting almost an octave higher than the *Tembung* scale as found in the *suling gambuh*. Attention is called to the wide distance of 854 *C.* between its first and fifth tones, with a correspondingly small interval completing the octave. Also to be noted are the unusually large intervals between *ding* and *dong*, and *dèng* and *dung*. The tonality of this particular gamelan, called *gamelan barong* since it played chiefly for the *barong* plays,[9] while remaining unmistakably *pélog* was utterly strange and captivating.

Four-tone *pélog* is found in only one ensemble, the *gamelan bebōnangan*, which furnishes music during processions. This gamelan, composed of isolated gongs of different sizes (Figs. 4, 5), may be a complete ensemble in itself or it may be assembled for the occasion by borrowing gongs from the *gamelan gong*. In any case, the lowest tone of the five-tone *pélog* scale, *ding*, is not employed. Chart 7 gives the scale as found in the *bebōnangan* ensemble of Sayan village, the instruments of which belonged to the village *gamelan gong*. The complete scale of this gamelan is given in Chart 5 (No. 3).

Chart 7. Four-tone pélog, gamelan bebōnangan, Sayan village

O		È					U	A
290		325					403	427
	197			373			100	
D		E					G#	A

The *sléndro* tonal system is far removed from that of *pélog*, a strange and apparently unrelated tonal sphere in itself. Essentially pentatonic, there is no place in this system for secondary tones. *Pélog*-like steps approaching a semitone or major third are unknown; instead the five intervals show more uniformity in size.

Sléndro has sometimes been defined as a system which divides or tends to divide the octave into five intervals of equal size. Each interval would thus be the equivalent of six-fifths of a tone or 240 *C.* The system is demonstrated in Chart 8. For the sake of later comparison with Balinese *sléndro*, F sharp has been chosen for point of departure.

---

[9] See Appendix 1.

Chart 8. Equidistant pentatonic

366		420		483		554.5		637		732
	240		**240**		**240**		**240**		**240**	
	200		300		200		300		200	
F♯		G♯		B		C♯		E		F♯
366		410.5		488		548		652		732

While Chart 8 may prepare the reader for the strangeness of the *sléndro* system, it cannot be said that it is ever approached in Balinese practice. When Balinese *sléndro* tunings are examined, each is found to create a scale composed of intervals of recognizably different size. While each interval in itself never appears to be too far from the abstract "ideal" interval of 240 *C.*, the scale steps follow in such a way as to produce a contrasting series of larger and smaller intervals. And though offering less contrast than those of the *pélog* system, there is sufficient difference in the intervals of the *sléndro* scale to produce a melodic line of pronounced character.

There is less confusion in the *sléndro* system than there is in *pélog*, possibly because the scale is found in one ensemble only, the *gendèr wayang* of the shadowplay. There are no different scale forms with distinguishing names, although there is the same latitude in tuning as there is in the *pélog* ensembles. Our first example of *sléndro* as found in Bali is shown in Chart 9 compared with the equidistant pentatonic scheme just given. The tuning is taken from the *gendèr wayang* ensemble of Kuta village, which was famed throughout Bali in the thirties, and which can be heard in Odeon recordings.

Although *sléndro* is an independent scale system it employs the same solfeggio method

Chart 9. "Ideal" and actual sléndro

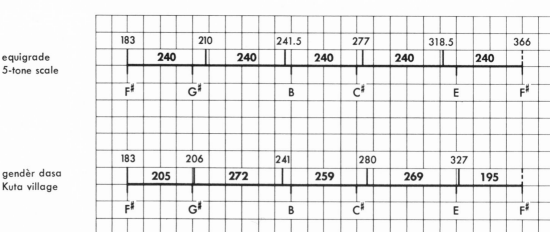

equigrade
5-tone scale

gendèr dasa
Kuta village

Order of tones:
dong   dèng   dung   dang   ding

used in *pélog*. The *sléndro* scale, however, as found on the ten-keyed *gendèr wayang*, starts from *dong* instead of *ding*, producing the series:

dong, dèng, dung, dang, ding,

and carrying this series an octave higher. In the past, when one-octave instruments were included in the ensemble to form the now obsolete *gamelan nandir*, their lowest tone was also *dong*.

In the following charts three *sléndro* tunings, beginning with that of Kuta, are shown for comparison. The first two scales, from villages some fifteen miles apart, resemble each other in general interval structure. Each begins and ends with an approximate major second. The other intervals remain about 250 C. In the third tuning, from a town farther away, the scale begins with a near minor third, followed by a near major second. Two intervals of about 250 C. then follow, with a final interval identical with that of Kuta.

Chart 10. Three sléndro scales compared

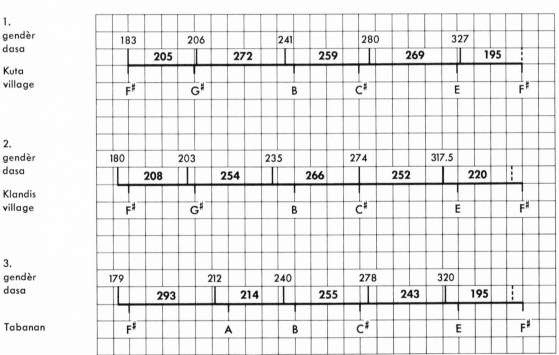

Order of tones in all three scales:
dong   dèng   dung   dang   ding

To illustrate further the Balinese *sléndro* system and the leeway in its tuning, three further examples are given below, all from the Bulelèng district in north Bali. As with the *pélog* tunings already presented, none of these *sléndro* tunings can be taken as the definitive scale form. What is perhaps most remarkable in their variability is that, unlike the *pélog* system, in which there are many different musical repertories, some heard in one scale, others in another,

51

in the *sléndro* system there is one basic repertory only, existing primarily for the shadowplay. This repertory is given endless variation in tonal color as it is performed by ensembles with widely divergent tunings.

Chart 11. Three additional sléndro tunings

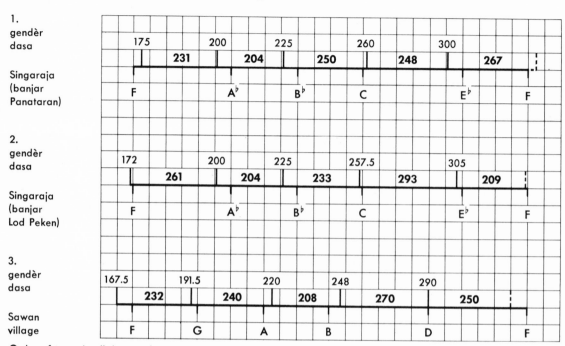

Order of tones in all three scales:
dong   dèng   dung   dang   ding

As in *pélog*, each of the five tones of the *sléndro* scale can in turn become the tonic or tonal center around which the composition revolves. It is interesting to note that despite the tonal differences of the two systems, for Balinese musicians there does exist a sufficient relationship between *sléndro* and *pélog* to allow for an occasional tone-for-tone transposition of a composition from one scale to the other. While transposition from *pélog* to *sléndro* is rare, the reverse is sometimes resorted to when, for instance, a composer wishing to create new music for a *pélog* gamelan draws from the *sléndro* repertory.

Chart 12. Pélog and sléndro scales compared

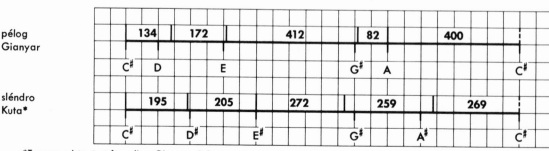

*Transposed to start from ding, Gianyar pitch.

What little the two systems have in common may be seen when a *pélog* scale and a *sléndro* scale are shown side by side, at which time the similarity and the contrast between the two are immediately apparent. In Chart 12 the *pélog* scale of the *gamelan gong* of Gianyar (Chart 5, No. 4) is shown with the *sléndro* scale of the Kuta *gendèr wayang* (Chart 10, No. 1). The *sléndro* scale has been arranged so as to start with *ding*, the first tone of the *pélog* series, and at the same time has been transposed so as to coincide in point of departure with the *pélog* scale.

The four-tone scale with *sléndro*-like intervals is known generally as the *saih angklung*, or

Chart 13. Four-tone sléndro

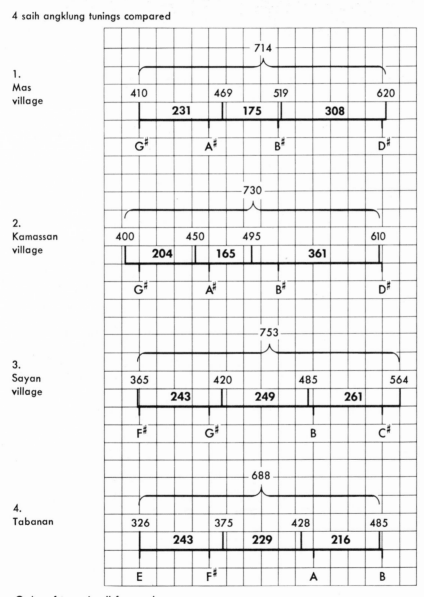

4 saih angklung tunings compared

Order of tones in all four scales:
dèng   dung   dang   ding

angklung scale, since it is employed exclusively by the four-tone orchestra known as the *gamelan angklung*. The Balinese consider this scale to be closely related to five-tone *sléndro*. In fact, it is said to be the *saih* of the *gendèr wayang*, except that it "lacks *dong*." In some districts the *gamelan angklung* is known as the *gamelan kembang kirang*, gamelan "lacking a flower," in reference to the "lacking" tone.

The *saih angklung* is by no means a curtailed scale, but a four-tone system complete in

Chart 14. Saih angklung; four unusual tunings

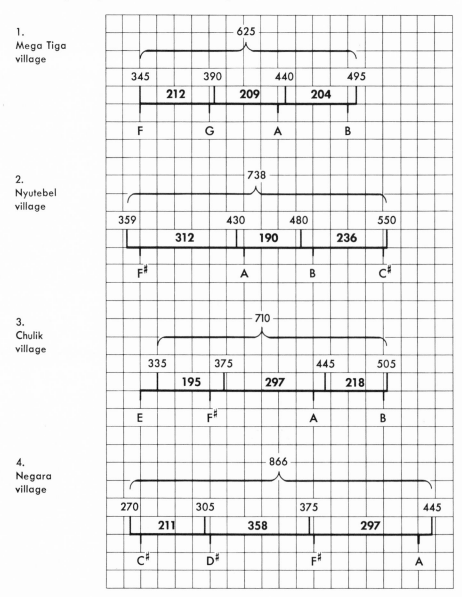

Order of tones in all four scales:
dèng   dung   dang   ding

itself. Unlike other scales, it never extends instrumentally to a second octave. All instruments of the gamelan are limited to a single octave, and the melodic line is confined to four tones whose normal range extends to around 700 *C.*, or a fifth.

In Chart 13, containing four characteristic *saih angklung* tunings, the distance between the two outer tones is shown to be fairly consistent, although the inner tones move about with the freedom typical of Balinese instrumental scales.

The *gamelan angklung* is found in almost every village in Bali, and while tunings will be found to vary in endless ways, the four scales shown in Chart 13 are sufficient to establish the general character of the *saih angklung*. The general pitch area for the scale lies between Nos. 1 and 4, and ensembles whose tunings are outside this area are rare.

Chart 14 presents four individual and most unusual forms of *saih angklung*. With these this survey of Balinese scales is concluded. Each came from remote villages in the Karangasem district of east Bali, where many archaic gamelans survive. Of special interest are the first and fourth scales—the former for its contracted range and its correspondingly contracted intervals consisting of three near whole-tones; and the latter for its unusually extended range of 866 *C.* and the curious position of the scale tones which create a scale consisting of a near major second followed by a neutral and a near minor third.

From the variability in the scales shown in the preceding charts, the impossibility of defining with finality the actual interval structure of any scale type is evident. Only the systems can be described and actual tunings given. Seven-tone *pélog* is found to be a scale with no fixed interval structure, whose tones are nameless until some five-tone scale has been established. Five-tone *pélog* and *sléndro* scales are found to be linked together by a common pentatonic solfeggio system which can only serve, however, to indicate a tonal sequence and the relative pitch of the scale tones. Nevertheless, this solfeggio system is useful here in furnishing an abstract key to the relation of the different scale systems.

5-tone pélog:	ding	dong	dèng	dung	dang
4-tone pélog:		dong	dèng	dung	dang
5-tone sléndro:		dong	dèng	dung	dang	ding
4-tone sléndro:			dèng	dung	dang	ding

The following pages will describe how these scale systems actually work.

Chapter 8

Notation and Terminology

SHOULD a Balinese composer wish to write down his music his only means of notation is a scanty set of symbols, derived from Balinese script, which can indicate scale tones but cannot express time values. In spite of the complex polyphony of the gamelan there is no way to indicate two voices at the same time. There is no way of expressing the intricate rhythms of the music itself. Only the bare melodic outline of the composition can be preserved, along with its basic punctuation by gong strokes and drum accents. In recent years numerals occasionally replace the original characters for the scale tones and some attempt is made to indicate melodic movement. Otherwise the system remains unchanged.

Notation, however, is not intended for use either at performances or during rehearsals. Indeed, few musicians in any gamelan are able to decipher a musical script if shown one. Notation is a simple mnemonic device for the music specialist, a musical code to be consulted should memory fail, its first use being to save from oblivion the melodic outline of ancient chants and ceremonial music so important to religious ritual. In preserving the basic melodic tones and the main punctuation which defines the metric structure of the composition this bare notation actually supplies all the necessary information. For the Balinese musician the rest is implicit. Polyphony, drumming, figuration and the various methods of orchestral organization—these have survived entirely through oral tradition, undergoing constant modifications and stylistic changes through revision by successive generations of musicians.

Like most classical Balinese literature, musical notations are ordinarily preserved in *lontar* form, inscribed on the prepared leaf of the *tal* palm.[1] The characters are scratched into the surface of the dried leaf with a small knife. The leaf is then waxed with *kemiri* nut, and soot or charcoal dust rubbed across the surface. When the surface is cleaned, dust remains in the engraved characters, making them legible. A second waxing seals them. The leaves thus prepared are held together by a cord passed through their centers or through one end of each leaf. The leaves are trimmed, and usually bound between two matching strips of bamboo or wood (Fig. 120). Nowadays pads and school note-books are also used for notations, which are written down in pencil or ink.

Only music in the *pélog* system is preserved in notation. Both the *sléndro* repertory of the shadowplay and the four-tone repertory of the *gamelan angklung* survive through memory alone. Moreover, in the *pélog* system the only seven-tone music which is written down is that of the *gambang* and *charuk* ensembles. No *lontar* containing the original repertory of the *gambuh* theater, which would throw considerable light on the *gambuh* scale system, is known to exist,[2]

---

[1] The palm, *Borassus flabelliformis*, whose broad leaf is still preferred for Balinese manuscripts. *Lontar* (metathesis for *ron-tal*), *tal*-leaf, refers especially to the inscribed leaf or leaves fastened together to form a book.

[2] A rare manuscript in my possession, *Dharma pegambuhan, Laws of the gambuh*, contains no reference whatever to music. My copy of *Dharma pewayangan, Laws of the shadowplay*, gives the lines to songs to be sung at certain places during the performance, but gives no musical notation.

nor even that of the derivative *gamelan Semar Pegulingan*, at least in its seven-tone form. These have survived through oral tradition alone. The *gambuh* repertory, however, when reduced to a single five-tone scale system, is occasionally preserved in notation, chiefly for use by the *lègong* ensemble.

The various musical repertories for which there is some form of musical notation can thus be summarized:

> seven-tone pélog
> > gending gambang and charuk
>
> five-tone pélog
> > gending gong gedé
> > gending gong kebyar
> > gending Semar Pegulingan
> > gending pelègongan
> > gending pejogèdan

The classical method of noting the melodic line to an instrumental composition or *gending* is simply to indicate the essential melodic tones as found within the limits of an octave. The basic or nuclear tones are called the *pōkok gending*,[3] the source-tones of the *gending*. Normally, the *pōkok* tones are of equal time value, a kind of cantus firmus from which the melody and figuration are realized. In the *gambang* ensemble, however, the *pōkok* tones are consistently syncopated throughout the *gending*, in a traditional style which is not indicated, though understood, in the notation (see Ex. 272).

Just when Balinese musical notation was developed is not known. It is assumed to be of local origin, possibly the invention of Hindu-Javanese migrating to Bali in the sixteenth century, who wished to preserve in some form their traditional music. This, however, is late in Balinese cultural history, and notation may well have been developed at an earlier period, either in Bali or in Java where, despite lack of actual evidence, it is believed that before the end of the Majapahit period some form of musical script had come into use.

The notation symbols themselves are for the most part borrowed from Balinese literary script, a script closely related to classical Javanese and deriving from Pali in the formation of its characters. The common Balinese name for musical notation is *grantang*, a word which at the same time means the symbol itself. *Pupuh*, melody or tune, is also used, although it refers more specifically to the actual melody than its notation.

Of all the repertories, only that of the *gamelan gambang* seems to have been preserved in consistent notation from one generation to the next. While the *gambang* system of notation, with its own special set of symbols, is reserved for a sacred repertory of music now played only at cremation rites, it serves as a point of departure for other derivative methods, and as such demands our first attention.

Unlike the *gambuh* method of shifting the solfeggio with transposition of the five-tone scale, the *gambang* solfeggio remains fixed, each of the seven tones having its permanent name regardless of scale change. Two tones bear the same name, *dong*, and two bear the name *dang*.

---

[3] The word *pōkok* is used in various ways, all referring to origin. *Pōkok yèh* is a water source or spring; *pōkok kayu* the living stump of a tree from which new shoots may sprout. *Pōkok* can also refer to the founders of a family, origins of a village, etc.

In each case the two tones are distinguished from each other by the terms, *ageng*, great, or low-pitched, and *alit*, small or high. Surprisingly, between the tones designated by *dong* (*ageng*) and *dèng*, normally adjacent, we find the tone *dang ageng*. Following *dang alit*, the sixth tone of the series, we find *dong alit*. When the two solfeggios are shown side by side, their differences are apparent:

saih 7	1	2	3	4	5	6	7
gambang	ding	dong ag.	dang ag.	dèng	dung	dang al.	dong al.
gambuh	ding	dong	dèng	p	dung	dang	p

Each tone of the *gambang* scale has its character or symbol. While these symbols are fairly consistently employed throughout the island, there are certain differences in their actual use. When several notations are compared, certain symbols may be found interchanged, or quite different ones substituted. Modern *lontars* usually include a key or clarification (*ketrangan*) to their contents, but most *gambang lontars* offer no such key. They are for personal use only, and most owners are reluctant to lend them. Actually, it may be said that no music *lontar* can be reliably deciphered without a key except by its owner, who may have inscribed it himself, or who may have inherited it along with its special method of notation.

The notation symbols themselves have names. Here again, the names can be misapplied, or changed as the symbols are modified. One example must suffice here to illustrate the basic system. The notation presented below, along with the nomenclature, is from a *lontar* loaned me by a *gambang* musician from Sukawati, whose ensemble furnished music for most of the cremation ceremonies of the region. The scale tones are given in ascending order from 1 to 7.

names of tones	characters	names of characters
1. ding	⌐	charik
2. dong ageng	⌐⌐	pōh or pa
3. dang ageng	—	pepet
4. dèng	Ɥ	talèng
5. dung	Ɥ, ᴜ	rōh
6. dang alit	ꙅ	bisah[4]
7. dong alit	ʊ, o, ૦	windu

The *lontar* contained in addition a small cross, +, ×, (*tapak* or *tampak dara*) to mark the endings of melodic sections.

So much for the seven-tone *gambang* notation system. All other Balinese notations employing characters derive from it, and are devised one way or another to preserve a purely five-tone melodic outline.

---

[4] In the Sukawati notation the character *bisah*, ꙅ, is an abbreviation of the complete and correct form, ꝫ . The character, *rōh*, Ɥ , is a common substitution for the more elongated character, *suku* ᴠ .

NOTATION AND TERMINOLOGY

While the repertory of traditional compositions of the *gamelan gong* are sometimes preserved in notation, complete *lontars* of such are not easy to find. It was only during the last year of my residence in Bali that I finally heard of one, said to belong to the *seka gong* of Pilan, a small hill village north of Sayan. Whether or not this was merely a legend I never found out, for although the musicians of Pilan promised on several occasions to produce the manuscript for my inspection on my next visit, it never was forthcoming. Old Lunyuh from Payangan, however, a specialist in *gending gong* and one of my most valued informants, surprised me one day by presenting me with a collection of *pōkok* tones to some forty different compositions of the *gamelan gong* repertory, including examples in all eight metric forms. These he had written down in traditional notation, penciled into a ruled school notebook.

Lunyuh's notation was consistently employed, and agrees in general with the *gambang* system shown above, although symbols for only five scale tones are necessary. His use of symbols indicating gong punctuation is a free adaptation of notation methods for music more metrically complex than that of the *gambang* repertory.

tones	characters	Lunyuh's names
1. ding	—	charik
2. dong	⌒	"pōh" (tedung correct)
3. dèng	⟩	talèng
4. dung	⟩⎮	"surang" (suku correct)
5. dang	⅔	bisah
kempli	✕	tampak dara
kempur	o	matan titiran
gong ageng	◎	(no name)

As in the *gambang* system, the notation shown here makes no attempt to express a melodic line extending into a second octave. It suffices, however, for the *pōkok* tones, as performed by one-octave instruments, along with basic metric scansion by different gongs. As we shall find later, drumming is implicit in the metric form, sufficiently defined, both in notation and performance, by the gong punctuation.

Modern Balinese notation frequently takes the *pōkok* tones for granted and attempts to record in outline the more lyrical melody, as performed by instruments with a wider melodic range. Additional characters are employed to designate tones lying above and below the basic one-octave scale. Indications for important drum-strokes may be included. An attempt is made to indicate secondary, ornamental tones in the melodic line; short slurs may bind together groups of tones that move at double speed, or indicate grace notes and short glissandos.

As illustration of this more elaborate method, the *ketrangan* or explanation to a *lontar* from north Bali, entitled *Pupuh gending lègong, Melodies to gending lègong*, is given below. This notation consists of characters for nine scale tones; the basic series from *ding* to *dang*, here distinguished by the term *panengah*, middle (register), plus two additional low (*ageng*) and two high (*alit*) tones. Four more characters indicate gong punctuation and melodic grace notes or glissandos (*ngorot*). This *ketrangan* was copied for me by the owner of the *lontar* into a notebook. The characters are well-formed and reliable, easily identifiable with their correct names given beside them. These names were not in the original *lontar* but given to me orally by the transcriber.

The ketrangan

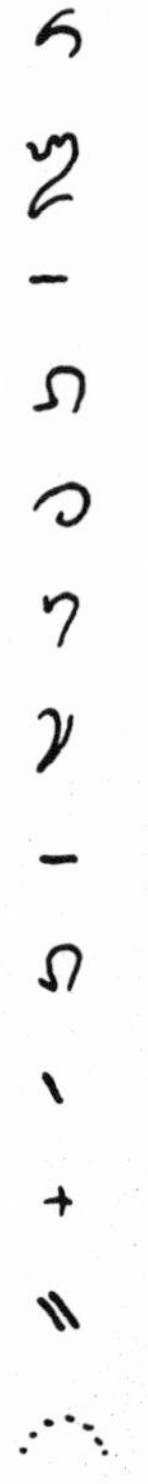

		names of characters
ᨀ	ndèng ageng[5]	é-kara
ᨁ	ndung ageng	u-kara
—	ndang panengah	chechek
ᨂ	nding panengah	ulu
ᨃ	ndong panengah	tedung
ᨄ	ndèng panengah	talèng
ᨅ	ndung panengah	suku
—	ndang alit	chechek
ᨆ	nding alit	ulu
\	angsel[6]	charik
+	atengah kajar[7]	tapak dara
\\	kajar	charik kali
⋰⋱	ngorot	tanda ngorot

A few additional characters may appear in manuscripts devoted to other types of *gendings*. These refer to technical details special to the *gending*, such as the terminal *gong* stroke, the *kumpung* and *kepek*—contrastingly deep and high-pitched drum passages—and occasionally the *pejalan gending*, groups of melodic tones in faster tempo. Some symbols substitute for

---

5 Ndèng, or nèng, for dèng, etc., is common usage among Balinese musicians, especially when singing the scale-tones.
6 Angsel, the accented phrase-break (see p. 175), is stressed by the kempur.
7 Atengah kajar, midway between kajar beats, is a metric point generally stressed by the kemong.

others. The characters given below practically complete the set of symbols which form the basis for Balinese musical notation.

symbol	term	term
(gong character)	gong	pemada
(character)		
x †		tapak dara
«	kepek	charik kali
x +	kumpung	tapak dara
⌒	pejalan gending	tanda pejalan gending
x +	kemong	tapak dara
(	dang ageng	surang
(character)	dong ageng	pa kapal

In the thirties, a few Balinese musicians had begun to follow the modern Javanese system of notation, using numerals to indicate the scale tones. Unlike the Javanese method, in which the ciphers 1 to 7 represent the seven tones of the full seven-tone *pélog* scale, the Balinese method normally employs only the numerals 1 to 5, which represent the tones *ding* to *dang* in their usual order:

ding	dong	dèng	dung	dang
1	2	3	4	5

The absence of the two remaining tones of the *saih 7* system is apparent only when the Balinese cipher notation is compared with that of Java:

Java:	1	2	3	4	5	6	7
Bali:	1	2	3		4	5	

A dot placed below a cipher indicates a tone lying below the basic series, while a dot above indicates a tone in the register above. These indications, however, are necessary only where an attempt is made to note the full melodic line. They are not necessary for the *pōkok* tones, which lie within the range of a single octave. The cipher method is used in the present study when Western musical notation is not employed.

The large Balinese musical vocabulary points to an elaborate musical practice with a wealth of technical resources. Partly inherited from Java, it includes a limited number of words of Sanskrit, Arabic and Malayan origin, some retaining their original form and meaning, others now applied in a purely local sense. A considerable part of the terminology is native to Bali alone, and refers to musical ideas and methods particularly Balinese.

The number of basic terms common to Bali and Java indicate the close connection between the musical practices of the two islands. Instrumental names such as *gendér*, *suling*, and *kendang*, musical terms such as *lagu*, melody, *gending*, instrumental composition, *gongan*, melodic period ending with a *gong* beat, and *pengelik*, melodic section in the high register—these are but a few of the words having an identical meaning in both places. It is where Balinese musical procedures take on a character quite their own that terms common to Java begin to acquire a different meaning. It is also likely that, owing to the survival of an earlier Javanese culture in Bali, many terms which are used differently in Java today retain their earlier significance. All names and terms found in the present book are used in their purely Balinese sense. Most colloquial Malayan words, which Balinese frequently substitute when speaking with a Westerner, have been avoided.

The compositions of different gamelans bear titles rich in poetic allusion and pictorial imagery. For the most part, the titles are not directly descriptive, though they may suggest the majestic or playful character of the music. Many derive from Hindu mythology and the legendary world of the Balinese theater. Some bear Sanskrit titles such as *Chandrakanta, Moongem; Brahmara, Bee; Durga* (Goddess of Death); *Suddamala, Freed of Evil.* Others, drawn from Javano-Balinese literary sources bear *kawi* names, like *Semarandhana, Fire of Love; Segara Wira, Raging Sea; Segara Madu, Sea of Honey; Bhimakrodah, Wrath of Bhima; Alas Harum, Scented Forest;* and *Chandih Rebah, Fallen Temple.* Most, however, are in everyday Balinese—*Galang Kangin, Light in the East* or *Dawn; Galang Bulan, Moonlight; Batuh Rubuh, Rock Falling; Sekar Puchuk, Hibiscus Blossom; Mangis Kuning, Yellow Mango.* Balinese fantasy is seen in the names of popular tunes played on the flute and by the *gamelan angklung*, such as *Chapung Manjus, Dragon-fly Bathing* or *Buya Mangap, Crocodile Snapping.* An extended list of these titles will be found on page 255. More unusual are the names, *Pis satus selaka loyang, One hundred coins in false silver,* and *Gontèng, Alarm-Clock,* inspired, according to its composer, I Lotring, by the chimes on a small clock. The list of such popular titles is endless, and new ones are constantly being invented.

Chapter 9

The Gamelan Gong

FOREMOST of Balinese gamelans is the *gamelan gong*, whose stately ceremonial music may be heard at all formal and festive occasions. As formerly maintained in the larger Balinese courts, this orchestra included some forty musicians and was known as the *gamelan gong gedé*, the gamelan with great *gongs*. Such large ensembles are now rare. Reduced to some twenty-five instruments this orchestra, while still including the large *gongs*, is generally referred to simply as the *gamelan gong*, and in almost every village is maintained primarily for temple festivals. All ceremonies of magnitude, religious or otherwise, are opened with a traditional repertory of pieces known as the *gending gong*, compositions for the *gamelan gong*. This orchestra is also used to accompany *tōpèng*, the historical mask-play, and *baris*, the formalized drill dance performed by men. In older villages the gamelan is also used to accompany ritual dances that take place within the temple. A modernized, more popular form of *gamelan gong*, sometimes referred to as *gong kebyar*, is now found in many towns and villages. In the present chapter only the traditional *gamelan gong* is discussed, as found in its older, most complete form.

Large or small, the traditional *gamelan gong* is organized according to a system which serves as the basis for most orchestral methods employed in Bali today. It is essentially an ensemble composed of various instrumental groups, each with its own characteristic function. There is no change in instrumental methods from one *gending* to the next. While each of the different gamelan types has its own highly individual orchestral style and color, resulting from the choice of instruments employed, within any given ensemble a single orchestral method is consistently used throughout. Only in recent times has variety in the orchestral texture been developed. With the exception of those small ensembles requiring no more than four or five players, all Balinese gamelans can be reduced to four main instrumental groups: those that are assigned the melody, in both its basic and extended form; those that perform figuration; those that can be classified as colotomic or punctuating instruments; and the drums, whose function is to lead the ensemble, controlling both tempo and dynamics.

This basic system, however, allows for much variability in instrumental balance in the different ensembles, as will be seen in the following chapters. In the *gamelan gong* the melodic section consists mainly of one-octave metallophones which sound the basic or nuclear melody. Extended melody is performed by a solo *trompong*. In larger ensembles this solo is generally doubled an octave higher by a second and smaller *trompong*, the *trompong barangan* or follower. Figuration is confined to the four-tone *réong*, and often is barely audible because of the almost overwhelming resonance of the cymbals and drums.

In setting out the gamelan, the instruments are arranged according to both their resonance and their function. The method described here, followed by the forty-piece *gamelan gong* of Sulaan village (Figs. 8–21) is typical. The two *trompongs*, whose melodic extension of the nuclear tones forms the heart of the music, are placed in the center of the ensemble, the leading *trompong* in front, the follower behind. In front and to the side of the *trompongs* are arranged the metallophones which sound or stress the nuclear tones of the composition. The more percussive *sarons* or *gangsas* of the group, whose tones are of relatively short duration, are placed, along with the *réong*, in the center of the gamelan, the large *gangsas* in front, the small one behind (Figs. 11, 15).

The more vibrant instruments of the *gendèr* group are divided into two balancing sets and placed along the sides of the gamelan. Arranged according to size, they stand in two diminishing rows. The *jegogans*, which arè lowest in pitch, and which do no more than stress the nuclear tones at regular intervals, are placed in front. Behind them stand the *jublags* and in the rear the *penyachahs*. These double the *gangsas*, adding sweetness and prolonging the nuclear tones with their vibrant resonance. In the center rear are placed the two drummers, and near them sit the cymbal players. At the very back are found the four vertically hung gongs, along with the *kempli* and *pŏnggang* (Figs. 16, 17).

Like most other ensembles of the *gamelan gong* type, the Sulaan gamelan was said to be tuned to the scale, *Selisir gong*. The Sulaan tuning is shown below, compared with the scale of the *gamelan gong* of Gianyar, already given in Chart 5 (No. 4). This latter scale is shown again because of all *Selisir* tunings given in the preceding charts it offers the most natural key to the musical illustrations which follow.

Selisir gong

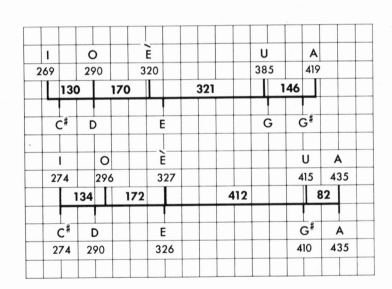

Expressed in Western notation with qualifying pitch symbols the two scales would appear thus:

Ex. 1. Selisir gong

Since the scale charts supply more precise information, this method is not employed in the present book.

With the general tonality of the *gamelan gong* thus established, the instrumental ranges can now be shown. Ex. 2 lists the instruments of the *gamelan gong* in Sulaan village, a large ensemble requiring forty-one players. The metallophone group, comprising twenty-four instruments, is unusually large; fewer *sarons* are normally employed, while two *jegogans* are standard. Those gongs whose final pitch is not stabilized but varies from gamelan to gamelan are indicated by an asterisk.

Ex. 2. Instruments of the gamelan gong; Sulaan village

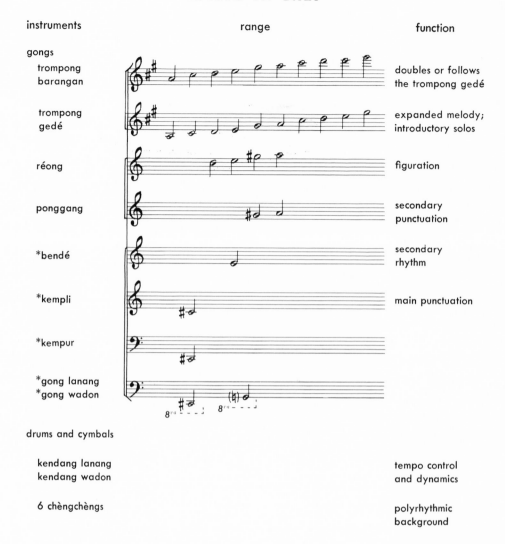

instruments	range	function
gongs		
trompong barangan		doubles or follows the trompong gedé
trompong gedé		expanded melody; introductory solos
réong		figuration
ponggang		secondary punctuation
*bendé		secondary rhythm
*kempli		main punctuation
*kempur		
*gong lanang / *gong wadon		
drums and cymbals		
kendang lanang / kendang wadon		tempo control and dynamics
6 chèngchèngs		polyrhythmic background

As can be seen, the nuclear melody or *pōkok gending* must be confined on each single-octave instrument to a five-tone range. Heard alone, without melodic realization, the *pōkok* tones offer little clue to the more fluid contour of the melody when fully expanded. Sounding in regular succession and periodically stressed by the *jegogans*, they provide a continuous cantus firmus which only in the longer and more elaborately constructed compositions will be broken by sectional pauses in the *gending*.

Ex. 3. Pōkok tones and jegogan stress tones; gending Silir ♩ = 46–60

pōkok

jegogans

Only with melodic expansion do the *pōkok* tones take on musical meaning, as shown in the following *trompong* realization of the tones given above. Because of the confined range, certain progressions in the *pōkok* tones, when compared with the *trompong* melody, are seen to be inversions.

Ex. 4. Trompong realization of pōkok tones; gending Silir

Performing the nuclear melody is a simple, almost mechanical act, requiring little more than the application of the collective memory of the group. Melodic realization by the *trompong* soloist, however, is a highly developed art. The leading *trompong* player is the one free spirit of the *gamelan gong*. The second *trompong*, if included in the gamelan, does little more than double the first an octave higher, and is used only in the sections for full orchestra. It is for the leading *trompong* player to introduce the composition to the rest of the musicians in a long, half improvised solo, transform the *pōkok* tones into fluid melody ornamented with light embellishments, and fill in the pauses between movements in the composition with solo interludes. He is free to interpret the nuclear melody with spontaneous rhythmic and melodic liberty. No two performances are ever quite the same. At the same time, he must preserve a nice balance between his own improvisational playing and the fixed *pōkok* tones of the composition. These he must know by heart and be able to anticipate melodically if his performance is to have flow and rhythmic elasticity. He must think of the *gending* in terms of sustained and constantly moving melody. While the other musicians pause at specific points during the course of the music, his solo part is the essential melodic thread, extending from start to finish, and bridging all sectional gaps in the composition. Although the *pōkok* tones may serve as melodic guides, he must at all times rely upon his own memory to tell him when the melody moves parallel to the *pōkok* tones and when it moves in contrary motion. Since many of the *gendings* take a good half hour to play through, this is no ordinary feat.

Style in the rendition of the *trompong* part is partly a matter of regional tradition, partly a question of the performer's individual taste. In the hill villages of south Bali the general tendency is toward simplicity and restraint. In the lowlands the melodic line is rendered more supple through the frequent introduction of embellishments and syncopations. This is especially so in gamelans which do not include a second *trompong*, and where the soloist is at complete liberty to perform as he pleases. In north Bali an extravagantly baroque style is favored. The nuclear tones of the composition serve as point of departure for floridly ornamental melody, executed with such sweeping and elegant gestures that the performance becomes almost a dance.

The solo is played without nuance or phrasing. Various forms of embellishment give the necessary emphasis to important melodic tones. These embellishments are standard and known everywhere. In its extended form the melody now moves almost entirely by conjunct motion; large intervals occurring in the nuclear melody are bridged by passing-tones and short glissandos. While skips do occasionally occur they are rare. Essentially the *trompong* solo furnishes the pattern for all Balinese instrumental melody.

Two ways of playing the melody are employed—in unison and in octaves. Unison passages are performed with both hands, which strike the gongs in irregular alternation. This style of playing is called *rangkep*, or *ngerangkep*, to perform with both hands held close together (Fig. 22). Octave playing is called *ngembat*, to perform with arms extended (Fig. 24). Both methods are used in the same composition. Passages in the lower register are of necessity played in unison; as the melody ascends to the upper register, the left hand reinforces the right in the octave below. The two methods are combined in many ways. *Ngerangkep* is especially adaptable to animated passages; *ngembat* is employed more consistently in the slower sections.

The most commonly employed embellishment in unison passages is called *numpuk* (to pile up), and consists of a short or extended group of rapid ornamental tones preceding a main tone, divided between the two hands in the following manner:

Ex. 5.

While the melodic tones are allowed to ring out freely, the *numpuk* is performed in a light staccato. The gongs are muted by allowing the sticks to rest on the bosses after striking, stopping the sound and producing a short, dry tone:

Ex. 6.

Swiftly executed, and with a delicacy of touch that contrasts strongly with the natural chiming legato of the *trompong*, the *numpuk* gives lightness and a unique tremulous grace to the melodic line. While shorter forms are used throughout the *gending*, the extended *numpuk* is heard only in the freely performed, quasi-recitative introductory solo by the leading *trompong*. Characteristic use of the *numpuk* is shown in the following example, the opening phrase of the introduction to the *gending*, *Tabuh Talōh*, which will be found quoted in full in Appendix 3, Ex. 348.

Ex. 7. Tabuh Talōh; trompong introduction

Other more or less stereotyped ornamental figures used in *rangkep* passages, popularly referred to as *kembang(an)*, flowers, give movement and suppleness to the melodic line, and may be simple or elaborate, according to the taste or momentary fancy of the performer. The next example shows a typical ornamental turn bridging two adjacent structural tones (*a*). The turn is given in simple form, along with characteristic variants.

Ex. 8.

Transposed to bridge two other adjacent main tones, the same turn becomes

Ex. 9.

In bridging wider intervals, the turn may take the following forms:

Ex. 10.

Rangkep passages may also be performed *tutug*, tones "following and catching up with." The term refers to the left hand, which repeats each tone sounded by the right.

Ex. 11.

Here the tones produced by the right hand are open, while the left stops them with an almost inaudible damping stroke. The tones which are actually intended to catch the ear sound on the offbeats:

Ex. 12.

69

Another form of *tutug*, used in more animated movements, combines stopped single tones with octaves. Extended passages, prolonged at will, are thus rhythmically shifted to the off-beat.

Ex. 13.

The passing from unison to octave playing is usually effected by means of the *ngorèt*,[1] a short three-note glissando leading to the octave. Extended glissandos are not used.

Ex. 14.

The *ngorèt* is also used in octave passages in slow tempo to embellish main tones within the phrase:

Ex. 15. Gending Lasem; excerpt ♩ = 46–60

A further embellishment in *ngembat* passages is the broken octave:

Ex. 16.

---

[1] To slide along in a line or graze, "like striking a match."

70

In addition to octaves, some *trompong* players introduce during *ngerangkep* passages sixths or fifths, which find their resolution in a following unison or octave:

Ex. 17. Gending Sanara; excerpt ♩ = 46–60

Attention is called in the following example not only to the fifths in the *trompong* part but to the rhythmic change in the *pōkok* tones which the fifths serve to intensify. Such changes are rare. Introduced well after the steady beat has been established, they create an arresting effect, momentarily disturbing the balance in the slow, regular flow of the *pōkok* tones.

Ex. 18. Gending Lasem; close of first movement ♩ = 46–60

In both unison and octave passages the *trompong* melody can be given still more flexibility by prolonged playing off the beat, consistently avoiding the *pōkok* tones or sounding in syncopated counter-rhythm. "Evading" the *pōkok* tones (*ngagol*), "following" them (*nganterin*), playing in a "deceptive" manner (*gebug* or *nelep maya*, from *maya*, meaning illusion), are popular terms referring to this method as opposed to the plain or *pōlos* style. Commonly heard is the term *ngarèn*, sounding afterwards (*ari*, coming or born later), although anticipation of the *pōkok* tones sometimes occur. In the following example the *trompong* part is less melodic than ornamental, the *ngarèn* figures merely filling in between *pōkok* tones.

Ex. 19.

A more complex *ngarèn* style can transform the melodic line into taut, highly syncopated continuity. Against the even beat of the *pōkok* tones, extended counter-rhythmic patterns are established which find partial resolution at structural points within the melodic period, but which reach full completion only with the terminal note. A strong, independent melodic line is the result, in rhythmic conflict with the basic tones and maintaining a high degree of tension throughout. While numberless examples might be given here, each with its special tendencies, the following example and the one found on page 73 are highly characteristic. These may serve at the same time as an introduction to the Balinese feeling for syncopation, which will be found expressed in many different ways in following chapters. Our first example consists of the repeating closing section to *gending Tembung*, a short composition in one movement.

Ex. 20. Gending Tembung; excerpt ♩ = 60

The above example, a complete melodic statement in itself, is seen to contain in the *trompong* version two pairs of contrasting phrases, *a, b, a, c,* although the *pōkok* tones give no indication of inner phrase structure. When the first phrase, *a,* of the *trompong* melody is written in its correct rhythmic notation, that is, expressed in terms of thirty-two fractional beats rather than in syncopated relation to the eight *pōkok* tones, its true independent metric structure becomes clear. The offbeats are no longer anticipations or retards, but main beats of a compound rhythmic pattern composed of inner rhythmic units of different lengths, which finds its silent resolution on the first beat of the following phrase, *b.*

Ex. 21.

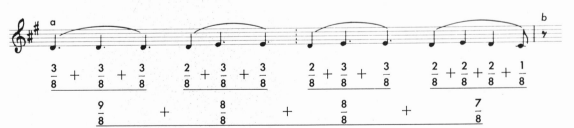

THE GAMELAN GONG

As a rhythmic unit composed essentially of disparate subunits, this compact pattern is clearly related in conception and impulse to Indian *tala*. Unlike *tala*, the pattern does not form the rhythmic basis for the entire period. The second phrase shows a quite different impulse. It is relatively relaxed, the syncopations mere filling-in tones between the basic beats. With the third phrase the initial tension is resumed. The fourth is again relaxed, with momentary cross-rhythmic tension toward the middle of the phrase.

In phrase *a*, the presence of $\frac{9}{8}$ at the beginning shifts the phrase forward a fractional beat, and is balanced at the end by a correspondingly reduced $\frac{7}{8}$. Such shifting and final balancing can be modified or developed in many ways. It is found not only in short rhythmic phrases but, in augmentation, frequently forms the basis in modern compositions for broad phrase structure in extended musical periods.

The above example can be performed without difficulty by two *trompongs*, the second player following or occasionally simplifying. The next example, ornate and rhythmically intricate, could not possibly be performed with a following *trompong*. It is characteristic of the true *trompong* solo, as performed in the lowlands. Here, alone, the performer can give free rein to his creative impulse. While similar in impulse to the preceding example, the following passage shows less orderly organization. The performer makes use of established rhythmic patterns but invents as he proceeds.[2] Definite counter-rhythm begins at *a*, and is maintained until *b*, when the pattern changes to purely ornamental filling-in tones. At *c* counter-rhythm is resumed, followed by more filling-in tones which continue till the repeat. Attention is called to the free relation of the melody to the *pōkok* tones at *e*.

Ex. 22. Gending Longgor; excerpt $\quad \quad \text{♩} = 76\text{–}92$

---

[2] This passage, obtained from my informant I Lunyuh, at my request was played several times over without significant change. Later repeats brought a wealth of variants.

73

Based on units of eight, sixteen, or thirty-two fractional beats, the counter-rhythmic passages occurring in the *trompong* solo give it vitality and rhythmic drive. The temporary disturbances of rhythmic balance thus created are intensified by the unbroken regularity of the *pōkok* tones, whose steady, slow beat offers strong rhythmic contrast to the freely moving solo. While the eight-beat unit, when divided regularly, offers little in the way of rhythmic variety it becomes a vital rhythmic source when irregularly divided, as shown in the permutations given below. In this form it lies at the heart of Balinese rhythm, a germinal rhythmic unit to be developed in endless ways. The larger units offer the *trompong* soloist wide scope for creating broader rhythm. A few examples of their breakdown into fractional beats, as noted during performance, are given here in illustration.

Ex. 23.

8 beats			16 beats						32 beats											
3	3	2	3	2	3	2	3	3	3	3	3	2	3	3	2	3	3	2	3	2
3	2	3	4	3	3	3	3		3	3	3	3	3	2	3	3	3	3		
2	3	3	4	4	3	3	2		4	4	3	3	3	3	3	5	4			
									8	4	4	3	2	3	2	3	3			

Such rhythmic subdivisions, as introduced in the *trompong* solo, are spontaneous rather than premeditated. They are improvisational disturbances rather than set metrical formulas for a complete musical period. Never repeated immediately, they lead directly to some relatively strong *pōkok* beat, for example the beginning of a new phrase or the end of a musical period.

Ex. 24.

4 3 3 3 3 | 1   or   3 3 2 | 1

At this point passage-work based on the fundamental beat is normally resumed, although some performers carry the preceding patterns well into the next phrase, as in *gending Longgor* (Ex. 22) at the end of the second and beginning of the third lines.

Ex. 25.

3 3 3 3 3 2 3 3 3 3 | 3 3 3 3 4 etc.

While the source for such rhythmic passages, based essentially on the dual conception of a single metric unit, may well lie in an early Indian *tala* system, they should be considered here in their independent Balinese context. A systematic classification of such pattern formulas as noted here does not exist in Bali. It is necessary, however, to define in these terms the rhythmic impulse of such passages, since they lead to the immediate understanding of the structure of so many rhythmically complex passages in Balinese music.

The translation of the *pōkok* tones into so taut and rhythmically intricate a melodic line is purely a *trompong* idiom, not met with in the melodic instruments of other ensembles. These ornate solos stand quite apart in present-day Balinese musical expression, and offer a fascinating glimpse of a past musical style. Performing them in what may be called the grand manner is a rapidly vanishing art. Stylistically, a certain parallel exists between the Balinese *trompong* solos and the far less elaborate solos performed on the Javanese *kolenang*, a similar instrument found in the *gamelan degung* of the Sunda district. A further echo of the style can be heard in the ornate solos of the Indian *jalatarang*, a series of graded small bowls containing water, which are also sounded with sticks. Here the similarity ends, however, because of the broad structure of Balinese compositions and the large-scale organization of the gamelan.

While the *trompong* translates the *pōkok* tones into extended melody, these are at the same time linked together by continuous, barely audible figuration executed on the *réong* by an interdependent pair of performers. This figuration is known as the *réongan*, and ripples gently throughout the composition in an unbroken flow of ornamental tones. Limited to a series of four tones, the *réongan* is the antithesis of the *trompong* solo in its confined range of movement. Each player controls two of the small gongs mounted in a horizontal row. These are tuned to the tones *dong*, *dèng*, *dung* and *dang*.

Ex. 26.

Within this narrow frame varied and constantly changing figuration is produced, deriving from a closely coordinated rhythmic interplay of the four tones. Through the irregular alternation of right and left hands, the two players create two separate voices which lock in essentially opposing rhythms to create a single and continuous stream of figuration. The basic system for the *réongan* is shown in the following example, which gives both the interplay and the resulting figuration.

Ex. 27. Réong interplay*

* Réongs sound here, as in the following examples, one octave higher.

It can readily be seen from this example that the two parts composing the *réongan* move not only in opposing rhythms but in essentially contrary motion. The core of the *réong* idiom lies in the two progressions:

Ex. 28.

Perfect balance in the interplay of upper and lower voices is preserved throughout the composition, a balance which seems well expressed in the following detail from a longer passage:

Ex. 29.

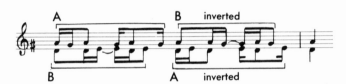

The normal speed of the *réongan* figuration is at the rate of eight tones to one *pōkok* tone. In animated movements where the *pōkok* tones move at double speed, the *réongan*, maintaining its basic tempo, sounds only four tones to one *pōkok* tone. Melodically, the pattern continuity of the *réongan* derives its impulse from the *pōkok* tones. Depending on their sequence, these tones are sounded simultaneously in either upper or lower voice. Characteristic linking of the *pōkok* tones is shown in the following example.

Ex. 30.

For the tone *ding*, missing in the *réong*, the tone *dung* is generally substituted, as in *a* in the following example, although occasionally other substitutions may be employed, such as that shown in *b*.

Ex. 31.

Two essentially different types of *réongan* may be distinguished: *a*) recurring patterns, based on short melodic ostinato units, which repeat more or less unchanged with each repetition of the motif; and *b*) unfolding patterns which develop over a more extended period. In the following examples, the recurring type is shown in *gending Longgor*, while the unfolding type may be seen in an excerpt from *gending Kambing Domba*.

Ex. 32. Gending Longgor; final section ♩ = 120

Ex. 33. Gending Kambing Domba; excerpt ♩ = 60

Like the *trompong* solo, *réong* figuration derives its continuity from the combination of two different kinds of rhythmic impulse. More or less regular ornamentation is created through simple two-part interplay based essentially on the established beat.

Ex. 34.

With a more complex interplay between the two parts, the *réongan* is transformed into a figuration composed of two interdependent but quite separate rhythmic elements. The germinal eight-beat unit can be broken up differently in upper and lower voices to create a variety of polyrhythmic patterns.

Ex. 35.

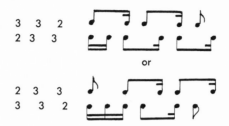

By letting one voice begin a fractional beat late, the pattern can be extended beyond its normal limit:

Ex. 36.

With the extension of the unit from eight to sixteen fractional beats—the duration of two *pōkok*-tones or beats—the interplay becomes increasingly involved, as shown in Ex. 37.

Ex. 37.

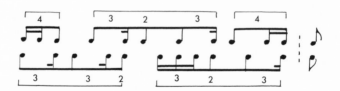

Depending on the length of the musical period, the *réongan* unfolds in continually changing patterns, its rhythmic structure kept constantly alive through the positive-negative relation of the two voices. While based on the *pōkok* tones, it forms at the same time a free variation of the melodic line; light clashes with the *trompong* are frequent, as may be seen in Ex. 38.

Ex. 38.

Like the *trompong* solo, the *réongan* is partly improvised but must at the same time follow the basic melodic line. But while the *trompong* solo is essentially an individual form of expression, the two *réong* players are completely interdependent. They must understand each other musically, must have had long experience playing together if smooth interplay between their two parts is to result. More essential than the actual sequence of tones is an unbroken rhythmic continuity. Since neither player sounds the two gongs at his disposal at the same time to create clashing seconds, a harmonious figuration will result even though accord between the two players is momentarily lost. There is no terminology to distinguish one part as more important than the other. Whoever finds the *pōkok* tone or tones within the range of his two gongs may be said to momentarily take the lead.

The *réongan* is often referred to as the *chandetan*, from *nyandet*, to perform two-part interlocking rhythmic patterns. This term is used generally in referring to two-part interplay of interdependent instruments. In the *gamelan gong* it refers particularly to syncopated interlocking rhythms that form part of the cymbal interplay.

The four or more men who compose the *chèngchèng* or cymbal section unite to create a continuous and tightly organized polyrhythmic accompaniment. Each player has his characteristic and unchanging rhythmic pattern; the different parts unite in an unbroken percussive figuration that moves at the same speed as the *réongan*. While two players alone are sufficient to create a steady flow of sound, four are considered a minimum for satisfactory interplay. In the largest gamelans, however, at least six performers, operating among them eight *chakap* (pair) of cymbals, are considered indispensable to support the powerful resonance of the orchestra (Fig. 20).

Through the use of the cymbals three distinct degrees of dynamic intensity are possible for the complete gamelan. Without change in dynamics by the main ensemble different passages can be made to sound fortissimo, a normal forte, or relatively soft, through a heavy or light underlining by the cymbals. A still lighter effect is obtained by their temporary or prolonged silence. Orchestral tuttis are generally referred to by the term, *rangkep*, complete or full.[3] Passages without cymbals are known as the *pengisep* (from *ngisep*, breathe in, take a breath). Following prolonged *rangkep* passages, the *pengisep* offers contrast and relief in its relative lightness. With the re-entry of the cymbals the initial splendor of sound is regained, often dramatically intensified by heavy unison cymbal accents.

The size and organization of the cymbal group varies somewhat from gamelan to gamelan, but all groups include a pair of musicians to stress in turn the beats and offbeats, and an interdependent pair to perform the syncopated *chandetan*. Unlike the *réongan* however, cymbal rhythms, simple or complex, do not unfold. Based on a unit of four, eight, or sixteen fractional beats, patterns are mere rhythmic clichés which are given an almost mechanical repetition. Because of the individual timbres of the different sized cymbals, each separate rhythmic current can be clearly distinguished. At the same time, all parts merge to create a homogeneous whole, a composite repeat-pattern in which each fractional beat is heard in one part or another.

---

[3] *Rangkep*, double, close together, has many musical meanings—twice as fast, crowded together, doubled. See Appendix 2, Glossary.

Typical six-part cymbal interplay is shown in the following example, the system employed in Sulaan. The cymbals are represented from top to bottom in the score in increasing order of size and resonance and corresponding descent in pitch. The upper sounds are thin and ringing, the lowest a powerful clash. The players sit in a circle, interdependent pairs facing each other, as shown in the diagram and in Fig. 20. The local nomenclature distinguishing the different cymbals is partly onomatopoeic, partly functional, referring both to sounds produced and to the characteristic rhythms. While four players sound their rhythms on single, upturned cymbals, the two who perform the *nichik* and *ngōbak* each control an upturned pair, striking them in regular alternation of left and right hand. Since the *bendé*, the special vertical gong with sunken boss, is auxiliary to the cymbal group rather than the gongs, it has been included here.

Ex. 39. Polyrhythmic cymbal interplay

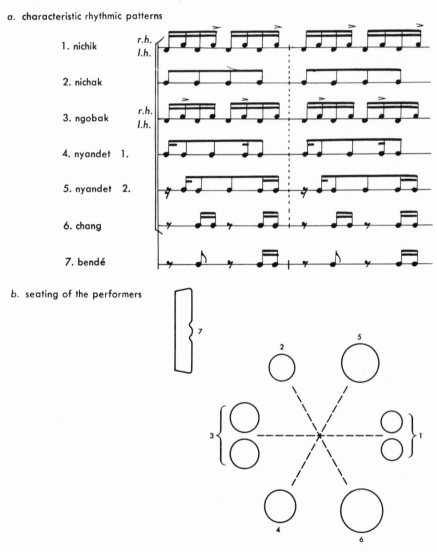

A more complex interplay, creating the same general effect but based on a somewhat different organization, is found in smaller cymbal groups commonly employed in the lowlands. In an ensemble of four, the players are divided into two interdependent pairs. One pair is assigned the two-part *chandetan*, performed on the smallest cymbals. The other pair is divided into the leading *nyachah*, (chop small), sounding on the beat, and the complementary *nyangsih* (differing) part, sounding generally on fractional offbeats. While the *chandetan* patterns are for the most part based on the unit of eight fractional beats, *nyachah* and *nyangsih* patterns usually extend to twice this length. Considerable polyrhythmic variety is possible in this type of interplay, and the close interlocking of the four parts creates a special dynamic energy and animation which the massive six-part ensemble cannot attain.

Ex. 40.

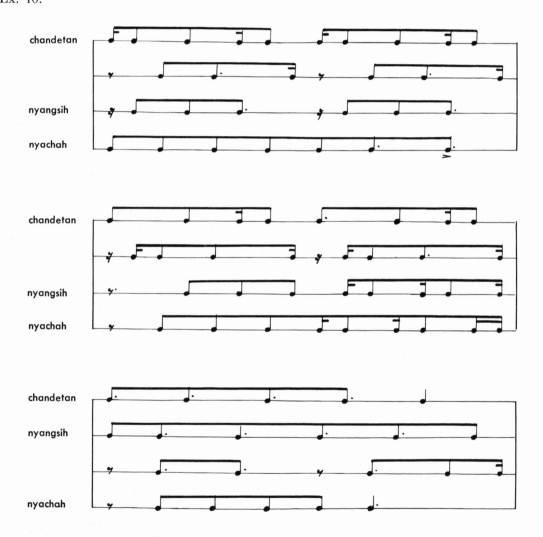

A fifth cymbal part, similar to the *chang*, is sometimes added to the quartet. The *chandetan* can also be assigned a single player, who controls two cymbal pairs. With irregular alternation of right and left hands, the *chandetan* now assumes various forms, of which the following are typical:

Ex. 41.

This polyrhythmic cymbal accompaniment is identical in rhythmic impulse with the many-part percussion accompaniment frequently performed to rice pounding. While women thresh the grain in a wooden trough, dropping their poles in regular alternation, different interlocking rhythms are beaten against the sides of the trough by a group of men. The combined patterns create an accompaniment, the *chandetan*, similar to that of the cymbal interplay. Just as each cymbal has its characteristic timbre, so each sound produced by striking the edge, side, or end of the rice trough has its special resonance. The rhythmic coordination of rice pounders with the *chandetan* is described in Appendix 1, p. 361. The object of the *chandetan* accompaniment is the same as that of the cymbal group. It adds a special rhythmic energy to the main activity, stimulating the workers as they raise and drop their poles. In the gamelan, the continuous interlocking patterns animate the orchestra, adding to the resonance in loud passages, and sometimes dropping out altogether in lighter sections.

The traditional ceremonial compositions of unknown authorship that form the basic repertory of the *gamelan gong* are commonly known as the *gending gong* or *pegongan*. They fall into two separate groups—those performed with *trompong* and those in which the *trompong* is not used. The former group consists of purely instrumental compositions of considerable length which are played on all important occasions. The second group, without *trompong*, is used to accompany formal plays and ritual dances. *Gendings* of this group are simple in structure, consisting mainly of short melodic units and motifs which, repeated indefinitely, create an ostinato accompaniment that can be prolonged to suit the occasion. *Gendings* of both groups are based on a wide variety of classical metric forms, each with its own colotomic structure, many of which serve as a basic for Balinese music composed today.

The ceremonial *gendings* with *trompong* fall into two main categories—the *gending ageng*, great *gendings*, which form the major part of any program, and the shorter, more animated *gending gangsaran*, quick *gendings*, played at the opening of any program and as interludes between the *gending ageng*. The great *gendings* consist of two separate movements, the first slow in tempo, the second relatively fast and slowly increasing in momentum until the end. Because of the slow tempo of the opening movement these *gendings* are also known as *gending lambat(an)* or *adeng*, slow *gendings*. The fast *gendings* are generally one-movement compositions, more immediately lyrical and fluid in melodic outline.

The *gending ageng* are constructed on an impressive scale. Eight separate groups are

82

distinguished, characterized by the length and metric punctuation of the first movement. All follow the same basic method of organization. A freely performed solo by the *trompong* begins in an improvisational manner, gradually introduces the melodic line of the *gending* to the musicians, and finally leads directly into the opening movement, the *pengawak* or "body" of the composition. The *pengawak* consists of a single melodic period which is repeated several times, with minor changes in the melody and the drumming made on the final repeat. The second movement, the *pengechèt* [4] or allegretto, is in contrastingly shorter meter. Unlike the *pengawak*, which is broken by a silence at each termination of the melodic period, the *pengechèt* is in constant motion. It contains several melodic sections, each based on a metrical contraction of the preceding meter, with a corresponding contraction in gong punctuation. The sections are closely linked together. Each section is repeated a number of times, and with the final metric contraction the movement ends in a short ostinato motif which may be prolonged indefinitely through repetition.

While the *pengawak* is essentially static in form and mood, the *pengechèt* is dynamically progressive, passing through successive phases of increasing animation and rising rhythmic tension. This rise in tension is effected not only by the metric contractions and increasing frequency of gong accents, but also through the rising tension in the drumming. During the *pengawak* the function of the drums is primarily quantitative. They scan the melodic period in slow tempo, alternating loud, explosive accents with sharp, muted accents. But with the *pengechèt* they take the lead, carrying the movement forward in an animated interplay that becomes, with the final ostinato, a steady roar of rapidly alternating stick beats. What with the successive diminutions of the meter, the regulated contraction of gong accents, and the corresponding increase in tempo and force of the drumming, the effect of the *gending* from start to finish is one of slow awakening, a gradual gathering of momentum in a series of transitions that build to a peak of maximum power and excitement.

All *gendings*, *ageng* and *gangsaran*, draw heavily on the principle of repetition for form, balance, and continuity. No melodic period, whether isolated or part of a more extended movement, is complete without restatement. While no fixed rule sets the number of repetitions to any movement or shorter melodic section within the movement, it may be said in general that repetition increases in ratio to metric condensation. The slow-moving *pengawak* of the *gending ageng*, constructed on the broadest of metric patterns, may possibly be repeated no more than once. With the final metric contraction of the *pengechèt*, the melodic line is reduced to a brief motif which, taking the form of an ostinato, can be repeated indefinitely.

Long or short, the melodic period can be described as circular in form, a melodic statement which reaches completion only when it has returned to its opening tone, with which it begins to repeat. This is the basis for all Balinese instrumental melody, from the compact ostinato motif to the most extended melodic period. Two differing types of melodic period, however, are to be distinguished: the closed and the open circle. In the former, by far the most prevalent, the melody repeats without a break. In the second type, employed mainly in the *pengawak* to the *gending ageng*, a rhythmic silence occurs after the return to the opening

---

[4] Said to derive from *ngechèt*, to travel at a half running pace when transporting a heavy load, such as rice. Two sheaves of equal weight are hung at each end of a bamboo pole which rests upon one shoulder of the porter. The easy trotting pace causes the sheaves to rise and fall in regular rhythm, considerably lightening their weight.

tone, lightly filled in by the drums to maintain the metric structure. Even here the gap before full resumption of the melody may be bridged by a *trompong* solo, indicating that the true melodic thread has not been broken.

The metric structure of the *gending* is defined, as stated earlier, by *gong ageng* (G), *kempur* (P), and *kempli* (k). Among them, these three *gongs* create a punctuation composed of three relative stress weights:

Ex. 42.

k	light	∨
P	medium	>
G	heavy	⊓

The natural order for the sequence of these three contrasting stress accents, from which a wide variety of colotomic patterns derive, is that of heavy, medium, light, medium—a basic reversal of the normal Western sequence of heavy, light, medium, light—which creates a feeling of continuous rhythmic tension and suspense throughout not only the melodic period but the whole *gending*. This feeling of suspense is heightened by the alternate use in the punctuation of the two large *gongs*, the higher pitched *gong lanang* (L), and the deeper voiced *gong wadon* (W), which between them create a "split" heavy stress accent:

Ex. 43.

L	heavy	⊓
W	heavier	⊔

Thus, in its most complete form, colotomic punctuation is based on the periodic recurrence of four contrasting stresses. All patterns derive, one way or another, from a basic sequence which, in its simplest form, can be expressed:

Ex. 44.

L   P   k   P   W   P   k   P

⊓   >   ∨   >   ⊔   >   ∨   >

The Balinese musician, however, makes no distinction between *lanang* and *wadon* when defining the punctuation of any *gending*, uniting the two under the single term, *gong*. Except in special cases, this double-pitched stress accent will be considered here as a single punctuating accent, represented in the examples to follow by the letter G. The above formula can thus be reduced to the pattern:

Ex. 45.

G   P   k   P   G   P   k   P

It is this sequence that serves as point of departure for all other colotomic punctuation.

Whether long or short, a broad melodic statement or a brief ostinato motif, the melodic period terminates with a *gong* stroke, marking the point where the period has come full circle and where it begins again. At the same time, the period is divided into sections of equal length by the *kempli*, whose first beat always coincides with that of the *gong*. A melodic period or *gongan* having four *kempli* beats thus shows the following *gong-kempli* structure:

Ex. 46.

k   k   k   k

G

Since the first *kempli* beat is practically inaudible owing to the greater resonance of the *gong*, it is often left out, and both orally and in notation Balinese reduce the above pattern to the basic sequence:

Ex. 47.

G   k   k   k

The interval between *kempli* beats depends on the metric breadth of the *gending*. In the shorter metric forms, employed in the *gending gangsaran* and the *pengechèt* of the *gending ageng*, the *kempli* accents each eighth, fourth, or even second *pōkok* tone. In the widely proportioned *pengawak* to the *gending ageng*, where metric structure attains its maximum breadth, the *kempli* beat falls with every sixteen *pōkok* tones.

The basic location for the *kempur* in the colotomy is exactly halfway between *kempli* beats, thus placing it within the complete melodic period in perpetual syncopated relation to the *gong* beat. This can be quickly demonstrated by the following two examples: *a*) a complete melodic unit of sixteen *pōkok* tones, with four *kempli* beats; and *b*) a single melodic section of sixteen *pōkok* tones, extending between two *kempli* beats, as found in the *gending ageng*.

Ex. 48.

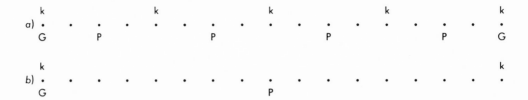

In the short *gangsaran* compositions, and in the *pengechèt* movements, various metric modifications are created through the omission of the first, or the first two, *kempur* beats in a unit containing four *kempli* beats. The metric pattern *a*), just quoted, is now transformed:

Ex. 49.

This sequence pattern can be further varied by the introduction of a second *gong* beat within the unit, so that the alternation of *lanang* and *wadon gongs* now becomes structurally organic.

Ex. 50.

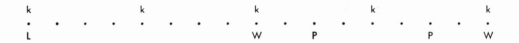

In its most contracted form, this pattern supplies the rhythmic basis not only to the ostinato finales of the *gending ageng*, but to all processional music and the various ostinato compositions that accompany most *tōpèng* and *baris* dances. In augmentation or maximum condensation it can be reduced to the formula:

Ex. 51.

G   •   k   •   G   P   k   P

further resolving itself in resonance, as heard from any distance, to:

Ex. 52.

G　·　·　·　G　P　·　P

The fundamental relationship of *gong*, *kempur*, and *kempli* in the punctuation of any *gending* is clearly seen from these few examples. *Gong* and *kempli* between them maintain a steady, primary beat, while the *kempur* creates strong secondary accentuation. The only time *gong* and *kempur* are heard in regular alternation is in the simple melodic compositions that accompany the women's ceremonial dances, *rèjang* and *mendèt*, where the relaxed rhythm created through their regular recurrence is stimulus enough for the gently swaying and essentially feminine movement of the dances.

Ex. 53.

G　·　P　·　G　·　P　·

The eight different species of *gending ageng* are distinguished primarily through the length and colotomic structure of the *pengawak* or first movement. The *pengawak* is a single melodic period ending with a *gong* stroke and repeating several times. This period is called the *gongan*, a general term for any melodic unit or statement extending between two *gong* beats. The period is also known as the *apada*, a literary term for stanza or strophe, in reference to its inner sectional, or phrase, structure.

The *gongan* or *apada* is based on a structural metric unit, the *palet* (a set), consisting of sixteen *pōkok* tones or the equivalent in beats. The *palet* contains one *kempli* and one *kempur* beat, while every fourth *pōkok* tone is stressed melodically by the *jegogans* (−).

Ex. 54.

·　·　·　·　·　·　·　·　·　·　·　·　·　·　·　·
—　　　　　　　　—　　　　　　　—　　　　　　　—
k　　　　　　　　　　　　　　　　P

The *palet* is further scanned by two contrasting drum beats, open (∧), and muted (+), the open sound deep and resonant, the muted sound short and dry, and delivered with explosive force. While complex patterns intermingle with these two basic beats they emerge as strong structural accents.

87

Ex. 55.

```
  .   .   .   .   .   .   .   .   .   .   .   .   .   .   .   .
  _           _           _           _
  k                       P
  ∧           +           ∧           +
```

The *gending* is classified according to the number of *palets* composing the *apada*, on which the *pengawak* is based. To distinguish the group, use is made of the word *tabuh*, here meaning struck, or sounded, and referring to the number of times *kempli* and *kempur* each occur in the *gongan* or *apada*. Thus a *gending* classified as *tabuh pat*, *tabuh 4*, will have for its first movement a melodic period based on an *apada* of 64 (4 × 16) *pōkok* tones, metrically divided into four *palets*, and containing four *kempli* and four *kempur* accents.

Eight *tabuhs* are known, with one to eight *palets* to the *gongan*. With the exception of the first, irregular because of its one-*palet* brevity, these eight metric variants form the basis for melodic periods of systematically increasing breadth.

tabuh	palets to the gongan
pisan or besik (1)	1
rōh or dua (2)	2
telu (3)	3
pat or papat (4)	4
lima (5)	5
nem (6)	6
pitu (7)	7
kutus (8)	8

Thus the melodic period of the different *tabuhs*, excluding *tabuh 1*, shows the following methodical increase of *pōkok* tones:

tabuh	pōkok tones
2	32
3	48
4	64
5	80
6	96
7	112
8[5]	128

---

[5] Following *tabuh 8* there is also, according to older informants in Sulaan village, *tabuh rohras* (*12*), with the further expansion of the melodic period to 12 *palets* and 192 *pōkok* tones. The gamelan of that village, however, no longer included any *gendings* of this type in their repertory, and the unusually broad dimensions of this metric form had already become half legendary.

Whether composed of two *palets* or extended to eight, the *apada* or *gongan* is a single melodic statement, with all tones at equal tension throughout. While the melodic line, especially in the longer *tabuhs*, shows elaborately organized phrase structure, it advances to no climax but moves inevitably toward the final tone of the *gongan*. In basic mood, one *tabuh* closely resembles another, the main difference being one of metric and melodic breadth. Each is performed at approximately the same speed, the basic tempo of the *pōkok* tones lying somewhere between M. 35 and 45.[6]

While the *apada* or *gongan* is metrically a closed circle, a melodic break occurs after the *gong* beat. For the equivalent of seven *pōkok* beats the main body of the gamelan is silent, entering with the *kempur* beat. The interval is melodically bridged, however, by the *trompong*, and rhythmically scanned by the drums. While the drum patterns remain unchanged with each *palet* they become rhythmically involved in the second half of the last *palet*, the closing phrase of the *gongan* which is called the *mipil*. Here the drums suddenly change from colotomic to agogic instruments and bring the melodic period to a majestic close with a broad rallentando that begins in the second half of the *mipil*. Tempo is gradually resumed in the orchestral pause that follows the *gong* accent.

The structural scheme of the *pengawak*, in all *tabuhs* from *2* to *8*, can now be shown. As illustration, *tabuh 4*, with four *palets* and four sets of metric accents, is given in Ex. 56. That part of the melodic period performed by all instruments is indicated by dots, which represent the *pōkok* tones. The small circles represent the time-equivalent beats intervening between the opening tone, sounded by the full gamelan, and the point where the gamelan resumes. These beats are filled in, one way or another, by the *trompong* solo, accompanied by the two drums.

Ex. 56. Tabuh 4; metric scheme*

* See Appendix 4, p. 394.

[6] Actual tempo, of course, is never final. The older ensembles preserve a traditional slow beat; the younger organizations show an inclination toward increasingly brighter tempos. Whatever tempo is felt to be most natural remains firmly established with the group as the basic speed for all the *tabuhs*.

While the first half of *palet* 1 is a silence for the main body of the gamelan, in musical notation it is usually filled in with *pōkok* tones, with the exception of an empty beat immediately following the opening tone, indicating that melodic continuity does actually exist between *gong* and *kempur* accents.

Ex. 57.

These tones, however, are generally sounded by the *trompong* only, the normal point of entry for the other instruments remaining on the *kempur* beat. Examples in notation of both the filled-in and the empty half of the first *palet* may be found in Appendix 4.

The *pengawak* ends with the *pengiwan*,[7] a melodic variant of the *pengawak* forming a coda to the movement. It is played at a contrastingly livelier tempo, with lighter drumming, performed mainly with the hands. While the *pengawak* is repeated several times, the *pengiwan* is played only once. With the final *palet* the original melodic line of the *pengawak* is resumed, along with the heavy drum accentuation with the sticks. Returning to the original tempo, the first movement comes to an end on the opening tone of the first *palet*.

Tabuh 1 differs from the other seven *tabuhs* in several respects. Classified as a *gending ageng*, it shows a closer relation to the *gending gangsaran*, both in colotomy and in the characteristic closed melodic periods that repeat and follow each other without a break. While essentially a one-movement form, the *tabuh 1 gending* has three contrasting but interconnected sections. It opens with the *pengechèt*, a one-*palet* ostinato repeating indefinitely, which frames a broader middle section composed of a *pengawak* and a *pengiwan*, each built on a melodic period of two or more *palets*. The *pengechèt* has the typical colotomy of the *gending gangsaran*, while the *pengawak* and *pengiwan* are based on the *pengechèt* colotomy in augmentation. Characteristic of *tabuh 1* compositions is the subtle tempo relation between *pengechèt* and *pengawak-pengiwan*. Opening with *pōkok* tones sounding at an animated tempo of M. 90 to 120, and slowing down with the last repeat of the ostinato to half speed, a feeling of still greater change in tempo is created because of a change in *gong* punctuation, which now stresses every fourth *pōkok* tone instead of every second. A return to the opening ostinato at the original tempo establishes a special unity typical of all *tabuh 1* compositions.

Gendings of this group show much freedom in the breadth of their middle section, which can be greatly extended through a series of melodically related periods. The following example presents the fundamental plan to this type of composition in its most concentrated form.

---

[7] Or *peniban*, in some regions. *Pengiwa*, from *kiwa*, left side, implies a transformation of some kind. *Pengiwa* is a book of black magic formulas for supernatural metamorphoses of humans into destructive shapes. The musical sense is obscure; it may refer to the melodic change, or the change in the tempo and style of the drumming. *Peniban* is generally used to indicate a musical section in quicker tempo.

Ex. 58. Tabuh 1; metric scheme*

```
                        •   =   120                              rall. (last time)
pengechèt           ‖: •   •   •   •   •   •   •   •   •   • •   •:‖
                       G       P       k       P       G       P       k       P

                        •   =   60
pengawak; palet  1. ‖: •   •   •   •   •   •   •   •   •   •   •   •
                       G           P           k           P

       palet  2.       •   •   •   •   •   •   •   •   •   •   • •
                       G           P           k           P             :‖

pengiwan; palet  1. ‖: •   •   •   •   •   •   •   •   •   •   •   •
                       G           P           k           P
                                                              accel. (last time)
       palet  2.       •   •   •   •   •   •   •   •   •   •   • •
                       G           P           k           P             :‖

                        •   =   120
pengechèt           ‖: •   •   •   •   •   •   •   •   •   • •   •:‖
                       G       P       k       P       G       P       k       P

                        •
                       G
```

* See Appendix 4, p. 390.

While the *pengawak* to the *gending ageng*, in its different metric variants from *tabuh 2* to *8*, remains firmly set in form, the *pengechèt* or second movement allows for considerable structural freedom. In general, it consists of an introductory section based on a one-*palet* ostinato of sixteen *pōkok* tones, a more extended melodic section, and a final section composed of a series of repeating melodic units that contract metrically to a closing eight-tone ostinato. In some districts the whole movement is called the *pengechèt*. Generally, however, it is considered to be composed of three distinct sections, the *pengaras*, the *pengisep*, and the actual *pengechèt*, known also as the *peniba(n)*. The introductory ostinato on which the *pengaras* is based is performed in forceful unison by the main section of the gamelan, emphasized by heavy cymbal and drum accents. In the contrasting *pengisep* the *trompong* interprets the melody with lyric freedom, while the drumming is lighter and the cymbals are for the most part silent. These two lyrical sections in the second movement prepare for the finale or *pengawak* proper. The *pengechèt* is marked by a return of energy, brought about partly by the vigorous drumming and cymbal playing and partly by a steady increase in tempo maintained till the end of the movement. As the melodic units contract in length the *trompong* solo either returns to the basic melody or develops a syncopated variation. As in the *tabuh 1* form of *gending*, there is a subtle tempo relation between the three sections. The *pengaras* begins in the relatively slow tempo of (approximately) M. 60 and leads through a slow accelerando to the tempo of the *pengisep*, M. 90. The *pengechèt* begins at this tempo but gradually increases speed to end, perhaps, at about M. 120. What with the gradual increase in tempo from the beginning, the

91

contracting melodic units in the *pengechèt*, and the quickening tempo of the drumming, one gains the impression of a controlled but steady accumulation of power throughout the movement.

No final formula for the structure of the second movement can be given. In contrast with the formal rigidity of the *pengawak* it is essentially a movement of freedom and release. Three different metric plans for the movement are shown in the following three examples. While each has its special form, all three show a fundamental structural conformity based on the principle of metric contraction. These three examples come from the same source, my informant I Lunyuh.

Ex. 59. Pengechèt Blandongan*

* See Appendix 4, p. 394.

Ex. 60. Pengechèt Penginyan*

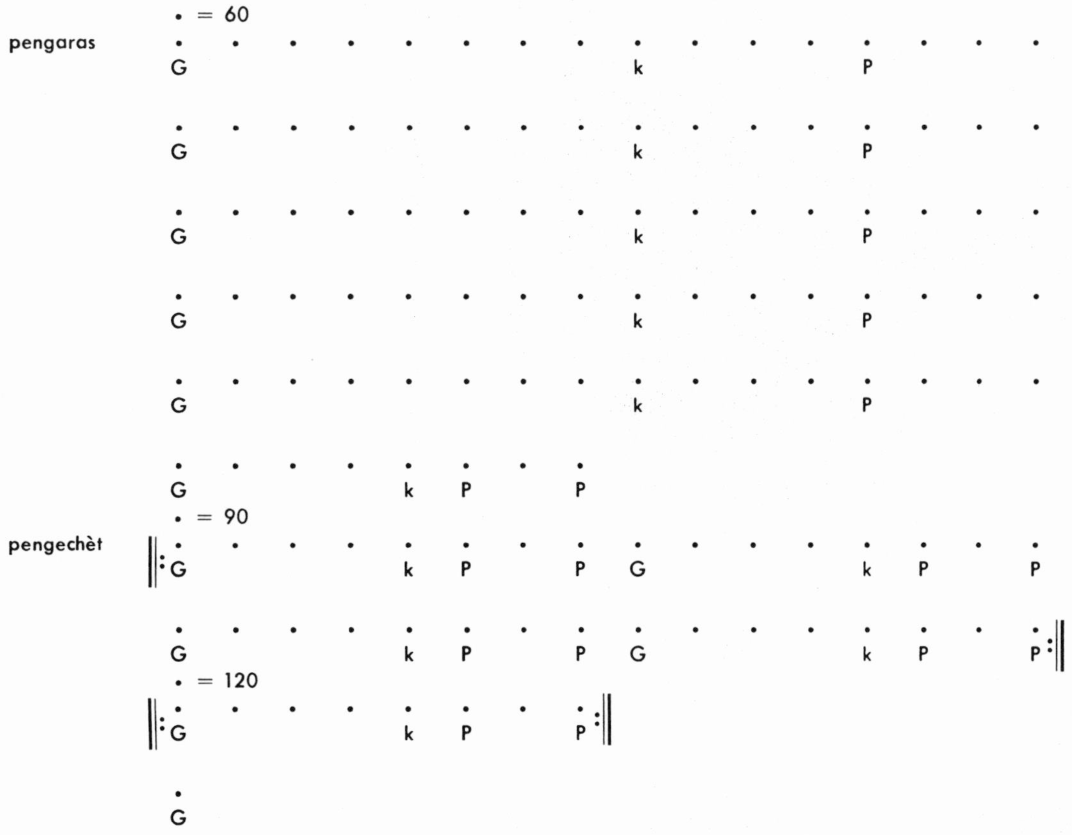

pengaras   ♩ = 60

pengechèt

♩ = 90

♩ = 120

* A short version of pegechet Blandongan (Ex. 59).

In the third example only the basic metric scheme is given. Each of the two metric units forms the basis for a chainlike series of ostinatos. The whole movement is considered the *pengechèt*.

Ex. 61. Pengechèt Sekarini*

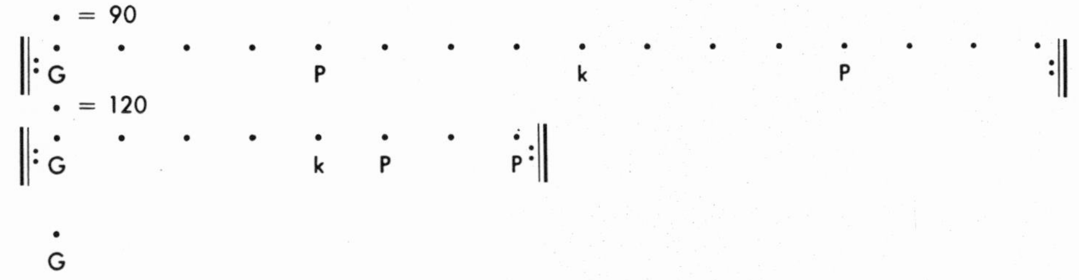

♩ = 90

♩ = 120

* See Appendix 4, p. 394.

The relatively short, one-movement *gangsaran* compositions are all related in colotomic structure. All are based on a *palet* of eight *pōkok* tones, moving at a general tempo of M. 60—about double the speed of the *lambatan* movements. The *palet* is given the same *gong* punctuation as that of the *pengechèt* in the *gending ageng*.

Ex. 62.

$$\begin{array}{cccccccc} \bullet & \bullet & \bullet & \bullet & \bullet & \bullet & \bullet & \bullet \\ G & & & & k & P & & P \end{array}$$

The *gendings gangsaran* show more variety and freedom of form than the *gendings ageng*. All, however, are based on the closed melodic period. Some consist of a single repeated period; others, more complex in structure, contain secondary melodic sections of contrasting character, or may consist of a series of linked melodic units which recur in changing order. These forms will be discussed later. The essential feature of all *gendings* of this type is a continuous melodic line, with the same punctuation by *gongs* throughout. Of all *gangsaran* forms the most condensed is the *gilak(an)*, an eight-or sixteen-tone ostinato based on the *gong* punctuation:

Ex. 63.

$$\begin{array}{cccccccc} G & \bullet & k & \bullet & G & P & k & P \end{array}$$

used without *trompong* realization for *baris* and *tōpèng* dances.

Both *ageng* and *gangsaran* compositions beging with a solo introduction played by the first *trompong*.[8] The introduction consists of two separate but imperceptibly linked parts: *a)* the *(se)sendon* or song,[9] a quiet, improvisational preamble which gradually outlines the melodic range of the *gending* to come, and finally leads into *b)* the *pengawit*[10] or thematic beginning. This is achieved by taking up the actual melodic line on the last *palet* of the *pengawak*, more or less freely at first, but becoming firmly settled with the *mipil*.[11] At this point the drums, which already have lightly accented the first half of the *palet*, take up the set drum phrase which underlies the *mipil*, setting the tempo and leading directly into the opening unison by the full gamelan, with which the *gending* actually begins.

---

[8] With the exception of those of the *tabuh 1* group, which are introduced by the drums alone.

[9] Sometimes called the *gineman* or *guneman*, from *meginem*, to converse or declaim; as in *peregina*, an actor with speaking lines.

[10] From *ngawit*, to alert, prepare beforehand. *Pengawit* is a holding in readiness, and "*Kawitan!*" means "Begin!" The *pengawit* is also known as the *penyumu(nin)*, from *dumun*, at first, beforehand.

[11] Balinese musicians say the *pengawit* is "taken up" at the *mipil* (*pengawit jemak ring mipil*). This clearly defines the thematic relation of the *pengawit* to the *pengawak*.

This prolonged solo introduction, in which the *gending* is approached in an oblique manner, is generally heard only once during a program, when it introduces the opening *tabuh talōh*, or beginning *tabuh*. Only after a long pause in the program may the soloist feel inclined to introduce the next composition with another extended prelude. Otherwise, the preliminary, purely improvisational part of the *sendon* is omitted. In this form the whole introduction is known generally as the *pengawit* and, while delivered freely, has rhythmic and melodic shape throughout.[12]

The *pengawit* may be shorter than the last *palet* but is more often considerably longer. Long or short, the essential thing is that the melodic line must be firmly established with the *mipil*. Two examples of the short *pengawit* are given below. In the first, a *tabuh 2* composition with two *palets*, the *pengawit* starts after the beginning of the second *palet*. In the other example, a *tabuh 8* composition, the *pengawit* commences just before the beginning of the eighth *palet*. For comparison, the *pōkok* tones to the *palet* are given in each example, although they are not performed. The first orchestral sound is the opening tutti, which is stressed by the *gong*. By comparing each *pengawit* with the *pōkok* tones given below, the definite establishment of the melodic line as the *mipil* is reached can be seen.

Ex. 64. Pengawit gending Mayat; tabuh 2 ♩ = 35

Ex. 65. Pengawit gending Ludira; tabuh 8 ♩ = 35–45

---

[12] In some regions the term *gineman* is used to indicate the *pengawit*, complete, or up to the *mipil*.

The *pengawit* is not always so brief. Some players, especially in the broader *tabuhs*, begin with the penultimate *palet*. In the following example, the *pengawit* remains melodically close to the *pōkok gending* throughout.

Ex. 66. Pengawit Kambing Domba; tabuh 8 ♩ = 35

The tonal organization of the *gending* and the structure of each melodic period is immediately apparent when the five scale-tones, *ding, dong, dèng, dung, dang*, are represented by the numerals 1 to 5. Presented thus, the skeleton structure shows indications of ordered and elaborate planning. Short melodic periods, which in the *trompong* version have wide and graceful contours, reveal in their nuclear tones a basic preoccupation with balance and logical tone sequence. The broad melodic periods show intricate and abstract design in their inner phrase structure. Recurring tonal patterns are seen to shift in relation to each *palet*, while tonal sequences and retrograde progressions are common.

There will always be the question of whether the *pōkok* tones are true nuclear tones which serve for full melodic realization, or whether, after all, they are no more than emphasis tones to a more freely conceived melody. In the shorter and more lyrical *gendings gangsaran* the latter could well be the case. Moreover, in the *gambuh* repertory, that classical melodic source for the Balinese, there are no *pōkok* tones nor instruments in the ensemble on which they could be played. But in the finely balanced proportions of the *gending ageng* and the planned arrangement of the nuclear tones, the *trompong* melody is clearly subordinate to what seems to be an intellectually conceived composition.

This tonal unity in the *gending ageng* can be seen in the following example, *gending Gerebeg*, which is based on the third tone, *dèng*, with which the composition begins and ends. This tone especially dominates the *pengechèt*, where it is found throughout at the beginning of each *palet*.

96

Ex. 67. Gending Gerebeg; tabuh 5, pōkok tones. M. 35

pengawak; palet	1.	‖: 3 G	•	3	3	4	4	2	1	1 P	1	3	4	5	5	3	2
	2.	1 k	2	1	5	4	4	1	2	1 P	1	3	4	5	5	3	2
	3.	1 k	2	1	5	4	2	2	3	2 P	2	2	3	1	3	2	1
	4.	2 k	2	5	4	2	2	5	4	5 P	5	3	2	5	5	3	2
	5.	3 k	3	5	1	2	2	5	5	3 P	3	3	3	2	3	1	2 :‖
pengiwan; palet	1.	3 G	•	3	3	3	4	3	2	3 P	3	4	4	2	3	1	2
	2.	3 k	3	4	4	2	3	1	2	3 P	3	2	1	3	2	1	3
	3.	4 k	4	4	3	5	2	2	3	2 P	2	2	3	1	3	2	1
	4.	2 k	2	5	4	2	2	5	4	5 P	5	3	2	5	5	3	2
	5.	3 k	3	5	1	2	2	5	5	3 P	3	2	3	1	1	3	2
final tone		3 G															

(pause)

pengaras	3 G	3	3 P	3	3 k	5	5 P	3	3 k	5	5 P	2	2 k	5	5 P	2
	3 G	3	3 P	3	3 k	3	5 P	5	3 k	3	5 P	2	2 k	2	1 P	3
pengisep	‖: 3 G	3	4 P	2	4	4	4 k	2	4	4 P	3	5	5	3	3	2
	3 G	3	5 P	2	2	4	4 k	2	2	5 P	5	2	2	2	5	4
	3 G	3	4 P	2	4	4	4 k	2	4	4 P	4	3	5	3	5	4 :‖
pengechèt	‖: 3 G	5	4	3	2 k	3 P	1	2 P	3 G	5	4	3	2 k	3 P	1	2 P
	3 G	3	3	3	3 k	3 P	2	3 P	4 G	4	4	4	4 k	5 P	5	4 P
	3 G	3	3	3	3 k	4 P	3	2 P	1 G	1	1	1	5 k	5 P	1	1 P :‖
	‖: 4 G	4	4	4	1 k	5 P	1	3 P :‖								
	‖: 3 G	5	4	3	2 k	3 P	1	2 P :‖								
final tone	3 G															

As already stated, any one of the five tones can become the tonic, the tone around which the entire *gending* revolves, and on which it begins and ends. This tonic is preserved not only throughout the first movement but generally prevails throughout the second as well. Five different modes can thus be said to exist within the five-tone *Selisir* scale. They are nameless, however, recognized only by the phrase, "the *gending* is taken from (or starts with) *ding*" (*gendingé ambil ring ding*).

No final statement can be made concerning the relative frequency with which the different tones are found as tonic. In fifty-two *gendings ageng* and *gangsaran*, the five tones appeared as tonic in the following frequency:

tonic	gending ageng	gending gangsaran
1 (ding)	8	4
2 (dong)	10	4
3 (dèng)	8	4
4 (dung)	7	2
5 (dang)	5	2

Occasionally there is a shift of tonal center during the *gending*, with or without a return to the opening tonic. A melodic period or a complete composition may begin on one tone and end on another. My notes show the following changes from one tone to another.

opening tone	terminal
1	2
2	1
2	4
3	2
3	4
4	2
5	2
5	4

Gendings with changing tonal centers are comparatively rare. A few examples will be found scattered through Appendix 4. Perhaps the final method of estimating the tonal balance of the *gending* is to consider first those tones which fall at the beginning of each *palet*, together with the relative weight of their stress accentuation by *kempli*, *kempur* and *gong*.

The different tempos in the *gending ageng* are subtly adjusted to each other. One may speak of three basic speeds or tempo zones at which the *pōkok* tones move:

lambat, slow; minimum speed; M. 30–46

gangsar, fast; M. 60–100

rangkep, double; maximum speed; M. 120–144

Lambat, the tempo of the first movement, remains fixed, once established, except for the rallentando which takes place at each close of the melodic period. *Gangsar*, the main tempo of the second movement, allows for more rhythmic elasticity, and may lead into *rangkep* tempo through a gradual accelerando. *Rangkep*, the tempo of the final section of the second movement, remains generally set, but allows for an accelerando leading to the end of the *gending*.

The drums normally move at the basic rate of four strokes to a *pōkok* tone in *lambat* tempo. In *gangsar* tempo the strokes may be increased to eight. Various transitions from one speed to another may be effected through a change of drum speed in relation to the *pōkok* tones. The following example of a change from *gangsar* tempo to *rangkep* is typical. Here a doubling in speed by the drums anticipates a doubling in the speed of the *pōkok* tones. The transition is further intensified by the gradual accelerando from *gangsar* to *rangkep*, often accompanied by a strong crescendo.

Ex. 68.

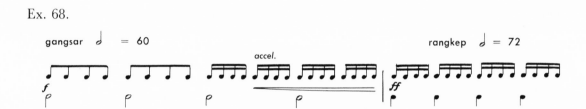

The functional character of the drums changes with the change of basic tempo. In *lambat* speed, the tempo of the *pengawak*, their role is primarily colotomic, their main beats reinforcing and sounding between *kempli* and *kempur* at fixed intervals. In *gangsar* tempo colotomic and agogic functions are combined; the melodic periods are animated by forward-moving drum patterns which nevertheless are always regulated by the metric structure. In *rangkep* tempo their rapid, continuous patterns are purely agogic, urging the music on to its closing tone.

Two different types of drumming or *kendangan* are employed, the *chedugan*, in which the drumstick is used, and the *gupekan*, performed by the hands alone. *Chedugan* drumming, based primarily on the interplay of stick accents between the two drums, prevails throughout the *gending*. *Gupekan* passages are introduced in secondary sections of the *gending* for sake of contrast.

As stated earlier, the drum is held across the lap, with the larger end, which produces the deeper sound, to the right. Only the right drumhead is struck with the stick. Two contrasting sounds can be produced with the stick, open and muted. When the left hand is free of the drumhead, the drum has a deeply resonant sound that carries for miles. When the left hand rests on the drumhead the sound is changed to a dry, explosive staccato. All main and structural beats in *chedugan* passages are sounded with the stick. Secondary accents are produced by hand at the left end of the drum. Hand strokes are performed either by the palm of the hand or by the fingers, held close together or spread apart, sometimes by the fingertips only.

The two drums together create a single rhythmic continuity of alternating essential accents and lighter filling-in strokes. While both drums are of equal importance, the *kendang wadon*, the female drum, plays the leading role, sounding the primary beats. The *kendang lanang*, the male, pitched a second or third higher, has an answering part, sounding the secondary beats and echoing the female on the final accent that marks the end of the *gending*. Through the contrasting pitch of the two drums and the interweaving of heavy drumstick beats with various hand strokes and muted sounds, a complex interplay is created that calls for perfect coordination between the two drummers.

The different types of strokes and main sounds of the two drums have distinguishing names:

chedug	the basic, unmuted drumstick stroke
kletek, tek	the muted drumstick stroke
dug	the open sound of the male drum, produced by stick
dag	the open sound of the female drum, produced by stick
pek	left hand stroke, produced by fingers
plak	left hand slapping stroke
krèmpèng	left hand fingertip stroke at the rim
nyantet	a double muted stroke by stick
chang kendang	the act of muting the drum

In addition to these basic strokes, the right hand produces a light, nameless, single stroke between *panggul* strokes, audible only to the drummer himself, which serves only to maintain a steady beat and help in the interplay between right and left hands. In *gupekan* passages, *pek* and *plak* hand strokes are also produced on the right-hand drumhead, alternating in irregular interplay with corresponding hand strokes at the other end.

Despite the variety of strokes, and the complex interplay between male and female drums, the drumming may be summarized and reduced to three elements which, combined, account for the rhythmic continuity:

a. inaudible finger strokes which help keep the main beats in place,
b. semi-audible finger or hand strokes, which create a filling-in interplay between main beats, with occasional secondary accentuation, and
c. loud, forceful strokes, produced by the drumstick, which help, along with *gong* punctuation, to define the metric structure in slow tempo, and which dominate the drumming in rapid tempo.

The following example illustrates the basic method of interplay between male (L) and female (W) drum and show how hand and stick strokes are interwoven in irregular but essentially balanced reciprocation. It will be seen that not only do the right and left hands of each drummer create a separate rhythmic continuity, but the two drums are at the same time entirely interdependent. The two left hands interlock to create a stabilizing, though secondary, rhythmic movement, against which the forcefully beaten *dug-dag* interplay (given alone below), which forms the main accentuation, stands out in full contrast.

Ex. 69.   ♩ = 60

1.   dug; open lanang sound, stick stroke

2.   dag; open wadon sound, stick stroke

3.   tek; muted sound, stick stroke

4.   pek; normal finger stroke

5.   inaudible finger stroke

6.   plak; loud slapping hand stroke

7.   krèmpèng; ringing finger-tip stroke, at rim

While the complexities of such a system of interplay offer fascinating material for study, our concern here is with the main and structural beats produced by the drumsticks. All secondary patterns derive from the interplay of the male *dug* and the female *dag* strokes, which will be referred to from now on simply as L (*lanang*) and W (*wadon*).

Although no final formula for fixed L W alternation exists to provide a convenient set of rhythmic patterns which can be recognized at a glance, there is, however, a basic system for interplay which is followed by the usual individual and recognized variations. This system may perhaps be most clearly demonstrated through an examination of the drumming to the *pengawak* of the *gending ageng*, which conforms to a general method of drumming practiced throughout the island.

With the exception of *tabuh 1*, which employs a *gangsaran* type of drumming, the drumming of the *pengawak* in all *gendings*, from *tabuh 2* to *tabuh 8*, remains fundamentally the same. The drumming is gradually stabilized in the first *palet*. In the following *palets* the drum patterns repeat without essential change, each *palet* receiving the same basic accentuation. In the final *palet*, the drumming develops rhythmic tension, ending, with the *mipil*, in a terminal drum phrase or rhythmic cadence which finds its resolution with the terminal *gong* stroke.

The drumming to the *pengawak* thus takes the following form:

opening palet	introductory
following palets	stabilized repeating patterns
final palet	concluding, generally with a rallentando

With the repeat of the *gongan* or melodic period, the basic tempo may be immediately resumed at the beginning of the first *palet*, or halfway through, with the entrance of the full gamelan.

Before discussing the drumming to the first and last *palets*, the basic, stabilized interplay between the two drums which underlines the intervening *palets* should be described.

The germinal pattern unit for repetition extends the length of eight *pōkok* beats, thus occurring twice within each *palet*. All but the first of the eight *pōkok* tones within the unit has its fixed W or L accent, sounded or implied through silence, and represented by the following scheme. In considering this scheme, it should be remembered that W represents the deeper-pitched, heavier, of the two drum sounds.

Ex. 70.

```
•   •   •   •   •   •   •   •
    W   L   L   W   L   W   L
```

Against the basic accentuation, secondary left hand patterns move continuously at the rate of four combined strokes to a *pōkok* beat.

Since the first of every eight *pōkok* tones is stressed in turn by *kempli* and *kempur* there is no need for drum accentuation at those points in the *palet*. The halfway point between *kempli* and *kempur*, however, is sharply accented by the *wadon* drum with a muted stroke. The complete formula for basic accentuation of the full *palet* by gongs and drums can be expressed in the following manner:

Ex. 71.

```
•   •   •   •   •   •   •   •   •   •   •   •   •   •   •   •
k                               P
    W   L   L   W   L   W   L       W   L   L   W   L   W   L
                +                               +
```

While this remains the essential scheme of W L alternation, two variants may be given, which may serve to emphasize the basic nature of the interplay.

Ex. 72.

```
•   W   L   L   W   L   W   L   general
                +
•   W   L   W   W   L   W   L   occasional
                +
•   W   W   L   W   L   W   L
                +
```

The variants tend to be regional rather than the optional choice of a single group. All are seen to agree in general principle, preserving balance between W and L beats, and all employ the muted *tek* sound in dividing the unit in half.

Around the basic scheme shown above a more animated drum continuity is developed by means of various additional strokes, as shown in the following example. The secondary, left hand interplay, of which the speed alone is indicated in *palet* 1, is to be taken for granted throughout. It is of importance only at the beginning of that same *palet* where it helps establish the tempo. From then on it is little more than a rhythmic filling in, often barely audible, and taking no part in the main accentuation. Our concern here is with W L interplay, and how it may be varied with each *palet*. The meter *tabuh 5* was chosen for illustration in order to include three *palets* of stabilized though varied drumming. It should be noted that while *kempli* and *kempur* beats are left unaccented by the drums, the *gong* stroke, which marks the end of the *gongan* and point of return, is given a *wadon* accent, followed immediately by a *lanang* accent. Similarly the important muted *tek* accent of the *wadon* drum that marks the midway point in each half *palet* is not complete without a following muted accent by the *lanang* drum. In the last *palet* a more active and energetic drumming is seen, anticipating the terminal *gong* stroke. This activity does not completely subside until the beginning of *palet* 2.

Ex. 73. Tabuh 5; basic drumming ♩ = 30

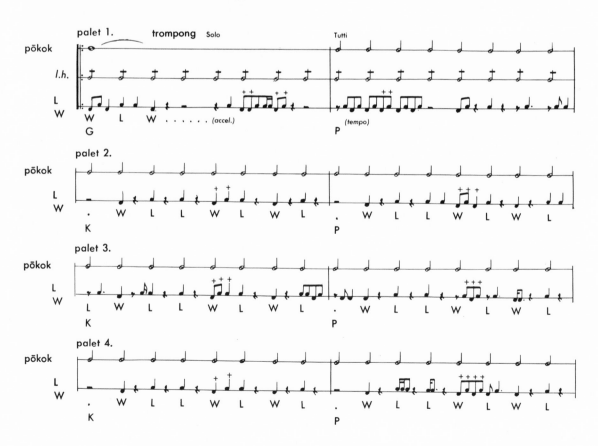

palet 5.

mipil

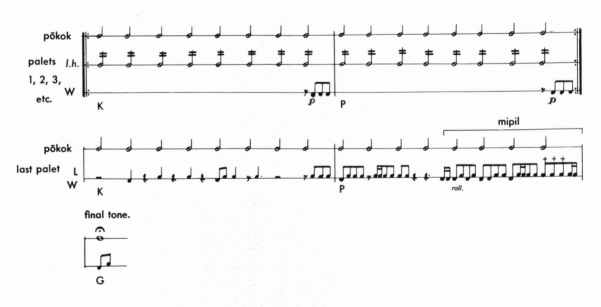

The basic system of W L alternation in the main *palets* is thus seen to remain fixed, although allowing for certain leeway of interpretation. Greater freedom is found in the drumming of the opening and closing *palets*. All drummers conform, however, in creating at the *mipil* a closing rhythmic phrase of maximum emphasis.

While the main part of the *pengawak* is heavily underlined throughout by drumstick accentuation, the *pengiwan*, the melodic variation with which the first movement ends, is accompanied by light animated drumming at double speed performed by the hands alone. In this contrastingly brighter section the cymbals are silent and the general tempo is somewhat faster. Twice during each *palet* the *wadon* drum scans the phrase with three lightly beaten stick strokes, in anticipation of the *kempur* and *kempli* accents. Only with the last *palet*, as the melodic line resumes its original form, does the drumming change. The tempo slackens to the earlier speed; the drumsticks are again employed; and the cymbals make their re-entry. In mood, melody, and drumming the final *palet* of the *pengiwan* is identical with that of the main *pengawak*.

Ex. 74. Pengiwan ♩ = 40

In the second movement the drumming maintains a purely agogic character throughout. The introductory *pengaras* is underlined by closely following drumstick accents based on a simple W L W L interplay. With the more broadly melodic *pengisep* which follows, the drumming changes to a light, animated interplay in *gangsar* tempo, in which the hands alone are used.

The drumsticks are resumed with the metrically contracted *pengechèt*, and closely knit interplay will now continue to the end. It is not easy to formulate the system of interplay, since the stick strokes now fall consistently off the *pōkok* beat. The *palet*, now contracted to eight *pōkok* tones, is given complete accentuation by *gong*, *kempli*, and *kempur*, and needs no further definition from the drums. Their restless movement derives from a rhythmic unit that seems to be based on the following scheme, quite different from that of the *pengawak*:

Ex. 75.

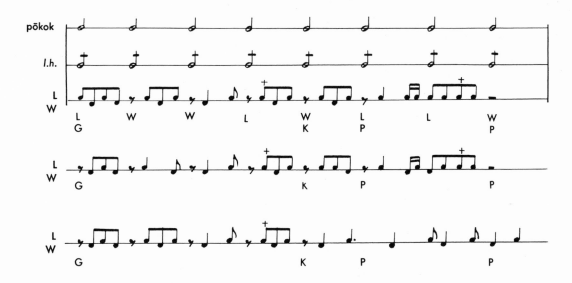

In any case, the *lanang* drum now plays a more prominent role, and later will be found to take the lead. The following example shows how rhythmic continuity is created through variation of a single basic pattern.

Ex. 76. Pengechèt   ♩ = 60–90

The final eight-tone ostinato phase of the *pengechèt* is taken at double (*rangkep*) speed. The L W interplay contracts correspondingly, while the patterns now are based entirely on the L W L W sequence. The sticks are used throughout; the left hands merely keep the rhythm steady. The few variants given below are enough to show the nature of this closing drumming to be an ostinato which, on count, has been known to repeat sixty to eighty times. It will be seen that the *wadon* drum now sounds on the offbeat throughout. The left hand strikes on the beat to maintain a steady rhythm but its sound is covered by the stroke of the *lanang* drumstick. Starting in a broken, syncopated manner, through the occasional omission of a *lanang* beat, the drumming gradually mounts in tension with the continuous repetition of the ostinato, to end in a steady, thunderous fortissimo.

Ex. 77. Pengechèt; closing phase ♩ = 120

A gradual increase in speed generally occurs as the ostinato gets under way. The movement may end in a rallentando—a sudden slowing up on the last repeat of the ostinato—or may break off abruptly at the height of rhythmic tension. Immediately before the terminal beat the drum pattern is adjusted to allow for *wadon* coincidence with the *gong* stroke.

Ex. 78.

The drumming thus has been shown in the three roles it plays in the *gending ageng*—colotomic, colotomic-agogic, and agogic. It is seen to be highly organic in giving the *gending* direction. It contributes to the subdivision of the *palet* in the *pengawak*, anticipates structural *gong* and *kempur* strokes, and maintains throughout a vigorous rhythmic impulse. The principles of interplay outlined here form the foundation for all Balinese drumming. With this basic technique as point of departure, an elaborate technique has been evolved, as will be later shown, to meet the different requirements of dance and drama.

The small group of *gending gangsaran*, fast *gendings*, are distinguished from the *gending ageng* by their brevity, continuous and fluid melodic line, bright tempo, and by drumming of a purely agogic nature. All are based on the closed melodic period, and all have the same phrase unit or *palet*, having the colotomic structure:

Ex. 79.

$$\cdot \qquad \cdot \qquad \cdot \qquad \cdot \qquad \cdot \qquad \cdot \qquad \cdot$$
$$\text{G} \qquad\qquad\qquad \text{k} \quad \text{P} \qquad\quad \text{P}$$

With the same basic punctuation, the *gending gangsaran* is closely related to the *pengechèt* of the *gending ageng*. The *gong* not only terminates the melodic period, but sounds within the period at the beginning of each *palet*. The melodic periods, however, are usually considerably longer than those of the *pengechèt*, and show much variety in phrase structure. The complete *gending gangsaran*, while remaining essentially a one-movement composition, often shows a complex and ingeniously planned form.

The *gendings* fall into four distinct groups, each with its own structural characteristics:

tabuh talōh   beginning or opening tabuh (often carelessly referred to as tabuh telu); a small group of short compositions, one of which is played at the start of any program,

Silir, Selisir   short compositions lying generally in the upper register of the trompong

Tembung   more extended compositions, commencing in the low register of the trompong and having a contrasting middle section in the high register,

Longgor   short ostinatos and more extended compositions characterized by heavy, rapid drumming, usually played at the end of the program

Of all four, the *gending Silir* group show the simplest structure, consisting of a single melodic period of four *palets*, sometimes three. It is introduced by a short *pengawit*, and is repeated as many times as wanted. In its simplest form the melodic line is a single, direct statement, extending the full length of the 4-*palet* period. Through tonal repetition of a *palet*, however, a more complex inner phrase structure is created, a leading characteristic of all *gendings* of the *gangsaran* type. Simple and relatively complex periods may be compared in the two following examples, which give the *pōkok* tones of two different *gendings* of the *Silir* group. The first is seen to consist of a nonrepetitive *a b c d* phrase or *palet* structure, while the second is based on the phrase sequence, *a a b c*.

Ex. 80. Gending Silir; Batuan village* M. 60

palet

1.	3	3	3	4	2	5	3	4	a
	G				k	P		P	
2.	2	4	2	4	2	4	2	3	b
	G				k	P		P	
3.	1	1	1	2	1	5	2	5	c
	G				k	P		P	
4.	4	3	2	5	4	3	2	1	d
	G				k	P		P	
	3								(a)
	G								

* For the sake of control in exploring the gangsaran forms of composition, all gendings examined here are taken from the same source, the gamelan gong of banjar Jeléka, Batuan village.

Ex. 81. Gending Silir M. 60

palet

1.	2	3	3	2	1	4	4	1	a
	G				k	P		P	
2.	2	3	3	2	1	4	4	1	a
	G				k	P		P	
3.	4	4	1	1	4	4	1	4	b
	G				k	P		P	
4.	2	4	4	2	2	4	2	1	c
	G				k	P		P	
	2								(a)
	G								

The inner phrase structure can be altered further. The *palet* sequences *a b a c*, *a b b c*, *a b c c*, all occur in my notes taken in Batuan. While the *Silir* type of *gending* is generally played as an interlude between longer compositions, it can also serve as the main melodic section in the second movement of the *gending ageng*, in which case it is followed by a closing *pengechèt*.

The *tabuh talōh* form is similar to that of *Silir*, except that it normally has a melodic period of five *palets*. There is little variation in *palet* sequence, and the following example, in which the first *palet* repeats, is typical. While stating that there were various *gendings* in this form, the Batuan musicians knew only one, which was virtually the same in structure and melodic line as that most commonly heard throughout the island. Since it opens the program, *tabuh talōh* is usually preceded by a preliminary *sesendon* or *gineman*.[13]

[13] See Appendix 3, Ex. 348.

108

Ex. 82. Tabuh talōh M. 60

palet

1.	‖: 3	4	4	5	3	1	1	4	a
	· G				k	P		P	
2.	3	4	4	5	3	1	1	4	a
	G				k	P		P	
3.	3	3	5	5	3	3	5	2	b
	G				k	P		P	
4.	1	1	3	3	1	3	3	1	c
	G				k	P		P	
5.	4	4	4	1	4	1	4	3 :‖	d
	· G				k	P		P ·	
	3								(a)
	G								

Far more complex and varied in structure are the *gendings* known as *Tembung*. These, while remaining essentially one-movement compositions, are based on the recurring alternation of two separate and contrasting melodic sections, a) the *pengawak*, a one-*palet* ostinato section melodically realized in the low register of the *trompong;* and b) the *pengelik*,[14] a more extended melodic section in the high register, usually performed in octaves.

The *Tembung* compositions are of unusual interest for their free yet balanced form and for their ingeniously planned inner phrase structure. The eight-tone *palet* is no longer merely a phrase unit for a broader melodic period. It is a complete melodic unit in itself, and through prolonged repetition forms the main section to the *gending*. The middle section or *pengelik* consists of a broader melodic section based on a planned sequence of *palets*. How this may be done is shown in the next two examples. Both compositions consist of a one-*palet pengawak* and an extended *pengelik*. Linking *palets* which are not repeated connect the main parts of the composition. In its basic plan, the *gending Tembung* can be expressed by the formula A B A, although in actual performance the plan is actually extended to A B A B A or longer. The *gending* always ends with the *pengawak*.

In the first example given here, the *gending* is seen to consist of a *pengawak*, a, a *pengelik* composed of *palets b c b d*, and a melodic link composed of *palets b c* which leads back to the opening *palet*, a.

[14] Known also as the *penyalit* or change (from *salin*, to change), because of the new melodic material and change in register.

Ex. 83. Gending Tembung M. 60

										palet	section
pengawak	‖: 1	2	3	1	4	1	4	2 :‖		a	A
	G					k	P		P		
pengelik	‖: 1	1	1	2	1	2	1	1		b	B
	G					k	P		P		
	4	4	4	1	4	1	4	2		c	
	G					k	P		P		
	1	1	1	2	1	2	1	1		b	
	G					k	P		P		
	4	2	2	2	2	3	3	2 :‖		d	
	G					k	P		P		
link	1	1	1	2	1	2	1	1		b	
	G					k	P		P		
	4	•	4	1	4	1	4	2		c	
	G					k	P		P		
pengawak	‖: 1	2	3	1	4	1	4	2 :‖		a	A
	G					k	P		P		
	1										
	G										

The next example is more complex. The *pengawak*, *a*, is followed in the *pengelik* by a non-repeating link composed of *palets b c d*, leading to the main section based on *palets e f g*. Two new *palets*, *e h*, form the link which leads back to *a*.

Ex. 84. Gending Tembung M. 60

										palet	section
pengawak	‖: 1	5	2	4	2	4	1	5 :‖		a	A
	G					k	P		P		
pengelik link	1	5	2	2	2	2	3	1		b	B
	G					k	P		P		
	5	5	5	1	2	2	3	1		c	
	G					k	P		P		
	5	5	5	1	5	1	5	1		d	
	G					k	P		P		
main section	‖: 3	4	4	3	2	5	5	2		e	
	G					k	P		P		
	4	4	4	5	4	5	5	1		f	
	G					k	P		P		
	3	1	1	3	2	5	1	4 :‖		g	
	G					k	P		P		
link	3	4	4	3	2	5	5	2		e	
	G					k	P		P		
	4	5	2	5	3	3	3	4		h	
	G					k	P		P		
pengawak	‖: 1	5	2	4	2	4	1	5 :‖		a	A
	G					k	P		P		
	1										
	G										

Further illustrations of the freedom and balance of the *Tembung* form can be shown through phrase structure alone. In the following tables, each small letter represents an eight-tone melodic unit or *palet*, which in the *pengawak* is given prolonged repetition.

Ex. 85.

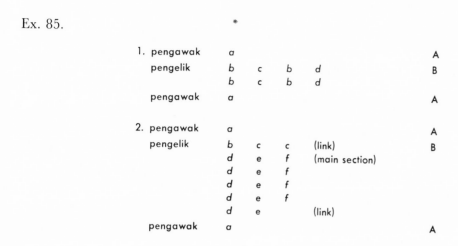

1. pengawak	a					A
pengelik	b	c	b	d		B
	b	c	b	d		
pengawak	a					A
2. pengawak	a					A
pengelik	b	c	c	(link)		B
	d	e	f	(main section)		
	d	e	f			
	d	e	f			
	d	e	f			
	d	e	(link)			
pengawak	a					A

In the following example an ostinato, represented by c, forms the main section of the *pengelik*.

Ex. 86.

pengawak	a			A
pengelik	b	b	(link)	B
	c		(main section)	
	b		(link)	
pengawak	a			A

Occasionally the *pengawak* consists of two melodically different *palets*, each repeated a set number of times:

Ex. 87.

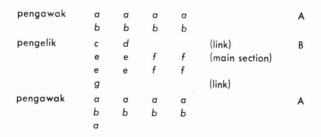

pengawak	a	a	a	a		A
	b	b	b	b		
pengelik	c	d			(link)	B
	e	e	f	f	(main section)	
	e	e	f	f		
	g				(link)	
pengawak	a	a	a	a		A
	b	b	b	b		
	a					

Variation of phrase structure in the *Tembung* compositions is endless. Almost every gamelan has its own special group of six to twelve *gendings*, each with its own individual form. While most show asymmetry in *palet* sequence, perfect balance is achieved as the composition

111

returns to the *pengawak*. Always of particular interest in this form are the linking passages which create pleasing metric irregularity in the broader melodic outline, but which also, as they recur, sound as secondary, thematic refrains.

The *Longgor* compositions are based on a simple A B, *pengawak-pengechèt* plan. Unlike the *Tembung* form, the *Longgor pengawak* is a broad melodic period, while the *pengechèt* is founded on the one-*palet* ostinato. No break occurs between the two movements, usually linked together by a transitional passage.

Palet structure in the *pengawak* may be simple or complex. Depending on its length, the *pengawak* may be repeated only once, or several times. The *pengechèt* is often played alone, and is frequently used as ending to the second movement of the *gending ageng*. While certain freedom of structure is known in the *Longgor* group, the following two examples, one simple, the other relatively complex, illustrate the basic plan of the composition and show characteristic *palet* organization.

Ex. 88. Gending Longgor

1. pengawak	*a*	*a*	*b*	*c*	*d*			A
	a	*a*	*b*	*c*	*d*			
	a	*a*	*b*	*c*	*d*			
	b	*e*					(link)	
pengechèt	*f*							B
2. pengawak	*a*	*a*	*b*	*c*				A
	d	*e*	*e*	*f*				
	g	*b*	*b*	*c*				
	d	*e*	*e*	*f*				
pengechèt	*i*							B

The eight forms of *gending ageng* and the four groups of *gending gangsaran* complete the set of musical forms that supply the basis for those compositions known as the *gending gong*. Few gamelans, however, are familiar with compositions in all these forms. All four types of *gending gangsaran* may be heard everywhere, but today the most generally known of the longer compositions are *tabuhs 1, 4, 5,* and *8. Tabuhs 3* and *6* are sometimes met with, while *tabuhs 2* and *7* seem to be the least known. Together, these compositions of the *gamelan gong* form an imposing collection. They impress the listener with their spacious and varied metric proportions, their melodic structure and solid formal balance. Their basic principles of organization are still drawn upon by Balinese composers today.

Chapter 10

The Gamelan Gambuh

THE ANCIENT and highly conventionalized *gambuh* theater, while rarely seen today, remains a main source for Balinese dances and dance dramas and for the music which accompanies these performances. The scene of action for the plays is East Java at the time of the last Hindu-Javanese dynasty, Majapahit. The costumes, stylized acting, and subdued orchestra of old and unfamiliar instruments evokes a legendary past which holds little appeal for Balinese audiences today. The slow-moving plays last from morning to nightfall and can continue for days. They deal with the wars and romances of kings and nobles as related in the *Malat* chronicle, of which Prince Panji is the central figure.

The large cast is composed entirely of men and youths, the few female roles taken by the latter. A reciter, the *jeru tandak*, and a small group of singers sit with the orchestra to explain and comment on the action. The actors, resplendent in elaborate crowns and brocade costumes, move with deliberation. Their lines are delivered in *kawi*, which few in the audience understand, and are declaimed in a highly artificial style. Noble characters of the *alus* type use the high upper voice, reciting each line in a thin falsetto that falls in a prolonged and gentle wail at the end of each sentence. *Kras* characters use heavy chest tones. Music continues throughout, the *gendings* changing with the entrance of each new character.

By the time I reached Bali in 1931 the *gambuh* theater had all but disappeared. Only three large companies survived, one maintained at the court of Tabanan, the other two in the villages of Batuan and Sèsétan. Smaller companies with reduced casts and small orchestras could be found in a few widely scattered villages. None appeared except on the most important formal occasions. The slow tempo and archaic style of the plays and music found little favor as popular entertainment.

Yet as a dramatic form, the *gambuh* theater provides the framework for popular dances and singing plays of today. Its stories are condensed, its stylized movements accelerated in the swift-paced choreographies of the *lègong* dance. Its classical melodies are now transformed into glittering compositions for the modern gamelan. These same melodies once formed the main repertory of the *Gamelan Semar Pegulingan* of the palace, and in the thirties they still could be heard occasionally at a temple festival, performed on the *trompong* of some old-fashioned gamelan that had passed from court to village.

While founded on a principle of metric structure similar to that of the *gending gong*, the *gambuh* compositions stand in a class apart. They are more lyrical in style; filled with poetic and dramatic associations, the repertory belongs essentially to the theater. Each *gending* is connected with a specific character, character type, or dramatic situation. The light and complex drumming, produced by the hands alone, gives an inner tension to the *gending*,

113

making it pre-eminently danceable. Whether performed in the *gambuh* play, the *lègong* dance, or by the *gamelan Semar Pegulingan*, each gending retains its special form of drum accentuation which both scans its metric structure and supplies impetus for gesture and movement.

The *gamelan gambuh* is primarily a melodic ensemble, under the direction of a pair of drums. Basic punctuation is supplied by two gongs of marked contrast in pitch and color, while light rhythmic background is supplied by small percussion instruments moving at different speeds. The following instrumental organization is that of the gamelan at the court of Tabanan:

a. melody or gending	4 suling gambuh
	1 rebab
b. main punctuation	kempur
	kajar
c. secondary punctuation	kenyir
	kelenang
d. agogic instruments	kendangs lanang and wadon
e. additional percussion	rinchik
	4 gumanaks
	2 kangsi

The large bamboo *suling* used in the *gambuh* ensemble is about 35 inches in length with a diameter of about 1¾ inches. It has a range of a little more than two octaves, starting in the neighborhood of F below middle C. The instrument is end-blown, with an embouchure already described on page 34.

On the upper side of the *suling* six fingerholes begin near the middle, the second located in the exact center of the tube. The holes are equidistant, with the exception of a double space between third and fourth holes (Fig. 25). The unusual length of the *suling* calls for fully extended arms to reach the fingerholes. The instrument is played with the open end resting on the ground, in the manner of similarly proportioned flutes to be seen in Egyptian tomb reliefs of the Fifth Dynasty, *c.* 2700 B.C.

The lower tones of the *suling gambuh* have the color, though not the vibrato, of the chalumeau tones of the clarinet, while the middle register has the sweetness of the flute. In the top register the tones, produced by violent overblowing, are forced and out of tune. The method of playing is such that the player is able to continue blowing while inhaling, producing a long unbroken melodic line.

With a more or less standard system of fingering, a series of twenty tones is obtained within the extreme limits of the *suling*, although certain microtonal inflections are possible through modified fingering. Within the first octave the basic scale of seven fundamental tones is produced, composed of intervals of considerable difference in size, beginning with a neutral third. In the third octave the scale ends chromatically. Although, as indicated in Chart 2, the *sulings* of Tabanan and Batuan show a slight difference in pitch and interval formation,

114

their scales agree in basic structure, which in the first octave of the Tabanan *suling* may be described as follows:

Ex. 89.

Compare with diagram a, page 116.

In the second octave an additional tone, produced by overblowing the bottom tone, F, to give the twelfth, is introduced between the fourth and fifth tones. This tone, indicated below by an asterisk, forms a structural part of the scale *Lebeng*, but is not used in the other scales:

Ex. 90.

Compare with diagram b, page 116.

With the beginning of the third octave, starting on an F already sharp—produced by overblowing the second of the fundamental tones—the tones become crowded together. Through forced overblowing they no longer agree with the two lower octaves, and are squeezed within the narrow range of an approximate major third, 412 *Cents* as measured in the Tabanan *suling*. From a sharp F of around 710 v., the scale thus contracts in a series of rapidly diminishing intervals:

Ex. 91.

Diagram *a*

Suling   gambuh;   Tabanan

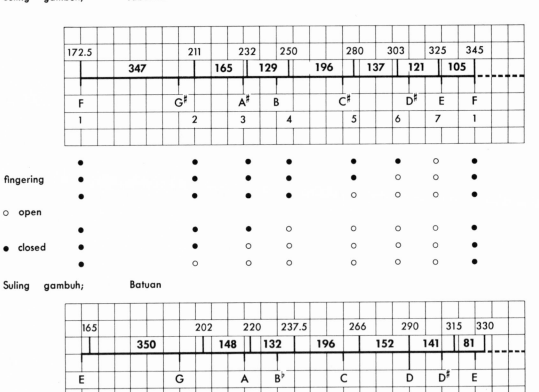

fingering

○ open

● closed

Suling   gambuh;   Batuan

Diagram *b*

additional
tone used
in tekep
lebeng

(suling
Tabanan)

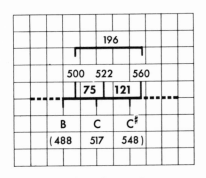

Expressed in *Cents*, the five tones of this octave stand in relation to the first five tones of the lowest octave:

3d octave	185	106	53	28	*Cents*
1st octave	347	165	129	146	*Cents*

Thus the different scales, so distinguishable from each other in their lower registers, take on the same cramped character in the top register; and melody played in these upper tones becomes a wild, shrill plaint, intensified by the strained blowing needed to produce the tones at all.

The upper tones of the middle octave can be made "sweeter," *manisan*, or slightly flattened, by altered fingering:

Diagram c

Use also is made of the half open fingerhole (*mipit, ngamis,* or *sibak*) which raises the pitch an approximate 50 *Cents*. The last five tones in the top register are fingered thus:

Diagram d

In the first octave of the *suling* the lowest tone, produced with all fingerholes closed, is never used. *Tembung*, the first of the five-tone scales, starts on the second tone.

The *sulings* are doubled in unison by the *rebab*, the Indonesian form of bowed lute. The body of the Balinese *rebab* may consist of half a coconut shell (*batok*) but is more often carved from wood. It is covered with a parchment of buffalo intestine (*babad kebo*). The bridge (*chanteng*) supports two wire strings (*kawat*) which are tightened by tuning pegs (*penguliran*). The two strings, *wadon* and *lanang*, are tuned respectively to the second and sixth tones of the *suling* scale, *ding* and *dung Tembung*, which stand a near tritone apart—627 *Cents* in the Tabanan *suling*, 628 *Cents* in the *suling* of Batuan.

The *rebab* is played with a loose bow, *sarad*, held between thumb and first two fingers,

117

while the fourth and fifth are passed between the bow and the hair to keep the latter taut. Resin (*sampang*) is used on the hair, and bowing is a continuous back and forth movement. A thin, rather acid tone is produced, with no expression and no distinguishable difference between the pushed bow (*nongsok*) and the drawn bow (*medèt*). A slight vibrato (*ngejèr*) is sometimes used, and the melody is occasionally ornamented with light, brief trills (*ngetor*). In slow movements long sustained tones are played with full bowing of unequal speed and pressure (*ngetetang*), giving the effect of an irregularly recurring throb during each tone.

While a fairly consistent unison is maintained in the group of *sulings*, the *rebab* interpretation of the melody is by comparison free and independent. This, in addition to its individual intonation which often far from coincides with the *sulings*, places it in a relation to the *suling* melody that can at times become extremely harsh. In small ensembles with one or two *sulings*, where the balance between *rebab* and *suling* is about even, this harsh relationship is intensified. But in full ensembles including four *sulings*, the *rebab* recedes to the background, now only faintly distinguishable by its sudden trills, light passing-tones, and occasionally syncopated paraphrasing of the melody.

Main punctuation is supplied by the *kempur*, which replaces the two *gongs* of the *gamelan gong*, and by the *kajar* or *cheluluk*, a small gong with sunken boss, which here corresponds in function to the *kempli* in the *gending gong*. The *kajar* is held in the lap, with the left hand resting on the surface to mute the sound as the gong is struck (Fig. 42). A light but resonant staccato tone is thus produced. The main function of the *kajar* is to stress the beginning of each *palet* in the longer melodic periods and to underline the *mipil* with syncopated accentuation. In short melodic periods such as the eight-beat ostinato it divides the *palet* in half, and it also serves on occasion as time-beater.

Because of the short duration of the muted *kajar* sound, main accents are intensified by a series of rapidly repeated strokes of unequal time value, their duration depending on the metric breadth of the melodic period. In the extended *pengawak*, where the equally extended *palets* set the *kajar* accents far apart, the strokes are continued long enough to give emphasis to the beginning of each *palet*. As the meter contracts, the number of strokes diminishes proportionately, so that in animated passages in march tempo (*batèl*), performed by percussion alone, the *kajar* accents, now following in close succession, become a rhythmic series of short double strokes.

Ex. 92.

With the beginning of the *mipil*, the second half of the last *palet*, the *kajar* begins a series of syncopated accents which lead to the terminating *kempur* stroke. Depending on the metric structure of the *gending* and the corresponding length of the *mipil*, the *kajar* accents are likewise prolonged or reduced in number:

Ex. 93.

a

b

Secondary punctuation is supplied by two interrelated colotomic instruments: *a*) the *kelenang*, a small high pitched gong mounted horizontally on a stand, and *b*) the *kenyir*, somewhat higher in pitch, a diminutive metallophone of the *saron* type, having three keys tuned alike to produce a softly ringing tone when struck with a triple headed mallet (Fig. 31). Pitched normally a semitone apart,[1] the two are generally found more or less coinciding, in the octave above, with the sixth and seventh tones of the *suling* scale. They are heard in alternation, sounding on secondary beats, the *kelenang* moving at double the speed of the *kenyir*:

---

[1] As found in Tabanan, Batuan, and in the Sèsètan *gambuh* recordings (see Appendix 6). Their pitch relation can vary, however, both to each other and to the *suling*. In Padang Haji the *kenyir* was tuned an approximate whole tone above the *kelenang*; in Kaba-kaba it stood a fourth higher.

Ex. 94.

In the Tabanan ensemble the two instruments stand in harmonious relation to the *kempur:*

Ex. 95.

A light, continuous rhythmic background is thus created, bridging the intervals between *kajar* accents and connecting these with the more widely spaced *kempur* tones. Although secondary, these accents play an important and integrating role in the musical punctuation. Without them, and with no steady succession of *pōkok* tones to maintain a basic tempo, the ensemble would fall apart. The speed at which these accents alternate is regulated by the metric structure of the *gending.*

Ex. 96.

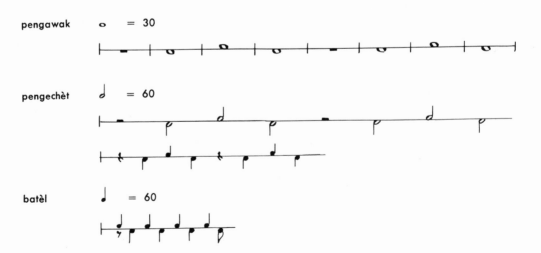

THE GAMELAN GAMBUH

Characteristic of the *gambuh* orchestra and found in no other ensemble is the *gumanak* or *kemenak*,[2] a small, cylindrical instrument of copper or iron which is held in the hand and tapped with a metal rod, giving a high clear sound similar to that of the triangle, though of shorter duration. Like the triangle, the cylinder is not closed; the sides of the strip of metal of which it is made are rolled over to almost meet, but to allow for a narrow separation extending the length of the cylinder. A handle usually projects from one end (Fig. 33). In smaller ensembles two *gumanaks* are generally employed. Of recognizably different pitches, they sound in alternation, filling in the intervals between *kelenang-kenyir* accents with lightly ringing tones that are barely audible above the other instruments. In the Tabanan orchestra four *gumanaks* were used, clear in pitch, and tuned approximately to C, D, E, F.[3] These, together with the *kangsi*—two pairs of very small cymbals mounted between forked sticks and struck against the ground, formed a complete and separate unit in the ensemble (Fig. 32). Like the cymbal group in the *gamelan gong*, the players performed continuous interlocking rhythmic patterns that ceased only with pauses occurring in the *gending*.

Ex. 97.

1st pair

gumanaks

2d pair

kangsi*

---

* Pitched at 830 and 875v. To be complete, the group should include a smaller kangsi barangan, sounding an octave higher.

The special cymbals or *ri(n)chik* used in the *gambuh* ensemble differ considerably from the heavy cymbals of the *gamelan gong* in their small size and brightly ringing sound. The top cymbal of each pair is attached to a stick, by means of a cord passed through a hole in its center, while the corresponding lower cymbals are loosely mounted, upturned, on a wooden stand with separate cylindrical bases for each cymbal (Fig. 29). Three or four such pairs are normally employed. The polyrhythmic interplay of the cymbals in the *gamelan gong* is not used here. So complex a rhythmic background would neutralize the intricate drumming which plays a leading role in directing gestures and movements of the actors. Instead, the *rinchiks* sound in unison, merely scanning the extended *palets* of the *pengawak* with occasional accents, and sounding simple rhythmic patterns in the *pengechèt*. Filled with little breaks or rests, the delicately sounded rhythms allow the drums to be heard on even their lightest accents. Only in the faster dances and scenes of action do the cymbals take on a more energetic character, now struck in rapid alternation of left and right hands to create a continuous tremolo.

---

[2] Similar, though modified in form, to the Javanese *kemanak*, and known in some villages, including Sèsètan, as *belana*.
[3] Pitched at 520, 570, 620, and 680 v. respectively.

121

Ex. 98.

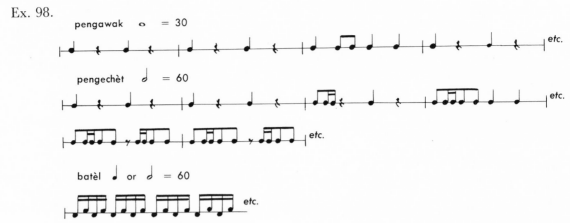

In addition to this group of lightly clashing and chiming percussion instruments that contributes so much to the unusual timbre of the *gamelan gambuh*, the *gentorak* or rack of small bells is sometimes included, to add to the continuous jingle of metallic sounds. This was found in Batuan, but no longer was included in the Tabanan orchestra.

The form of *kendang* or drum used in the *gambuh* ensemble is considerably smaller than that used in the *gamelan gong* and is immediately recognized by its higher pitch and brighter tone. It is more commonly referred to by the alternative name, *gupek*, and the drumming, in which the hands alone are employed, is generally known as the *gupekan*.

As in the *gamelan gong*, an interdependent pair of drums leads the orchestra, composed of a larger and lower-pitched *wadon* and a smaller, higher-pitched *lanang*. The natural, open tone of each *gupek*, produced at the larger end by the right hand, is known as *dag*, and the two open tones of the drum pair are distinguished by the names, *dag wadon* and *dag lanang*. These two resonant, fundamental tones supply the basic accents in the interlocking drum rhythms. They have a more definite, musical pitch than those of the *kendang gong*. The *wadon* drum is generally tuned to sound in the vicinity of the *kempur* tone, while the *lanang* is pitched a fourth or fifth higher. In order to distinguish more clearly between the relative weight of the two sounds, Balinese musicians generally refer to *dag lanang* as *tut*, so that in describing a basic drum pattern a drummer will say, for example, *dag, dag, tut, dag, tut, tut, dag, tut*.

The patterns and interplay between the two drums are far more intricate and varied than those which animate the *gending gong*. In addition to the *tut-dag* accents, secondary accentuation and complex filling-in patterns are created through a variety of tones and sounds of contrasting weight and color, produced by the full hand, the fingers, or the finger-tips or thumb alone, while the drumheads are struck in the center, near the edge, or on the rim. These, combined with the more widely spaced main accents which follow each other in irregular but balanced alternation produce a dynamic inner movement within the metric structure of the *gending*. It is this inner movement that gives impetus and direction to the actor's dance and movement about the stage. This he listens to rather than the actual melody, for without the drumming he cannot move a step. Balinese musicians consider *gambuh* drumming as the most difficult of drum styles. This difficulty, however, is not due to the need for technical virtuosity, for tempos are leisurely and the interplay between the two drums cannot compare in complexity with that of high speed *lègong* and *kebyar* drumming. The difficulty lies partly in the strangely suspended character of the ensemble itself, with its free and syncopated *suling* melody and lack of any instruments to supply a stabilizing progression of *pōkok* tones. But the main difficulty lies in the unusually broad metric dimensions of the slow movements, where only the most experienced drummers know how to maintain a rhythmic continuity between the widely spaced *kajar* accents.

Gambuh drumming is based on the interplay of three basic and contrasting sounds— open, muted, and harmonic. These occur at three markedly different pitch levels, and are known by the differentiating names, *dag*, *pek*, and *krèmpèng*. The *dag* tone is highly resonant, and is used for main accentuation. The *krèmpèng* tone, the most definite in pitch, is tense and penetrating. It sounds an octave or twelfth above the *dag* tone, depending on how it is produced, and is used for secondary accents. *Pek* is a short neutral sound of indefinite pitch, which might be described as lying halfway between the *dag* and *krèmpèng* tones. It is used chiefly for creating filling-in patterns. The sounds are produced in the following way:

a. *dag*, the deep-pitched open tone, is sounded at the larger end of the drum by the right hand. It is produced by striking just inside the rim (*bibih*) with the central part of the hand or by striking a little further in with the thumb. The fingers of the left hand are free of the other drumhead, allowing for full resonance of the drum (Fig. 53).

b. *pek*, lighter in sound, is produced by the left hand at the smaller end of the drum. The four fingers are spread out, striking near the center of the drumhead with the last two joints only. The sound is lightly muted by stopping the right drumhead with the thumb (Fig. 56).

c. *krèmpèng*, the ringing overtone, is produced by the finger tips near or at the rim of the left drumhead while the right drumhead is lightly muted with the hand. Only the last three, or two, fingers are used. Some drummers prefer the fourth finger alone, producing a delicate, vibrant tone. Since the *krèmpèng* tone of the higher pitched *lanang* drum is shrill and overpenetrating, most drummers lower the pitch by striking a little further in from the rim, so that while the two *dag* tones may sound a fourth apart, the two *krèmpèng* tones usually sound an approximate second apart (Figs. 50, 54).

Thus, in the interplay between the two drums there is a basic series of six clearly distinguishable sounds, four musical, two neutral, lying at contrasting pitch levels:

left hand	krèmpèng	L W	• •	
	pek	L W	• •	
right hand	dag	L W	• •	(tut)

Interplay between the *pek* sounds of the two drums is known as *gumpek* or *gupekan*. It forms a light but integrating rhythmic background, setting and maintaining the tempo with its continuous interlocking patterns. Since the *dag* tones produced by the two right hands occur at wider and irregular intervals, the alternating beats of the left hand *gumpek*, not always following in regular order, are kept rhythmically in place by light filling-in finger strokes per-

123

formed by the right hand when not producing a *dag* tone. These, however, are almost inaudible, and play no significant part in the rhythmic interplay. The *gumpek* rhythm itself may become inaudible, heard only by the two drummers. Normally struck, the *gumpek* beats carry to both actors and audience, and in moments of dramatic action, or to signal a faster tempo, they emerge in a sudden forte.

The *lanang* drum is considered the leader of the pair, although sounding on essentially secondary beats. The *wadon*, though sounding generally on main beats, plays no part in introducing a change in tempo or dynamics.[4] The *lanang* has, accordingly, several additional strokes and sounds which are not employed by the *wadon* drum:

d. *tut chenik*, "small" or high *tut*, a lighter, modified *tut*, or *dag lanang*, tone, produced in the same way, but with the left hand muting the left drumhead. The pitch is raised slightly, while the tone is shortened to a half staccato.

e. *krumpung*, a modified, lower-pitch *krèmpèng* tone, produced by striking further in on the drumhead, and using the last two joints of the fingers instead of the fingertips. The right drumhead is muted. The sound is substituted for the more brilliant *krèmpèng* in passages where the latter would be too prominent (Fig. 55).

f. *plak*, a sharply accented *pek* sound, used as signal for an immediately slower tempo. Sounded several times in quick succession the *plak* accent leads into a faster tempo.

The basic method in which the six principal strokes, along with *tut chenik*, are combined is shown in the following example. Here the three main interplays, *tut-dag*, *gupekan*—interlocking *gumpek* sounds—and *krèmpèngan*—interlocking *krèmpèng* tones—are shown. The *tut-dag* is accompanied by the *gupekan* alone, while the *krèmpèngan* fills in an empty beat. In the first measure the basic beat of the two drums is seen to be regular; in the last half of the second measure the beat is varied through syncopated interplay of the two basic tones.

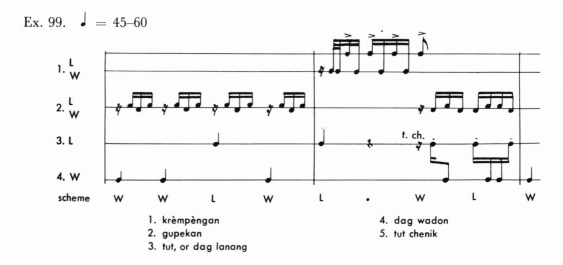

Ex. 99. ♩ = 45–60

1. krèmpèngan
2. gupekan
3. tut, or dag lanang
4. dag wadon
5. tut chenik

[4] According to Tabanan and Batuan informants, and to I Lunyuh, who in former days was *lanang* drummer in the *gambuh* orchestra at the palace in Payangan.

124

Like the drumming of the *gending gong*, the basic *dag* accents alternate throughout the *gending gambuh* in irregular but essentially balanced order. Their relative position in the metric structure of the composition is such that the *dag* accent of the *wadon* drum falls primarily on all main structural beats, or is deliberately silent on these beats; the *tut* or *dag lanang* essentially stresses the secondary and offbeats. While during the course of the composition the *dag wadon* may be omitted on *kempur* and *kajar* beats, it always occurs on the *kempur* stroke which terminates the melodic period of the complete composition. Here it is the final drum sound to be heard, for it is not followed by an answering *lanang* accent.

While the basic *tut-dag* interplay is constantly varied through the introduction of additional beats, displacement and syncopation, it can be reduced to a basic scheme of beat sequence. Thus the following passage, in which the main accentuation and filling in *krèmpèngan* are given (the *gupekan* may be taken for granted), can be basically expressed by the pattern created by the alternating *dag* and *tut* tones.

Ex. 100.   ♩ = 45–60

This basic pattern is in itself an amplification of a more elementary eight-beat unit at half the speed which, when completely filled in, can be expressed by the lower of the two formulas:

```
 W   W   L   W   L   L   W   .   .   L   W   W   .   W   L   L
 W   W   L   W   L   L   W   .   .   L   W   W   .   W   L   L
 W       L       L       W       L       W       W       L
```

This characteristic eight-beat unit of alternation, in which the second half is seen to be an inversion of the first, can be reduced further to the formula W L W W, and finally is found to be based on a regular alternation of W and L strokes. By leaving out certain basic beats, as shown above, and filling in with *krèmpèng* and *gupek* passages, rhythmic monotony is avoided and the drumming acquires buoyancy.

The drums contribute, along with the *kajar* and *kempur*, to the colotomic accentuation. The system of subdividing the melodic period differs from that of the *gending gong* in that the normal *palet* of the *pengawak* or first movement of the *gending gambuh* contains thirty-two beats instead of the normal sixteen beats to the *palet* in the *gending gong*. The basic scheme for alternation of *wadon* and *lanang dag* accents is followed for the first eight beats then modified:

125

```
palet 1.  W    W    L    W    L    L    W    W
          P
          L    .    .    .    L    L    W    W
          L    .    .    .    .    L    W    W
          L    .    .    L    W    L    W    L
palet 2.  W
          k
```

Following *palets* are given basically the same accentuation, while the final *palet* begins with a *lanang* accent, and *lanang* beats dominate throughout. Thus the four main structural drum accents within the *palet*, along with the *kempur* and *kajar* beats, occur in the following order:

```
W    L    L    L    W    L    L    L    W    L    L    L    L    L    W    L    W
P         k              k                   k                        P
```

Since the *wadon* beat coincides with the resonant and rapidly repeated strokes of the *kajar* accent, it is often eliminated, while the *kajar* accent is intensified by *krèmpèngan* drumming. The *palet* thus may be subdivided in a number of ways:

```
.    L    L    L
k
.    L    .    L
k
.    .    L    L
k
```

By omitting basic accents and replacing them with *gupek* or *krèmpèng* passages performed at double or quadruple speed the drumming is kept in constant motion. The *gending* thus is given contrasting light and shade, firmly supported at times by a succession of structural accents, at others left suspended indefinitely over a barely audible drumming composed entirely of combined *gupek* and *krèmpèng* interplay.

The compositions of the *gambuh* repertory are known as the *gending pegambuhan*. They show a similarity in form to the *gending gong*, although there is not the same variety of metric structure. Two separate groups of compositions may be distinguished—those in two movements, and of broad metric dimensions, which are classified, because of their metric punctuation, as *tabuh telu, tabuh 3;* and those in one movement and metrically contracted, which are known as *tabuh besik, tabuh 1*.

The two-movement *gendings* consist of an extended *pengawak* in slow tempo, followed by a more animated *pengechèt* which is more tightly condensed in metric structure. There is no break or pause between movements although either may be played alone. The *tabuh 1* compositions are in fast (*gangsaran*) tempo, and are relatively short in length. While they also consist of a *pengawak* and *pengechèt* they are usually performed at a uniform tempo throughout, though in some the *pengawak* is taken at half speed. Since both *pengawak* and *pengechèt* are closely interwoven and follow each other without a break they are actually contrasting and

126

complementary melodic sections rather than separate movements. These shorter compositions usually begin with the *pengechèt*, proceed to the *pengawak*, and then return to end with
the *pengechèt*.

Because of their quiet, nondramatic character, and because they accompany quiet scenes
and the entrances of leading characters of the *alus* type, the two-movement compositions are
known as *gending alus*. In these compositions the *pengawak* accompanies the formal entrances
or serves as musical background for the dialogue, while the *pengechèt* accompanies those
episodes which are danced. The short animated compositions are known as *gending kras*,
since they accompany dramatic scenes, *kras* characters and *alus* heros when roused to action.
During the performance the *gendings* follow each other without a break, one passing almost
imperceptibly into the next or linked to it by the half improvisational *sesèndon* performed by
sulings and *rebab* alone. These free and often prolonged passages in which the rest of the
orchestra is silent offer points of repose in the drama, marking a change of locale, a moment
of indecision, or a pause in the action, and establishing the new scale in which the next
gending will be performed.

Considering the metric classifications of the *gending gong*, one would expect the *pengawak*
to the *tabuh 3* form of *gending pegambuhan* to be based on a melodic period of three *palets*.
Instead, it is composed of four *palets* of 32 beats, thus equal in length to *tabuh 8* of the *gending
gong*, which has eight *palets* of 16 *pōkok* tones. The term *tabuh 3* refers to the three *kajar* accents
which follow the *kempur* stroke, marking the beginning of the second, third, and fourth
palets and dividing the melodic period in the following way:

P   k   k   k

Three types of *pengawak* are found in the *tabuh 3 gendings*:

a. in which the musical statement is complete with a single melodic period of 128 beats,

b. in which the complete musical statement is of double length, composed of two 128-
beat units, each containing four *palets*, and given the basic punctuation,

P   k   k   k   P   k   k   k

c. in which the *pengawak* is composed of two separate but melodically related four-*palet*
periods, which are linked together by a short interlude for *sulings* and *rebab* alone. All
three forms of *pengawak* are played at more or less the same speed, based on a beat at
M. 36–46.

The *pengechèt* is played at double speed—that is, the basic beat is now at M. 72–92.
Structurally it is a contraction of the *pengawak* to one-fourth its metric dimensions, reducing
the melodic period to 32 beats and proportionately shortening the *palets* to 8 beats. The
four *palets* are marked at the beginning by the same basic accents, P k k k. Following an
extended *pengawak* of eight *palets*, the *pengechèt* is accordingly extended to 64 beats, with eight

127

palets and the corresponding basic punctuation, P k k k P k k k. This eight-palet *pengechèt* occasionally follows a four-*palet pengawak*, although this is unusual. A third, though rare, form of *pengechèt* includes a third 32-beat melodic unit. Short or long, however, the *pengechèt* is a single musical statement which, unlike the *pengawak*, is only complete with repetition, and is usually repeated several times.

A less frequently employed *tabuh 3* form of composition is the *gending* in which an unusually expanded section called the *pengrangrang* is inserted between the *pengawak* and *pengechèt*, and forms the main part of the *gending*. Here the *pengawak* is identical with the *pengechèt* in structure and tempo—a 32-beat melodic period played at the fast speed of approximately M. 120, thus lasting about fifteen seconds. This opening tempo is firmly established during the several repetitions of the *pengawak*. With the *pengrangrang* time suddenly seems to stand still. The beat drops to four times as slow—M. 30—and the preceding *pengawak* is played in corresponding metric augmentation, now lasting one minute. But this 32-beat melodic period is no longer a period at all. It is now treated as a single *palet* to a broader melodic period. Three similar *palets* follow, in which the melodic line of the first *palet* is given three transpositions, beginning each time on a different degree of the scale. The four *palets* are marked by the same basic P k k k accentuation, but one minute now elapses between each stroke, and four minutes must pass before the *kempur* is heard again. After a repeat of the *pengawak* the opening tempo is resumed and the melody assumes its original form, but now transformed into *pengechèt* through the change in drumming, which is performed at twice the speed of the *pengawak*.

Because of their faster tempo the *gendings* classified as *tabuh 1* are compositions which, like the *pengechèt* of the *tabuh 3* group, are intended primarily to accompany danced episodes. These *gendings* normally open with the *pengechèt*, an ostinato unit of 8 or 16 beats which can be repeated indefinitely, according to the requirements of the dance. They are classified as *tabuh 1* because of the alternating punctuation of *kempur* and *kajar*, which mark the beginning and halfway point in the *pengechèt*.

The *pengechèt* is followed by the *pengawak*, based on a similar metric structure, but sometimes expanded to a melodic period of 32 beats. In this case the basic punctuation changes to the *tabuh 3* system.

The *pengawak* may be played at the same speed as the *pengechèt* or be taken at half speed. It generally is not danced to, but accompanies dialogue of an animated nature. It may be repeated or not, as needed. It is followed again by the *pengechèt*, with which the *gending* ends.

In addition to the *gendings* in *tabuh 3* and *tabuh 1* forms there are a number of 8- and 4-beat ostinatos which are used for the dances of secondary characters and which have no metric classification. And finally there is *batèl*, a 2-beat unit used only at the height of dramatic action. These all show a punctuation similar to *tabuh 1*.

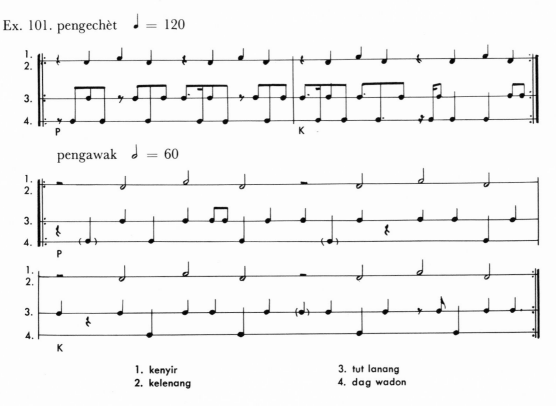

The drumming to the *gending kras* is agogic throughout. There is no place in the contracted metric scheme for secondary colotomic accentuation by the drums. Instead, there is a continuous interplay of *tut lanang* and *dag wadon* beats which now follow in close alternation. The following example gives the basic drumming to *gending Biakalang*, a *tabuh 1* composition consisting of two 18-beat ostinato motifs, the second taken at half the speed of the first. Both sections are given the same P k punctuation. Here the interlocking of drum beats with *kenyir* and *kelenang* accents can be seen. In the *pengechèt* the drum patterns are essentially offbeat. In the *pengawak* the same basic interplay takes place at half speed.

Ex. 101. pengechèt   ♩ = 120

pengawak   ♩ = 60

1. kenyir
2. kelenang
3. tut lanang
4. dag wadon

As the metric unit contracts to 8 or 4 beats, the drum patterns contract accordingly:

Ex. 102.

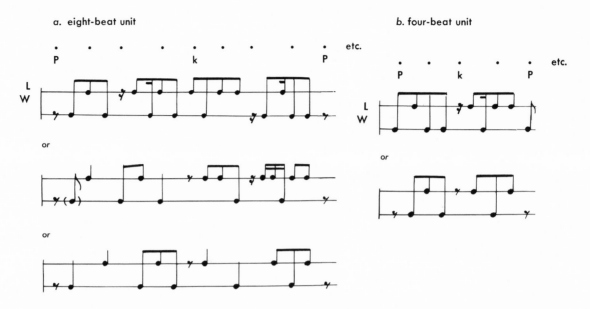

In the animated, 2-beat *batèl* which accompanies scenes of combat the drumming becomes further contracted; it now rings with *krèmpèng lanang* accents while *tut-dag* interplay occurs on the extreme offbeats:

Ex. 103. Batèl ♩ = 120

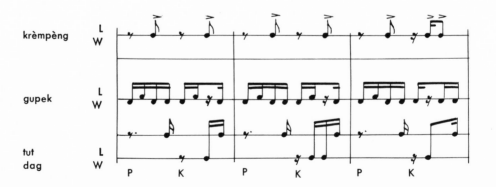

Extended *krèmpèng* interplay between the two drums may substitute for basic W L accentuation in the *pengawak*. The following drumming to a single 32-beat *palet* of a *tabuh 3* composition is typical. Here *krèmpèng* alternates with *gupek* for three measures before *tut-dag* beats occur.

130

Ex. 104. ♩ = 45*

* The five staff lines represent, from top to bottom, krèmpèng lanang, krèmpèng wadon, gupek, tut lanang and dag wadon.

The first three *palets* are given more or less the same accentuation. In the concluding *palet* or *mipil* continuous *tut-dag* interplay throughout finally gives solidity to the long suspended melodic period and prepares for the *kempur* stroke, while the *krèmpèng* is heard only once, immediately before the end.

Ex. 105. Mipil ♩ = 45

With the *pengechèt* the drumming changes to a light and animated interplay of *gupek* and *tut-dag* beats. *Krèmpèng* accents, which played so prominent a part in the *pengawak*, are now entirely absent. The first three *palets* are underlined by the same basic drumming, which is intensified in the *mipil*. A feeling of suspense is given to each *palet* through the omission of the *lanang* accent. Only when the *pengechèt* has been repeated for the last time are the last two beats of the *mipil* filled in with concluding *tut-dag* interplay.

131

Ex. 106. Pengechèt   ♩ = 92–120

The *gending pegambuhan* are essentially pentatonic in character and lie in four different five-tone scales, of which the fingering on the *suling* is fairly standardized. The lowest scale, *Tembung*,[5] begins on the second degree of the seven-tone *suling* scale, and the five tones, *ding, dong, dèng, dung, dang,* are produced by means of the following fingering:

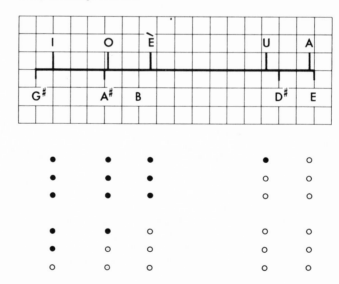

Tekep Tembung; Tabanan

The second octave is produced by overblowing, with modified fingering for the highest tones.

Characteristic use of the *penyorog* tone lying between high *dang* and higher *ding* is shown in the following example, *gending Tembung*, of which the *suling* melody is given in full. The

5 Called *Sunarèn* in Batuan.

gending belongs to the *tabuh 1* group, opening with the *pengechèt*, which lies in the low register of the *suling*. The *pengawak* lies in the contrasting upper register and here the *penyorog* is introduced at *a* and retained through the following measure, giving the effect of a temporary modulation. As the *pengawak* falls to the middle register the opening tonality is resumed. The syncopated, continued playing off the beat (*ngarèn*) is characteristic of the *suling gambuh* style, and usually becomes more and more involved as the melody is repeated. The *gending* is played for the entrance of the *kadian Melayu*, the pair of attendants who introduce Prince Melayu.

Ex. 107. Gending Tembung ♩ = 112

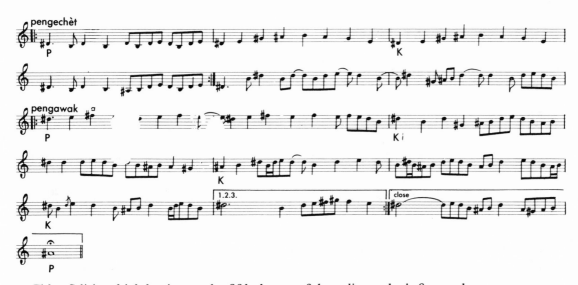

Tekep Selisir, which begins on the fifth degree of the *suling* scale, is fingered:

Tekep Selisir; Tabanan

133

Apart from its higher pitch and brighter color, the *Selisir* scale creates a quite different effect from *Tembung* through the relatively greater distance between the tones *dèng* and *dung*, and the relatively higher place of the fifth tone, *dang*, in the series. The ear, however, soon adjusts to it during a performance, accepting it as one more variation of the five-tone *pèlog* scale. Ex. 108, the *pengechèt* to the *gending, Sumbambang Bali*, shows characteristic *Selisir* melody. No *penyorog* tones occur—these are rare in *Selisir* compositions—and the melody remains pentatonic throughout. The *pengechèt* belongs to a *gending* of the *tabuh 3* group, and accompanies the entrance of the *pramisuri*, queen or married princess.

Ex. 108. Pengechèt Sumbambang Bali ♩ = 88

Use of the *penyorog* tone in *Selisir* melody will be seen in Ex. 109, *Bapang Selisir*, a short composition of the *tabuh 1* group, consisting of an eight-beat ostinato *pengechèt* which is followed by the contrasting *pengelik* or *pengumbang*.[6] The *gending* ends with the opening *pengechèt*. Here the *penyorog* tone appears in the *pengechèt* at *a*, but is not heard in the *pengelik*. This *gending*, a condensed *tabuh 1*, accompanies Prince Panji and other nobles during a more dramatic episode in the play.

---

[6] That part of the *gending* where the actor no longer dances but moves freely about, covering the whole stage. *Ngumbang* means to stride about, like a bee (*kumbang*) flying around within a small area. Here dialogue takes place, while the cymbals are silent and the drumming is almost inaudible.

Ex. 109. Bapang Selisir $\quad \downarrow = 60$

Starting a tone higher than *Selisir*, on the sixth degree of the seven-tone scale is the scale *Baro*, with the fingering:

Tekep Baro; Tabanan

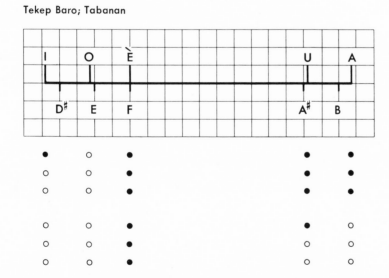

Relatively few compositions are played in this curiously distorted scale, which is used mainly for dances of a bizarre character. Through transposition, the three lower tones of the scale lie near semitones apart, while the distance from *dèng* to *dung* now extends to an approximate fourth. In the octave above, the scale tends toward a more normal form through the higher pitch of the tone, *dèng*, resulting from overblowing.

The following *gending*, *Jaran Sirig*, *Rearing Horse*, which is used for the entrance dance of

135

the *prabu kras*, vigorous prince, shows typical use of the *Baro* scale. The composition begins with a so-called *pengawak*, actually a *pengechèt* in tempo and spirit. It is followed by the *pengelik*, and the *gending* ends with a return to the *pengawak*. The *pengawak* motif forms the basis for endless variations with each repetition, while the *pengechèt*, introduced by the *pengelik*, consists of the *pengawak* motif in augmentation, transposed an octave higher. A final statement of the augmented motif transposed to a lower tone series, *a*, allows the melody to regain its original contour. The *gending* now returns to the *pengawak*, and new variations follow with each repetition until the close.

Ex. 110. Gending Jaran Sirig ♩ = 90

In the scale known as *Lebeng* the five main scale tones are found in their most unusual relationship. Beginning on the seventh degree of the *suling* scale, the second interval is of necessity a neutral third. By skipping the next tone in the usual way to locate the tone, *dung,* a second large interval results, this time a near minor third. The last tone of the series, *dang,* is produced as shown in Ex. 90, which places it less than a semitone above *dung.* In addition, a second *dang* may be substituted, located a near semitone above the first, so that one may speak of *Lebeng* as actually a six-tone scale, with a first and a secondary *dang.*

Tekep Lebeng; Tabanan

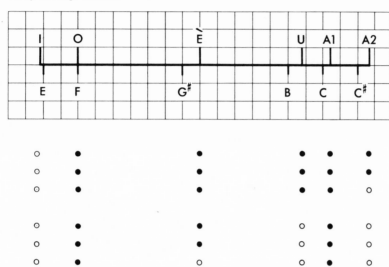

Although lying in the middle register of the *suling, Lebeng* is rarely used in the octave below. Because of the mellow register and the unusual interval structure, compositions played in this scale have a purity of timbre and an elusiveness of tonality which the unaccustomed ear finds enchanting. In Ex. 111, *gending Biakalang,* characteristic *Lebeng* melody is shown. In this composition there is no substitution of secondary *dang* during the course of the melody. In the upper register, however, *ding Lebeng* is replaced by *ding Baro,* thus lowering it a semitone in pitch, as can be seen by the tone indicated by *a.* The *gending* belongs to the *tabuh 1* group, with an opening ostinato *pengechèt* which is repeated with variations. It is followed by the *pengawak* in the high register, and ends with the *pengechèt.* In the *pengawak* further alteration of the scale occurs; the tone, *dèng,* is now lowered a semitone at *b* through modified fingering.

Ex. 111. Gending Biakalang   ♩ = 96

Ex. 113, the *pengechèt* to the *gending*, *Sumbambang Java*, illustrates the special use of the secondary *dang* tone, indicated by the figure 2, in its alternation with the basic *dang*, indicated by 1. With *dang* 1 as the tonic or final tone, the movement plays back and forth between two separate but interlocking tonal series, the one containing a primary *dang*, 1, the other a modified *dang*:

Ex. 112.

The *pengechèt* belongs to a *tabuh 3* composition, used to accompany the appearance of the *putri* or princess. It is a single melodic statement composed of two four-*palet* periods. It begins on the third *palet* of what is actually the first period, once the two periods take their proper relative position with the repetition of the *pengechèt*. The brief appearance of high *dung*, indicated by *a*, is purely ornamental, and need not be taken into account when considering the basic melodic structure.

Ex. 113. Sumbambang Java; pengechèt ♩ = 100

The four scales described here form the complete tonal range of the *gambuh* musical repertory as it is heard today. By far the greater number of compositions lie in the *Selisir* scale, considered ideal for the *gending alus*. Because of its darker color, *Tembung* is found more suitable for the *gending kras* which accompany leading characters of the vigorous type as well as leading opponents; while *Baro* is reserved for the entrances of subordinate characters, such as heralds, officials, and buffoon attendants. *Lebeng* is used later in the performance, sometimes for the *gending alus*, but especially in scenes of recrimination and dramatic action.

As one *gending* follows another without pause, the effect created is that of a continuous melodic line, fluid in tempo, and constantly changing color through change in scale and drumming. With its gongs of fixed pitch that sound in different relation to the melody with each change in scale, and with its faintly ringing chromatic accompaniment by *gumanaks* and *kangsi*, the *gamelan gambuh* is a completely atonal ensemble.

139

Chapter 11

The Gamelan Semar Pegulingan

IN GENERAL appearance and instrumental organization the *Gamelan Semar Pegulingan* bears a resemblance to the *gamelan gong*, but it is far sweeter and more delicately chiming in sound. In its complete form this gamelan is a *saih 7* orchestra, so constructed in order to perform the compositions of the *gambuh* repertory in their original scales. It is more often found, however, as a five-tone ensemble tuned to *Selisir*, and pitched somewhat higher than *Selisir gong*.

The leading melodic instrument of the orchestra is the *trompong*, brighter and more ringing in tone than the *trompong* of the *gamelan gong*, and having a wider and higher range. Wide-range *genders* may be included to accompany certain dance performances, notably *lègong*. The present chapter, however, is mainly devoted to the old, seven-tone form of gamelan, and the manner in which the music of the *gambuh* theater is transformed when adapted to a gamelan of bronze instruments.

The sweeter, lighter sound of the *Semar Pegulingan* orchestra is due primarily to the absence of heavy sounding *sarons* and the many large cymbals used in the *gamelan gong*. Instead, the *pōkok* tones here are played entirely by one-octave *genders*, while in the highest octave small *saron*-type instruments perform light filling-in passage work. As in the *gambuh* ensemble the main colotomic accentuation is supplied by the *kempur* and *kajar*, while the *kemong*, or *kentong*, is used in certain compositions for additional gong punctuation. The *kenyir* and *kelenang* are replaced by the more resonant *pōnggang* for secondary accents. The pair of drums used are somewhat larger than those used in the *gambuh* ensemble, and the drumming derives directly from the *gambuh* drum method, giving buoyancy and life to the ensemble. One set of small cymbals similar to those used in the *gambuh* orchestra underlines the drumming with animated clashing, and occasionally the *gentorak*, the chime of small bells, is included in the gamelan.

Like the *gambuh* theater, the seven-tone *Semar Pegulingan* had all but vanished by 1931. There were several six-tone orchestras, so formed as to make possible the playing of separate repertories in the two scales, *Tembung* and *Selisir*. But only two seven-tone ensembles could be found in any state of activity. One, which was badly out of tune, and whose musicians knew only a small repertory of compositions, belonged to the village of Kamassan in Klungkung. The other, in excellent condition, belonged to a Brahman priest of Tampak Gangsal, a *banjar* in the town of Badung, and was heard now and then on ceremonial occasions. The present account is based on information received from the musicians of this ensemble, for they still played with assurance and knew compositions in four different five-tone scales. The full seven-tone scale of the Tampak Gangsal gamelan has been given in Chart 2 (No. 4), but is shown again here for sake of reference to the derivative five-tone scales which follow. By comparing it with the *saih 7* of the *suling gambuh* it will be found to begin a near minor seventh higher.

Saih 7 scale; Tampak Gangsal

310	337	365		425	457	485	560	
144	138	264	126	102	249	177		
Eᵇ	F	Gᵇ	A	Bᵇ	B	Dᵇ	Eᵇ	
307.5	345	366	435	461	488	548		

The Tampak Gangsal musicians knew *gendings* in the scales *Tembung*, *Baro*, *Lebeng*, and *Selisir*. These were said to start on the first, second, third and fifth tones of the *saih 7* as found in the first octave of the *trompong*. Already a change from the *gambuh* system is seen, not only in pitch, but in scale relationship.

first tone	scale	saih 7, trompong	saih 7, suling gambuh
ding	Tembung	1st tone	2d tone
ding	Lebeng	2d tone	7th tone
ding	Baro	4th tone	6th tone
ding	Selisir	5th tone	5th tone

This scale relationship corresponds to that of the Kamassan gamelan, with the exception of *Lebeng* which there began on the sixth tone of the *saih 7*.

In its complete and extended form the melody can be performed by the *trompong* in any of these scales. But because of the restricted one-octave range of the metallophones, the *pōkok* tones can only find their natural sequence in the first two scales, *Tembung* and *Lebeng*. The remaining two scales can be expressed only through inversion of the basic tone series, thus often forcing the *pōkok* tones to travel in opposite direction to the *trompong* melody. The above four scales are found on a one-octave instrument in the order:

	1	2	3	4	5	6	7
saih 7	1	2	3	4	5	6	7
Tembung	I	O	È		U	A	
Lebeng		I	O	È		U	A
Baro	U	A		I	O	È	
Selisir		U	A		I	O	È

Of the four scales, *Tembung* and *Selisir* are most frequently used. *Gendings* in *Lebeng* and *Baro* are rarely performed, since, in the original *gambuh* repertory, the majority of these *gendings* are of the contracted *tabuh 1* type, primarily dramatic and, because of their repetitive, ostinato character, of less appeal as instrumental music.

The *trompong* style of the *Semar Pegulingan* orchestra has a lightness and grace very different from the majestic style of the *trompong* of the *gamelan gong*. With a fourteen-tone range and with no second *trompong* following in the octave above, the soloist has far greater freedom in the interpretation of his part, and transforms the original *suling* melodies into metallic music of elegance and rhythmic charm. While the slow-moving *pengawak* is performed with relative simplicity, the more animated *pengechèt* becomes a supple dance movement, ornate with graces and passing-tones, and continually enlivened by syncopated passages that take their impulse from the drums. The basic contour of the *suling* melody is preserved; the colotomic accents and drumming of the composition remain unchanged. But because of the change in instrumental timbre and the precise, percussive attack of the *trompong*, to say nothing of the difference in pitch and tuning of the orchestra itself, the original soft and dreamlike music is translated into something entirely new, familiar in contour but strange in intonation.

To the Western ear the most potent factor in effecting this change is the modified interval relation which takes place within each scale when transferred to the *trompong*. This may readily be imagined when the Tampak Gangsal versions of each scale are compared with the corresponding scales of the *suling gambuh*:

Tekep Tembung; Tampak Gangsal

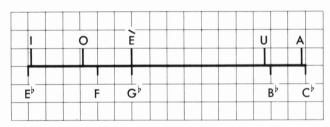

As illustration of *trompong* melody in the *Tembung* scale the *pengechèt Bramara* is given in Ex. 114. Just how far this adaptation follows the original *suling* version in contour and at the same time translates it into an ornate solo may be seen by comparing it with the melody in *gambuh* form given in Appendix 3, Ex. 357, where it will be found lying in the *Selisir* scale. While in *gambuh* form this *pengechèt* is irregular in metric structure, when transferred to the *Semar Pegulingan* orchestra it becomes a conventional *tabuh 3 pengechèt*, composed of two balanced four-*palet* interdependent melodic periods. The first period is entirely pentatonic but at the beginning of the second period a secondary tone, *a*, makes a brief appearance. Here it has less melodic importance than in the *gambuh* version. According to the Tampak Gangsal musicians, it is simply considered as a *bèro* or false tone. Introducing it is simply to "*ngaras bèro*," "graze a false tone," or "*ngaras dèng Selisir*," "graze *dèng Selisir*." In the following example the *trompong* melody is given in full. The *pōkok* tones and *jegogan* tones, here stressing every second *pōkok* tone, are given for the first period only. The steady beat of the *pōkok* tones, sounding in three octaves, should be kept in mind when estimating the effect of the syncopated passages in this and later passages of *trompong* melody.

142

Ex. 114. Pengechèt Bramara ♩ = 60

Tekep Lebeng; Tampak Gangsal

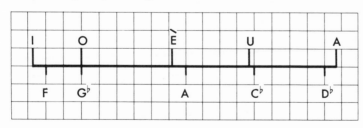

The *Lebeng* melody given in Ex. 115, *Sumbambang Java*, has been quoted in its *gambuh*
form in Ex. 113. In metric structure they are identical, starting on the second half of the

143

second melodic period and ending, after repetitions, on the opening tone of the first. On comparing the two versions, the general melodic line will be found to be essentially the same. Certain changes, however, occur in the transference of the *suling* melody to the *trompong*. In its *gambuh* form the movement opens and closes on the tone *dang*, while there is continuous alternation between the two *dang* tones throughout. The *trompong* version of the melody is transposed so as to open and close on the tone *dong*, in order to make use of the top register of the instrument and allow for the widest possible range for playing in octaves. The tone which would correspond to the secondary *dang* in the *gambuh* melody disappears, since it does not exist on the *trompong*. Instead, a purely ornamental *bèro* tone, not found in the *gambuh* version, is introduced at *a*, where it substitutes for the tone *dèng*. Sounding only once during the movement, as though by accident, it becomes more firmly established with each repetition, adding a delicate inflection each time to the otherwise pentatonic melody. In performances by five-tone ensembles this tone too disappears without affecting the main melodic line.

Ex. 115. Pengechèt Sumbambang Java $\quad \downarrow = 60$

Tekep Baro; Tampak Gangsal

Ex. 116, *gending Sekar Gadung*, though brief, must suffice as illustration of *Baro* melody, since it was the only composition in this little-used scale included in the Tampak Gangsal repertory. Like the original *gambuh* version, the melody is pentatonic throughout. The *trompong* style here is more direct than in the previous example, making much use of repeated tones (*tutugan*) and playing after the beat (*ngarèn*).

Ex. 116. Gending Sekar Gadung ♩ = 60

Tekep Selisir; Tampak Gangsal

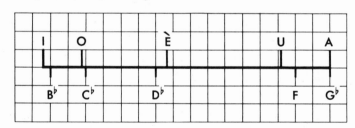

As in the other scales, *gendings* in *Selisir* make occasional use of a sixth tone, or even employ all seven. Ex. 117 is of unusual interest for the strong functional use of a sixth tone, *a*, situated between *dang* and upper *ding*. With its appearance at *a* and persistence for two *palets*, this tone, considered as *penyorog* by the Tampak Gangsal musicians, becomes an integral part of the melody, replacing the tone *ding*. The effect of a new and strongly contrasting tonality, dominated by the *penyorog*, is created. The opening tonality is seen to return later, at *b*, but is only firmly established toward the end of the last *palet* but one in the complete melodic period.

Ex. 117. Pengechèt Semuradas 𝅗𝅥 = 60

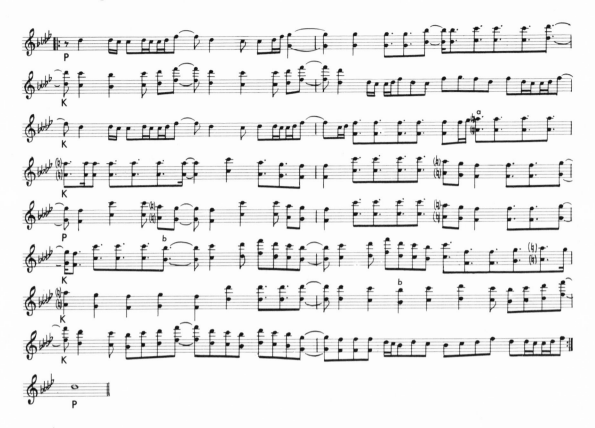

Yet even in this *gending*, the *penyorog* tone, despite its strong organic part, can be omitted and the piece performed by a five-tone ensemble. When teaching this composition to the members of my own five-tone *Semar Pegulingan* in Sayan, my old informant, Lunyuh, played a simplified version on the *trompong*, replacing the *penyorog* tone throughout with the tone *ding*. The effect of modulation to a new tonality was lost, but as he remarked, "If *saih 7, penyorog* is *possible;* if *saih 5,* not."[1]

In Ex. 118 all seven tones of the *saih 7* are made use of. At *a* a single ornamental *bèro* tone is sounded in passing, while toward the end of the melodic period the *penyorog*, entering at *b*, effects a momentary change in tonality similar to that in Ex. 117.

Ex. 118. Pengechèt Lèngkèr 𝅗𝅥 = 60

---

[1] " *Yèn saih pitu, dados, yèn saih lima, tan.*"

146

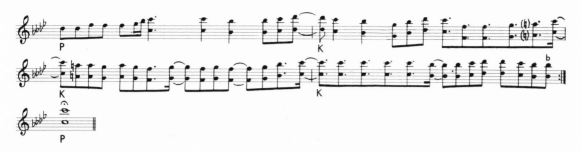

The above examples can only suggest the melodic possibilities of the *saih 7* system, now unfortunately falling into disuse. The Tampak Gangsal gamelan offers a glimpse of an earlier practice and style. It is impossible to determine just how representative of past *saih 7* gamelans is the particular tuning of this ensemble. It differs considerably from the diatonic sounding scale of the Kamassan gamelan, given in Chart 2 (No. 3). Furthermore neither scale resembles in interval structure the scale of the *suling gambuh*, as noted in either Tabanan or Batuan. What clearly emerges from the system is the basically pentatonic character of the different scales, and the subordinate role played by the two secondary tones in the melodic line.

The instrumentation of the *Semar Pegulingan* orchestra is simple and transparent, with all attention centered on the *trompong* solo. The *pōkok* tones are sounded in octaves by *jublags* and *penyachahs*, and linked together in the octave above by repeated tones played by small *gangsas* and *kantilans*. A constantly moving and lightly chiming background is thus created, against which the *trompong* rings out clearly, clashing from time to time with the *pokok* tones in momentary dissonance. Ex. 119 and 120 are from the five-tone *Semar Pegulingan* of *banjar* Titih, whose unusual scale, *Tembung Chenik*, is given in Chart 6 (No. 1).

Ex. 119. Pengechèt Sumbambang Bali; excerpt ♩ = 52

Ex. 120. Pengechèt Seduk Maru; excerpt   ♩ = 60

1. kantilans and gangsas
2. jublags and penyachahs
3. trompong

4. jegogans
5. kempur

While the *gendings* of the *gambuh* repertory, as performed in the *gambuh* ensemble, survive entirely through oral tradition, when transferred to the *gamelan Semar Pegulingan* they are sometimes preserved in outline by noting the *pōkok* tones. The same system of notation is used as that employed for the *gending gong*, and since there are no symbols to indicate secondary tones these *gendings* are noted only as performed by a five-tone *Selisir* orchestra.

Although no actual *lontar* containing collected compositions came to light during my stay in Bali, my informant, I Lunyuh, once presented me with a notebook containing the *pōkok* tones to fifteen *tabuh 3 gendings* which he had written down in pencil. This had taken him a month, for it was, he said, a long time since he had thought of them. Yet he never hesitated when playing them on the *trompong*, and when playing them again a week later they remained essentially the same, both in contour and ornamentation.

With the orderly *pōkok* tones and the transference of the sometimes intangible *suling* melody of the *gambuh* ensemble to the *trompong* it was now possible to define more clearly the melodic structure of these compositions. The *pōkok* tones to four *gendings* will be found in Appendix 4. Just how they differ in proportions and metric accentuation from the *gending gong* can be seen at a glance. One is struck first of all by the metric breadth of these *gendings* which are based on a *palet* of 32 *pōkok* tones instead of the 16-tone *palet* of the *gending gong*. In the first example, the *pengawak* contains 128 *pōkok* tones, the equivalent in length of *tabuh 8* of the *gending gong*, but with the *gong* punctuation of *tabuh 4*. In the following two examples the *pengawak* is extended to double the length, and contains two interdependent melodic periods of 128 *pōkok* tones each. The length of the *pengechèt* is likewise double the length of that found

148

in the first example. The last example, described as *rangkep*, contracted, is irregular. The *pengawak* contains 64 *pōkok* tones, while the distance between both *kempur* and *kajar* accents is reduced by one half. In the *pengechèt* of Example 3 and throughout Example 4 the *kemong* (M) is introduced to supply secondary accentuation. No matter what the length of the *pengawak* may be, it is not complete without at least one repetition. It is probably because of the slow tempo and unusual breadth of the opening movement to these compositions that they have lost their appeal for Balinese audiences of today. It is significant that the last example, *Lagu Tabuh Gari*, is still played occasionally at the end of a *lègong* performance, reorchestrated once more, and often drastically cut. It is the shortest in length, the most metrically contracted, and shows the most variety in its punctuation by *gongs*.

Chapter 12

The Gamelan Pelègongan

THE *gamelan pelègongan*, intended primarily to accompany the *lègong* dance, is actually an enlarged five-tone *Semar Pegulingan* orchestra with the *trompong* omitted and replaced by four wide-range *gendèrs*, two large *gendèr gedé*, and two smaller *gendèr barangan* pitched an octave higher. The group of one-octave metallophones is augmented and the *pōnggang* is discarded. Otherwise the orchestra remains the same, except that the two drums are somewhat smaller and more vibrant in sound. With these instrumental changes, and with a new and richly polyphonic orchestral style, the Balinese gamelan reaches its peak of development. More delicate and less percussive in resonance than the *gamelan gong*, it transforms the music of the *Semar Pegulingan* into a shimmering web of sound. Tempos are swift, dynamics change with dramatic suddenness, while the music glows throughout with ornamental figuration in the high register of the gamelan.

The orchestra is used to accompany a large repertory of dances and dance plays drawn mainly from the *gambuh* theater and Hindu mythology. Peopled with kings and princesses, gods and demons, witches, apes, and magic birds, this colorful theatrical world still holds a strong appeal for Balinese audiences. While some of the performances may be extended to full-length plays, the most popular form of presentation is the *lègong*, which is danced by three small girls who take different parts in turn. Here drama is transformed into dance. The choreographies derive in style from the *gambuh* tradition of movement, but with dance and music tempos greatly speeded up and scenes condensed, which creates an atmosphere of excitement and dramatic tension.

According to their means and ambitions, clubs may specialize in *lègong*, *barong*, or *Chalonarang*, each with its special repertory of compositions. In addition to the required repertory, most clubs include a number of purely instrumental compositions, recently composed, which may be played at a performance as preliminary show-pieces and interludes. While the traditional *gendings* for the most part derive directly from the *gambuh* repertory or else show similar form and metric structure, the recent compositions, generally referred to as *gending baru*, new *gendings*, reveal unlimited imagination in their freedom of form and rhythmic invention. Deriving in structure and melodic line from the older music, each *gending* shows on analysis a distinctive form of its own, while the melodic line, now liberated from the quadratic metric formulas of the past, takes on unexpected freshness and lyric grace. These recent compositions, created by some talented member of the club or taught by a visiting composer, are the real recreation of the music club. They are learned with enthusiasm and played for several years but are eventually discarded and replaced by new ones.

Because of the complex polyphony, the intricate figuration, and the quick changes in tempo and dynamics dictated by the dramatic action in the choreographies—all demanding a new precision in ensemble playing—the question of intensive rehearsal continued over a long period of time now enters our study for the first time. As already shown, in the *gamelan gong* and the *Semar Pegulingan* only the slow-moving and simple filling-in parts are doubled or played by a unison group. The *trompong* soloist may interpret his part as he pleases; tempos are slow and generally steady, while the system of orchestration is simple enough to prevent few difficulties in ensemble playing. No rehearsal is needed beyond an occasional run through of the traditional repertory to refresh the memory of the group.

But the *lègong* orchestra, with its main melody now assigned to a quartet of *gendèrs*, its rapid figuration played in unison by a large group of *gangsas*, and its highly syncopated drumming, is a virtuoso orchestra where smooth performance can only be achieved after long practice. Balinese standards are high in regard to rhythmic precision, and a performance where musicians and dancers are even a fractional beat apart on a sudden accent is sure to call forth criticism.

We can best understand the organization of this gamelan and its relation to dance movement if a short synopsis is given of how a *lègong* dancer learns a new choreography. For the first rehearsals, only the dancing-master, the three pupils, the leading *gendèr* player, the *kempur* and *kemong*, the two drums, and the cymbals are present. Guided by the teacher, the child learns the *gendèr* melody phrase by phrase, together with its basic punctuation and drumming. The music "enters" the pupil together with the choreography; accent and gesture become one. Once the three basic elements of the *gending*, melody, punctuation, and drumming, have been coordinated with movement and gesture, the whole elaborate overlay of gamelan polyphony can be added without confusing the dancer. In the last analysis it is the drumming which is her guide, controlling her speed and preparing her with accented cues for an approaching pause.

The musicians learn a new composition by the same method. All are present, but the teacher devotes his first attention to the *gendèr* melody, punctuation, and drumming. As a melodic period is being memorized by the leading *gendèrs*, the instruments sounding the *pōkok* tones gradually join in, followed by the smaller *gendèrs* that paraphrase the melody an octave higher. The teacher now turns to the group assigned the figuration. Deriving in principle from the two-voiced *rèongan* of the *gamelan gong* (Ex. 30-38), though performed with one hand only, this figuration is generally known as the *kōtèkan*,[1] but is also called the *kantilan*[2] or *chandetan*.[3] The two interlocking voices of the *kōtèkan* must be learned separately before they can be fitted together. Much attention is given to the *kōtèkan;* the two separate parts are continuously syncopated, constantly changing, and difficult to remember. Yet the *kōtèkan* group usually consists of the youngest members of the gamelan, often little older than ten or eleven.

With the addition of the *kōtèkan* the orchestration is all but complete. A small horizontally mounted gong, the *kelenang* (Fig. 41), is added, to sound on secondary beats, while the *kajar* is included to mark the beginning of the *palets* (in extended melodic periods) or else (in fast sections) merely to beat time. A *suling gambuh* is occasionally added, but is usually

[1] From *ngōtèk*, to slide or scratch, here referring to the quick, almost sliding movement of the striking mallet from one key to the next.
[2] From *kantil*, a kind of small aromatic blossom.
[3] Because of its similarity to the interlocking *chandetan* rhythms in the cymbal group of the *gamelan gong* (Ex. 39 and 40).

greatly out of tune with the gamelan. The *gentorak* may also be included, its small jingling bells adding a touch of metallic color.

For the following account of instrumental methods employed in the *gamelan pelègongan* and for most of the musical examples included in this chapter I have gone to the *lègong* orchestra of the village of Kuta. This gamelan, with its thirty musicians under the direction of the composer, I Lotring, was one of the outstanding gamelans of Bali in the thirties, and made a series of recordings for Odeon in 1928.[4] These are well worth listening to today, for they are remarkable both for their technical perfection and above all as a documentation of Balinese music at the time.

The tuning of the gamelan was said to be *Selisir pelègongan;* somewhat higher in pitch than the average *Selisir gong,* thus adding greatly to the special brilliance of the gamelan. The table in Ex. 121 lists the instruments and their ranges.

Selisir pelègongan; Kuta village

	I		O		È					U		A
	295		315		350					435		465
		115		183				376			116	
	D	Eᵇ			F					A	Bᵇ	
	290	307.5			345					435	461	

It will be noted that the *kemong* is tuned outside the five-tone scale, adding a sixth tone to the gamelan. This is general practice, and contributes greatly to the special tonal color of the orchestra. The pitch relation is not always the same in different gamelans, but it is generally such that the penetrating and unusually beautiful tone of the *kemong* is emphasized. This small gong is of particular importance in the *lègong* gamelan. It functions both in the regular colotomic punctuation and also as special signaling instrument for an approaching end to a melodic period, when its distinctive, prolonged sound rings clearly through the rest of the instruments.

The basic system for instrumental organization may be seen in the orchestral cross-section, Ex. 122. Although the passage is merely an eight-tone ostinato motif, the example may well serve as a point of reference for the following musical illustrations in this chapter. While this system is followed in general by all *lègong* orchestras, most gamelans have their own individual ways of varying the *kōtèkan* patterns, the *gendèr* melody and paraphrase. Gong punctuation and drumming, here reduced to the open tones of the two drums, remain stabilized.

---

4 See Appendix 6, Recordings.

152

Ex. 121. Gamelan pelègongan, instrumental ranges; Kuta village

2 gangsa jongkok chenik

2 gangsa jongkok gedé

4 kantilans

4 penyachahs

4 jublags

2 jegogans

2 gendèr barangan 13

2 gendèr gedé 13

kelenang

kemong

kajar

kempur

2 kendangs, rinchik, gentorak

Ex. 122. Garuda ostinato-motif; gamelan pelègongan, Kuta village

1. and 2. gangsas chenik and kantilans, divided
3. and 4. gangsas gedé and penyachahs, divided
5. jublags
6. jegogans
7. gendèrs barangan
8. gendèrs gedé
9. kelenang
10. kajar
11. kemong
12. kempur
13. kendangs L. and W.; tut-dag interplay
14. rinchik and gentorak

The melodic core of the gamelan is formed by the four *gendèrs*, which may either play in unison or break into free polyphonic weaving around the main melodic line. The leading role falls to the large *gendèrs*, which replace the *trompong* in function, preceding the *gending* with a solo introduction and carrying the true melody throughout. The smaller *gendèrs* are not used in the solo passages; they are part of the main orchestra, and either double the leading *gendèrs* an octave higher or enrich their melody with a faster moving paraphrase. Their role is primarily acoustic, and in smaller gamelans they are often left out.

Gendèr playing requires both a special technical skill and a high degree of musicianship. The instrument is played for the most part in octaves, but the hands may break away and move in opposite directions. There is no arm motion involved in striking the keys with the pair of mallets, which are held lightly between the first two fingers; a quick finger stroke is needed instead, as delicate and precise as that of a pianist. At the same time a smooth legato is produced by a rolling motion of the hand which carries the mallet from key to key.

When played softly the tone of the *gendèr* is limpid, cool, almost flutelike in quality. At the same time, a light, percussive click accompanies each tone, caused by the wooden head of the mallet as it strikes the key. In this the tone color differs markedly from that of the Javanese *gendèr*, on which soft, shockless tones are produced by a mallet whose disc-shaped head is enveloped in a half-inch band of rubber. With the Balinese *gendèr*, in soft passages the click is hardly audible, but in louder playing the percussive attack is pronounced, while the tone color of the instrument becomes metallically vibrant. Like the rest of the metallophones, the *gendèr* pair consists of a *pengumbang* and a *pengisep*, which is pitched slightly higher. The difference in pitch is small, but enough to produce a humming vibrato between the two, especially in the lower register.

The melodic direction of the whole gamelan thus lies with the pair of large *gendèrs*. They not only carry the melody, but perform the preliminary solo, here known as the *pengawit*, *gineman* or *pengalian*.[5] Since this passage is played freely, almost rubato, a complete sympathy, born of long association, must exist between the two players. In the main melodic passages a strict unison is not maintained throughout; as will be shown, a certain amount of liberty is allowed in each part, although a feeling of unity must be maintained at all times. This is also true of the paraphrasing *gendèrs*, both in relation to each other and to the leading *gendèrs*. Unlike the rehearsed patterns of the *kōtèkan*, no two performances by the *gendèr* quartet will ever be exactly the same.

As interpreted by the leading *gendèrs*, the melodic line is always supple and flowing, and performed with elegance. Various forms of ornamentation add grace or emphasis to the melody. Light, staccato tones and short, percussive tremolos embellish the solo introductions and interludes, while the melodic line is kept in fluid motion through the use of passing-tones, grace notes and the short glissando or *ngorèt*. An initial idea of the *gendèr* style may be gained from Ex. 123, the introduction for *gendèrs* alone to *Lagu Lasem*. Rhythmically free, it is played in an improvisatory manner until the entry of the drums at *a*. The passage can be played by either a single *gendèr* or, if their ensemble is sufficiently good, in unison by the two, each introducing his own embellishing tones.

---

5 From *ngalih*, to seek. The three terms are interchangeable.

Ex. 123. Pengawit Lasem   ♩ = 70

1 and 2: right and left hands
a: entry of the drums
P: kempur stroke and entry of full gamelan

In full orchestral passages the *gendèrs* are given more independence. The melody may then be played in unison or may break into two separate voices, as shown below in *pengechèt Biakalang*. In this and other short ostinato melodies the general practice is to play the first few repeats in unison, and then to vary the parts as the ostinato is continued.

Ex. 124. Pengechèt Biakalang*   ♩ = 60

both gendèrs

gendèr 1.

gendèr 2.

M—kemong

* It is interesting to compare this Selisir version of the pengechèt to gending Biakalang with the Lebeng version of the same pengechèt as played by the sulings in the gamelan gambuh (Ex. 111). The melodic contour remains the same in both examples, based on the tonal series, o è u a u a è i. The change in interval structure is great, and the special gendèr style completely transforms the original suling melody.

156

In more extended melody each *gendèr* is free to fill in the larger intervals in the *pōkok* tones according to his taste, providing the general melodic line is not obscured. It is here that good musicianship and mutual accord between the two players is especially called for, so that the different parts at all times remain harmonious and converge on the melodic tones that coincide with the *pōkok* tones. A characteristic example (Ex. 125) of this is shown in the *penyuwud* or closing section (*suwud*, finished) to the *gending, Lagu Jōbog*.

Ex. 125

Penyuwud Jōbog ♩ = 46–52

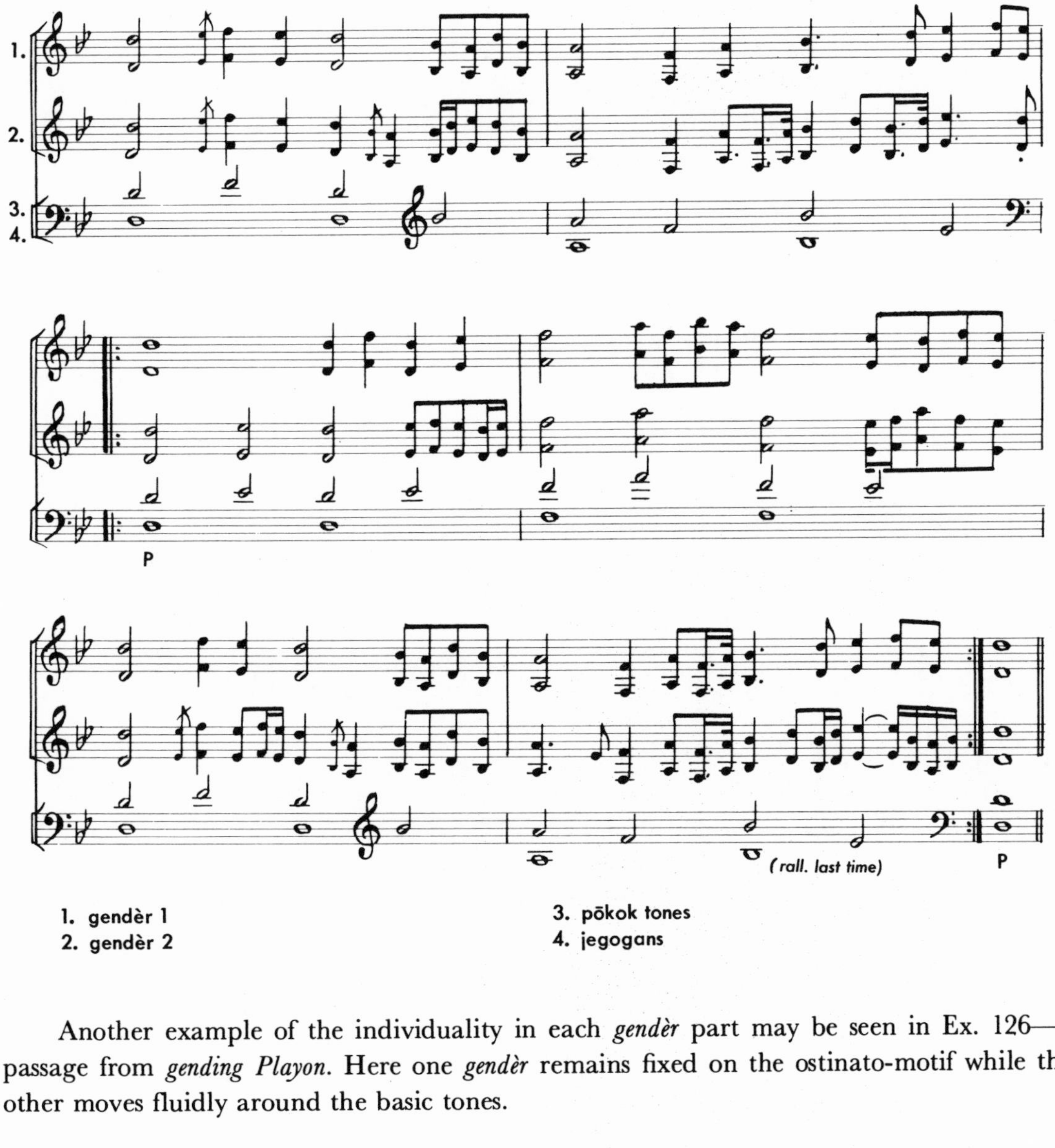

1. gendèr 1
2. gendèr 2
3. pōkok tones
4. jegogans

Another example of the individuality in each *gendèr* part may be seen in Ex. 126—a passage from *gending Playon*. Here one *gendèr* remains fixed on the ostinato-motif while the other moves fluidly around the basic tones.

Ex. 126. Gending Playon; episode   ♩ = 60–84

Owing to its limitations of range the thirteen-keyed *gendèr* occasionally must make certain adaptations in the melody when playing in the high register which may not be necessary at all on the *gendèr* with fourteen or fifteen keys. Since the top note of the thirteen-keyed *gendèr* is *dang*, a melody that ascends to a higher *ding* can only be played by the left hand. The right hand either omits this tone or substitutes the adjacent lower *dung*, as shown in Ex. 127. Here the melody, as given in form *a*, can be played only on the fourteen- or fifteen-keyed *gendèr*. Version *b* represents its adaptation to the thirteen-keyed *gendèr*. Even on *gendèrs* with a wider range this version is often preferred for its richer acoustic value; often both parts are played simultaneously by the two *gendèrs*. I have included the Kuta tuning of the *kemong* and *kempur* here, to suggest how these two gongs not only punctuate the melody but give it special color through their individual pitches.

Ex. 127. Pengechèt Jōbog   ♩ = 66–84

a gendèr 14 or 15
b gendèr 13
1. jublags

2. jegogans
3. kemong
4. kempur

⌒ = closing tone; also opening tone of the pengetog which follows. See Ex. 162.

Should the melody rise still higher to *dong*, the right hand of the *gendèr* 13 simply remains silent, while the *gendèr* 14 now makes the adaptation shown above, the right hand descending from *ding* to the adjacent *dang*.

The two smaller *gendèrs* do not have the interpretive leeway of the two leading *gendèrs*. For sake of clarity they must double each other more closely in their paraphrasing passages, which are purely ornamental. Although not organically essential, these add greatly to the sensuous charm of the orchestral texture, amplifying the resonance of the melodic line and softening with their flowing legato continuity the percussive passage-work of the *kantilans* and *gangsas*.

Characteristic paraphrasing by these two instruments is shown in Ex. 128. Here the two *gendèrs* perform identical parts in octaves throughout, weaving around the main melody a free and occasionally dissonant figuration. It is in paraphrasing passages such as those shown on the following page that the technical skill required for *gendèr* playing is especially called for, in order that the passages may be executed with perfect ease and grace.

Ex. 128. Pengipuk Lasem; Sayan village* ♩ = 44–60

1. paraphrasing gendèrs   2. leading gendèrs

* Cf. Ex. 161.

In compositions based on the short ostinato, such as *Bapang*, of which two forms are given below, the figuration of the two *gendèrs* may remain fixed at a certain level throughout, or may be varied with a more flowing continuity.

Ex. 129. Bapang; Klandis village   ♩ = 60

1. paraphrasing gendèrs   2. leading gendèrs

In Ex. 130 the right hand part in the paraphrase will be seen to move more independently, introducing little breaks for the sake of variety.

160

Ex. 130. Pengipuk Jōbog; Klandis village ♩ = 54–66

1. paraphrasing gendèrs   2. leading gendèrs

In the *pengawak*, because of the slow tempo, the leader of the paraphrasing *gendèrs*, should he have the skill, may perform his figuration at double speed. In Ex. 131 the *gendèr* quartet is now found moving in three separate streams, the two leading *gendèrs* playing in unison while the two paraphrasing *gendèrs* break into an ornamental duet.

Ex. 131. Pengawak Jōbog, excerpt; Klandis village ♩ = 36–42

1 and 2. paraphrasing gendèrs   3. leading gendèrs

A very different kind of musical training is required for the syncopated, percussive *kōtèkan* figuration, performed at high speed by a group of eight or ten players. Composed of two rhythmically opposing parts which, like the *rèongan* of the *gamelan gong*, interlock to create a perpetual flow of sound, the *kōtèkan* adds sheen and intensity to the music, and calls for the utmost rhythmic precision. Absolute unison in each group of instruments assigned to the two separate parts is necessary if the *kōtèkan* is to sound as it should. There is no place at all here for individual variation.

The *kōtèkan* lies in the top register of the gamelan, and is performed by the large and small *gangsas* and the *kantilans*, thus sounding in octaves. Since these are all instruments with a one-octave range, the players are able to concentrate on speed and rhythmic complexities. The keys of these instruments are arranged in a different order from that of the larger instruments. The highest in pitch is placed to the left of the series, so that the keys and the five tones are now found in the following order:

Ex. 132.

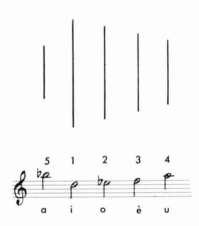

In many gamelans the *kōtèkan* instruments possess a sixth key, a second *dang* of the same pitch lies in its normal place at the right, so that the keys now appear in the order:

5   1   2   3   4   5

thus facilitating quick interplay between fourth and fifth tones.

The *kōtèkan* is performed in varying degrees of martellato. A small mallet with a hammer-shaped head of horn is used to strike the keys. The strokes are swift and incisive, produced from the wrist. As the right hand quickly passes from key to key, the left hand closely follows, muting the tone by momentarily grasping the end of the vibrating key (Fig. 98). Both hands are thus in constant, rapid motion, often traveling in opposite directions as right hand passes over muting left to strike the following tone.

The two interlocking parts which form the *kōtèkan* are known as the *mōlos* (simple, direct) and the *nyangsih* (differing). These two opposing parts, one as rhythmically complex as the other, might be compared to positive and negative. United they create a continuous current of figuration that pauses only at the close of an episode or at an accented phrasing break in the music.

The *mōlos* plays the leading part. Deriving directly from the *pōkok* tones, it is taught first at rehearsal.

Ex. 133. ♩ = 60–72

Once the syncopated patterns of the *mōlos* are well established, the *nyangsih*, which closes all gaps of the *mōlos* with filling-in tones, can be worked out.

Ex. 134. Kōtèkan, pengipuk Jōbog ♩ = 60–72

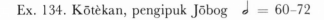

Combined, the two parts create the figuration,

Ex. 135.

No matter how fast, this dovetailed figuration is performed with extraordinary smoothness. The rhythmic vitality of the two interdependent parts causes the passage-work to ring with tireless energy. Through a change in striking force, rapid percussive crescendos and diminuendos are possible which, reinforced by the drums and cymbals, keep the music in a state of constant animation. Generally an even balance of tone is kept between the two parts, but occasionally one will ring out above the other, its syncopated rhythm in clear relief against the rest of the gamelan.

While the *mōlos* derives more directly from the *pōkok* tones, there are endless ways of shifting the balance between the two parts, so that the lead passes back and forth. In Ex. 136 the *mōlos* takes the lead in the first half of the figuration pattern, the *nyangsih* in the second.

Ex. 136. Kōtèkan; Bapang*

* Cf. Ex. 129b.

In short ostinato episodes the *kōtèkan* is merely a simple cliché pattern repeated without change. With the extension of the ostinato the cliché pattern is correspondingly extended.

Ex. 137. Kōtékan, Lagu Sisyan; Anggabaya village   ♩ = 64–72

In broader melodic periods like *pengechèt Jōbog*, given in Ex. 127, the *kōtèkan* is expanded into a figuration whose ever-changing patterns only recur with the repetition of the complete melodic period. In the beautifully integrated *kōtèkan* given in Ex. 138, the *mōlos* will be found to follow closely the *gendèr* melody while the *nyangsih* plays throughout a filling-in role. Dynamics which may occur within the period, though not with each repetition, have been indicated to suggest their expressive nature.

Ex. 138. Kōtèkan, pengechèt Jōbog; Klandis village ♩ = 66–84

1. mōlos 2. nyangsih 3. gendèrs

In the passages quoted so far, *mōlos* and *nyangsih* interlock in such a way as to create a single-voiced figuration. A more complex form of *kōtèkan* may be preferred, in which *mōlos* and *nyangsih* no longer meet at the unison but on different tones of the scale, causing the figuration to break into two separate voices. The *kōtèkan* given in Ex. 139 is by the composer, I Lotring, famed for inventing intricate figuration. The composition, given here complete, is from the *lègong* repertory, and consists of two ostinato sections: *a)* the *lagu* or melody, with which the piece opens and closes, and *b)* the *penyalit*, given on the following page, in contrasting high register. The *kōtèkan* as it actually sounds appears on the top line.

Ex. 139. Lagu Chondong; Kuta village ♩ = 58–66

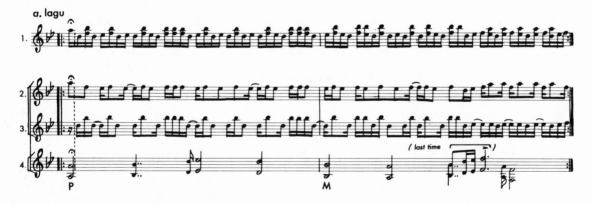

a. lagu

b. penyalit

1. kōtèkan as sounding   2. mōlos   3. nyangsih   4. gendèrs

In such ingenious ways, the *kōtèkan* animates the music throughout and brings a restless glitter to the orchestra. It is more than mere ornamentation, however. Closely related to the drumming, it reinforces all important accents and intensifies the sudden changes in dynamics which play so dramatic a role in this music.

The colotomic group in the *lègong* gamelan consists of *kempur, kemong, kajar,* and *kelenang.* The system of punctuation is based on that of the *gambuh* and *Semar Pegulingan* ensembles but is given more variation through the addition of the *kemong*, which plays an important part.

To meet the requirements of the swift-paced theatrical choreographies of the *lègong*, interplay between the four gongs is more diversified and animated than in the older systems. The *kempur* now not only marks the opening and close of the melodic period, but may recur within the period, sounding in regular alternation with the *kemong* as shown in Ex. 138.

The *kemong* plays a double role. In longer melodic periods, especially in the *pengawak*, where it has been silent throughout, it acts as a signal instrument anticipating the close of the period. In ostinato passages it divides the ostinato motif in half, as may be seen in Ex. 137 and 139. In the extended *pengechèt* of eight *palets*, such as found in Ex. 115 and 117, the *kemong* now replaces the *kempur* in the middle of the melodic period, so that the formula for gong punctuation to the whole period now becomes

P   k   k   k   M   k   k   k   P

In shorter melodic periods such as *pengipuk Lasem* (Ex. 128) the *kemong* accent occurs in the middle of the second *palet*, although occasionally the middle of the first *palet* is stressed as well. Ordinarily, the melodic period contains but one *kemong* beat, occurring near its ending, or else the period is punctuated by alternation of *kempur* and *kemong*.

The *kelenang* retains its usual function of stressing the offbeats. In quick tempo passages it occurs between the *pōkok* tones, as shown in Ex. 122; in extended slow tempo sections like the *pengawak* every second *pōkok* tone is stressed.

The *kajar* is by far the most active of the four gongs. In more extended melodic periods it marks the beginning of each *palet*, either with a single stroke or a series of repeated strokes in the *gambuh* style. In animated sections, as in Ex. 122, it acts as time-beater. It may also reinforce the main accents of the drums in broader melodic periods, creating a continuous rhythmic undercurrent.

For these different types of accentuation a variety of sounds are produced by striking the *kajar* on the boss or on the surface. Two main sounds are distinguished; *a*) the *cheluluk*, produced on the boss, which is hollow and penetrating but of short duration, and *b*) the *klèntèng(an)*, produced on the surface, which is brassy and ringing in quality. Both sounds can be reduced to a muffled staccato by muting the *kajar*, the left hand resting on the surface as the gong is struck. The *klèntèng* sounds can be further varied by striking while open and muting immediately afterwards.

The *cheluluk* is considered the male or *lanang* of the two sounds. Open, it marks the beginning of the *palet*. Muted, it alternates with the *klèntèng* accent, or is used throughout in episodes where the *kajar* is used as time-beater.

The *klèntèng* is the female or *wadon* of the two sounds, alternating with the *cheluluk* tones, and generally coinciding with the *dag* accent of the *wadon* drum. While the drum interplay in *gambuh* drumming is here less complex, it remains essentially the same, and the *kajar* player must be well acquainted with the interlocking patterns to coordinate his part with that of the drum pair.

The method of muting the *kajar* is illustrated in Ex. 140. The *klèntèng* and *cheluluk* accents, produced on surface and boss respectively by the right hand, are noted on the top and middle lines, while the muting left hand is noted on the bottom line. In example *a*, the left hand rests on the *kajar* throughout, while the right hand strikes the boss. In example *b*, the surface of the gong is struck, then muted by the left hand. In example *c*, *klèntèng* and *cheluluk* accents are shown combined, the latter sometimes muted.

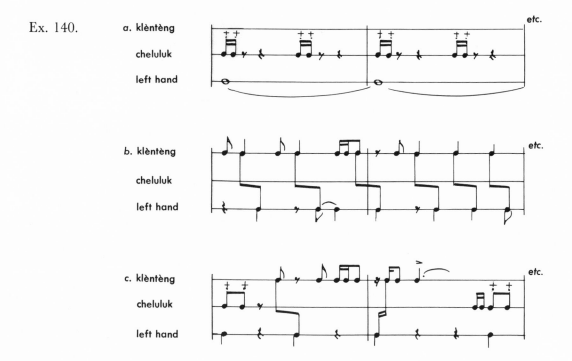

Ex. 140.

167

Ex. 141 shows typical *kajar* accentuation to a *palet* in the *pengawak* of *Lagu Lasem*, a *tabuh 3* composition with *lègong* choreography. Here the close relation between *kajar* and drums can be seen. With the exception of the strong opening accent, all *cheluluk* beats, struck on the boss of the gong, coincide generally with the *lanang* drum, while the more metallic *klèntèng* accents, sounded on the surface, coincide in principle with the *wadon* drum. The silences which occur in the *kajar* part follow the two main points of accentuation, the beginning and the middle of the *palet*. The apparent breaks in the drumming are, of course, filled in with light, barely audible *gupek* interplay.

Ex. 141. Kajar and drums ♩ = 60

1. klèntèng (wadon)   3. kendang lanang (tut)
2. cheluluk (lanang)   4. kendang wadon (dag)

THE GAMELAN PELÈGONGAN

The *kajar* is thus seen to be closely related to the drums in function. For the benefit of the dancers it emphasizes the main accents in the drumming, which may be no longer always audible through the resonance and complex polyphony of the gamelan. Although the *kajar* is not always present at dance lessons and rehearsals, for a performance it is as indispensable to the dancers as the drums.

The traditional repertories of the *lègong* gamelan fall into three main groups—those intended for the *lègong* dances; those which accompany the *barong*, the Balinese equivalent of the Chinese New Year lion, which takes part in both ritual and plays; and the dance drama dealing with witchcraft, known as *Chalonarang*. Of all three repertories, that of the *lègong* draws most heavily on *gambuh*. The *barong* compositions form a separate group, while the *Chalonarang* repertory, though not large, borrows partly from *gambuh* but also includes compositions which are exclusively its own. Since the *barong* plays a part in this performance, various *gending barong* form part of the *Chalonarang* repertory.

This last dramatic form, in which dance, acting, and music are combined, is of special interest when considering the role of music in the Balinese theater. Played partly as dance drama and partly as half-improvised comedy, the performance is a series of related episodes—charming or menacing dance scenes in which the main characters appear, thrown into relief by one or more interludes of comedy and burlesque. The lines declaimed by the leading characters are delivered in *kawi* in traditional *gambuh* style, while the dialogue of the comedy interludes is in a colloquial Balinese that even the youngest child can follow.

The play dramatizes the old Javanese account of the conflict between the evil sorceress Chalonarang and the holy man Mpu Bharadah. The witch, together with her pupils—beautiful young girls who can transform themselves into demons—have spread plague throughout the land and people are dying in large numbers. The holy man seeks to destroy her and end the plague. He sends the heroic Pandung to kill her, but the witch puts him to flight. The holy man himself sets forth and the final scene of the play takes place. The witch now appears in supernatural form, represented by a demonic mask and fantastic costume, and is confronted by the holy man, also magically transformed and represented by the *barong*. After a symbolic dance of conflict the play comes to an end. Neither character has been defeated.

No script for the play exists, and clubs interpret the story to suit themselves. Sometimes the heroic Pandung represents the warrior prince sent by the king, sometimes the holy man himself. All versions, however, agree in general form. The play opens in the graveyard, where the pupils enter and await the witch, who first appears as an old woman. The scenes of the comedy interludes are the broad highway and the forest, where villagers are fleeing the plague. The comedy consists mainly of malicious pranks played on the terrified people by the pupils of the witch, now wearing demonic masks and grotesque costumes. The main drama leading to the final confrontation takes place after the comedy, and the final scene is once more in the graveyard. To the crackle of firecrackers, the transformed witch makes a dramatic entrance. After a prolonged slow dance the music suddenly quickens and the drumming grows tense and rapid. The *barong* appears, and the closing dance takes place.

The graveyard is represented by a papaya tree, planted in the center of the stage and

169

symbolizing the tall *kepuh* tree, sacred to Durga, Goddess of Death, which grows in every Balinese graveyard. The other locales, such as the king's court, a village road, the hermitage, and the forest, are left to the imagination. The house of Chalonarang is sometimes represented at one end of the stage by a raised bamboo hut with a plank leading up to it. According to the club's means, the cast may be either large or small. At least one pair of *sisyas*, pupils, is essential for the opening dance, and larger clubs may have three pairs. Also essential is the witch, both as *dadong*, old woman, and transformed as *rangda*, widow; a few comedians; the witch's daughter and her maid; and the *barong*, representing the holy man. A full cast may include, in order of appearance:

dancers	2 sisyas (pupils)	girls	music
	2 sisyas		
	2 sisyas		
	dadong (witch as old woman)	man	
	2 penasars (heralds)	men	
	patih (prime minister)	man	
	prabu (king)	man	
comedians	anak glem (sick person)	man	no music or intermittent
	anak beling (pregnant woman)	man	background music
	parakan (attendant)	man	
	dukun (doctor)	man	
	léyaks (transformed sisyas)	girls	
	temedis, butas (imps, demons)	boys	
dancers	chondong (lady-in-waiting)	boy	music
	Larung (witch's daughter)	girl	
	Pandung (hero)	man	
	rangda (the witch transformed)	man	
	barong (the holy man transformed)	two men	

The most appealing dances in the play are those of the *sisyas*, small girls who have received rigorous dance training. Although performed mainly to the simple ostinato form of composition, the dances are richly varied in gesture and movement, and progress for the most part at high speed. The dance of the maid-in-waiting, generally performed by a youth, holds a similar appeal for its grace and swiftness. More leisurely and classical in style are the portrayals of stock characters such as the heralds, prime minister, king, and hero. The dances of the witch, both as old woman and as widow, are simple; the former merely pantomimes a feeble old woman leaning on her walking stick while the latter is a kind of grotesque prance.

Most elaborately organized, both choreographically and musically, is the opening scene, in which the pupils enter, singly and in pairs, to gather around the tree awaiting the arrival of the witch. This dance prologue may last as long as two hours, as my notes taken at a *Chalonarang* performance in the village of Anggabaya, show:

9.15 P.M. The gamelan begins a program of modern recreational compositions as the audience is arriving. Offerings are laid out on the stage and the village priest officiates.

10.00 Firecrackers. The gamelan begins the four-note ostinato motif called *Sisyan;* entrance of the first *sisya*— a child of perhaps seven.

10.15 Enter the second *sisya*—a child of the same size; the other joins her and they dance together.

10.20 The music changes to *pengechèt Ampin Lukun,* a melody of greater breadth.

10.30 The second pair of *sisyas*—a little taller—enter together to a new ostinato motif.

10.43 The music returns to *pengechèt Ampin Lukun.*

170

10.50	The third pair of *sisyas*—girls of perhaps eleven—enter together to a new ostinato motif.
11.00	The music returns to *Ampin Lukun,* this time starting with the *pengawak* before taking up the *pengechèt.*
11.09	Enter the witch as old woman, to *Tembung* ostinato motif.
11.15	The witch begins a slow dance to the composition, *Tèrong,* a long composition in *pengawak-pengechèt* form.
11.45	*Penarik* and *sesendon;* heavy accent in repeated tones for unison gamelan, followed by melodic interlude for *gendèrs* alone; the witch addresses the pupils in *kawi;* they answer in the same language, their childish voices rising and falling in soft wailing unison.
12.00	The gamelan begins the animated *Bapang* ostinato, and they all quickly leave the stage.

Intermission.

It will be seen here how both dance and music depend heavily on the ostinato form. The main musical interest, however, is not in the melody but in the drumming, which is rapid and complex. The dancers are free to rush about the stage, winding in and out in graceful spirals and half-circles. A musical device not found in other dramatic repertories is used here. The different ostinatos are thematically related, for they turn out to be transpositions of a single motif, *Sisyan,* which, when commencing on the first degree of the scale, *ding,* appears in the form:

Ex. 142. Sisyan motif; Pliatan village

Gendèr realization of the motif takes the melodic form:

Ex. 143.

A variant of this *Sisyan* motif may be heard in the Odeon recording of the Kuta gamelan.[6] Here the motif starts on the second half of the ostinato just shown.

Ex. 144. Sisyan; Kuta village

[6] See Appendix 6, Recordings.

While the *Sisyan* motif is complete as a four-tone ostinato, it can be extended to eight *pōkok* tones. In this form it supplies the basis for a melodic period of sixteen *pōkok* tones; the first half of the eight-tone unit is repeated once, and the second half given similar repetition. In the following example will be found the five transpositions of the *Sisyan* motif in its extended form. The motif retains its basic form on the first two degrees of the scale, but from there on is inverted, because of instrumental limitations.

Ex. 145. Sisyan motif and transpositions

			complete unit						
		motif			extension				
		repeat once			repeat once				
ding	‖: 1	4	3	2 :‖: 1	4	3	5 :‖	1
dong	‖: 2	5	4	3 :‖: 2	4	5	1 :‖	2
dèng	‖: 3	1	5	4 :‖: 3	1	5	1 :‖	3
dung	‖: 4	2	1	5 :‖: 4	4	1	3 :‖	4
dang	‖: 5	3	2	1 :‖: 5	4	3	4 :‖	5
	P	M		P	M				P

Stated in these terms, the table of transpositions in Ex. 145 appears to be a purely numerical formula. *Gendèr* realizations of the *pōkok* tones, however, show the melodic possibilities of the system.

Ex. 146. Sisyan, gendèr realizations; Pliatan village ♩ = 84

All five variants of this motif are rarely heard in the same performance. The first form, starting on *ding*, may be considered as the basic motif. With this the dance prologue opens. The choice of variants to follow and the order in which they occur is optional.

Two important factors transform the ostinato into an extended composition of great animation and vitality. A restless drumming at double or *rangkep* speed, light, syncopated, and filled with ringing *krèmpèng* tones, carries the ostinato buoyantly along with constantly changing dynamics. This racing stream of sound, however, is checked from time to time by a sudden pause in the music known as the *angsel*, which supplies a momentary breathing space for both dancers and orchestra.

The complex interplay between the two drums is best illustrated by examining first the patterns of the male drum, which takes the lead. In Ex. 147 the relative frequency of *tut* and *krèmpèng* tones can be seen. These are the important, most audible tones in the continuity; the *pek* strokes in the right hand merely fill in, while the complete interplay is stabilized with left hand *pek* strokes and an occasional *krumpung* tone, deeper in pitch than the *krèmpèng*.

Ex. 147. Kendang lanang continuity   ♩ = 120

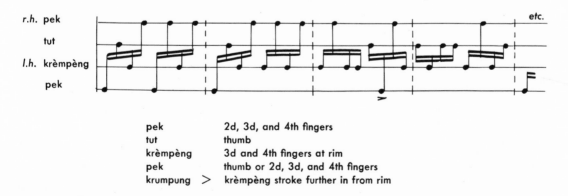

pek	2d, 3d, and 4th fingers
tut	thumb
krèmpèng	3d and 4th fingers at rim
pek	thumb or 2d, 3d, and 4th fingers
krumpung >	krèmpèng stroke further in from rim

Some idea of the way the two drums interlock may be gained from the cross-section in Ex. 148, where the two drum parts are shown separately. What actually emerges from the combined patterns as pre-eminently audible and of main importance is shown beneath, in the reduction composed of combined *krèmpèng* strokes and *tut-dag* interplay.

173

Ex. 148. Lanang and wadon interplay $\quad \downarrow = 120$

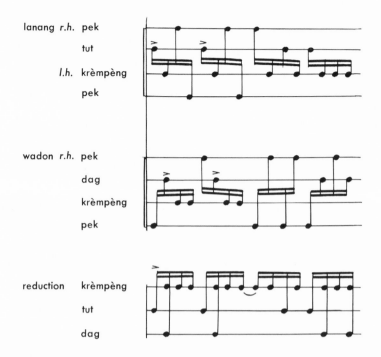

In such interplay the two drums are evenly balanced, dovetailing with an accuracy that comes only after long playing together. With a less expert *wadon* player, or with a *lanang* drummer preferring to play a more prominent leading role, the *krèmpèngan* is sounded throughout on the *lanang* drum, and the patterns are more freely expanded. The *wadon* drum is now reduced to a secondary complementing role. Fundamental *dag* tones answer the *tut lanang* tones, linked together with light *gupekan* patterns. The greater freedom of the *krèmpèngan* which now results can be seen in Ex. 149, which gives the *kendang lanang* in full, together with the *dag* tones of the *kendang wadon*.

Ex. 149.

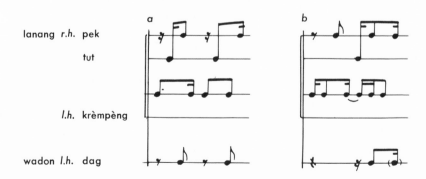

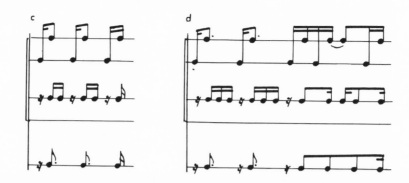

With the *angsel*, dancer and musicians come to a momentary halt on a sharply accented offbeat, to immediately resume movement and music without a break in the tempo. On this beat the dancer is arrested in a sharply defined pose which brings to fulfillment the movement of the preceding passage and at the same time serves as point of departure for the next. The *angsel* may be described as a comma, a fractional pause both visual and audible, dividing dance and music into phrases of varying length. It may also precede a sudden change in tempo, and it always precedes the closing phrase, which is generally taken at a markedly slower speed. While the term *angsel* primarily means the actual stop or break in both movement and music, it is also used by the musicians to indicate the accented beat or syncopated rhythmic unit which interrupts the regular flow of dance and music.

Depending on the length of the dance phrase, the ostinato motif is repeated a varying number of times before the end of the passage is punctuated by the *angsel*. The break normally occurs on the third beat before the *kempur*, in which the dancer pauses for the duration of a beat and a half before resuming movement. Two types of *angsel* may be distinguished, single and compound. In the compound *angsel* two halts in close succession replace the single halt, and movement is resumed on the last half-beat before the *kempur*.

In the gamelan, the *angsel* is determined primarily by a break in the drumming. The rhythmic unit which makes up the compound *angsel* is sounded in unison by drums, cymbals and the *kōtèkan* group. Since the *angsel* can take place without any change in basic tempo, the *gendèrs* and instruments sounding the *pōkok* tones are free to pause at this point or to continue undisturbed, while the main colotomic punctuation remains rhythmically intact.

An example of the simple *angsel*, in which the dancer pauses only once will be found in Ex. 150. In it a number of details are to be noted.

1. The dancer halts instantly on the accented beat, *a*, and resumes movement leading into the following passage at *b*.
2. Drums, cymbals (*rinchik*), and *kōtèkan* figuration, all moving at the same speed, come to a stop on the same beat, reinforcing it with an accent. They lightly stress the off-beat, *b*, on which the dancer resumes movement, while the drums fill in the remaining two half-beats.
3. The *gendèr*s may choose at *c* between joining the *kōtèkan* in unison or continuing as noted.
4. *Pōkok* tones and main gong punctuation continue undisturbed.

175

5. The dual metric structure of the 8-beat unit at this point is clearly demonstrated by the *kajar* accents, which divide the eight beats in such a way that instead of 8/8, they become 5/4 plus 6/8. With the following *kempur* beat the normal 8/4 meter is restored.

Ex. 150. Angsel, Sisyan; Kuta village ♩ = 120

It may be gathered from Ex. 150 that while the *angsel* is a phrasing pause for the dancer it is not a point of relaxation. Instead, the same tension level at which the former passage was performed is preserved in the momentarily rigid pose, and carried over to the following passage. This tension is emphasized in the syncopated, strongly accented compound *angsel* known as the *angsel kras*, forceful or strong accent, in which the break is filled in by a rhythmic unit based on the same shift to 6/8 as that shown in the preceding example. Ex. 151 gives three examples of the *angsel kras*, as sounded in unison by drums, cymbals, and *kotèkan* group. In the first two, the dancer makes two definite halts, on beats *a* and *b*, filling in the interval with coinciding rhythmic movement, and beginning the new passage at the end of the *angsel*. In the third example the *angsel* begins earlier and is still more forceful. Here the dancer halts on the first beat, after which he may make a quick quarter-turn on each of the following two, marking them with hand gestures, or he may emphasize all three beats with a stamp of the foot.

Ex. 151. Angsel kras

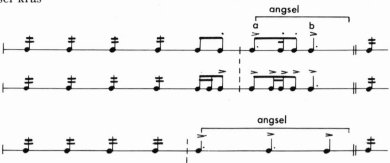

Only an actual performance can demonstrate the extraordinary vitality the *angsel* brings to the ostinato form of composition, when the sudden syncopated and sharply accented rhythms which unexpectedly break the continuity are given visual meaning through the flashing gestures and brittle movement of the dancer. While space does not allow for full quotation, some idea of the rhythmic continuity and the variety in breaks may be gained from Ex. 152, *Lagu Chondong*, already given in Ex. 139. As noted earlier, the composition is based on two contrasting sections, the opening melody in the low register, and the more animated *penyalit* in the high. The dance begins with a slow advance downstage, broken by short detours to right or left. The opening motif is given here, and below it a more extended drum continuity is suggested by the rhythmically identical cymbals.

Ex. 152. Lagu Chondong, cymbal continuity; Sayan village* ♩ = 72

* Noted during daily dance rehearsals at my house, 1934

177

In the more animated *penyalit* the dancer moves about the stage with greater freedom. There is finally a return to the stage center, and the opening movement is resumed. Vigorous cymbal accents introduce the *penyalit* before the cymbals subside to a normal tremolo:

Ex. 153. Lagu Chondong, penyalit; cymbal continuity ♩ = 80

With swift *rangkep* drumming and a variety of breaks which divide the ostinatos into broad, sweeping phrases, the long dance prologue to the *Chalonarang* play has a continuous flow that is maintained to the end of the scene. Only at one point is there a prolonged break in the rhythmic tension, when *gendèrs* alone perform the *sesendon*. Here all dance movement is suspended as the witch addresses her kneeling pupils.

The various *Sisyan* motifs used for the different pairs of *sisyas* can be linked together in different ways, according to the form of the choreography. They may follow one after the other, separated by the briefest of pauses. Or each dance episode may end in a more leisurely *pengechèt* movement before the entrance of a new pair of dancers. With the entrance of the witch the music expands into the broad *tabuh 3* form, with a slow *pengawak* and a more animated *pengechèt*. At the end of the prologue, tempo is speeded up again with the two-note ostinato, *Bapang*.

The basic organization of the prologue may be outlined:

dancers	gending	drumming	tempo
1st sisyas	Sisyan pengechèt Ampin Lukun	rangkep tabuh 3	animato moderato
2d sisyas	Sisyan pengechèt Ampin Lukun	rangkep tabuh 3	animato moderato
3d sisyas	Sisyan pengechèt pengawak pengechèt	rangkep tabuh 3	animato moderato andante moderato

178

THE GAMELAN PELÈGONGAN

dadong	pengawak	tabuh 3	andante
	pengechèt		moderato
	sesendon	no drumming	recitativo
exit music	Bapang	rangkep	animato

The *gending barong* used in the play consist of a separate group of ostinato motifs and a few compositions composed of a *pengawak* and *pengechèt*. Only one or two of the longer compositions will be played, however, depending on the planned length of the finale. For the *barong* a single drum is used, struck partly with the hands, partly with the stick. Loud *chedugan* drumming animates those dance passages expressing the more menacing nature of the *barong*.

The dramatic entrance is usually accompanied by the loudly played *pengilak*, a two-note ostinato underlined by vigorous drumming.

Ex. 154. Pengilak ♩ = 60

The drumming finally subsides to light, hand-beaten patterns while the *gending* changes to *pengechèt Pèrong*, a metrically irregular melodic period composed of two *palets* of ten *pōkok* tones each.

Ex. 155. Pengechèt Pèrong; Klandis village ♩ = 50–60

179

Here the dance of the *barong* becomes light and humorous, expressing its more playful nature, and offering contrast to the dramatic opening dance. It is followed by a return to the *pengilak*, after which the *barong* retires to one end of the stage.

The *pengilak* is continued for the equally dramatic entrance of the witch in supernatural form. Once again the music finally subsides, to be followed without a break by the *pengawak* to the *gending Tunjang*.

This movement is of special interest for its unusual melodic structure. The complete melodic period is composed of five subordinate periods of equal length, each of which is repeated once. The melodic line of the first period sets the pattern for the others, two of which are transposed to other degrees of the scale. The *gendèr* melody of the first period is given in Ex. 156 in full, along with the second ending which leads to the first transposition.

Ex. 156. Gending Tunjang, pengawak; Kuta village*   ♩ = 45

* Recorded in abridged form by Odeon. See Appendix 6, Recordings.

With transpositions, the *pengawak* becomes an extended musical statement, with the inner structure:

period		opening tone
1	statement	dong
2	transposition 2 tones downward	dang
3	restatement at original pitch	dong
4	transposition 2 tones above	dung
5	restatement at original pitch	dong

The tonal unity of the complete *pengawak* can be seen from Ex. 157, which gives the opening phrase to each inner period, together with its second ending.

Ex. 157. Pengawak Tunjang   second endings

This quiet movement in slow tempo is followed by a sudden return to the animated *pengilak*, which heralds the re-entry of the *barong*. The final dance of conflict between transformed witch and transformed holy man now takes place. After a prolonged repetition of the *pengilak*, extended to fit the half-improvised choreography, a signal accent from the *lanang* drum directs the musicians to the closing phrase with which the drama ends.

Ex. 158. Pengilak and closing phrase; Kuta village   ♩ = 60

The complete *gending* is seen to be organized around the tone series:

The tone *dong* (e flat), on which the *gending* opens and closes, remains throughout the pivot tone around which both *pengawak* and *pengilak* revolve. This is perhaps most strongly demonstrated in the last half of the closing phrase, where the eight tones preceding the terminal note sum up, as it were, the essential tonal structure of the entire composition.

The *lègong* performance calls for two leading dancers, the actual *lègongs*, who should match in size and general appearance, and a third dancer, the *chondong* or maid-in-waiting, a part often given to a boy. The *lègongs* perform the main dances, while the *chondong* introduces

181

them with a preliminary dance, hands them their fans, and retires. The *lègong* choreographies may tell some well-known story, in which case the three dancers take different parts, or may be purely formal and abstract.

The choreographies vary considerably in length, taking from perhaps fifteen minutes to almost an hour to perform. The performance opens, generally in the late afternoon, with a long dance prologue for the *chondong,* followed by the two *lègongs.* This is followed in turn by two separate, elaborately composed dances, the first usually abstract, the second based on some legend. Each consists of several connected movements of contrasting tempo and mood, and the storied choreography can be extended into a lengthy dance suite of possibly twelve connected episodes. In the pause which separates the two dances, during which the dancers rest, instrumental interludes are played by the gamelan.

Training is rigorous and calls for at least a year of practice before a first appearance. A large dance vocabulary testifies to the variety of hand positions and gestures, the different head and arm movements, the play of the eyes, the body postures, and the steps and movements about the stage. Before their public appearance around the age of eight, the little dancers will have learned some four or five extended choreographies, and will spend the next few years learning others. With the approach of adolescence they are withdrawn and the club begins to train new dancers.

Storied or not, the *lègong* choreographies all show the same basic structure. Each dance begins with a formal opening movement, the *pengawak,* followed by a contrasting *pengechèt* in a more animated tempo, and ends, after various episodes introduced according to the choreography, with a formal epilogue, the *penyuwud,* or conclusion.[7] Since the different elements of the *lègong* dance, formal, interpretive, and dramatic, are utilized to the fullest extent in the *Lasem* choreography, an account of its musical continuity will illustrate the elaborate organization of a composition intended for a *lègong* dance with a story. An outline of the story, taken from the *gambuh* repertory, should first be given.

The scene is medieval east Java at the time of the Majapahit Empire. Lasem, ruler of a small kingdom of that name, has abducted the princess Langkasari, ward of his vassal Metaun, and married her against her will. She shuts herself in her apartments within the palace and refuses to see him. Lasem learns that her brother is coming to her rescue. He prepares for battle, and implores Langkasari to admit him before he leaves. She opens her door, only to reject him. On his way to battle Lasem encounters evil omens. He strikes his foot against the wheel of his chariot; blood flows from the wound. A raven flies across his way, a black forecast of death. In the duel Lasem is killed and the princess is taken home. In *gambuh* form the play may take all day. As a *lègong* dance it is condensed to an hour.

The dance is divided into three sections: the prologue, which tells no story; the part in which the story develops; and the epilogue, which is a return in mood to the abstract prologue. The dramatic part of the dance presents in turn the love dance of Lasem who is continually repulsed by Langkasari; the leave-taking; the departure of Lasem with an attendant; the dance of the raven, performed by the *chondong;* and the duel, with closed fans indicating krises. The action ends with the death of Lasem, killed with the tap of a fan.

Longest of all episodes is the opening *pengawak,* which forms the first half of the prologue.

---

7 From *suwud,* finished.

182

In *tabuh 3 pegambuhan* form, in which the melody extends the length of 128 *pōkok* tones, this movement is the most difficult for the dancers to perform, because of its metric breadth. The movements of the two dancers are identical; the dance phrases are controlled throughout by the *palet* structure and metric punctuation. Only with the stroke of the *kemong*, heard for the first time on the final quarter of the last *palet*, do the dancers pause, to begin the *tanjek* or terminal dance phrase which ends with a final pose. Repeated once, or even twice, the *pengawak* is performed each time in exactly the same way.

With the *pengechèt* the mood of both dance and music changes to one of lightness and animation. The musical period contracts to thirty-two *pōkok* tones with four correspondingly shortened *palets*. While the basic tempo for the *pengechèt* remains around M. 60, light drumming transforms the movement into one of resilience and delicate rhythmic tension. The four *palets* that compose the melodic period are marked in turn by *kempur*, *kajar*, *kemong*, and *kajar*, thus giving variety in tonal color. While the *gendèr* melody, quoted in full in Ex. 159, is played without phrasing, brief *angsels* in the drums, cymbals, and dance mark the ends of *palets*, 1, 2, and 4 at the points indicated by *a*, dividing the period into two short phrases and a balancing phrase of double length.

Ex. 159. Pengechèt Lasem; Sayan village ♩ = 60

1. gendèrs
2. pōkok tones
3. rinchik
4. kendangs; tut-dag interplay

With the end of the *pengechèt* there is a sudden, dramatic change in the music. The *penarik*,[8] a loud unison passage based on a single, reiterated tone, rings out in a swift accelerando, announcing that the narrative part of the dance is about to begin. The signal is sounded three times, while the dancers break apart, rapidly circle the stage in opposite directions, and come together once more. They are now Lasem and Langkasari, and they stand back to back, gently swaying from side to side as the two leading *gendèrs* softly play the half-improvised phrases of the introductory *gineman*. Should the club include a *jeròh tandak*, singer and reciter, he now sings the *sesendon*, poetic stanzas that summarize the plot. At the end of this free interlude an accent from the *lanang* drum indicates a return to a set tempo, and with the *pengipuk* or love scene music the interpretive part of the dance at last begins.

Coming immediately after the polyphony of the preceding two movements, this sudden unison creates a striking contrast in its resonance and tension. Each accelerando is marked at the beginning with a *kempur* stroke and terminated in the pause that follows by a *kemong* accent. The whole passage is further intensified by the use of *krumpung* strokes on the *lanang* drum, deeper in pitch than the *krèmpèng*, which are employed simultaneously with heavy *dag* beats by the *wadon* drum.

Ex. 160. Penarik and gineman, Lasem; Sayan village

_____

[8] In music, a signal for attention, from *tarik*, to pull or draw tight, referring to the accelerando with which the passage is performed. In some places it is known as the *penarèk*.

THE GAMELAN PELÈGONGAN

gineman; gendèr solo

1. metallophones (sounding in 4 octaves)
2. kajar and rinchik
3. kemong
4. kempur
5. kendang lanang; krumpung tones
6. kendang wadon; dag beats

⌢ indicates the fermata

With the *pengipuk,* the music for the following love scene, there is a return to fixed metric form and a set tempo, while the *kōtèkan* is resumed and the music regains its former orchestral shimmer. In this opening scene Lasem expresses his love for Langkasari, following her as she moves about the stage in a winding path of evasion. From time to time he is allowed to draw near; each time he attempts to touch her he is repulsed by an impatient gesture, intensified by a simultaneous accent in the music. Warm emotional color is given to the scene through short crescendos and sudden breaks in the drumming. Much use is made of the resonant *krumpung* tones of the *lanang* drum, repeated at lightning speed, throbbing and suggestive as it underlines some erotic gesture. Lasem's dance throughout conveys anguish and despair, and the constantly changing dynamics in the music give the episode a moving pathos and feeling of anxiety.

The *pengipuk* consists of a short melodic period of sixteen *pōkok* tones, repeated a number of times with everchanging drum patterns. A secondary melodic period of equal length, the *penyalit* or variation, may be introduced later to form a middle section and allow for contrast and change in mood. In both sections the drumming is varied with each repetition, according to the planned choreography, so that dance movement may be freely developed in interpreting the scene. The dance thus becomes a theme with variations, its continuity extending beyond the limits of the melodic period, yet at the same time always controlled by the period's metric structure.

Some idea of the rhythmic continuity and variation in the drumming may be gained through Ex. 161, which includes:

a. The first statement of the main melodic section, with opening drumming.

b. A later phase, first *palet*, with cymbal continuity indicating the speed of the drumming. The crescendos indicate the approaches of Lasem, while the accents mark the gestures of repulse.

c. The *penyalit*, without drumming, included here to complete the melodic line. The movement closes on the opening tone of the first section.

Ex. 161. Pengipuk Lasem; Sayan village ♩ = 60, 80–112, 60

The tone sequence   1   2   3   4   5   represents the drum strokes.

1. dag wadon   4. pek lanang
2. tut lanang   5. krumpung lanang
3. pek wadon

When included, the *penyalit* ends with a return to the first section, which is repeated several times and ends with the opening tone. This tone is allowed to last for the duration of four *pōkok* beats, when suddenly the *pangkat* or departure motif is heard, a four-note ostinato with *rangkep* drumming (Ex. 162). The dancer who has played the part of Langkasari now takes the role of *penasar* or attendant, and the two cover the stage in march steps, with rapid paced arcs and sweeping loops to indicate their progress through plains and forest.

Ex. 162. Pangkat Lasem $\quad \downarrow = 72$

The scene ends with a dramatic interruption as the *penarik* is sounded for a second time, in preparation for the entrance of the raven. As the dancers leave the stage the *jerōh tandak* announces the change in scene by singing in *kawi* the stanza which starts,

> Now begin all omens of disaster . . .

to the soft accompaniment of the two *gendèrs*. As the *gineman* draws to a close the *chondong*, who has been kneeling in front of the gamelan, takes up a pair of gilded wings. A sharp accent from the *lanang* drum is a signal for the *guak* or raven melody,[9] an eight-note ostinato with a short secondary section or *penyalit* and agitated *rangkep* drumming. The two sections alternate many times before the dance comes to an end.

Ex. 163. Guak motif, or Lagu Garuda $\quad \downarrow = 70–120$

---

[9] Known also as *Lagu Garuda*, after Vishnu's bird-mount, and used in all dance scenes where a legendary or magic bird appears.

Animated by the turbulent drumming, which now has gained a new intensity, the *chondong* begins the dance on her knees, while her concealed hands cause the wings to flutter violently. She rises to her feet to circle the stage, sweeping freely about in erratic flights of arcs and spirals. The dance is long—the technical climax of the entire choreography. The suggestion of a bird in a high wind is effected through the stormy dynamics of the music and by the soaring movements of the wings, which incline one way, then another. At the height of the dance Lasem enters the stage, and the bird now swoops across his path, attacks him with beating wings, withdraws, and attacks again.

On the same motif, and without change in tempo, the other *lègong* appears as rescuing brother. The bird departs, and the final scene begins at the same level of tension. The adversaries face each other in a dance of challenge; the closed fans are flourished with elegant menace. With the duel there is one more dramatic change in the music. The gamelan breaks off abruptly, and the fight takes place to a percussive accompaniment, the *batèl*, which is used in all scenes of maximum dramatic tension. The gongs sound in close alternation, while the high-pitched *batèl* drumming, ringing with *krèmpèng* tones, heightens the mood of excitement and suspense.

Ex. 164. Batèl   ♩ = 90–138

To this theatrical accompaniment the duel takes place, a swift and stylized dance in which the closed fans never touch. The fatal thrust is dealt with the lightest of taps, and the life blood seems to flow before our eyes as Lasem suddenly releases all body tension to droop like a wilted flower. At this moment all action ends. As the epilogue begins the dancers resume the opening dance position of the *pengawak*. Characterization is over, and from now until the end, movement will have the formal, abstract quality of the prologue.

While the closing *penyuwud* varies in length with different dances, it is based on the repetition of a short melodic period. The *penyuwud* to *gending Lasem* consists of a two-*palet* period of thirty-two *pōkok* tones. It is thus, metrically, an abridgment of the opening movement, equal in length to a single *palet* of the *pengawak*, and containing two *palets* instead of four. The movement is played twice at the speed of the *pengawak*, but the third and last time is enlivened by a sudden animato, which lasts for the duration of a *palet*. On the second and final *palet* the original tempo is resumed, and the dancers begin the *tanjek* or ornamental

188

closing dance phrase which ends with the terminating *kempur* stroke. With the resumption in the *penyuwud* of the opening tempo, tonality, and mood, balance is restored.

Mention should be made here of an important structural passage frequently found in *lègong* compositions but not employed in *gending Lasem*. This is the *pengetog* (*ngetog*, strike repeatedly), a strongly accented rhythmic transition which connects two movements, modulating through a gradual and controlled accelerando from slow to quadruple speed. Starting with the terminal note, or beat, of the preceding movement, it accomplishes the change in tempo within the limit of eight, twelve, or a maximum sixteen *pōkok* tones, and is effected entirely by the drums, with the whole gamelan sounding the *pōkok* tones in strongly accented unison.

In Ex. 165, the *pengetog* from the *lègong* composition *Siyat*, the transition takes place within the compass of twelve *pōkok* tones. The two-note motif, *a*, which forms the basis for the succeeding movement, is sounded six times, starting at half the speed of M. 35 and ending at M. 70, the tempo of the new episode, *c*. The passage begins with sharp "*plak*" accents by the *lanang* drum—loud slapping strokes by the left hand. As the accelerando begins, these subside to light *pek* strokes, while *tut-dag* alternation becomes firmly established. The new tempo is reached at *b*, with the last *pōkok* tone of the passage. Here signaling *krèmpèng* accents by the *lanang* drum introduce the new movement, which now breaks into *kōtèkan* figuration.

Ex. 165. Pengetog Siyat; Kuta village ♩ = 35

The series  represents the drum strokes,

1. dag wadon 3. plak (>) and pek lanang
2. tut lanang 4 krèmpèngan lanang

The principal types of movements, episodes, and transitional passages which can be linked together in one way or another in *lègong* compositions have now been mentioned. All choreographies and musical accompaniments show ingenuity and craftsmanship in their organization and balance of longer and shorter episodes. How each dance has its own choreographic and musical form may be seen by comparing the following structural outlines of three compositions:

Lasem	Jōbog	Kuntul
1. pengawit	1. pengawit	1. pengawit
2. pengawak	2. pengawak	2. pengawak
3. pengechèt	3. penarik	3. batèl
4. penarik	4. gineman	4. pengetog
5. gineman	5. pengechèt	5. pengechèt
6. pengipuk	6. pengetog	
7. pangkat	7. pengipuk	
8. penarik	8. penyuwud	
9. gineman		
10. garuda		
11. batèl		
12. penyuwud		

Chapter 13

The Gamelan Pejogèdan

THE BRITTLE resonance of the *gamelan pejogèdan*, the village orchestra of xylophones, transforms the music of the *lègong* gamelan into a lively staccato accompaniment for the popular *jogèd* dance. The *jogèd* club is organized primarily for village entertainment; the boys and youths of the gamelan frequently help in making their instruments, which is easy enough to do since no casting of *krawang* is involved.

The *jogèd* dance usually takes place at night, along the road or in the market place, and never fails to draw a crowd. The *jogèd*, a girl in her early teens or perhaps younger, performs various display dances derived from the *lègong* repertory. These, however, are merely interludes in the main dance, repeated as long as there are onlookers, in which the *jogèd* is joined by one partner (*ngibing*) after another. The musical accompaniment is often dimmed by the laughter of the crowd as some adventurous *ngibing* draws too close to the *jogèd* and is expertly evaded. In some villages the performance is given by the *gandrung*, a boy of ten or twelve, in *jogèd* costume.

The solo dances require a *lègong* training, and are usually chosen from some episode in the *lègong* repertory. The dancer may even give a condensed version of a dance as elaborate as *Lasem*, taking the part of Lasem, princess, raven, and rescuing brother in turn. The main dance, the *ganderangan*, in which partners may join, is simple and uniform in movement throughout. It requires little more than learning the swift steps that will enable the dancer to circle about the clearing, the places where gesture must coincide with *angsel* breaks in the music, and generally how to adapt to the dancing of the partner.

The gamelan is modeled after the *lègong* gamelan, though reduced to a dozen players at the most. The keys of all instruments are suspended over bamboo resonators, *gendèr* fashion. The *pōkok* tones are played by a pair of *jegogans*. The expanded melody performed by the leading *gendèrs* of the *lègong* orchestra is here played by a pair of large *rindiks*—xylophones with a similar range. Figuration is performed by a pair of smaller *rindiks*, pitched an octave higher. The *rindiks* are played in octaves throughout, and since the tones are of short duration no effort is made to stop the sounds.

The main punctuation is supplied by a special instrument known as the *kempur kōmōdong*, composed of a thick slab of bamboo suspended above a narrow-mouthed earthern jar which acts as resonator. Secondary accentuation is produced by a special form of two-keyed xylophone found only in this ensemble, usually referred to as the "*kempli*." Each key rests loosely above a horizontal bamboo resonator, a single joint closed at each end but having a narrow opening beneath the key. The two bamboos are usually joined together with a brace, forming an H, and are given to a single player. The pair is sometimes separated and assigned to two different players, in which case they are generally known as *kempli* and *kempyung*. A set of *rinchik*, operated by one player, and a single drum, somewhat larger than the *wadon* drum of the *lègong*, complete the gamelan.

The general effect of all music performed by this ensemble is one of lightness and gaiety. Various stylistic devices are employed to compensate for the short dry tones of the xylophones. The sustained melody of the *gendèrs* in the *gamelan pelègongan* is now changed to an incessant staccato of repeating tones. The small *rindiks* break up the melodic line into animated *kōtèkan* figuration. Through this continuous hail of interlocking rhythms the *jegogans* sound with unusual penetration. The basic tones are transformed into freely moving counter-melody, in constant motion throughout the composition. In order to produce a more sustained tone, the two *jegogans*, now played by a single musician, are struck in continual and rapid alternation, creating a constant tremolo that may break only at the end of a melodic section. Each tone, which ordinarily would be sounded by the two *jegogans* in unison, acquires an intensely vibrant quality, augmented by the difference in pitch between the *pengumbang* and *pengisep* instruments. The soft, strangely throbbing melody can be heard at night for miles.

To reproduce the prolonged tone of the bronze *kempur*, the bamboo key of the *kempur kōmōdong* is struck in quick succession, amplifying the tone and causing it to pulsate within the earthen jar below as long as the strokes are continued. In this bamboo orchestra whose resonance depends entirely on rapidly repeated tones, only the *kempli* accents are sounded with a single stroke; the two keys may be struck separately or, for greater emphasis, simultaneously. In either case the sharp, hollow tone produced is clearly distinguishable through the rest of the ensemble. The drum combines the main accents of the two *lègong* drums in a style known as *bebanchian*, bisexual, while the *rinchik* reinforces the drumming throughout as in the *lègong* gamelan.

A special characteristic of the *gamelan jogèd* is its generally lower pitch. The scale of my own *jogèd* ensemble, made in the village of Batuan and brought to Sayan for the purpose of forming a *gandrung* club, is typical:

jogèd scale	ding	dong	dèng	dung	dang
pitch vibrations	257	276	312	380	408
Western tempered tuning	C	D♭	E♭	G	A♭
pitch vibrations	258.5	274	307.5	388	410.5

This general lowering in the pitch of the scale softens the hard tone of the *rindiks* and adds a more attractive resonance to the whole ensemble. Pitched in the more brilliant range of *Selisir pelègongan*, *jogèd* ensembles sound thin; the tones have not the same resonance, and the carrying power of the whole gamelan is considerably diminished.

A change in the standard arrangement of tones in the *jegogan* lends a new and distinctive character to the basic melody. Instead of extending from *ding* to *dang*, the series begins with *dèng*, the third tone, and ends with *dong*.

Ex. 166.

This unusual arrangement frequently gives the *pōkok* melody a quite new character, changing its original contours and at times transforming it into a counter-melody that freely diverges from that of the large *rindiks*.

Since the simply constructed bamboo *kempur* is made at the same time as the other instruments, and easily tuned to any desired pitch, its tonal relation to the scale is deliberate rather than accidental, as is so often the case in bronze ensembles. It is generally tuned to either *ding* or *dèng*, according to preference. The most common tuning of the *kempli* is to the tones *ding* and *dung*. In my own *gamelan jogèd* the two instruments stood in the following harmonious relation to each other and to the rest of the orchestra:

Ex. 167.

Transferred to the *rindik*, *gendèr* melody loses its original legato and repose, now changing to a staccato figuration which is continued throughout the composition. Only at the end of the melodic periods, or at the *angsel* breaks which mark the inner phrases, do the restless patterns come to a momentary halt, soon to be resumed with the same tireless energy. The transformation of the ostinato melody, *Lagu Chondong* (cf. Ex. 139), from *gendèr* to *rindik*, as shown in the following illustration, is typical. Here the *rindik* version from Sayan village is compared with the standard *gendèr* version. The basic tempo remains the same.

Ex. 168. Lagu Chondong ♩ = 60

While many clubs follow the practice of having the melody played in unison by the two large *rindiks*, others divide the pair so that the second *rindik* follows the first a sixteenth-note

193

later, thus filling in between the tones of the first *rindik* and turning the melody into continuous *kòtèkan* figuration. The part performed by the first *rindik* is now called the *mōlos*, plain, while that of the second is now termed the *nyangsih*, differing, part. In Ex. 169 two different styles of *nyangsih* are shown, one, *a*, sounding always between the main *mōlos* tones, the other, *b*, joining the *mōlos* from time to time by means of additional filling-in tones. Either type is used consistently through the *gending*.

Ex. 169. Lagu Chondong; rindik kōtèkan ♩ = 60

Played with utmost rhythmic precision, at the high speed of M. 60 or more, and shifted thus a fraction off the beat, the *nyangsih* part must be heard to be believed. Similar passages may be found in the modern *gamelan gong kebyar*, performed by the *gangsas* assigned to the *nyangsih*. But *gangsa* technique is different, since it is not based on octave playing. In passages like that in Ex. 169, the right hand would play consistently off the beat, but the left hand would silence the tones on the beat, thus giving the performer a rhythmic point of support. No such physical support exists in the *rindik* passages, where both hands are engaged in performing the part in octaves. These passages, shifted off the beat for extended periods or even throughout the entire composition, call for a rhythmic sense far different from our own. It is hard to imagine Western musicians performing them with the same precision. Yet in small Balinese villages far from any musical center boys with no musical training beyond that picked up at club rehearsals will accurately perform this offbeat part with all the ease imaginable.

The interlocking *mōlos* and *nyangsih* parts thus transform the melodic line into a continuous tremolo, against which the softer tremolo of the *jegogans* sounds in striking contrast. In Ex. 170 the basic relation of *rindik* part to the *jegogan* melody is shown, together with the *kempur-kempli* punctuation which substitutes for *kempur-kemong* accents in the *lègong* gamelan.

Ex. 170. Lagu Chondong

194

A typical instance of the free relation of the *jegogan* melody to that of the *rindiks* is shown in Ex. 171, the *jogèd* version of *pengipuk Lasem* (cf. Ex. 161). Here the *jegogan* part moves fluidly within its five-tone frame, frequently traveling in contrary motion to the *rindik* melody. Attention is called to the repeating final tone, a characteristic method of prolonging its sound.

Ex. 171. ♩ = 60

The smaller *rindiks* may either double the large *rindiks* if these are performing two-part *kōtèkan* figuration, or break into independent *kōtèkan* of their own. In a passage from a *ganderangan* composition (Ex. 172), as performed in Sayan, the two pairs of *rindiks* break into four separate interlocking parts, forming with the *jegogans* a five-part polyphonic stream which may be prolonged, by means of sectional and complete repetitions, to a half-hour's duration.

195

Ex. 172. Ganderangan; Sayan village ♩ = 60–66

small rindiks

large rindiks

jegogans

kempli

The lively rhythm of the second *kempli* (or *kempyung*) is an elaboration of the normal single accent (>) and is maintained throughout. It may be varied in the following manner:

Ex. 173.

_____

* The similarity of these rhythmic patterns to those of the claves (two hardwood sticks beaten together) employed in small Cuban dance bands is striking.

These patterns are found only in the *gending ganderangan*, and give a special resilience to the music. For solo dances and instrumental compositions the *kempli* functions in the usual way, sounding a single accent in the punctuation.

The *gending ganderangan* form of composition is of unusual interest for its immediate adaptability to the length of the dance it accompanies, determined by the number of dance partners who may follow one another. It can be kept going indefinitely, and may be described as a "perpetual motion" in rondo form, with an introduction and coda, and having an ostinato middle section or trio around which the rondo revolves. By avoiding the coda and returning to the point where the actual rondo begins, the composition can be extended to twice its length or more. By omitting the trio a second time, or jumping straight to the coda, the composition can quickly be brought to an end.

Various *ganderangan* compositions are known, but all resemble each other both in general structure and thematic material, and are little more than variants of the same basic composition. One version is enough for the average club. The following analysis is based on the *gending ganderangan* played by my own *gamelan jogèd* in Sayan, taught to the musicians by I Lotring of Kuta, and which I was able to note as it was learned.

The lively introduction, during which the *jogèd* circles about alone, sets the bright mood for the dance. Flexible in its duration, it can lead immediately into the main composition or be prolonged through repetition, becoming an independent preliminary section. It is non-thematic, growing out of the repetition of a single tone and finally breaking into *kōtèkan* figuration that will continue throughout the piece. Unlike the main part of the composition, which has no *kempur* punctuation except in the trio, the introduction is marked by *kempur* accents which follow in close succession.

Ex. 174. Ganderangan; introduction   ♩ = 60–66

The thematic material of the actual rondo is slight. The whole movement is based on a single rhythmic motif:

Ex. 175.

The rondo opens with this motif, which is repeated once and then extended, to be followed by two transpositions. A return to the motif in its original form is followed by more transpositions in a new order. A transition leads to the ostinato trio, which can be prolonged at will. A restatement of the opening motif on a new tone series forms a second transition which leads back to the point of repeat in the main movement, but can lead as well directly into the coda, in which three of the earlier transpositions recur, but in a new sequence.

Ex. 176 gives the basic motif in its opening form, followed by two transpositions, and sets the pattern for the complete rondo.

Ex. 176. Ganderangan; opening to main section

Ex. 176 thus shows the following structure:

A	motif on dung	extension of 3 measures
B	motif on dong	extension of 4 measures
C	motif on dang	extension of 1 measure

With the return to the motif in its original form (A) the sequence changes; A and B are restated then followed by a new transposition:

A	motif on dung	extension of 3 measures
B	motif on dong	extension of 3 measures
D	motif on dèng	extension of 3 measures
B	motif on dong	extension of 1 measure

A new, subordinate theme (E) is now heard. It does not repeat, and merely serves as a transition, leading directly into the trio (F).

Ex. 177. Ganderangan; transitional passage

At the point indicated by F, a new phase in the composition is reached. The melodic line no longer moves forward but remains fixed in an ostinato passage that can be extended indefinitely. Thematic interest shifts to the *jegogan* part, which is varied with each repetition. The *kempur* is now heard, alternating with the *kempli* and marking each recurrence of the ostinato.

Ex. 178. Ganderangan; trio

A short extension leads from the trio to a restatement of the opening motif, this time beginning on *ding*, the one transposition not used up to this point. Structurally, this is a transitional passage that can lead either to the coda or back to the beginning of the rondo.

Ex. 179. Ganderangan; second transitional passage

The musicians now find themselves at the point (A) where they may either repeat the rondo or proceed to the coda, based on the structure:

A	motif on dung	extension of 2 measures
C	motif on dang	extension of 3 measures
B	motif on dong	extension of 3 measures

A terminal phrase (H) leads to the closing tempo of M. 54. Here the *jogèd*, now alone, assumes the final pose, coming to rest on the final tone, *dung*, on which the rondo began. Since the gamelan cannot produce a sustained tone except through close repetition of the note struck, the final note is played as shown on next page.

Ex. 180. Ganderangan; closing phrase

The *gending* is thus seen to be composed on the following plan:

introduction							
main section	A	B	C	A	B	D	B
transition	E						
trio	F						
2d transition	G						
coda	A	C	B				
closing phrase	H						

Chapter 14

The Gendèr Wayang Ensemble

BALINESE MUSIC perhaps finds its most perfect form of expression in the music that accompanies the *wayang* or shadowplay. For this miniature theater the instrumental ensemble is reduced to a quartet of *slèndro* tuned *gendèrs*, here known, because of their tuning and special function, as the *gendèr wayang*. With these four instruments, unaccompanied by gongs or drums, a fascinating musical background is created, light and transparent in resonance and, because of the *slèndro* tuning, unique in tonal color. A repertory of compositions heard nowhere else, miniature in scale, sparkling with intricate figuration, and ingeniously contrived, underlines the different episodes of the plays. The repertory consists of various compositions to be played before the performance begins, the opening music or "overture," and the different *gendings* that are played during scenes of tenderness, strife, denunciation, clowning, and deep sorrow.

The plays, enacted by small shadow puppets, are drawn mainly from *kawi* translations and adaptations of the *Mahabharata* and *Ramayana*, which hold a particular appeal for Balinese audiences when presented in this form. The puppets are flat leather figures with jointed arms which are controlled by thin sticks attached to the hands. From the head down through the center of the figure runs a slender brace of horn which extends beyond the feet and serves as handle. The puppets are painted in glittering colors, and the crowns and costumes are so stamped with tiny holes that when held against the light the puppets seem to be made of lace.

The performance takes place at night. Beginning late in the evening, it often lasts till dawn. A raised booth is set up in the open, by the temple, in the marketplace, or perhaps before the house of one who has engaged a performance in honor of some private celebration. At the front of the booth is stretched a semi-transparent sheet of white cloth, illuminated from behind by a hanging lamp, through which the puppets appear in silhouette. Beneath the lamp sits the *dalang*, who operates the puppets and recites their lines, with his puppet box beside him. An assistant sits at each side, to receive the puppets from the *dalang* and set them up at the right and left sides of the screen, thrusting the handles of the figures into a banana stalk that lies along the bottom of the screen. This is a long ceremony. Gods, heroes, and all their allies and attendants are crowded to the right of the *dalang;* while demons and adversaries are set up to the left. Back of the *dalang* sit the musicians, encircled by a gathering of boys and men who prefer the glitter of the puppets in the lamplight to the black and white version which the main part of the audience will watch from the other side of the screen.

The plays most frequently performed are drawn from the *Mahabharata*. Should the *Ramayana* be presented, a percussion group called the *batèl* is added to the *gendèr* quartet, which now is augmented by *kempur*, *kempli*, *kajar*, *rinchik*, and drums, a sufficient addition to lend excitement and noise to the battles that take place between the demons and Rama's allies, the apes. The ensemble is now known as the *gendèr wayang batèl*. The additional instruments, however, merely supply a rhythmic background to certain compositions that are musically complete without them. The present account deals entirely with the music played during a *Mahabharata* performance, since the repertory is larger and more varied, and because of the special beauty of an instrumental style free of a percussive background.

As the puppets are set up on the screen the musicians play the *pemungkah*[1] or opening music, a long chain of melodically related episodes which can be extended or shortened as required. One of the first figures to appear on the screen before the play begins is the *kayon*, a conventionalized tree, placed there to establish the legendary world of the *wayang*. It also appears from time to time during the performance, waved about to represent fire, wind, or rain. When all the puppets have been removed from the box, the *kayon* is picked up and flourished, thus informing the audience that the play is about to begin. The *dalang* gives a signal for a change in music by striking the side of the puppet-box with the *chempala*, a small wooden block held in his right foot, which is also used throughout the play to punctuate the dialogue and add noise to battle scenes. The musicians now begin the quiet melody, *Alas Harum, Perfumed Forest*, while the *dalang* chants in *kawi* the customary opening stanza introducing a *Mahabharata* play, beginning with the line, *Rahina tatas kemantian*:

> Thereupon day breaks.
> Drums, cymbals, and conches sound with a roar.
> The shouting troops assemble
> And set forth in procession.
> The royal brothers have put on splendid garments
> And travel in gleaming chariots;
> King Yudistira is at the head,
> Preceded by Bimasèna,
> Nakula, and Arjuna.[2]

The *dalang* now recites the *penyachah parwa*, a few lines explaining the origin of the *parwa*, the eighteen books of the *Mahabharata*. This is followed by a stanza introducing the particular episode to be performed. This stanza is called the *penyarita*, story. On its termination the *kayon* is removed from the screen, the leading characters are introduced, and the story now can get under way.

The special instrumental style of the *gendèr wayang* quartet calls for a high degree of technical skill and rhythmic coordination. The free polyphony of the *gendèrs* in the *lègong* gamelan is developed into the most closely integrated interplay. The *gendèr wayang* player must be trained to both think and feel contrapuntally, for his right and left hands perform entirely different parts most of the time. While the *lègong gendèrs* are mainly played in octaves,

---

[1] From *bungkah*, to open up—earth, box, the box of puppets. The *pemungkah* is also known as the *gineman wayang*.

[2] This stanza is from the twelfth century Javanese poem, *Bharata-Yuddha, War of the Bharatas*, adapted from part of the *Mahabharata*. The translation is my own. It will be found musically quoted in Ex. 208. For *Ramayana* performances the melody, *Rundah*, is played, and a stanza from the *Ramayana* is sung.

the two hands of the *gendèr wayang* must acquire complete independence, since they are usually engaged in two completely opposing rhythmic patterns.

The quartet is organized in the following way. Two large *gendèrs* form the leading unit. The two players integrate their individual parts in various ways. In quiet, purely melodic compositions with no figuration the two players perform identical parts, their left hands sounding in unison the main melody while the right hands create a form of counter-melody, as shown in Ex. 188. Complex interplay between the two *gendèrs* begins with the more animated music. Here both left hands perform the same basic melody, but the right hands break into separate interlocking parts, forming rapid *kōtèkan* figuration. Each of these continually syncopated right hand parts must not only interlock with each other but must also be coordinated with the left hand part, which often moves with a restless syncopation of its own. The two left hand parts may also break and travel separately, thus creating a four-part polyphony between the two *gendèrs*.

All this is doubled with great accuracy by two smaller *gendèrs* which form the second unit of the group and sound an octave higher. In order to achieve a precision of ensemble the four players sit facing each other, as in a string quartet. The instruments are placed close together, the musicians of each pair sitting opposite each other, where they may catch each other's eyes and watch each other's movements. The two interlocking parts thus play across to each other; the men seated side by side play identical parts, sounding an octave apart.[3]

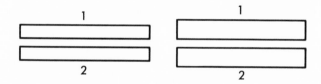

The special form of *gendèr* used in this quartet is smaller than that used in the *lègong* gamelan, and is popularly known as the *gendèr dasa*, or ten-keyed *gendèr*. These ten keys give it a scale that extends through a second octave. The playing method is essentially the same, though more exacting, calling for a greater flexibility of wrist and sensitivity of touch. A wider range of dynamics is employed, for the quartet of *gendèrs* must at times suggest a large gamelan. In soft passages the *gendèrs* are sweet and vibrant. The color changes in the loud passages; here the full weight of the hand is thrown down to produce bright metallic tones and clanging accents.

The *slèndro* scale, as found in the *gendèr wayang*, begins invariably with the tone, *dong*, and extends through a second octave to the tone, *ding*. The following scale, already given in Chart 9, is that of the Kuta ensemble, as found in the large *gendèr pengumbang*. It is with this tuning in mind that the musical examples given in this chapter may most easily be read. The reader, however, may widen his conception of *slèndro* tonality by referring the examples to more elusive tunings presented in Charts 10 and 11.

---

[3] As shown in Fig. 57. In another arrangement players 1 and 2 of the small *gendèrs* exchange places, so that the two first players of the quartet now sit diagonally across from each other.

Sléndro, gendèr wayang, lowest octave; Kuta village

	183		206			241		280		327		
		205		272		259		269		195		
	F♯		G♯			B		C♯		E		(F♯)
	O		E			U		A		I		(O)

As in the *pèlog* system, each of the five tones of the *slèndro* scale can become the tonal center, the tonic of the composition, on which it opens and closes. This tonal center, however, may shift several times during the course of the composition. Many pieces owe their extended form to the procedure of transposing, tone for tone, ostinatos, longer melodic passages, and even extended episodes to different degrees of the scale, establishing each time a new tonality. This practice of transposition is most completely shown in the *pemungkah* or opening music to the *Mahabharata* performance, of which an analysis is given in the following pages. In the varied series of little episodes that form this elaborately constructed composition may be found all the elements of *gendèr wayang* style. Free recitative unison or two-voiced passages alternate with animated sections in three- and four-part polyphony. The mood changes constantly, passing from calm to agitated, lyrical to rhythmically energetic. As the different episodes return in transposed form they take on new tonal color. Before the *pemungkah* has come to an end it has passed more than once through all five tonalities as the tonic shifts from one scale-tone to another. The following step by step account of this composition is based on the version played by the *gendèr wayang* ensemble of Kuta village, of which the composer, I Lotring, was the leader. The composition was obtained through musical dictation. Lotring and a second *gendèr* player remained for two weeks at my house in Sayan while the music was transcribed.

The *pemungkah* opens with a short, freely performed introduction which ends with a loud rap from the *dalang's chempala*, announcing that he will begin taking the puppets from the box.

The introduction, which is given in Ex. 181, consists of two sections, a freely performed preliminary passage, *a*, followed by a form of cadenza, *b*, which leads directly into the opening section of the composition, *c*. The opening passage begins on the tone, *dung*, on which the entire first section is based, and which will serve as tonic for several successive episodes before the piece shifts to a new tonal center. The main tones are sounded in broken octaves, and embellished with ornamental tones and swift tremolos that ring out in sudden crescendo. In the two-voiced cadenza, the voices move for the most part in so-called fifths, but resolve to the octave at the end of the passage. In the example below the complete introduction is given as played by the two leading *gendèrs*. The second pair of *gendèrs*, doubling an octave higher, is implied, as elsewhere in this chapter. All four instruments perform this passage, up to *c*, in unison. Right and left hand parts are indicated by upward and downward stems.

204

Ex. 181. Pemungkah; introduction

Reduced to its essential tones, the introductions can be expressed quite simply:

Ex. 182.

In this embryonic polyphony, with its delayed octaves creating canonic imitation and its fifths that resolve into octaves, lie the germs for a more fluid movement of parts which can be developed with much imagination to form the basis for *gendèr wayang* technique.

With the return of the introduction to the opening tone, *dung*, the first episode of the actual composition begins, in a suddenly rapid tempo. A simple repeating figure is heard, based on the opening tone, and rhythmically accompanied by the tapping of the *dalang's chempala* as the puppet box is opened. Beginning softly, the passage breaks off in a sudden fortissimo when the *dalang* is ready to set up the puppets. Here the two *gendèrs* begin to perform independent parts. While the two left hands remain in unison the right hands move in opposite directions, creating between them alternate unisons and fifths.

Ex. 183. Pemungkah; opening section ♩ = 60

The *chempala* tapping is discontinued with the setting up of the first puppet. The repeating figure of the opening passage now changes to an ostinato figure in the lower voice, accompanied by two-part *kōtèkan* figuration divided between the two right hands.

Ex. 184. Pemungkah; opening section continued

* From here on, in similar passages, the above method of transcribing the two gendèr parts will be followed.

There is much to be noted in the preceding example. In the first part of the passage three separate yet interlocking rhythmic patterns move at different pitch levels. In the *kōtèkan*, resonant sixths create a syncopated cross-rhythm against the restless ostinato. The right hands of the two performers create quite different rhythmic patterns against the same rhythmic bass, presenting two separate problems of execution. The above passage, based on repetition, is relatively simple to perform. More extended and intricate passages will be found in later examples. Despite the high speed of M. 60 or more, extended episodes based on interplay such as that shown here are performed with utmost precision, all the more remarkable since there are no gongs or drums to furnish a rhythmic background. Also to be noted in the above example is the contraction of the *kōtèkan* to a strident alternation of sixths and seconds, terminating the passage in a sudden burst of energy.

Following the *angsel*, or break, the opening section enters a new phase. The ostinato is continued at the same level, but the *kōtèkan* is transposed a step down. Upper and lower right-hand parts retain their relative distance, but with a change in intervals, fifths now occurring in place of sixths. For a short time the *kōtèkan* remains fixed at this level, but toward the end of the passage it rises again in a quick crescendo to break off at the former level. This marks the end of the opening section. A strong unison passage now carries the music downward, swiftly modulating to an entirely new tonality.

206

Ex. 185. Pemungkah; conclusion of opening section

The modulating passage signalizes the appearance on the screen of the *kayon*, marking a new phase in the *dalang's* formal preliminaries. Before it is fixed in the center of the screen, the *kayon* is given a series of elegant flourishes and twirls, causing its shadow on the screen to appear and vanish mysteriously. A new motif in the music is heard as the first main section of the *pemungkah* begins. The ostinato form is retained allowing the *dalang* to flourish the *kayon* as long as he pleases.

Ex. 186. Pemungkah; first main section, opening motif $\quad \downarrow = 60$–84

With many repetitions, the passage is played at varying speeds and changes in nuance, beginning softly, at a moderate tempo, and increasing to a strident animato as the *dalang* waves the *kayon* more vigorously. As this preliminary performance concludes, the music slows down, to end in a brief coda. The ostinato loses its syncopated character and is now transformed into smoothly flowing melody that gradually comes to rest on the tone *dèng*, which will be the point of departure for the next episode.

Ex. 187. Pemungkah; first main section, close of first episode   ♩ = 44–60

The rap of the *chempala* is heard on the closing tone, marking the end of the *kayon* episode. The *dalang* fixes the *kayon* in the center of the screen; from now on to the end of the *pemungkah* he is occupied with setting up the puppets.

The music now enters a new phase. Growing out of the preceding closing tone, a quiet passage is heard, sounding in simple two-part polyphony based on a succession of octaves and fifths. Only a nonmensural notation can be used here, since the passage is played with complete rhythmic freedom. It repeats only once, without change in nuance, and serves as an introduction to the following section.

Ex. 188. Pemungkah; first main section, second episode   ♩ = 66

A free variation of this passage begins at letter G. Mainly two-voiced, from time to time three tones sound simultaneously as the right hands of the two players move in contrary motion. The variation is repeated several times, twice in moderate tempo, then gaining in speed, to break off abruptly in the middle of the phrase with a sharp accent. The preceding passage, F, is then resumed.

Ex. 189. Pemungkah; first main section, second episode (variation)

The return to the earlier passage, F, prepares for an animated finale, H, to this series of related episodes which together form a complete movement in itself. In the following example the lower voice in Ex. 188 becomes stabilized in a broad ostinato which is varied with each repeat. The *kōtèkan*, however, remains a stationary repeating figure until the end of the episode where, in the extended closing phrase, the figuration is carefully worked out in relation to the melody, resolving with it on the final tone. Since the *kōtèkan* remains unchanged until the end of the episode, it has been given here in only the opening and closing phrases.

Ex. 190. Pemungkah; first main section, closing episode ♩ = 92

A brief codetta follows, and with it this short movement, which forms the first half of a larger main section of the *pemungkah*, is complete, coming to rest on the tone, *dang*.

Ex. 191. Pemungkah; first main section, codetta

The halfway point of the first main section of the *pemungkah* has now been reached. A complete restatement of all that has gone before immediately follows, starting with the *kayon* motif (D), but now transposed two steps higher in the scale. Balance is thus given to the musical form, which up to this point has been asymmetrical. At the same time both melody and figuration take on a new and contrasting color through the change in pitch and subtle alteration in interval relation. A new tonal sphere is created by the substitution of the series:

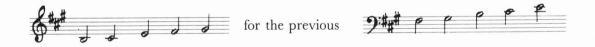

Before this tonal variation begins, however, a transitional passage growing out of the previous codetta acts as a modulating link, joining the new section to the first both melodically and through change in tempo, so that there is no perceptible point where one ends and the other begins.

Ex. 192. Pemungkah; transitional passage

With the accelerando—the actual transitional point in this passage—several things happen at the same time. The opening tempo of M. 60 is resumed; the termination of the *kōtèkan* on the tone, *dung* (*b*), marks the end of the preceding section; and at the same time the lower voice, while appearing to come to rest on the tone, *ding* (*e*), has already entered the transposed *kayon* motif, now established on the tones, *dung, dang, ding* (*b*, *c♯*, *e*). For a time, as the motif repeats, the upper voice remains fixed on the tones *e*, *c♯*, *b*, but as it descends to the point D2 indicated in the above passage, tone for tone transposition of the earlier episode, D, has begun.

The different episodes now recur in their former order, each transposed to the new tone series. Variations within the episodes, however, may occur to keep the restatement from being rigidly mechanical. Episode E, for instance, which would appear, automatically transposed, as:

Ex. 193.

is given the following variation:

211

Ex. 194. Pemungkah; transposed restatement of E

The episode F2, and its variant, G2, will be found to be an exact transposition of episodes F and G to the new tone series.

Ex. 195. Pemungkah; transposed restatement of F and G

The earlier animato section, H, now follows in transposed form. Only the last repeat of the ostinato, followed by the closing phrase, is given here. In the closing phrase both melody and figuration move downward, returning to the original tonality to end, as before, on the tone, *dang.*

Ex. 196. Pemungkah; first main section concluded

The first part of the *pemungkah* ends with the conclusion of the restatement. The following section is a free interlude composed of two melodic sections which are linked together by an ostinato. There is no transposed restatement of the three passages.

The first episode is unusual in its irregular phrase structure and rhythmically complex melodic line. A short introduction leads directly into this passage, an animated melodic period with continuous *kōtèkan* figuration. Performed without phrasing breaks, and with no audible beat to give a rhythmic clue, the melody is metrically bewildering with its irregular repetitions and frequently shifting rhythm. Yet when, as shown in Ex. 197, a theoretical beat of M. 60 is supplied throughout the melodic period, a hidden structural order is immediately revealed. The whole passage, from the preliminary beat on which the melody, followed by the *kōtèkan*, begins, to the final tone, extends to the equivalent of a thirty-two beat period.

The melody is quoted below in full, with the regular, but purely imaginary, beats indicated by numerals. The *kōtèkan*, in sixteenth-notes, is omitted. The melody will be seen to start firmly on the beat at *a*, be already off it at *b*, return to it at *c*, and finally become stabilized at *d* in a balanced and ornamental closing phrase.

Ex. 197. Pemungkah; interlude, first episode

The complete melodic period, from *a* to the closing tone, is organized in the following ways:

- *a.* opening section, with melodic contractions starting at *a¹*;

- *b.* inversion of *a*, shifted off the beat, with contractions at *b¹* balancing those at *a¹*, and the extension at *b²* leading to

- *c.* a variation of *b*; here the rhythmic balance is momentarily restored as the first tone of the phrase falls on the beat;

- *d.* closing phrase, firmly on the beat, extended to fill out the period to a normal metric length.

This episode is followed immediately by the ostinato passage which links it to the second episode. Starting at a lively tempo, the ostinato gradually slows down to prepare for the following episode. This passage is an echo of E2 of the preceding section; the lower voice retains its original form, but the upper is transposed a tone higher.

Ex. 198. Pemungkah; interlude, linking passage ♩ = 66

The second episode opens with a short repeating passage in which not only the figuration but the lower part is now divided into two separate voices, thus creating four-part polyphony. This prepares for the closing section of the episode, a quiet, melodic passage continuing the four-part polyphony. A more extended melodic period may be included between the two passages at the place indicated in the following example by the letter *a*, but the episode is complete without it.

Ex. 199. Pemungkah; interlude, closing section ♩ = 80

The second main section of the *pemungkah*, similar in structure to the first, now follows. A short sequence of episodes is stated first on one tone series, and then restated, transposed to another. This time the transpositions take place one degree higher in the scale instead of two, as in the first section.

214

Episodes that lie in the range:

are transposed to the series:

Secondary episodes lying within the range:

are restated on the tones:

This new main section opens with a short introduction (N) leading to the tone, *dung*, *b*, with which the first episode (O) begins and ends. With the later restatement, the transposed introduction (N2) leads to *dang*, *c♯*. The contrasts between the two tonalities may be seen if the two introductions are ranged side by side.

Ex. 200. Pemungkah; second main section, first and transposed introductions ♩ = 120

The first episode opens with a repeating passage composed of two contrasting sections—*a*, in which upper and lower voices move mainly in parallel motion, and *b*, a brief motif accompanied by *kōtèkan* figuration.

Ex. 201. Pemungkah; second main section, first episode ♩ = 100

215

With the repetition of the above passage, section *b* expands into a broader melodic period, which in turn is given several repetitions before leading to the final tone which terminates the complete episode.

A lively concluding episode, based on the ostinato form, now follows and eventually brings the main section to a halfway halt. In the following example the ostinato figure on which this passage is based will be found to be a variant of the motif, D, in the first section of the *pemungkah* (Ex. 186). It supplies the background for an elaborate figuration worked out at three different tonal levels, indicated here by the letters *a*, *b*, and *c*. The ostinato undergoes a rhythmic change at *c*, and finally expands and slows down in the closing phrase, *d*.

Ex. 202. Pemungkah; second main section, second episode ♩ = 92

A short transitional passage leads away from *dang*, the final tone of the preceding episode, to establish the tone *ding*, a step higher in the scale, preparing for the transposed restatement which will follow.

Ex. 203. Pemungkah; second main section, linking passage ♩ = 96

With the tone *ding* thus established, the transposed introduction, given in Ex. 200, leads to the first episode in the new tonality. Because a real transposition of the opening phrase would take the top voice beyond the range of the *gendèr*, certain melodic adjustments must be made which affect the passage throughout.

Ex. 204.

While in its original form this passage was two-voiced, it is now enriched by a third voice, as shown in Ex. 205, giving it an entirely new color. In the second phrase, which is lower in range, note for note transposition occurs in all parts.

Ex. 205. Pemungkah; transposed restatement of O

The transposition of the second episode (P2) is almost note for note throughout, as may be seen by comparing the following example with the earlier version given in Ex. 202. In the first two measures the lower voice retains the original tone, *dung*, on the secondary beats, but from then on the transposition is exact. The closing phrase shows some adjustment in the upper parts, but the episode ends on the opening tone, *ding*, which was established earlier by the linking passage given in Ex. 203.

Ex. 206. Pemungkah; transposed restatement of P

The second main section of the *pemungkah* has now been brought to an end. The *dalang* has finished setting up the puppets, and the stage is crowded with figures. While the musicians play the closing section the *dalang* clears the center of the screen; the rest of the puppets are left massed at the sides, framing the screen in a forest of shadows.

It is during this final part of the *pemungkah* that the melody seems at last to expand and flower, unfolding in a series of lyrical phrases. Like the interlude, the closing section is not repeated later on a new tone series. It is a complete movement in itself, the most unified of the entire *pemungkah*.[4]

This concluding section is introduced by an animated ostinato passage, based on the motif that served for the linking passage in the interlude:

Ex. 207.

[4] This last part of the *pemungkah*, as played by the Kuta ensemble, was recorded by Odeon. See Appendix 6, Recordings.

With repetition, the motif slows down to half speed, setting the final tempo. The passage ends as the ostinato changes to a simple rhythmic figure, played at exactly double the speed of the preceding tempo. This figure forms a stationary accompaniment to the first half of the closing movement, throwing into relief the fluid movement of the melody.

Ex. 208. Pemungkah; closing section, first half   𝅗𝅥 = 72

The passage in Ex. 208 illustrates the breadth and suppleness of the melodic line in this final section of the *pemungkah*, but it does not reveal how the melody is divided between the two *gendèr* players. It is not performed throughout in unison, but is broken up into two separate interlocking parts. Two different ways of dividing the parts are given in Ex. 209. The first is from Kuta village; the second, in which a second voice is added to the melody, is from Mas.

Ex. 209.

220

In Sayan, the musicians broke up both accompaniment and melody, performing the whole passage in the following unexpected way:

Ex. 210.

Ex. 211 illustrates further the Sayan method.

Ex. 211.

Space does not allow for the continuation of the closing section beyond the point indicated by S in Ex. 208, at which a new and contrasting melodic section in a livelier tempo begins.[5]

---

[5] This can be found given in full in the author's transcription for two pianos of the last part of the *pemungkah*, entitled *Pemoengkah* and included in the series, *Balinese Ceremonial Music* (G. Schirmer, New York, 1940). See Appendix 5.

221

Ex. 212 gives the concluding passage to the closing section; the *pemungkah*, now complete, is found to end on the tone *dang*, a step higher than the tone on which it began.

Ex. 212. Pemungkah; conclusion ♩ = 80

The *pemungkah* is thus seen to be a series of miniature episodes which, linked together, form an extended composition marked by a constantly changing tonal center, and by a fluctuating tempo that revolves around a basic pulse of M. 60. Despite its apparent freedom, the form is completely integrated; the chain of episodes will be found organized on the following plan:

introduction							
opening section	A	B	C				
first main section:							
statement	D	E	F	G	F	H	I
modulating link	J						
transposed restatement	D	E	F	G	F	H	I
interlude	K	L	M				
second main section:							
statement	N	O	P				
modulating link	Q						
transposed restatement	N	O	P				
closing section:							
introductory passage	L						
statement	R	S	T				

The balance of the composition as a whole and the symmetry achieved through paired statements and restatements are immediately evident in this plan. No two ensembles, however, will perform the *pemungkah* in quite the same way. The episodes, while following in the same order and tonality, can be altered through melodic variation, and extended or shortened according to individual taste. Nevertheless, in spite of minor stylistic changes from region to region, the basic form of this elaborately extended composition remains intact.

With the center of the screen cleared of puppets, the *kayon* is taken up for a final flourish. The musicians return to the first two ostinato passages of the *pemungkah*, A and B, which accompanied the preliminary appearance of the *kayon*, and continue until the *kayon* is put down. The *gending* known as *Alas Harum* is now begun, to which the *dalang* chants the stanza beginning with the line, "*Rahina tatas kamantian*," or "Thereupon day breaks."[6] The lines are sung with great freedom, in the top register of the voice. Each syllable is prolonged to a great length. Pauses between phrases are greater still. The chant is softly supported by the music, a quiet two-voiced composition of irregular phrase structure, played in a quasi-improvisatory manner. The following excerpt, Ex. 213, gives the first two lines of the stanza, with *gendèr* accompaniment.

Ex. 213. Gending Alas Harum

---

6 Given on p. 202. The music is recorded, without voice, by Odeon. See Appendix 6, Recordings.

Ex. 213 continued

⌢ indicates the fermata.

The formalities of opening the performance end with the introduction of the leading characters, during which the *pengalang*, the special music for this procedure, is played. From now on the music is intermittent.

The lines of the play are improvised from epic *kawi* texts which the *dalang*, who must be a scholar before all, knows by heart. His popularity depends upon the skill with which he can transform narrative to dialogue, and also on the spontaneity of his jokes and puns in comedy scenes. A number of set stanzas, the *peretitala dalang*, may be sung to the music played when gods or demons are introduced upon the screen, and in scenes of love, grief, and death. Both the songs and the dialogue of the leading characters are delivered in *kawi*, and all spoken lines are given a free translation into colloquial Balinese by the everpresent attendants, who at the same time are the comedians. The *dalang* must also have an expressive and flexible singing voice, and know how to embellish the song with graceful ornamental tones.

The choice of *gendings* performed before the performance begins is left to the musicians. The musical repertory played during the performance is standard, consisting of a number of softly played compositions of an *alus* type, which are heard during quiet scenes, and a number of vigorous pieces that accompany the departures to war, battles, pursuits, and flights that fill the play. The *alus* compositions are free in form, generally two-voiced throughout and similar in style to *Alas Harum*. Complete in themselves, they may be played alone or used as musical background to the *dalang* as he sings a stanza appropriate to the scene. The pieces that accompany any action on the screen are based on the useful ostinato form which allows them to continue without break for the full length of the scene.

Two types of *gending* are used for this action music, the *batèl*, based on an ostinato unit of two beats, and the *angkat-angkatan*,[7] in which the *batèl* unit is extended to four beats. All *gendings* in both groups are based on the same thematic material. They vary in form, however, due to different sequences of transpositions, restatements, figuration patterns, and the alternation of unison with polyphonic passages. The following example gives the thematic point of departure for the two forms of composition. Simple as they are, the motifs, when developed, add excitement and suspense to the action taking place on the screen.

Ex. 214.

A typical *batèl* composition, played during scenes of strife, is given below. Characteristic technical devices are displayed which, combined, maintain unbroken tension throughout the piece. Any of the repeating units can be continued indefinitely.

---

[7] Or *angkatan*, an expeditionary force (*kawi*).

Ex. 215. Batèl ♩ = 60–76

A	the motif is repeated indefinitely, sharply accented with fifths in the upper parts
B	the fifths break into figuration, which may be developed with changing patterns
C	the upper parts shift a tone higher, while the motif remains stationary
D	new figuration, with possible extension of patterns
E	linking phrase, in which the motif prepares to shift
F	transposition of all parts a tone higher
G	figuration transposed a tone higher
H	linking passage, returning to the opening tonality
A	closing passage, or point for the repeat of the piece

This percussive composition, with its swift tempo, contrasting dynamics and metallic accents, supplies effective background for a battle on the screen, during which the *dalang* holds a cluster of puppets in each hand and clashes them together. The resonant three-tone close is characteristic of *batèls* ending on the lowest tone of the scale, *dong*. For endings on other tones, the combinations in Ex. 216 are generally employed.

Ex. 216.

The *angkatan*, which accompanies quick motion scenes such as those of armies in pursuit, or the flight of gods through the air, has an appropriately wider sweep, with its extended and syncopated ostinato. Intricate figuration with everchanging patterns hurries lightly above the restless bass, creating an impression of continuous movement that is broken only by a sudden *angsel* or phrasing break. The basic form is similar to that of *batèl*. The ostinato figure repeats a number of times, shifts by means of a linking phrase to a new tonal series, and then returns in a second linking phrase to its original tonality.

Some idea of the intricate patterns and constant movement of the figuration, which here occupies the foreground, may be gained from Ex. 217. Two different types of interplay are to be noted. In one, *a*, the interlocking upper and lower parts combine to create unison figuration which is essentially melodic; in the other, entering briefly at *b*, the interlocking parts are two separate voices. Either style may be used consistently throughout, or combined.

226

Ex. 217. Angkatan ♩ = 120–138

The restlessness of this music is intensified by sudden changes from pianissimo to forte and back. The following excerpt, a passage leading to a phrasing break is from an *angkatan* played by the Kuta ensemble. The sudden cross-accentuation against an already syncopated ostinato is typical of I Lotring's special love for rhythmic complexities.[8]

Ex. 218. Angkatan; Kuta village ♩ = 120–132

----

[8] Recorded by Odeon under the name *Batèl*.

When played at half speed, and slightly modified rhythmically, the *angkatan* ostinato can serve as accompaniment in short compositions in which the upper part becomes melodic. This may be seen in the following example, *Lagu Délem*, played with the appearance of Délem, one of the leading attendants. In this miniature piece the form is perfectly balanced; the melodic period is divided equally into *a*) statement, and *b*) restatement transposed a tone higher. The melodic period is repeated several times, either in its original form or transformed into figuration.

Ex. 219. Lagu Délem; Kuta village　♩ = 69

Ex. 220. Lagu Délem; figuration

For scenes of love, *gending Rebong* is used, a composition in three connected parts—the opening, to which words may be sung by the *dalang;* an interlude; and a final section for the *gendèrs* alone. The first two parts are slow in tempo, softly played, and accompany the tender love scene between prince and princess; the last episode is a loud and animated movement, played for the burlesque and usually indecent love scene between Tualèn, the chief attendant of the prince, and the *chondong,* the maid-in-waiting of the princess. Like the other brief stanzas sung during quiet scenes, the text used here describes the situation through poetic imagery. The essence of the little poem is contained in the first two lines:

> *Sekar guntang anggitang madori putih*
> *Pusung buyar madia rengkiang mangedin*

> The crimson lily[9] is sought by the white *madori* flower
> The bud has opened out; the lovely center is disclosed

The *dalang's* singing is now very different from the loudly intoned stanza with which the performance opened. He now uses his "sweet" voice, nasal, languorous, almost falsetto in the high tones. The long, supple phrases are sung freely, and embellished from time to time with ornamental passing-tones. The melodic line has a wide range. It adds a third voice to the already complete two-part polyphony of the *gendèrs,* joining them in unison at the end of each phrase. In Ex. 221 the first two lines of the song are given, as sung by Ida Bagus Gedé, the famous Brahman priest and *dalang* in the village of Bangkasa.

Ex. 221. Gending Rebong; first section

---

[9] *Gloriosa superba,* a species of climbing lily with blossoms resembling the Turkscap lily.

∩ indicates the fermata.

As these lines are sung, the shadow figures on the screen move in a quiet dance, passing each other or merging briefly into a single shadow of embrace. The onlookers easily identify these movements with the stylized movements of living dancers in similar scenes. The song is complete with the singing of the sixth line of the text, although there are more lines which can be sung later should the *dalang* care to prolong the scene. The dance on the screen continues during the playing of the interlude, an extended and metrically balanced melodic section with figuration. It is, however, interrupted halfway through by a return to the opening section, at which time the *dalang* may sing another line or so of the poem. The interlude is then resumed and continued to the end. It is immediately followed by the closing section, or *pengiwa*, a syncopated version of the first half of the tranquil interlude melody, played at double speed. This section is a complete episode in itself, and can be repeated as long as the *dalang* cares to continue the comedy scene.

Ex. 222. Gending Rebong; interlude, first half ♩ = 76

Ex. 223. Gending Rebong; pengiwa or closing section ♩ = 132–144

The *pengiwa* is a musical parallel to the action on the screen. While the two attendants caricature the preceding love scene, it transforms the languid melody of the interlude into an episode of energetic movement. Should the *dalang*, however, prefer to end his love scene on a more gentle note of poetry and romance, the final scene and its music are left out.

At the end of the play, which may come unexpectedly if rain should suddenly start falling, the closing music, *Tabuh Gari*,[10] is played while the *kayon* is replaced in the center of the screen. The *Tabuh Gari* is no more than a short melodic flourish which can immediately follow or be introduced into the middle of any composition and bring it to a quick conclusion. The passage is familiar to everyone in the audience; before the brief outburst is over, all have risen to their feet and begun to leave.

Ex. 224. Tabuh Gari; Kuta village   ♩ = 60–69

Because of the few musicians required, and the delicate sound of the music itself, the *gendèr wayang* ensemble is often engaged for private feasts such as weddings and birthday celebrations of very young children. The musicians enliven the event with a program of *rerosian*, animated compositions which are played before the start of a shadowplay performance. At a time of death in the family, the musicians may be called again, to go through their repertory of quiet melodies while the priest officiates, and afterward to repeat them off and on throughout the night.

If the deceased is of high rank, the two leading *gendèr* players take a special part in the actual rites of cremation that will follow at some later date. Then they supply special music for the progress of the tower in which the corpse is borne from house to cremation ground. The two men sit with their instruments on a bamboo platform supporting the tower, borne on the shoulders of a shouting crowd of men. Beside them are seated the priest and the *dalang*, both present to perform a series of rites which will protect the soul from malignant spirits during the journey. Along the road are danger spots. Crossroads, a turn or fork in the road, a stream, the edge of the cremation grounds, all are demon-haunted. At these points, the tower is swung around three times; offerings of Chinese coins, rice, and shredded *dadap* leaves are thrown out by the *dalang; mantras* are recited by the priest, and music considered appropriate to each act is played by the musicians. As the tower is carried along the road, the percussive *batèl* (Ex. 215) rings stridently. At the danger spots the *gending Rundah*, used in the shadowplay to accompany demons, is played, after which *batèl* is resumed. At the edge of the cremation grounds the musicians begin the music, *Tunjang*, associated with the sorceress

---

[10] Known also as *Lagu Abughari*. This latter name is a combination of two words, *abhog*, in India the closing section of an instrumental composition, and *ari* (Bal.), something which follows or comes last.

Chalonarang, protegée of Durga, the Goddess of Death. And finally, as the tower is set upon the ground, the musicians begin the melody *Mèsem*, which in the shadowplay is heard in scenes of grief.

That night the musicians play again at a special shadowplay performance in the house of the bereaved, or, if the cremation has been a communal one in which many families have participated, in some clearing near the center of the village. Six weeks later, after the ashes have been dispersed in the sea, another shadowplay is performed as part of the rituals celebrating the final departure of the soul.

Chapter 15

The Gamelan Angklung

THE GAMELAN ANGKLUNG has always been a ceremonial orchestra of the village and was never employed, I have been told many times, at the court. Heard at temple anniversaries and called upon to play at all village festivals, this essentially folk orchestra is perhaps the most useful ensemble to the smaller community, supplying bright ceremonial music of a lighter character than that of the *gamelan gong*. In smaller villages, especially in the Karangasem district, the *gamelan angklung* often replaces altogether the *gamelan gong* for ceremonial occasions, and is brought out only at the time of temple anniversaries and village cremation rites.

While the name of this gamelan would seem to indicate an orchestra composed of, or at least including, a number of *angklungs*, these ancient instruments have long since been abandoned in most of Bali. For the majority of Balinese the *ganelan angklung* is an ensemble made up of metallophones and various small gongs, distinguished from all other gamelans by its four-tone scale. We may thus speak of two forms of this orchestra, one in current use throughout the island, and an older form including *angklungs*, which is found chiefly in a few scattered villages of Karangasem.

Whether *angklungs* are included or not, this ensemble is made up primarily of four-keyed *gendèrs* of different sizes, supplemented by a set of antique *réongs*, *kempur*, *kempli*, two drums, and a set of *rinchik*. The instruments are small and light enough to be carried and played in processions, suspended from poles born on the shoulders of a single file of marching musicians (Fig. 66). Ceremonial expeditions of the village to some distant shrine or temple are accompanied during the journey by frequent outbursts of lively melodious music, familiar and heartening to all.

Although almost obsolete, the older form of gamelan is of great interest, partly because of its particular instrumental methods, but above all for the unusual technique of the *angklungs* which gives the orchestra a unique color. The organization of the gamelan is simple. The main body of the ensemble is composed of four-keyed metallophones—two *jegogans*, four or six large *gendèrs* or *gangsa gantung* (Fig. 67), and a corresponding number of small *gendèrs* an octave higher in pitch. There are no *pōkok* tones to be melodically developed. Instead, the complete melody is played in octaves by the *gangsa gantung* group and stressed at regular intervals by the *jegogans*. An ornamental paraphrase of the melody is performed by the *chungklik*, a xylophone with a two-octave range, and the *grantang*, similar in range but having for keys a series of bamboo tubes. Figuration accompaniment is furnished by a set of four *angklungs* and a set of four *réongs*. The *kempur* supplies the main punctuation, while secondary accentuation is sounded by the *kempli* or omitted altogether. Two very small drums are included, the *kendang angklung*, which are beaten with sticks. In the more remote Karangasem villages where this form of gamelan generally substitutes for the more powerful *gamelan gong*, several pairs of large cymbals are added to the ensemble.

THE GAMELAN ANGKLUNG

Occasionally a two-octave *trompong* is included in the gamelan, on which florid solos are improvised against the unison melody of the *gangsas*. In the village of Abang, far up in the hills, I discovered an unusual instrument, described as "*trompong misi bruk*," *trompong* supplied with "*bruk*" or open coconut shells. Here thick slabs of sugarpalm (*jaka*) wood substituted for gongs, and the coconut shells, hung in a row beneath the keys, acted as resonator (Fig. 75). A solo instrument with a two-octave range, however, is unusual in the *gamelan angklung*, which is essentially an ensemble that is melodically confined to the limits of the basic four-tone scale.

The *angklung* included in this orchestra is found in two forms. The one most generally employed is furnished with three bamboo tubes of different lengths which are hung within a light wooden frame and tuned to sound a single tone in three octaves when the frame is shaken (Fig. 62). The other form is supplied with four tubes; two larger tubes of equal length produce the basic tone, while two smaller tubes sound the tone an octave higher (Fig. 63). Each tube is open at the top and ends in a tongue which extends beyond the actual tube in order to amplify its basic tone.[1] The closed lower ends of the tubes have short extending strips. These fit loosely into individual slots cut in a transverse bamboo tube which forms the base of the *angklung*. The tubes are separated from each other by thin wooden rods, ornately terminating in spearheads and decorated with ribbons or feathers (Figs. 64, 65). Small bells are sometimes hung inside the frame, adding a faint jingle when the instrument is in motion.

In Java the *angklung* is generally shaken back and forth to produce a tremolo tone. In Bali a single or quickly repeated double tone is preferred. The frame can be given a single jerk, causing each tube to knock against one end of its slot only, producing a sharp staccato tone; or it can be shaken so that the tubes knock once against each end of the slots, giving an

accented tone with a fainter echo ♫ . The tone produced is hollow and musical, amplified

by the doubling in octaves. Four instruments, each tuned to a different scale-tone, complete the set. Each is operated by a separate player. The instruments are sounded in close succession, creating figuration patterns that continue without a break throughout the composition.

The nature of the *angklung* patterns and their relation to the melodic line can be seen from Ex. 225. Here the four *angklungs* combine to form a simple rhythmic accompaniment that is repeated with little variation. They combine in such a way, however, as to give a secondary, cross-rhythmic accentuation to the passage, created by the sounding of two *angklungs* at the same time. In the excerpt the *angklung* patterns are given both as performed and as they actually sound. In order to show more clearly the individual rhythmic impulse that activates each separate part, the different rhythms are written in single tones, although the double-tone method can be used in producing those tones that move in slower tempo. The example given here, as well as most of the following, is taken from the *gamelan angklung* in

[1] A *pandé krawang* from the Karangasem village of Tiyingan made me a set of *angklungs* by the following method. Each tube was cut to its approximate length, after which the tongue was cut. The tube itself was then tuned by cutting down, the *pandé* blowing into it from time to time and listening to ascertain the pitch. As a model for tuning, a *gangsa* from the ensemble for which the *angklungs* were intended was used. When the right pitch had been reached, the tongue was then cut down until, when tapped against the cement floor of my house, it gave the same tone as when the tube itself was blown into. The *pandé* explained. "The tongue is the key (*don*) and the tube its resonator (*bumbung*). Key and tube must correspond in tone as in other instruments."

235

the village of Chulik, whose scale is included in Chart 14 (No. 3), and whose instruments and players are shown in Figs. 61 and 62.

Ex. 225. Pengechèt Sutrian; excerpt ♩ = 92

In more extended melodic passages the *angklung* figuration breaks away from the simple repeating pattern and follows the broader melodic line, as shown in the next example. Here the four *angklungs* are seen to double the *réong* accompaniment, the first *angklung* coinciding with the right hand of the first *réong* player, the second *anklung* with his left hand. Although a certain leeway may be found between *angklung* and *réong* patterns because of the different instrumental methods of performing, essentially unison figuration is maintained at all times. In Ex. 266 the four *angklung* parts are performed in double notes throughout, creating a continuous tremolo.

Ex. 226. Gending Guak Maling Talōh; Chulik village ♩ = 100

actual angklung figuration, measure 1

Grantang and *chungklik* play a minor role in the ensemble. These have individual paraphrasing parts; the weak sound of the two instruments contributes little to the orchestral resonance. Each is played in octaves, adding staccato filling-in tones to the melody as performed by the *gangsas*. The difference in style between the two instruments may be seen in Ex. 227. The *grantang* figuration continues unbroken throughout the *gending*, as shown, while the *chungklik* patterns are consistently offbeat. Each soloist is free to follow the *gangsa* melody as he pleases, and unison between the two parts is not strictly observed.

Ex. 227. Gending Guak Maling Talōh

The *chèngchèng* section in these older gamelans is heavy in relation to the size of the orchestra. Five pairs of cymbals are used, ranging in size from six to ten inches in diameter. Polyrhythmic patterns similar to those heard in the *gamelan gong* underline each *gending* throughout. The distinguishing names for the different cymbals are local, rarely used outside the Karangasem district. Largest and loudest is the pair of *penyelah*, whose heavily accented

237

rhythms are clearly heard above the rest. Next in diminishing size is the *penengah*, which
sounds between the main beats. The still smaller *chongé-chongé* sounds the same offbeat rhythm
at double speed. The polyrhythmic interplay of this cymbal group is completed by the interlocking rhythms performed by two pairs of small *kichak*.

Ex. 228. Gending Guak Maling Talōh

While the four upper cymbals repeat the cliché patterns with little, if any, variation, the
penyelah creates a feeling of forward movement by developing its basic rhythm and intensifying
the pattern as the point for the repeat of a melodic period approaches. Each recurrent rise in
tension finds immediate release with the *kempur* stroke which marks the point of repeat, where
the gradual build-up in tensions begins again.

Ex. 229. Gending Guak Maling Talōh; penyelah rhythm

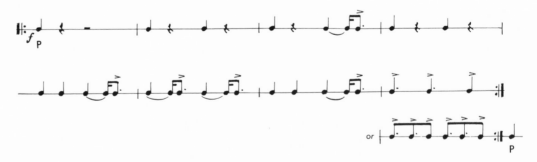

Since tempo and dynamics never change, the pair of small, high-pitched drums used in
this gamelan play no part in regulating tempo, and merely supply a light, rhythmic accompaniment. The pair consists of a *kendang wadon* and a somewhat smaller *kendang lanang*,

usually tuned to the two lowest tones of the scale, *dèng* and *dung*.[2] The drums are struck at the larger end with a light stick; there is no interplay of hand strokes on the smaller drumheads, and the two drums are often assigned to a single player. The pair agree rhythmically with the two larger *angklungs* and the two lower *réongs*. They sound in irregular alternation, their interlocking rhythms occasionally overlapping. Their close relation to the *réongs* (and *angklungs*) may be seen in Ex. 230. More expanded patterns will be found in the full score transcription of *gending Guak Maling Talōh* in Appendix 3.

Ex. 230.

The general orchestral effect of these older ensembles is one of strength and fullness. The expressionless *gangsa* melody rings metallically above the complex blend of sounds produced by *angklungs*, *réongs*, and xylophones, through which the throbbing tones of the *jegogans* penetrate at regular intervals. The drums are scarcely heard, but the cymbals add an energy to the music that seems almost mechanical in its steady flow. All compositions are played in the same manner, with no change in dynamics, and no noticeable difference in tempo from one *gending* to the next.

The compositions played by these gamelans with *angklungs* are simple in structure. The *pengawak-pengechèt* form is rare; most *gendings* consist of a single short melodic period which is repeated again and again. The leading *gangsa* player introduces the composition with a preliminary solo, the *pengawit*, more often referred to in Karangasem as the *gihing*.[3] Unlike the prolonged and half-improvised solos that precede the compositions of the *gamelan gong* or *pelègongan*, the *gihing* is brief and immediately thematic, picking up the melody at some point after its beginning and leading directly to the *kempur* stroke which marks the beginning of the actual *gending*. In spite of such distinguishing titles as *Croaking Frog*, *Hibiscus Blossom*, or *Waves*, the musicians of the gamelan rely entirely on the *gihing* to indicate which *gending* they will play. With these Karangasem groups I soon found that the only way to be sure of hearing a certain *gending* again was to note the introductory solo immediately, the first time the piece was played. When I wished to hear a certain composition again, if instead of asking for it by name I would play the introduction on a *gangsa*, then the desired piece was sure to follow.

---

[2] Tunings vary to a certain degree. While the *dèng* remains fixed, the *dung* may be slightly raised, placing the drums an approximate minor third apart. Most *angklung* drums, however, are pitched around a major second apart.

[3] In Karangasem the word *gihing*, meaning backbone or spine, refers both to the introduction and to the *pōkok* or nuclear tones of a composition.

For although the musicians, including the leading *gangsa* player, could always give the name of the *gending* after playing it, to ask for it by name beforehand often produced a quite different piece, even immediately after its performance. This, of course, is understandable since, because of the small melodic range, one *gending* closely resembles the next; the actual titles are of little help in suggesting the melody to follow.

Yet in spite of the narrow range of the *gamelan angklung* scale, each *gending* has its own individual form and melodic contour that somehow set it quite apart from the rest. Here variety in the metric structure compensates for the restricted movement of the actual melody. While some compositions are based on the regular melodic period of sixteen or thirty-two beats, many are irregular in form, contracting or expanding the normal balanced period. In those few two-part compositions having a first movement or *pengawak*, followed by a second part which in this region is known as the *peniban*, there is little difference between the two movements except for the change in melodic line. The same metric structure prevails throughout; each movement is preceded by a thematic introduction or *gihing*, and each can be performed separately.

It is, however, the short, one-movement *gendings* of irregular length that form the greater part of the repertory still played by these all-but-obsolete gamelans of eastern Karangasem. Four of these, as played by the metallophone group, are given below, in Ex. 231–234. Note should be made that the *jegogans* do no more than stress the *gangsa* melody at regular intervals. Since there is no instrumental group to supply a simplification of the *gangsa* melody, we may consider this as the true *pōkok* of the *gending*.

In Ex. 231 the *gihing* has been included. It will be seen to take up the melody after the third *jegogan* tone in the actual *gending*, skip the following measure, and proceed without further melodic alteration to the opening tone of the *gending*. Various modifications of the melody may occur in the *gihing*; the important melodic clue, however, lies in the last part, which must be melodically recognizable.

Ex. 231. Gending Sekar Puchuk; Chulik village ♩ = 100

240

Ex. 232. Gending Jaran Putih; Chulik village ♩ = 100

Ex. 231 and 232 are from the *gamelan angklung* of Chulik village, whose scale is given in Chart 14 (No. 3). Ex. 233 and 234 are from Mega Tiga, whose scale will be found in the same Chart (No. 1).

Ex. 233. Gending Lelasan Megat Yèh; Mega Tiga village ♩ = 100

Ex. 234. Gending Méong Megarang; Mega Tiga village ♩ = 100

The *trompong*, when included in the gamelan, replaces the *grantang* and *chungklik*, and is assigned to a soloist who improvises a highly syncopated version of the *gangsa* melody. The free relation of *trompong* to the *gangsa* melody may be seen in the following example, *Guak Maling Talōh*, as played in Prasi village. The *gending*, given in full, is an extension of the composition by that name played in Chulik (Ex. 226). Whereas the Chulik version, consisting of a single repeating melodic period, is complete in itself, the Prasi version adds a *pengechèt* based on a series of short ostinato motifs and ending with a coda or *penyuwud*. The solo is performed for the most part in octaves (*ngembat*), but the more rapid passages are played in single tones (*numpuk*). The soloist is free to elaborate at will on the *gangsa* melody, introducing variations as the different sections are repeated. The scale of the Prasi gamelan was very close to that of Chulik; the performance tempo was somewhat faster.

Ex. 235. Gending Guak Maling Talōh; Prasi village ♩ = 60

1. trompong   2. gangsas   3. jegogans

242

The next example is from the village Abang, where the *trompong* solo was played on the special xylophone with coconut shell resonators known as the *trompong bruk*. The village proudly claimed this instrument as the only one of its kind.[4] Two different styles of octave playing are shown here. The *pengawak*, with which the piece opens, is performed in plain octaves; in the following *pengechèt* the right hand adds filling-in tones, while the left hand remains simple. Here the right hand of the player performs what is termed the *nyandet* part, while the left hand plays the *pōlos* or plain part. While I neglected to note the actual tuning of this gamelan, the scale followed the usual structure found in the *angklung* gamelans of central Bali, as shown in Ex. 237, though when compared with this latter it will be found considerably lower in pitch. The title to the *gending* was not known.

Ex. 236. Trompong bruk solo; Abang village ♩ = 80

Bright young musicians from central Bali who accompanied me on my expeditions to these remote villages found their old-fashioned orchestras utterly absurd. They would sit in polite silence while the musicians played, but could hardly wait until we drove off to comment on the "plain" (*pōlos*) style of the music, the "stiff" (*kaku*) way of playing, and to gaily parody the preposterous accompaniment of the *angklungs*.

Nevertheless, when in 1938 I organized in Sayan a *gamelan angklung* composed entirely of small boys, I decided to include a set of *angklungs* in the orchestra. At first the children

---

[4] I came across another, however, lying in disuse in the temple at Kaangkaang, another village of the same district. Dr. V. E. Korn's study of the Karangasem village, Tenganan (*De Dorpsrepubliek Tnganan Pagringsingan*, Santpoort, C. A. Mees, 1933) contains one photograph of a purely local *gamelan glunggangan*, a small ensemble composed of similar instruments, two with ten keys and one with four.

ignored these instruments entirely, but they soon became intrigued with their unusual sound, and there was much discussion—in which I took no part—as to who should play them. I engaged a young musician from Karangasem to teach the club and train the four boys to whom the *angklungs* had been assigned. These latter caught on to the unfamiliar style with surprising rapidity. Within a few months this club of children—a complete novelty in Bali—had acquired a repertory of compositions, some short, others of considerable length, which they played with complete assurance. Their first public appearance at a temple *ōdalan* in Sayan created a local sensation, partly because of the youth of the musicians, some of whom were no more than five or six, but especially because of the novelty of the *angklungs*. The word spread, and soon the club was in demand for festivals in other villages; the gamelan with *angklungs* had proved a success. Today, I am told, these almost forgotten instruments have become familiar to everyone, and have even been adopted by other *angklung* orchestras in central Bali.

In spite of the revival of interest in the *angklung*, the standard *gamelan angklung* of Bali today remains essentially a bronze ensemble, and has a very different resonance from that of the older Karangasem ensembles. With the elimination of the *angklung*, *grantang*, and *chungklik*, and the substitution of a set of small *rinchik*-type cymbals for the massive *chèngchèng* group, the orchestral sound becomes light and transparent. While the gamelans of north Bali vary considerably in the number of their instruments, those of south Bali are of generally uniform size, employing some eighteen or so players. The metallophone group, which forms the main body of the orchestra, consists of two *jegogans*, four large, one-octave *gendèrs* or *gangsa gantung*, and four smaller *kantils*, pitched one octave higher. The rest of the gamelan is composed of two *réong angklung*, or "*klèntèng*," as they are often called,[5] *kempur*, *kempli* or *kelenang*, two small drums, known as *kendang angklung*, and *rinchik*. The instruments are generally arranged in the order followed by the larger gamelans, the *gendèrs* forming the first row, and the *kantilans* the second. Drums, cymbals, and *kempur* are placed at the rear, while the *réongs* are in front or on one side (Figs. 70, 71).

Compared with the unusual tunings of Karangasem, the scale of the *gamelan angklung* of central Bali is relatively stabilized. The tuning of the gamelan belonging to Mas village given in Chart 13 (No. 1) is typical, and may serve as a key to the musical illustrations which follow.

Saih angklung, Mas village

È			U		O			I
410			469		519			620
	231			175		308		
A♭		B♭		C			E♭	
410.5		461		517			615	

----

[5] The gamelan itself is occasionally referred to as the *gamelan klèntèng(an)*.

The instrumental range of the gamelan is unusually high, imparting to the ensemble a peculiarly sweet and aerial sound. The *kempur*, as may be seen in Fig. 66, is considerably smaller than that found in other gamelans, and is generally pitched a little below the lowest tone of the *jegogan*. The two small drums are normally tuned an approximate major second apart, and correspond in pitch to the two lowest tones of the scale.

Ex. 237. Gamelan angklung; instrumental ranges

The dissonant tonal relation of the *kempur* to the rest of the gamelan, as shown above, is characteristic. While occasionally found coinciding in pitch with the lowest tone of the *jegogan*, the *kempur* is generally pitched to sound some tone not included in the four-tone scale, in order to give a greater salience to its accentuation. Most *kempurs* sound either an approximate major second or major third below the lowest scale-tone, the latter tuning being perhaps the most frequently employed. This small *kempur* is remarkable for its soft yet vibrant and penetrating tone. To a Western ear the tonal color of the whole gamelan is affected by its pitch, as can be seen from the following examples, one from Mas village, the other from the neighboring village of Batuan.

245

Ex. 238. Kempur pitches compared

a) Mas village

kempur

b) Batuan village

kempur

Like those played in Karangasem, the *gendings* of the standard gamelan show great variety in structure and melodic line. Free of the balanced metric forms and elaborate punctuation systems found in the *gending gong* and *pegambuhan*, they reveal a flexibility of form similar to the compositions of the *gendèr wayang* repertory.[6] Like these, the *gending angklung* are not preserved in notation of any kind, but survive entirely through oral tradition.

Two different types of *gending* may be distinguished: *a*, those in which simple basic melody—the *pōkok gending*—is sounded by the *jegogans*, while *gendèrs*, *kantils*, and *réongs* unite in continuous accompaniment; and *b*, compositions in which the melody—the *lagu* or *gending*—is played by the smaller metallophones and *réongs*, while the *jegogans* merely underline the melody at intervals.

Ex. 239.

a)

gendèrs*
réongs

jegogans

etc.

b)

gendèrs*
réongs
jegogans

etc.

* The genders are doubled an octave higher by the kantils.

---

6 Indeed, many *angklung* gamelans include in their repertory compositions said to be "drawn" (*ditarik*) from the *gending pewayangan*. *Angklung* compositions such as "*pemungkah*" and "*lagu gendèr wayang*" are based on four-tone ostinatos and melodic episodes taken directly from the *wayang* repertory—a practice showing how closely related the two scale systems are considered to be by the Balinese.

246

Gendings of type *a*, with their structural *pōkok* melody, show more compact and clearly defined metric form than do the more lyrical *gendings* of type *b*. Shorter compositions may be based on the simple ostinato unit, or consist of a single extended melodic period repeated at will. Longer compositions follow the traditional *pengawak-pengechèt* plan. All forms show, however, a surprising freedom in metric structure. Ostinato units contain not only the usual eight or sixteen *pōkok* tones, but often consist of ten, eleven, or twelve. Extended periods show a similar irregularity. This can immediately be seen from the following examples, in which the *pōkok* tones are expressed by the numerals 1 to 4, representing the four tones of the *saih angklung—dèng, dung, dang,* and *ding.* It will also be seen that no secondary punctuation subdivides the melodic period in any way. The *kempur* supplies the only structural accents; the *kempli* merely marks the offbeats between *pōkok* tones.

Ex. 240.

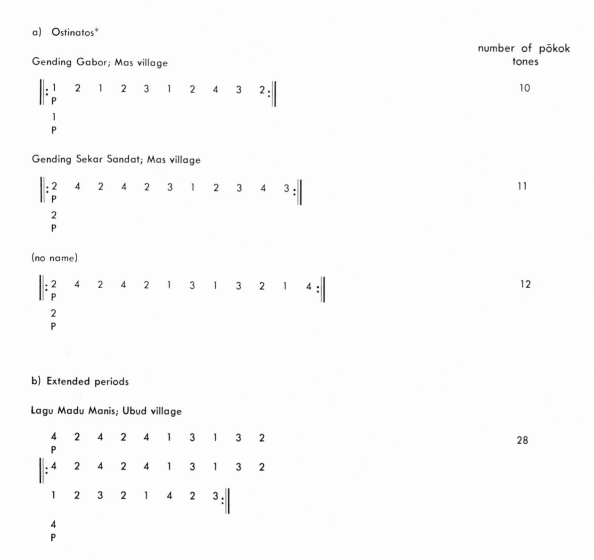

a) Ostinatos*

number of pōkok tones

Gending Gabor; Mas village

10

Gending Sekar Sandat; Mas village

11

(no name)

12

b) Extended periods

Lagu Madu Manis; Ubud village

28

247

number of pōkok
tones

Gending Chelunjuk; Payangan village

```
‖: 1  2  1  2  3  2  3  2                    40
    P
   1  2  1  2  3  2  3  2

   2  3  2  1  3  2  3  4

   2  3  2  1  3  2  3  2

   4  2  4  3  1  2  3  2 :‖

   1
   P
```

*The basic tempo of the pōkok tones in these and the following examples remains essentially the same—M. 48–60.

So far, the *pōkok* tones are all seen to have the same time value. In many *gendings*, however, the *jegogan* melody becomes more fluid, with certain tones extended to two, three, or even more times their normal time value.

Ex. 241.

number of pōkok
tones or time
equivalents

Gending Sekar Jepun; Mōgan village*

```
‖: 1  .  2  1  3  .  .  2  1  .  2  1  3  .  .  2        52

   3  1  3  2  4  .  2  1  4  .  2  1  4  2  3  1

   2  .  3  1  2  .  3  1  2  3  1  2  3  .  .  3

   3  1  3  2  3  .  .  .  . :‖
                Pt
```

Lagu Gendèr Wayang; Sayan village

```
‖: 1  .  .  3  2  .  3  .  1  .  .  3  2  .  3  .        80
   P
   1  .  2  1  2  .  .  .  3  .  4  .  2  .  .  4

   3  .  4  .  2  .  .  4  3  .  4  .  2  .  3  4

   3  .  .  .  .  .  .  2  3  4  3  2  3  .  .  2

   3  4  3  2  3  .  .  .  .  .  .  .  1  .  3  . :‖

   1
   P
```

*This gending is recorded by Odeon. See Appendix 6, Recordings.
†The kempur stands here in an unusual position, terminating the period, but not marking the point for a new beginning.

In *gendings* with a *pengawak-pengechèt* construction the *pengawak* does not always return immediately to the opening tone, as in the *gending gong*. The *pengawak* to *gending Bèrong*, for example, contains sixty-four *pōkok* tones plus a terminal tone lasting the equivalent of eight *pōkok* beats.

Ex. 242. Pengawak-pengechèt form, gending Bèrong; Mōgan village*

																number of pōkok tones or time equivalents

pengawak

‖: 2   3   2   4   2   4   2   1   3   1   3   1   3   1   3   1   64 + 1 +

   2   3   2   4   2   4   2   1   3   2   3   2   1   3   2   1   7 beats

   3   2   3   2   1   3   2   1   3   2   3   2   1   3   2   1

   4   3   4   3   4   3   2   3   1   3   1   3   2   4   3   2

   1   •   •   •   •   •   •   •   •:‖
   P

pengechèt; transition

   3   •   •   2   4   •   •   2   3   •   •   2   4   •   •   2   26

   3   •   •   2   3   2   4   2   3   2

main section

‖: 2   4   2   4   2   4   2   1   3   1   3   1   3   2   1   4 .:‖   16
  P
  2
  P

---

* Recorded by Odeon, with the titles, Bèrong pengawak and Bèrong pengechèt. Each movement begins with the usual solo introduction or pengawit. See Appendix 6, Recordings.

Pengechèt and *pengawak* are usually played without a pause in between, and are frequently linked together by a transitional passage which leads from the *pengawak* to the main section of the *pengechèt*, recalling the *pengaras* of the *gending gong*. The *pengechèt* is often thematically related to the *pengawak*. In the above example the main part of the *pengechèt* consists of a sixteen-tone ostinato deriving from the first sixteen *pōkok* tones of the *pengawak*, as may be seen when the two sixteen-tone units are compared.

Ex. 243.

pengawak Bèrong   2   3   2   4   2   4   2   1   3   1   3   1   3   1   3   1

pengechèt   2   4   2   4   2   4   2   1   3   1   3   1   3   2   1   4

The transitional passage that introduces the *pengechèt* is sounded in unison by the metallophones. Starting at the tempo of the preceding *pengawak*, whose *pōkok* tones move at M. 48, it gradually increases in speed to approximately twice as fast, when the basic melody of the *pengechèt* is heard for the first time. A gradual rallentando brings the passage to a close at approximately the tempo at which it began, and the main section of the *pengechèt* can now begin. Ex. 244, *pengechèt Berong*, is transcribed from the Odeon recording, and includes the opening transitional passage and one statement of the ostinato which forms the main part of the movement. It is a typical realization of the *pōkok* tones, in this case the tones already given in the *pengechèt* section of Ex. 242.

Ex. 244. Pengechèt Bèrong, transition and main section; Mōgan village

Some gamelans like to vary the figuration as the ostinato is repeated. Variety may also be given to the movement through a change in instrumentation. In the Odeon recording of the Mōgan gamelan a *suling* is included in the ensemble—an unusual practice today. Twice during the *pengechèt* the main body of the gamelan stops playing; the figuration is continued by the *suling* alone, sounding against the *jegogan* melody, which now moves at double speed.

Ex. 245. Pengechèt Bèrong; suling variation

With the approach of the *kempur* accent the other instruments enter in unison, and break into figuration as the ostinato returns in its original form.

Ex. 246. Pengechèt Bèrong

The *pengechèt* is not always as closely related thematically to the *pengawak* as it is in *gending Bèrong*. It may even be an independent movement, based on a more extended form than that of the single ostinato unit. Variation in metric structure is limitless; the principle of metric contraction as the movement proceeds, which dictates the form of the *pengechèt* in the *gending gong*, is employed in endless ways. Two examples may suffice as illustration. The first, *pengechèt Sekar Uled*, shows more regularity of form in its immediate contraction from the eight-tone ostinato units to a series of four-tone units. *Pengechèt pemungkah* has greater metric freedom, introducing a twelve-tone unit (divided in half, however, by a *kempur* stroke) between the initial eight-tone unit and the final four-tone section.

Ex. 247.

Pengechèt Sekar Uled; Ubud village*

‖: 3 2 4 2 1 3 4 2 :‖
   P

‖: 3 1 2 3 1 3 4 2 :‖
   P

‖: 3 4 1 4 :‖
   P

‖: 3 2 1 4 :‖
   P

‖: 3 1 2 4 :‖
   P

‖: 3 2 1 4 :‖
   P

‖: 3
   P

Pengechèt Pemungkah; Sayan village

‖: 2 3 4 2 3 • 3 2 :‖
   P

‖: 2 3 2 3 2 1
   P

   3 4 3 4 3 1. :‖
   P

   3 4 3 4 3 2
   P

‖: 1 2 3 4 :‖
   P

   1
   P

* For melodic realization see Appendix 3, Ex. 355.

The group of compositions in which figuration is replaced by clearly defined and fluid melody are more loosely constructed than those just examined. While some of the *gendings* of this class have contrasting *pengawak* and *pengechèt* movements, the great majority are completely free in form. Each has its own individual shape, not too different from the others, but organized in its own special way. Chains of short melodic sections are interwoven with syncopated linking passages; ostinatos with figuration accompaniment are introduced for contrast. Like the *gending pewayangan*, which they greatly resemble in their elasticity, these compositions can be extended or shortened during performance through prolonged or limited repetition of the various episodes.

Typical of these melodic *gendings* is Ex. 248, the *pengawak* to gending *Jaran Sirig* (*Rearing Horse*), as played by the *gamelan angklung* of Selat village. The whole movement, with its various repetitions of inner melodic units, is free in structure, and has no conclusive ending. As *pengawak* to the complete *gending* it can only be considered ended when, after several repetitions of the whole melodic period, the *kempur* sounds for the first time at the point indicated below by (P), accenting the tone which links the *pengawak* with the *pengechèt*.

252

Ex. 248. Gending Jaran Sirig, pengawak; Selat village ♩ = 58

The *gending* in Ex. 248 is played without solo introduction, the full gamelan entering in a resolute tutti. The *pengawak* begins with the top line, is repeated once or twice, and ends with the *kempur* stroke (P). The *pengechèt*, given on the following page, overlaps, beginning without a break on the same *kempur* stroke. Starting in an animated unison, it slows down to a tempo slightly brighter than that of the *pengawak*, breaks into figuration derived from the opening melody, and continues to the end of the movement. No elaborate transition prepares for the main section of the *pengechèt*, as in *gending Bèrong*. Instead, the opening melody, which will later dissolve into figuration, is stated twice, with rhythmic emphasis underlined by the slower moving *jegogan* tones which will later supply the melodic interest.

253

Ex. 249. Gending Jaran Sirig; pengechèt ♩ = 76

Despite their limited range, the figuration patterns have an animation that cannot be conveyed in condensed notation. The constant interlocking of *mōlos* and *nyangsih* parts, and the sudden rhythmic breaks that occur from time to time, maintain a steady tension throughout the music. These patterns differ from the more mobile figuration patterns on five-keyed instruments inasmuch as they must remain stationary. The *mōlos* part is confined to the two upper tones of the scale, the *nyangsih* to the lower two.

In order to strengthen the figuration or *kōtèkan*, as performed by the *gendèrs* and *kantils*, certain clubs ingeniously add a third interlocking part. This is called the "binder" or *kilitan* (*lilit*, vine), which binds together *mōlos* and *nyangsih* parts in order that the *kōtèkan* is not "broken" (*apang kōtèkan sing pegat*).

Ex. 250.

For this type of playing the metallophones are divided in the *gendèr wayang* manner; the *pengumbang* and *pengisep* instruments are arranged in separate parallel rows, with the two lines

254

of interdependent musicians facing each other. Two instruments in each quartet perform the *mōlos* part, while the other two are divided into *kilitan* any *nyangsih*.

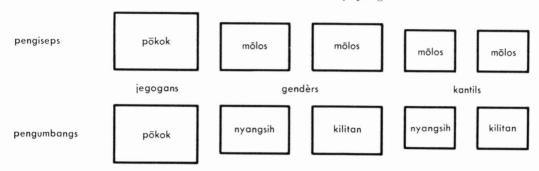

The popular nature of the *gamelan angklung* is perhaps most clearly shown in the tunefulness of its music and the picturesque titles of the actual compositions. I give some of the more colorful ones here, obtained from different parts of the island. Those starred were known only in Karangasem.

asep menyan[7]	burning incense
*chapung manjus	bathing dragonfly
*chapung ngumbang	circling dragonfly
chelagi manis	sweet tamarind
*dongkang menak biyu	treefrog climbs coco palm
*dongkang menak gedang	treefrog climbs papaya
glagah puwun	burning grass fields
guak maling talóh	crow steals eggs
jaran putih	white horse
jaran sirig	rearing horse
*jero dagang	market woman
kambing slem	black goat
*katak nongkèk	croaking frog
kupu-kupu metarum	playful butterflies
*lelasan megat yèh	lizard parts water (swim)
*lindung pesu	eel comes out
*lutung megulut	embracing apes
*méong megarang	fighting cats
ombakan	waves
pipis satus	one hundred coins
*sampi nginem	drinking cow
sekar cambodia	cambodia blossom
sekar puchuk	hibiscus blossom
sekar sandat	sandalwood blossom
tumisi kuning	yellow snail

In spite of their graphic titles, such *gendings* as those listed here are purely instrumental compositions, in no way descriptive or associated with any texts or dances. Many are said to have their origin in the simple folk tunes known as the *gending gènggong*, which are strummed on the *gènggong* or jew's harp by boys and men all over Bali.[8] They form a large part of the traditional repertory of the *gamelan angklung* which, alternating with the more stately music of the *gamelan gong*, rings brightly through the temple courts at festival time.

---

[7] The Balinese noun comes first, followed by the adjective or verb.

[8] An account of the relation of the *gending gènggong* to the *gending angklung* will be found in the author's study, "Children and Music in Bali" in *Childhood in Contemporary Culture*, Margaret Mead and Martha Wolfenstein, eds., Chicago, 1955.

Chapter 16

Four Sacred Ensembles

IN A SMALL number of villages scattered through Bali there may still be found certain instrumental ensembles, carefully preserved and surviving from an unknown past, which are heard only on special religious occasions.[1] Stored away when not in use, the treasured heirloom instruments may not be brought out and played before offerings have been prepared in their honor and prayers recited by the village priest for their protection. Four quite different types of ensemble may be distinguished, all related through the use of a seven-tone scale system. Each has its special instrumental method, its own repertory of sacred music, and its traditional role in rites and ceremonies. No new music is composed for these ensembles; even the slightest stylistic change in the traditional way of performing the music is inconceivable. The sacred repertories are treasured as highly as the instruments themselves. In some villages they are believed to be of divine origin, but more often they are considered to have "come down from Majapahit"—the last Hindu-Javanese empire.

The *gamelan selundèng*

Possibly the oldest of all four ensembles is the *gamelan selundèng*, whose name is mentioned occasionally in twelfth century Javanese literature. Composed of cumbrous, primitive metallophones furnished with great iron keys (Fig. 85), this crude but astonishingly resonant ensemble survives in only two or three remote mountain villages, where it supplies the main music for periodic religious festivals. Taking the gamelan from its special storehouse is a solemn event, and the villagers assemble and squat in reverence as the instruments are carried to the *balé selundèng*, the special pavilion that stands in the center of the village. Special care is taken at this time to protect them from the desecrating touch, no matter how accidental, of an outsider from some other village, which would render the gamelan *sebel*, ritualistically soiled. Should this happen, the instruments may not be played again before they have been cleansed with the necessary offerings and rites of purification, an elaborate ceremony that may bring the whole festival to a standstill. The gamelan, moreover, may not be taken out of the village except when it is periodically carried to the sea for purification. In its course along the road it may not pass beneath bridges or water conduits. On occasion, telephone wires have been cut to avoid overhead desecration, and repair expenses rather reluctantly paid on government demand.

Legends surround the *gamelan selundèng* with romance. In Kayubihi, a small mountain

---

[1] These continue to survive, I was informed in 1952 by Anak Agung Gedé Mandera of Pliatan, whose gamelan appeared in New York that year.

256

village in the Klungkung district, the gamelan is known by the title, *Ratu Maospahit*, Lord Majapahit, and was a gift from the sea god (*déwa laut*).[2]

Said my informant, the *klian dèsa* (village headman):

Long ago, as the men from Pujung Sari (the old name for Kayubihi) were making their annual offerings by the sea, they heard the sound of music coming from the waves. They returned to their village, and the next day, after a meeting of the *krama dèsa* (village elders), they brought offerings to the place where the music had been heard and made a *slamatan* (ceremony of honor). From the water appeared a gamelan unlike any ever seen, and the men waded out and brought it ashore. They carried the instruments back to Pujung Sari, and stored them in the *Pura Panataron*, Temple of the Kings. For a long time the gamelan remained untouched, for no one knew how to play the instruments or dared to strike them. One day there came an *utusan*, messenger, from heaven in the form of a white raven, which taught them how to play. It sang from a tree in the temple court, and taught the men seven *saihs*, melodies.[3] The seven *saihs* were taught in the following order: *Memiyut, Malat, Demung, Wargasari, Gerapet, Panji,* and *Madura.* To this day the *selundèng* of Kajubihi plays these *saihs* in the same order. The instruments are still kept in the *Pura Panataran*, but no one other than the priest and I know exactly where they are stored.

The rather meager information I have to offer here on actual *selundèng* methods was obtained in Tenganan, a mountain village of Karangasem, where long acquaintance with the *klian dèsa* and the musicians themselves made investigation easier than in Kayubihi. Even so, this could only be carried on when the instruments had been taken out for some festival, and mainly during actual performance. Tenganan festivals are not frequent, and to notify me of some event the *klian* would send a messenger who traveled partly by bus, mostly on foot, to my house in Sayan, some sixty miles away.

Tenganan, an isolated village of grave but friendly people, prides itself on its aloofness, its *Bali-aga* (pre-Hindu Balinese) culture, and its strict adherence to a traditional and ancient way of life. The village moreover is unique in possessing not one but three complete *selundèng* ensembles, all equally holy and enmeshed in taboos. On feast days the three gamelans are set up each in its own pavilion. These stand, some distance apart, in the middle of the cobbled main street that climbs in terraces through the center of the walled-in village. The three gamelans are known as the *selundèngs kaja* (north), *tenga* (central), and *kelod* (south), named after the locations where, since time immemorial, they have been set up. Alternating with the *selundèng* pavilions stand three Ferris wheels, rough constructions of wood, each containing four swinging seats that will hold two. Sedate rides in these are taken by the *dahas*, unmarried girls of the village, dressed in ceremonial clothes—a traditional part of the festival program. Time-honored groans and squeaks are heard as the ungreased framework is slowly turned by the unmarried boys.

---

[2] My informant used the literal Malayan phrase, giving no proper name to the actual god.

[3] Ordinarily, *saih* means scale. That the *klian* meant tune, as well as its proper scale, may be gathered from the actual names of the "*saihs*," all names of *gendings* in the repertories of the *charuk* and *gambang* ensembles.

Although the three gamelans are considered to be perhaps the most precious possessions of the village, I was told that they were no more than reproductions of the original and holiest gamelan, "a gift from heaven," which is never taken out, and which few have ever seen. I was also told that the keys of this gamelan have holes for mounting bored at one end only, a sign that they were not meant for use.

The Tenganan festivals are temple anniversaries in which the main events, other than actual services, take place in the village main street. Here the three gamelans accompany in turn the ceremonial processions around the gamelan pavilions, the various processional dances of youths and maidens, and the ritualistic *perang duwi*, fight with thorns, a series of duels between paired youths armed with shields and vicious bundles of thorny rattan. Equally important during the festival is the playing of Tenganan's own secret repertory of inherited sacred music, the *gending pingit*, whose very names may not be given to a stranger. The musicians from all three gamelans must be present when these *gendings* are played by any one ensemble. There are no special restrictions for villagers about touching the instruments, although there is a rule that a child whose first forelock has not yet been cut in ritual may not play in the gamelan. But an outsider who has touched a part of any instrument, above all one of the iron keys, must pay a fine sufficient for the purification offerings.

One reason for such concern over the *gamelan selundèng* is the fact that the keys of the instruments are cast not in bronze but in iron, a magically dangerous, but also magically protective metal. In temple grounds throughout Bali miniature weapons of iron are buried as protection against evil forces. Thus the iron-keyed *selundèng* has magic power, and must be kept in a constant state of purity. The actual keys are held to be of divine origin, and even to correct their tuning is sacrilege. Yet there is evidence that restorations have taken place in the course of time. On an early trip to Tenganan I noticed an embossed inscription on one great iron key which, on cautious examination proved to be no ancient text but merely the statement in plain English: "Made in Sweden."

When compared with the elegant *gangsas* and delicately adjusted *gendèrs* of other Balinese gamelans the large, unwieldy metallophones seem primitive indeed. No attempt is made to soften their rough appearance. The heavy iron keys are suspended over low, thick-walled soundboxes hewn from heavy blocks of wood. In the larger instruments the longest keys reach the length of some twenty-five inches (Fig. 84). The keys are mounted in a special way, using an ancient method followed by other keyed instruments described in this chapter. Toward each end, but far enough in to lie within the walls of the soundbox below, two holes are bored, through which the supporting strings are passed from below (Fig. 85). Between each pair of keys lie wooden cross-bars, through which are looped the supporting strings, thus preventing the keys from coming in contact with the soundbox. Each instrument in its complete form has eight keys, but is constructed in two separate parts, each part having four keys and a separate soundbox. In performance, the two parts of each instrument are placed together to form a row of keys that ascend in pitch from left to right. The instrumental pairs are usually left free of each other, but can be lashed together for convenience (Fig. 84). A stout wooden mallet is used in playing the smaller instruments, while the larger ones are struck with club-shaped sticks (Figs. 83, 84).

Yet despite their rough appearance the instruments of the *selundèng* ensemble create music of surprisingly sweet and mellow resonance. The large instruments produce sounds rich in overtones, resembling those of deep bells, while the timbre of the smaller instruments is clear and chiming. On hearing the gamelan perform the sacred *gendings*, one gains the impression of listening to the most serene, the most impersonal music to be heard in Bali. There is no percussive shock or throb of drums to lend excitement. Dance and sacred music alike are played without the slightest change in tempo or dynamics. After the ceremonies of the day, the three gamelans continue to play throughout the night, sounding in turn from their separate pavilions, and filling the air with quiet, melodious polyphony.

When the instruments are arranged in order, the Tenganan *gamelan selundèng* is found to consist of five eight-keyed metallophones which overlap to produce a seven-tone scale that

extends from an approximate 𝄢 to an approximate 𝄞 . Two of the instru-

ments, however, are divided into two component parts, each furnished with four keys. The two larger instruments are each assigned to a single player; the others are assigned as shown below. Tenganan has its own terminology for the instruments. Commencing with the largest, they are known as:

gong		8 keys	1 player
{ inting gedé	(large inting)	4	1 player
{ inting chenik	(small inting)	4	
{ penem		4	1 player
{ petuduh		4	1 player
nyonyong gedé	(large nyonyong)	8	1 player or 2
nyonyong chenik	(small nyonyong)	8	1 player or 2

A set of small cymbals, *chèngchèng*, are included in the ensemble to be used when accompanying the dances. Two players are employed for each of the *nyonyongs* when *gendings* with two-part figuration for these instruments are performed.

While requiring separate players, the *penem* and *petuduh* together constitute a single instrument. Although not ordinarily a melodic instrument, the *penem-petuduh*, as will be shown later, actually forms the tonal core of the gamelan. It is the only instrument of the ensemble in which the *saih 7* scale is found in its basic form, with the scale-tones named in their customary order. The solfeggio system of the *gamelan selundèng* is the same as that used by the *gambang* and *charuk* ensembles discussed in this chapter. As stated on pages 57–58 this system differs from that of the *gambuh* system in that the names of the scale tones remain fixed and do not shift with a change in mode or tonality. On the *penem-petuduh*, the *saih 7* commences with the tone, *ding*, and the ascending scale-tones are named in the following order:

1. ding		I
2. dong		O
3. dang ageng	(great or low dang)	A
4. dèng		È
5. dung		U
6. dang alit	(small or high dang)	a
7. dong alit	(small or high dong)	o
8. ding alit	(small or high ding)	i

The Tenganan *selundèng* scale which follows was taken from the *penem-petuduh* of the *selundèng kelod* gamelan, whose instruments at the time (1937) were most consistently in tune.

Saih 7 selundèng; penem-petuduh

	I		O		A		È		U		a				o		i
	310		345		383		420		460		496				575		630*
		184		181		159		158		131			255			158	
	Eb		F		G		Ab		Bb		C				D		Eb
	307.5		345		387.5	410.5		461		517				580	615

* 26 Cents sharp.

To show the unusual overlapping of tones which can be heard as the instruments produce the full orchestral scale, the different instrumental ranges are given below. All instruments except the *nyonyong chenik*, which doubles the *inting* two octaves above, are seen to begin on different scale-tones. In both *gong* and *inting*, the third and fourth tones are found to repeat, thus producing an incomplete seven-tone scale. The remaining instruments each have a full eight-tone scale.

Ex. 251. Gamelan selundèng, instrumental ranges; Tenganan village

This methodical overlapping engenders a unique form of orchestral integration. Characteristic movement and interplay of the different instruments may be seen in the following example. Here the melodic line is found in the right hand parts of the two *nyonyongs* and doubled two octaves below by the *inting*. Left hand parts of all three instruments are purely rhythmic filling-in. Interlocking figuration is produced by the *penem-petuduh*. The so-called *gong* creates an undercurrent of movement, functioning not unlike the drums of a larger gamelan.[4] Special attention is called to the *gong* and *inting* parts. As stated, these instruments, while each having eight keys, produce only six different scale-tones, two of which are repeated. The eight keys of each instrument fall into a lower and upper set of four, at the disposal of left and right hands respectively:

	left hand					right hand		
1	2	3	4		3	4	5	6

Certain tones in *gong* and *inting* parts are thus seen to occur at the same time in both left and right hand patterns, binding them together in rhythmic unity.

Ex. 252. Gilakan selundèng; Tenganan village   ♩ = 100

1. nyonyong chenik	3. petuduh	5. inting
2. nyonyong gedé	4. penem	6. gong

---

[4] Worth noting here is the quite different and more familiar instrumental nomenclature of the Kayubihi *gamelan selundèng*. Compared with the corresponding Tenganan instruments they were named as follows:

Kayubihi	Keys	Tenganan
chèngchèng	4	gong
gong-kempul	4	
penengas	8	inting
gangsa	8	penem-petuduh
trompong	8	nyonyong gedé

261

Ex. 252, an adaptation of a *gilakan* ostinato composition from the *gamelan gong* repertory, and used in Tenganan as part of the music played for the men's ceremonial dances, is purely pentatonic in character. More complex both in scale and organization is the following example, an extended melodic period, complete in itself, which belongs to the repertory of processional music. The melody is here transferred to the *gong*, divided between the right and left hands. Rhythmic movement is supplied by the *inting*, which sounds throughout on the offbeat. Figuration is created by the *penem-petuduh*, and is freely doubled an octave higher by the two *nyonyongs*, not included here.

Of main interest, however, is the use of a full seven-tone scale, containing the following five head tones and two secondary or *pemèro* tones:

Ex. 253.

The sudden appearance in all parts of these *pemèro* tones creates the effect of a quite unexpected change in tonality. This abrupt shift is most prominent in the *penem-petuduh* figuration, where the *pemèro* tones, indicated by (p), enter the patterns at two different places. The *gending* ends, after many repetitions, on the opening tone.

Ex. 254. Gamelan selundèng; processional music   ♩ = 76

1. petuduh
2. penem

3. inting
4. gong

The Tenganan musicians claimed to know at least three different scales or modes. These bore no distinguishing names; perhaps they had been forgotten, but quite possibly they were withheld as part of the Tenganan secret. In referring to the different scales the usual terms employed in the *gamelan gambuh*, *tekep* (cover) and *jalan* (go by way of) are used. Thus the musicians would say, *jalan* (or *tekep*) *rèjegan* (the name of a *gending* played for the ceremonial *abuang* dance performed by the young men), or *jalan ijang*, the music played for the same dance performed by the girls. In explaining how the *jalans* differed, they said, "If you go by way of *rèjegan*, *dèng* and small *dong* become *pemèro*."[5] And, "By way of *ijang*, large *dong* and small *dang* become *pemèro*."

The three modes in general use in Tenganan are located in the basic *saih 7* scale in the following order:

saih 7	1	2	3	4	5	6	7	
tones	I	O	A	È	U	a	o	
	I	O	A	p	U	a	p	tekep rèjegan
	I	p	A	È	U	p	o	tekep ijang
	I	O	p	È	U	p	o	no name

Thus, with the exception of a fixed solfeggio, and a somewhat different order in the naming of the scale tones, the system is seen to be essentially the same as that of the *saih 7 pegambuhan*. It will be found more methodically developed in the other ensembles included in this chapter.

---

5 *Yan jalan rèjegan dèng teken dong alit jadi pemèro.*

Certain *selundèng* compositions, especially the shorter ostinato forms, may be transposed from one tone series to another where, because of change of pitch and interval formation, they assume an entirely different tonal color. In the following example the *gilakan* ostinato given on page 261 is now found transposed a tone higher, lying in the scale referred to as *tekep rèjegan*. The transposition is note for note, except for the *inting* part, which must omit the highest melodic tone since it is beyond the range of the instrument.

Ex. 255. Gilakan selundèng, tekep rèjegan; Tenganan village

Transposition to *tekep ijang* would necessitate considerable changes in pattern because of instrumental limitations. How the melodic line can thus be affected is better shown in Ex. 278, where an extended melodic period in the *gending Lilit*, as played by the *gamelan Gong Luang*, is presented in six different scalar transpositions.

The sacred *gending pingit* of the Tenganan *selundèng* are not preserved in notation. All that I heard consisted of a series of repeating melodic periods which were sometimes played without a break, sometimes with pauses between the periods. They are related in form to the *gendings* of the *gamelan Gong Luang*, of which one is examined for phrase structure and changing tonalities later in this chapter. I was told that many of the *gendings* played for the ceremonial dances were taken from the repertories of the *charuk* and *gambang* ensembles. "The way of playing them is changed to make them more pleasant to dance to." In fact, the general *selundèng* method of instrumental organization shows much in common with that of the *Gong Luang* ensemble, despite the absence in the *selundèng* of regular *pōkok* tones or colotomic punctuation of any sort. The rhythmically integrating role of the *penem-petuduh* in the *selundèng*, and the manner in which the two players create two-voiced melodic figuration, corresponds to the part played by the so-called *trompong* of the *Gong Luang*. An examination of the technique of this latter instrument, as shown in Ex. 284, offers a useful clue to the more elusive and restricted method of the *penem-petuduh*.

The *charuk* ensemble

Less surrounded with legend and taboo than the *selundèng*, the rare *charuk* ensemble is still found in a few villages of Karangasem, notably Tenganan, Asak, and Selat, and in Krōbōkan, a village in Badung, which also possesses a *gambang* ensemble and a *gamelan Gong Luang*.

The *charuk* ensemble requires no more than two players, and takes its name from an antique form of bamboo-keyed xylophone, the *charuk*.[6] Like the instruments of the *selundèng*, the *charuk* is composed of two separate parts, each consisting of a wooden soundbox over which are suspended four keys (Fig. 76). The complete instrument produces a seven-tone scale plus the octave. The keys, however, are arranged in irregular order, in a manner that will be described later.

Two *sarons*—a *saron gedé* and a smaller *saron chenik*, sounding an octave higher, complete the ensemble. These are played by a single musician, who performs the *saron* melody in octaves. Simple figuration, closely following the *saron* melody, is played by the *charuk*. The united effect of the two *sarons* and *charuk* is one of ringing, metallic melody lightly supported by a continuous accompaniment of staccato ornamental passage-work.

The *charuk* ensemble is played only at temple anniversary ceremonies and during cremation rites, when it substitutes for the customary *gambang* ensemble. In regions where both *charuk* and *gambang* are known, the *charuk* is considered merely a simplified form of *gambang* ensemble, having the same scale system and the same repertory of sacred music.

Like the *gambang*, the *charuk* was formerly used to accompany the singing of certain ancient *kawi* texts known as *kidung*, narrative poems of historical-legendary character. The singing of these texts, notably *Malat*, from which the *gambuh* plays are taken, and *Chupak*, a moralistic romance well known to the Balinese, formed, like the shadowplay, an important part of the ritualistic program. While the texts may have been chanted in part by a group, it is more likely that only a singer trained in the florid *kidung* style could perform any of these extended narratives from start to finish. Composed in different classical Javanese meters, of which there are many forms, the *kidung* consists of a series of episodes, each based on a specific stanza form having a fixed number of lines, a set number of syllables to each line, set vowel

---

[6] In Krōbōkan, where the word *charuk* is not known, the ensemble is known as the (*gamelan*) *saron*, while the *charuk* is simply referred to, inaccurately, as the *chungklik*.

endings to the lines, and its individual name referring not only to the stanza itself but also to its special chant form.

Today the practice of singing *kidung* to the accompaniment of the *charuk* or *gambang* ensemble has long been forgotten. A few of the more familiar *kidungs*, or at least certain passages from them, are still heard in the temple during worship, chanted without accompaniment by a group of men and women. Trained *kidung* specialists are still engaged for the elaborate weddings and cremation ceremonies of high-born Balinese. Occasionally a short *kidung* episode is included as a vocal interlude in a modern *kebyar* composition for dancer and gamelan, when the singer is heard during a pause in the instrumental music. But the *charuk* and *gambang* ensembles today play their inherited repertory of *gendings* bearing the names of ancient chant forms unaccompanied by the chanting of their texts. The playing of the music alone is ritualistically sufficient. The preservation of the different melodies in their instrumental form is considered important enough for them to be written down and carefully guarded.

Attempts on my part to find any older singer who was able to chant *kidungs* to *charuk* or *gambang* accompaniment met with no success. One singer, however, was finally discovered in Blahbatu who claimed to have sung with the *gambang* ensemble of that village in his younger days, and did actually succeed in singing several stanzas to *gambang* accompaniment at my request. His method will be discussed later. For our present purpose, both *charuk* and *gambang* ensembles are considered entirely from an instrumental standpoint—as they survive today, completely severed from their former role.

The *charuk* and the two *sarons* together produce a seven-tone scale extending three

octaves, and ranging from an approximate to an approximate

As stated above, the *charuk* is furnished with eight keys, its scale ending with the octave or *penangkep*. Both *sarons*, however, have seven keys only, and lack the eighth tone of the *charuk*, *ding alit*. It is significant that the *saron*, the leading melodic instrument of the ensemble, is considered complete with seven keys only. The *ding alit* does not belong to the basic *saih 7* series, and is never found in the notation of *charuk* and *gambang* melodies.

As might be expected, there is the usual leeway found in the tuning of *charuk* ensembles. The *charuk* scale given below is taken from the *saron gedé* of the Krōbōkan ensemble. It is chosen in order to compare it with the *saron* scale from the *gambang* ensemble in the same village, already presented in Charts 1 and 2. Both these ensembles belonged to the same musicians, who claimed that their repertory of *gendings* could be played with either set of instruments.

Two *saih 7* scales compared, Krōbōkan village

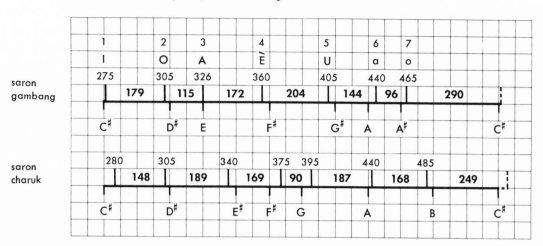

These are different tunings indeed for two ensembles which play the same music and are considered interchangeable. Different again is the tuning of the *gambang* ensemble of Sukawati, which presents still another version of the *saih 7* scale. It is this tuning which is chosen here to represent the *charuk* and *gambang* scale system as described in the following pages.

Saih 7, saron gambang, Sukawati village

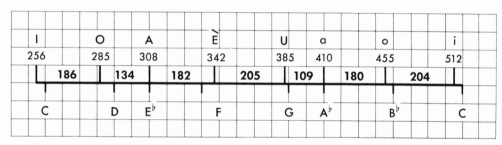

When the two component parts of the *charuk* are placed together, the eight keys are found arranged in an unusual order, with the four higher tones of the scale located at the left. Similarly, the highest tone in the *saron* scale, *dong alit*, lies to the left of the instrument. The full instrumental scale of the ensemble is found, from the positions of the players, in the order:[7]

Ex. 256. Charuk ensemble; instrumental ranges

---

[7] On occasion I have found the two parts of the *charuk* placed in reverse order, and the larger turned around, so that the series of keys ran, 4 3 2 1 6 5 8 7, as though it were of no importance to the player which way the sequence ran. I have observed this elsewhere, musicians playing rapid *kōtèkan* passages on a reversed instrument with equal ease.

Wherever questioned, *charuk* musicians invariably claimed that the *gending charuk* and the *gending gambang* were the same. Only the styles of playing were different. While manuscripts specifically labeled *gending charuk* are rare, collections of *gending gambang* are relatively common. I finally discovered, however, in the village of Selat, an old manuscript containing seventeen "*gending charuk*," inscribed in Balinese notation. The owner, an old acquaintance, agreed to copy the contents, and later presented me with a notebook facsimile. The notation system agreed with that of the Sukawati *gambang* notation system, shown on page 58, with the exception that the symbol for *dong ageng* was modified, and the symbol, *suku*, substituted for *rōh* to express the tone, *dung*.

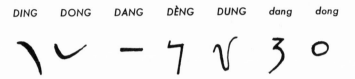

DING   DONG   DANG   DÈNG   DUNG   dang   dong

The *gendings*, copied in their original order, are systematically arranged according to scale formation, of which the *lontar*, however, made no mention, the name only of each *gending* appearing at the beginning of its notation. Some *gendings* are entirely pentatonic throughout; some employ a sesondary, *pemèro* tone. Others include two *pemèro* tones making full use of the seven-tone scale. In the following table these *gendings* are listed in the order found in the original *lontar* and later transcribed. They are grouped and numbered here according to their basic scale formation. *Pemèro* tones are underlined. The right-hand column gives the opening and final tones of each *gending*.

Saih 7; saron			I	O	A	È	U	a	o	
scale type	gending				scale formation					first and final tones
1.	Genihyat		I	•	A	È	•	a	o	A – A
	Demung									A – A
	Pangrus									A – È
	Malat									I – a
	Pamadana									A – È
2.	Manyura		I	•	A	È	U	•	o	A – A
	Pelugon		I	•	A	È	U	a	o	È – I
	Jabugarum		I	O	A	È	U	a	o	O – I
	Martamasa									I – È
3.	Panji Marga		I	O	A	•	U	a	•	A – O
	Wasih									A – A
	Nyurang Danu		I	O	A	•	U	a	o	A – È
4.	Wargasari		•	O	A	•	U	a	o	A – A
	Megatkung									A – U
5.	Chupak		I	O	A	È	U	a	o	U – U
6.	Madu Alas		I	O	•	È	U	•	o	U – U
1.	Pengalungra		I	•	A	È	•	a	o	I – a

FOUR SACRED ENSEMBLES

Of the six different scale types given here, only one—No. 3—is found in its basic form, located thus on the *saron:*

Ex. 257.

Because of the one-octave range of the *saron,* the other scales are found in various forms of inversion. When the ensemble accompanied vocal melody, such inversion must have been less evident, since the voice would be free to travel up or down beyond the *saron* range, giving the melodic line its full extension.[8]

The method of performing the *gending charuk* is extremely simple. The basic melody is sounded in octaves by the two *sarons,* while the *charuk* closely follows the melodic line, filling in with repeated notes and passing-tones. The passage-work is divided between the right and left hands. The first tone of the *charuk* scale, *ding (ageng),* is always sounded together with the eighth tone, *ding alit,* to produce the octave. Otherwise the figuration remains in unison. Just how the irregular distribution of the *charuk* keys affects the division of right and left hand parts may be seen in the following example. The excerpt includes the introduction and beginning of the first melodic period from the *gending, Manyura,* belonging to the second scale type shown above, and containing no *pemèro* tones.

Ex. 258. Gending Manyura, charuk ensemble; excerpt $\quad \boldsymbol{\lozenge} = 56$

---

[8] It was gratifying to find in the Selat *lontar* as many as ten *gendings* whose names not only appear in the listing of *gambang* melodies by Kunst some twenty years before in *Toonkunst van Bali, 1,* Table 15, but are located on the very same scale tones. I have numbered the different scale types in the order they occurred in the Selat *lontar,* since that is the order in which the repertory was said to be played. Kunst, following his own method, lists my third scale type as type 1. A comparison of the above table with that of Kunst's, however, shows those *gendings* found in each to have the same scale formation. Absent in Kunst's table is the scale I have listed as No. 6, of which there was only one example in the *lontar.* It is evident that while actual tunings in the *charuk* and *gambang* ensembles may vary considerably, an established and ancient scale system still survives.

269

1. sarons gedé and chenik
2. charuk

Ex. 258 is typical of the *charuk* style; all *gendings* are played alike, without change in tempo or dynamics. Attention is called to two stylistic clichés, both rhythmic: *a)* the little breaks in the otherwise monotonous continuity of the *charuk* figuration,

Ex. 259.

and *b)* the sudden syncopated change in the steady progression of the *saron* melody which occurs at the end of the introduction:

Ex. 260.

This characteristic rhythmic change is generally found near the end of a melodic section, as though to stress the approach of the closing tone or anticipate the beginning of a new melodic period. It becomes a prominent feature of the *saron* melody as played in the *gambang* ensemble.

270

The *gending charuk* all show the same basic form. The *gending* is composed of a series of extended melodic units separated from each other by the *charik*, the comma or break. These melodic units, also referred to by the term, *charik*, are of unequal length, and in the Selat *lontar* each *gending* contains four *chariks*. The complete *gending* may be considered as a single stanza or statement, and ends with the *charik kali* (double *charik*) which corresponds to the period. The complete stanza is repeated several times.

Since there is no punctuating instrument to mark the *charik*, this may be achieved through a slight pause in the music, or by a short break in the *saron* melody while the *charuk* figuration continues without interruption. Occasionally the entire *gending* is played through with no perceptible break in the melody other than passing syncopations such as those shown above.

While the notation of the *gendings* includes *charik* punctuation, it offers no clue for the uninitiated as to how the melody is to be scanned. In actual practice, as shown in the following example, the melodic line begins with an "upbeat."[9] This is not only borne out through the interpretation of the melody by the *charuk* figuration but is more strongly confirmed, as shown later, in the *saron* melody as played in the *gambang* ensemble, and in *gambang* compositions when rearranged for the modern *gamelan gong kebyar* or *pelègongan*.

Several examples of *saron* melody, as performed in the *charuk* ensemble, are given here. The first, the opening *charik* to *gending Megatkung*, belongs to scale type 4 of the table on page 268.

Ex. 261. Gending Megatkung, charuk ensemble.

Had the *saron* a sufficient range, a more natural flow of the melody would seem to be:

Ex. 262.

Lying more naturally within the *saron* range are those *gendings* belonging to scale type 3.

---

[9] The writer is forced to use the far from ideal Western term here for lack any Balinese term even remotely suggesting an upbeat.

Ex. 263. Gending Panji Marga; first charik

As an example of *saron* melody in which two *pemèro* tones occur, the first *charik* to *gending Jabugarum* is given here. Despite the two additional tones, this *gending* belongs to the same scale type as that of *gending Manyura*, already quoted in Ex. 258. The two *pemèro* tones are indicated by the symbol, (p).

Ex. 264. Gending Panji Marga; first charik

The *gambang* ensemble

Heard only during the *ngabèn* ceremonies attending the cremating of the dead is the *gamelan gambang*, the small ensemble of xylophones and one or two *sarons* that plays off and on through the three days preceding the actual cremation. The repertory of compositions is essentially the same as that of the *charuk*, but here the simple style of the *charuk* ensemble has been transformed into the most complex form of polyrhythmic interplay known in Bali. The system of instrumental organization remains basically the same. The melody is usually sounded in octaves on a pair of seven-keyed *sarons* similar to those used in the *charuk* ensemble. Figuration accompaniment is performed by a quartet of large bamboo-keyed xylophones of a special type known as *gambang*.[10] This figuration is composed of four separate but interlocking parts which dovetail in a complicated manner to create a rapid and unbroken continuity.

The method of involving the four *gambangs* in this complex interplay is of particular interest here, not only in itself but for its historical value. Instruments identical to those used in Bali today may be seen in the reliefs of the Panataron, immediately recognized because of their unusual shape and the peculiar arrangement of their keys. Because of their construction and the Y-shaped form of the sticks used in striking the instruments, little if any change in

---

[10] Not to be confused with the Javanese *gambang*, a form of xylophone similar to the Balinese *chungklik*.

instrumental technique could have taken place through the years. By its very nature the *gambang* ensemble requires specially trained musicians, who usually devote themselves to this form of music and no other.

The *gambang* is actually a more highly developed form of *charuk*, with a seven-tone scale that extends through a second octave. The fourteen keys are strung together in the method used for the charuk and the instruments of the *gamelan selundèng*, and are suspended over a low, hollowed wooden base which forms the resonator (Figs. 77, 78). The playing is done with a pair of forked sticks, the *panggul gambang*. The forks spread at such an angle as to sound the octave when the keys are struck. Right and left hands strike in irregular alternation, creating rhythmic patterns which interlock with those of the other *gambangs*. At first glance, the fourteen *gambang* keys appear to be shuffled in complete disorder, three shorter keys to the left, the two longest to the right, and the remaining keys arranged in ascending order between the two outer sets. The arrangement, however, is far from haphazard, and proves to be an ingenious system by means of which the forked sticks may produce octaves at all times without having to encompass the unwieldy span of eight keys.

The *saron gambang*, like the *saron charuk*, produces the *saih 7* scale in its basic form, beginning with the tone, *ding:*

Ex. 265. Saih 7 gambang; saron gedé

I   O   A   È   U   a   o*

---

* The last tone, dong alit, is actually found to the left of the series, as on the saron charuk.

The four *gambangs* differ in size and range, each starting the *saih 7* scale on a different tone, and extending through a second octave. The four instruments have distinguishing names, which vary regionally. They are listed here starting with the smallest, with their names as found in the village of Blahbatu.

Ex. 266. The four gambang ranges

1. pametit

2. penyelat

3. pemèro

4. pengentèr*

---

* Pametit; small one; penyelat, in between; pemèro, in between (as the pemèro tone); pengentèr, leader. In the village of Krambitan, the instruments are named: 1, pametit, 2 and 3, pemèro, 4, pengedé. Kunst gives seven variants in gambang nomenclature.

The keys of each *gambang* are arranged in the order shown in the following diagram. In the *pengentèr* these keys produce the scale in the sequence given below. Dotted lines indicate the position of the cross-bars which support the strings and divide the keys into two groups of three each, and four groups of two's. For reasons explained presently, the normal division between right and left hand movement lies between the seventh and the eighth keys.

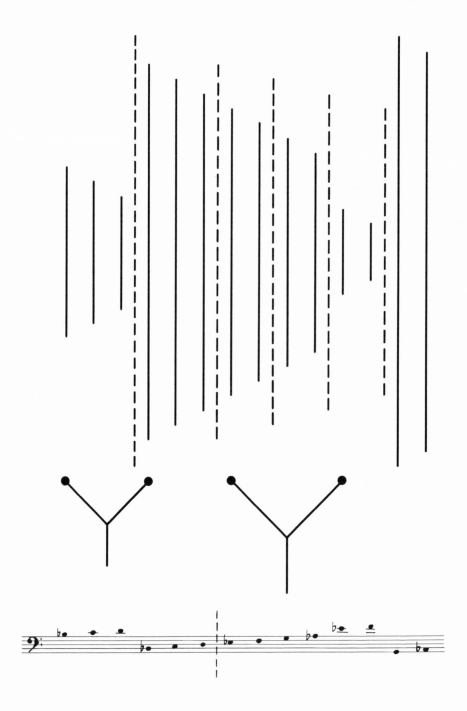

It will be seen from the diagram that the angles of the two forked hammers are not the same. The left fork must skip two keys to produce the octave. The right fork has a greater span; owing to the different arrangement of the keys, three must be skipped to sound the octave. If the left hand passes a step or so above the normal range, fourths are produced, while if the right hand passes below, fifths result. These smaller intervals are occasionally heard in the figuration, but octave playing is the normal *gambang* method. Ex. 267 gives the *gambang* scale as found on the four instruments, with left- and right-hand octaves produced by each.

Ex. 267. Arrangement of gambang keys and resulting octaves

The reason for the existence of so involved a system merely to produce octaves probably lies in the nature of *gambang* passage-work, which is primarily rhythmic and based, as will be shown, on patterns produced by the irregular alternation of right and left hands. This gives each part in the figuration a special rhythmic vitality that would be completely lacking were both hands to travel continuously in parallel octaves. Combined, the four *gambangs* produce an unbroken and staccato polyrhythmic accompaniment, of peculiar, rather hollow resonance because of the octaves and relatively low pitch of the instruments. Above this the ringing *saron* melody, likewise sounding in octaves, offers strong contrast and is clearly audible at all times.

The *gending gambang* differ from the *gending charuk* only in that the repertory is much larger. All show the same basic form—a series of melodic units of different lengths separated from each other by the punctuating *charik*. During the melodic sections the four *gambangs* develop a complex figuration accompaniment that is constantly changing as it follows the melody as played by the *saron*. The *charik*, which marks the end of each melodic section, may be indicated by a short break in the music, or by an extended pause in the *saron* melody while the *gambangs* continue, filling in the melodic pause with repeating patterns that are now rhythmic rather than melodic.

Characteristic interplay between the four *gambangs* is more easily shown in the passage-work heard during a break in the *saron* melody. In Ex. 268 the fourth *gambang*, lowest in pitch, is seen to furnish steady rhythmic support. The first and third *gambangs* supply interlocking figuration, simple or syncopated, while the second *gambang* is more or less a filling-in instrument.

Ex. 268. Gambang accompaniment

The surprisingly harmonic nature of *gambang* figuration is more apparent when a passage such as the above is reduced to condensed notation:

Ex. 269.

The frequency of thirds and extended "chords," resulting from the movement of the different parts, is characteristic of all *gambang* figuration, giving an unusual fullness to the ensemble, while the parts dovetail in such a way as to produce a continuous succession of repeated tones.

When such a passage as the above is transposed to another scale type, the parts must change because of instrumental limitations. In the following example, the patterns of Ex. 268a are transposed a fourth lower. Because of the disposition of the *gambang* keys the interplay of left and right hands in each part is found to be reversed.

276

Ex. 270. Transposition of Ex. 268, a fourth lower

The *saron* melody is performed in an unusual and characteristic rhythmic manner, of which, however, there is no indication in the *lontar* notations. Instead of allowing each tone the same time value, the melody is played in what seems to be a casual, almost faltering way, as though the musician could not follow with precision the basic beat and was playing a careless 3/4 against a 4/4 unit of *gambang* accompaniment:

Ex. 271.

This, however, proves to be far from the case. So lax a beat is completely foreign to the feeling for rhythmic tension shown by the Balinese at all times. Careful listening reveals that the *saron* part is actually played in the syncopated form noted in the following example, a rhythmic style associated exclusively with the *gending gambang*. We shall later find this traditional style exploited by Balinese composers seeking new material and effects (Ex. 294, 337, 338). The melodic excerpt given here is from the last *charik* of *gending Manyura*, already quoted in *charuk* form in Ex. 258. Toward the close will be found rhythmic changes similar to those in the *charuk* melody.

Ex. 272. Gending Manyura; saron gambang ♩ = 120

Characteristic accompaniment of the *saron* melody by the *gambangs* is shown in Ex. 273. The figuration now moves freely and is in a state of constant change. The first and fourth *gambangs* are seen to follow the *saron* melody, while the remaining two fill in with characteristic patterns.

Ex. 273. Saron melody and gambang figuration ♩ = 120

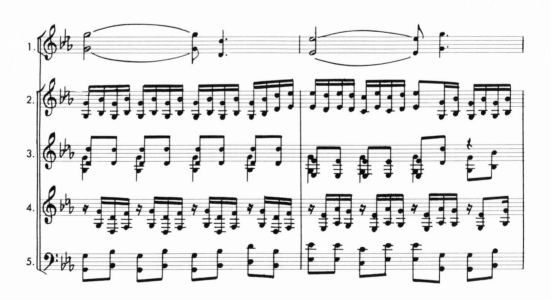

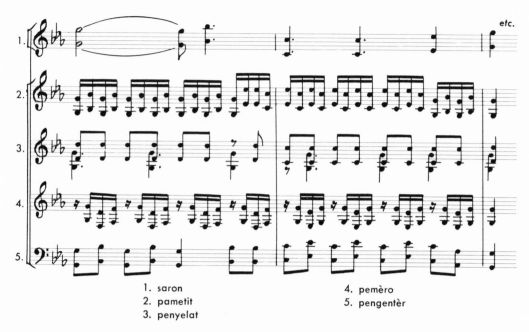

1. saron
2. pametit
3. penyelat

4. pemèro
5. pengentèr

Ex. 273 hardly begins to show the variety in patterns and freedom of movement in the different parts. It can only suggest the general style and organization of the *gambang* ensemble. The total effect is one of sustained melody which is at the same time kept in constant vibrato by the incessantly repeating melodic tones in the *gambang* accompaniment.

Occasionally, instead of a large and small *saron* pitched an octave apart, a pair of large *sarons* tuned in approximate thirds is used, so that the melody is played throughout in thirds instead of octaves.

Ex. 274.

sarons   1.
         2.

I found the effect of the *saron* melody when sounded in thirds strangely melancholy and unforgettable, for these were thirds impossible to obtain in a tempered system of tuning. Moreover, the two *sarons* may be quite out of tune with each other. I once heard in Kabakaba village a pair of *sarons* whose tuning I did not obtain but which, according to my notes, transformed the melody into something like the following:

Ex. 275.

sarons

279

Ensembles with *sarons* tuned in thirds, however, are rare. Two *sarons* pitched an octave apart are generally employed, and occasionally the large *saron* is used alone.

It is difficult to imagine how so resonant and complexly organized an ensemble could once have served to accompany singing. It would completely cover a single voice, and its rhythmically taut continuity is very different from the relaxed *kidungs* which men and women intone in the temples today. Long drawn-out phrases, separated by pauses, follow one another in the leisurely manner of Gregorian chant. The melodic line always moves conjunctly, passing from tone to tone with none of the wide leaps which characterize the *saron* melody.

Such leaps were not uncommon, however, with singers specially trained in *kidung*. This was demonstrated for me by the *kidung* specialist whom I found in 1937 in Blahbatu village. He was a man of perhaps sixty, and although he stated he had not sung with *gambang* for a great many years, he was willing to try at my request. The attempt was not too successful. The Blahbatu *gambang* players with whom he had once sung were no longer alive, and the present musicians knew few of the *gendings* known to my informant, who in turn had forgotten the texts. Singer and musicians finally succeeded in getting through a few stanzas of the *kidung, Manukaba,* of which the opening *charik* is given here. Unfortunately, I do not have the *kawi* text to accompany the excerpt. The singer succeeded in paralleling the *saron* melody closely enough, introducing little embellishments from time to time. The relaxed attack of the voice, however, which was not so precisely on the beat as the *saron,* seemed to negate the syncopated nature of the *saron* melody, more nearly approaching the rhythmic notation given in Ex. 276.

Ex. 276. Kidung Manukaba; first charik ♩ = appr. 90

FOUR SACRED ENSEMBLES

It is, of course, impossible to determine just how representative Ex. 276 is of *kidung* melody when sung to *gambang* accompaniment. The excerpt is included here as part of the scant information available about a long discontinued practice. The many leaps of a seventh, when an adjacent tone in or from the other direction would seem more vocally natural, could be influenced by the restrictions of the *saron* melody. Such leaps, however, are common in *kidung* melody as sung by trained soloists of today.[11] The discontinuation of *kidung* accompanied by *gambang* is a regrettable loss. Any survival would have thrown much-needed light on an earlier relationship existing between vocal and instrumental melody.

The *gamelan luang*

With the *gamelan luang*, sometimes referred to as the *gong luang*, the group of sacred ensembles with a seven-tone scale is complete. This small orchestra of eight or nine instruments has somewhat the appearance of a *gamelan gong* reduced to essentials. For the separate rites connected with death, cremation, and the later dispersal of the ashes in the sea, it is still the custom in certain districts to engage this ancient gamelan to play a special repertory of sacred compositions known as the *gending luang*. With a slight change of instruments the orchestra may also be used in the temple, substituting for the customary *gamelan gong* as it accompanies the various ceremonial dances performed by men or women.

The antique instruments included in the *gamelan luang*, the seven-tone scale, and the old style of performing, have gradually brought about the almost complete abandonment of this ensemble, whose lovely resonance and tranquil music set it quite apart from the other orchestras. In the thirties there were perhaps no more than ten still active in Bali, six to my actual knowledge, the rest by hearsay. In the few villages where unbroken sets of instruments still remained but were no longer used, the word was always the same; the *seka* had long since broken up and no new players were to be found. In Singapadu, however, a village some ten miles south of Sayan, there were two complete and active gamelans, one in *banjar* Sèséh, the other in *banjar* Ampuan. Both were frequently engaged by nearby villages, and the Ampuan gamelan, the better known, was often booked for three weeks running in villages more distantly located.

The following pages deal with the *gamelan luang* of Ampuan, which was identical to that of Sèséh, but whose instruments were in better condition. The musicians, a group of middle-aged men, not only played with authority but gave their information with simple conviction. The gamelan was frequently brought to my house in Sayan where, in long and relaxed music sessions, *gendings* could be repeated and passages interrupted on request. By happy chance, the tuning of the Ampuan gamelan could be approximated with my piano without too much distortion, as may be seen from the following chart, and my notations of the polyphonic figuration characteristic of this ensemble were constantly checked in play-back.

---

[11] This can be heard in various Odeon and Beka recordings of *kidung* and *kekawin*. See Appendix 6, Recordings.

281

Saih 7, gamelan luang, gangsa gedé; banjar Ampuan

275		305		345	371		410		466		515	(550)

| | 180 | | 213 | | 126 | | 173 | | 222 | | 172 | | 114 | |

| D♭ | | E♭ | | F | G♭ | | A♭ | | B♭ | | C | D♭ |
| 274 | | 307.5 | | 345 | 366 | | 410.5 | | 461 | | 517 | 548 |

For the *gending luang* ten players are required for the gamelan, which is composed of the following instruments:

instruments	players
1 gangsa chenik ⎱	1
1 gangsa gedé ⎰	
2 jegogans	1
1 bamboo saron[12]	1
1 16-gong trompong	4
1 kendang wadon	1
1 gong ageng	1
1 set of chèngchèngs	1

In the temple, the bamboo *saron* is omitted; its archaic figuration is too static for music intended for dance accompaniment. A *kendang lanang* is added to form the necessary pair of interlocking drums, and the colotomic section of the ensemble is enlarged by the addition of *kempur* and *kelenang*.

The method of orchestration combines the systems of the *charuk* ensemble and the *gamelan gong*. The *pōkok* tones are sounded in octaves on the two *gangsas*, and stressed at regular intervals by the pair of *jegogans*. The *saron* performs typical *charuk* figuration shown in Ex. 258. The unique feature of the *gamelan luang*, however, is the so-called sixteen-gong "*trompong*," here played by four men who create a special form of melodic polyphony deriving from the *pōkok* tones of the *saron*.[12] The single drum is no longer an agogic instrument, but alternates at fixed places with the *gong ageng* in punctuating the musical period. For dance accompaniment, the *trompong* takes the place of the *gangsas* in the *gamelan pelègongan*, playing animated two-part figuration similar to the *kōtèkan*.

The solfeggio system of the *gamelan luang* differs from the other ensembles discussed in this chapter, following the *gambuh* system in which the five head tones, *ding, dong, dèng, dung, dang*, have no final position in the seven-tone scale, but shift with transposition of the basic five-tone scale. The two secondary tones are known as *mèro* or *pemèro*.

No *lontars* containing notation of the *gending luang* are known to exist. While the repertory of music played for temple ceremonies is more or less standard, the number of *gending luang*

---

[12] The *saron* listed above is actually a xylophone of the *charuk* type. The true *saron* is here called *gangsa*. Because the bamboo "*saron*" is included in the *luang* ensemble the gamelan is also known as the *gamelan saron*.

performed today is small. The Ampuan men knew only four *gendings* or *tembang*,[13] as they more often called them, and six *jalans* (ways) or scales in which the *tembang* could be played. In referring to the different *jalans* they also used the words *ambah* (go by way of) and *tekep* (cover). Thus they would say, in announcing a composition they were about to play, "*Tembang Lilit, jalan Panji Chenik*," "the *tembang, Lilit*, by way of *Panji Chenik*." Their small basic repertory could thus be varied by transposing the four compositions from one scale to another.[14]

The seven *jalans* are located on the *gangsa* in the following order:

Ex. 277.

gangsa								name of jalan*
1.	i	o	è	•	u	a	•	Panji chenik
2.	•	i	o	è	•	u	a	Panji gedé
3.	a	•	i	o	è	•	u	Wargasari
4.	u	a	•	i	o	è	•	Nyura gedé
5.	•	u	a	•	i	o	è	Panji miring
6.	è	•	u	a	•	i	o	Nyura chenik
7.	o	è	•	u	a	•	i	Kartika

* These names may partly derive from the gambang repertory. Wargasari and Panji are the names of two different kidungs, the first chanted today in the temple. Nyura, or Manyura, peacock, and Kartika, or Kartikaya, the war-god of Hindu mythology, are the names of two Indian ragas.

Not all seven *jalans* were used by the Ampuan musicians. Their preference seemed to be for the first four, and of these the most frequently heard were *Panji chenik* and *Wargasari*. I was told that much of the music played in the temple, especially for the women's dances, was played "*jalan Wargasari*," the scale which closely resembles *Selisir gong*, though pitched somewhat higher.

To demonstrate the system of transposition, my informants once played two complete *tembangs* in six of the seven *jalans*, although they were ordinarily played in only three— *Panji chenik, Wargasari*, and *Nyura gedé*. They began with *Panji chenik*, the first and lowest of the *jalans* listed above, and announced each *jalan* in turn. As the transpositions rose step by step, more and more melodic adjustments had to be made on the one-octave instruments. Allowing for these adjustments, the transpositions proved to be remarkably faithful, as the different versions of the *gangsa* melody given in the following example will show. These,

[13] Ordinarily, *tembang* means a stanza form in poetry, but also implies its particular scale form and melodic structure.

[14] Kunst, in *Toonkunst van Bali, 1*, 35s, states exactly the reverse, giving three scale forms, of which *Lilit* is one, and six *gendings*.

noted tone for tone as they were played, vary only in an occasional substitutional tone. The excerpt given here consists of the first melodic period in *tembang Lilit*, metrically classified as *tabuh 8*. The period is seen to have eight *jegogan* stress tones, indicated by the symbol, >, and the equivalent of sixty-four *pōkok* tones when the final tone is given its full time value. Thus the period is half the metric length of *tabuh 8* in the *gending gong*. The period terminates with a gong stroke, preceded by three drum accents, >, which always recur in exactly the same place. Except for these accents the drum is silent. The complete *tembang* consists of eleven similar metric units having the same drum accentuation, some joined together, some separated by brief *trompong* interludes.

Ex. 278. Tembang Lilit, gamelan luang; six gangsa variants ♩ = 72

The melodic transformations which take place with transposition are less noticeable in the *gamelan luang* than in the *charuk* and *gambang* ensembles, where the *saron* takes the melodic lead. In the *gamelan luang* the *gangsa* melody plays a less prominent part, serving as support for the polyphonic development of the melody by the *trompong*.

284

FOUR SACRED ENSEMBLES

The *trompong* of the *luang* ensemble is similar to the *bonang* of the Javanese gamelan, and older musicians frequently call it by that name. It consists of sixteen small gongs, similar to those found in the usual *trompong*, though smaller and mounted horizontally in the usual way. The gongs are arranged in a double row (Fig. 80), and produce the two-octave scale in the following order:

16	15	14	13	12	11	10	9
1	2	3	4	5	6	7	8

The four players sit on the outside of the two rows in facing pairs, each with four gongs at his disposal. But when playing in scales pitched higher than *Wargasari* the players change their position, the first taking, say, gongs 3 to 6, the second, now moving to the end of the instrument, taking gongs 7 to 10, as may be seen in Fig. 80. The third player shifts accordingly, while the fourth drops out. The essence of the *trompong* melodic figuration, here known by the old name, *sekatian*, lies in the interlocking parts of the first two players, the other two for the most part doubling an octave higher.

The relation of the *sekatian* to the *gangsa* melody may be seen in the following excerpt, Ex. 279, the introduction and beginning of *gending Galuh*, in the *jalan, Wargasari*. The introduction, the *penyumu*, is divided between the first two *trompong* players, the other two entering shortly before the actual *gending*. It is interesting to note how the tones of the *gangsa* melody occur first in one part then in the other, the two parts uniting in melodious polyphony. Where three tones are shown simultaneously in the *trompong* figuration, the highest, which completes the melodic line, belongs to the part performed by the third player. The *gending* itself is part of the temple repertory, played for the slow processional dance, *gegaluh*, which is performed by the unmarried girls of the village.

Ex. 279. Gending Galuh; jalan Wargasari ♩ = 44–50

Like all the functional music played by the *gamelan luang* in the temple, this *gending* is completely pentatonic ("*tan medaging pemèro*," or "it doesn't contain *pemèro*"). Three of the four actual *gending luang*, however, make use of a sixth tone or *pemèro*, situated between the tones *dèng* and *dung*. The *pemèro* may occur in the melody merely as an occasional passing-tone. More often it is treated as a substituting tone, giving the effect of a complete change in tonality. Thus, for example, a *gending* opening in the scale form known as *Panji chenik* can change tonality with the substitution of the *pemèro* tone for the third tone of the basic scale, *dèng*. By reintroducing the original *dèng* and dropping the *pemèro* tone the *gending* returns to its original tonality.

Ex. 280.

Just how the two modulations are instrumentally accomplished may be learned from the next two examples. They could hardly be smoother or more natural had they been worked out on paper. Characteristic of these changes is the appearance of the modulating passage in the figuration prior to the tonal change in the basic melody.

Ex. 281. Modulation to new tonality

286

Ex. 282. Return to opening tonality

The *gending luang* have a formal structure quite their own. Each consists of a single movement, composed of a series of melodic units of equal length, which, joined together, give the effect of broad, continuous melody that is only completely stated with the closing *gong* stroke at the end of the *gending*. The melodic unit is here called the *palet*, the term ordinarily used for a phrase unit within a melodic period. Two of the four *gendings* known to the Ampuan men, *Ginada* and *Saih Miring*, are classified as *tabuh 4*. These have thirty-two *pōkok* tones or the metric equivalent to the *palet*, and four *jegogan* stress tones. The other two *gendings*, *Lilit* and *Ririg*, are classified as *tabuh 8*, having sixty-four *pōkok* tones and eight *jegogan* stress tones to the *palet*. The drumming is the same for all four *gendings*. As shown in Ex. 277, the drum is silent throughout the *palet* until the approach of the *gong* stroke which marks the end of one *palet* and the beginning of the next. Three anticipatory accents are given, using the drum stick, and the *gong* stroke is intensified by a final accent.

Of unusual interest, both for melodic structure and for constant shift back and forth between two different tonalities is the *gending*, *Saih Miring*, an analysis of which will give some idea of the unusual form of the *gending luang*. Nothing short of quotation in full of this composition can reveal the involved melodic plan and subtle interplay of two opposing tonalities.

As already stated, *Saih Miring* belongs to the *tabuh 4* category. It consists of eight *palets* of thirty-two *pōkok* tones or their metric equivalent, with four *jegogan* stress tones to the *palet*. Each *palet* is introduced with a *gong* stroke which at the same time marks the end of the preceding *palet*. In basic form the *gending* is constructed on the A B A pattern. *Palet 1* (A) consists of a complete musical statement, ending with a short pause, which returns as the concluding *palet 8*. The main body of the composition (B) extends from *palet 2* through *palet 7*. Here the *gending* continually unfolds in a series of melodic units which keep returning in changed order, always in a new relation to the basic metric plan.

The version of *Saih Miring* given here is that of the *gending* as it is played in the first and lowest *jalan*, *Panji chenik*. By means of a substituting *pemèro* tone, tonal change similar to that described above frequently takes place; the *gending* will be found to be based on the interplay of the two tonalities given in Ex. 280.

The balance between the two tonalities may be seen from the following table, in which the tonal changes are listed as they occur during the course of the *gending* and as they are found in relation to *palet* structure:

	palets	tonalities		
A	1.	1	2	1
	2.	1	2	
	3.	2	1	
	4.	1		
	5.	1	2	1
B	6.	2	1	
	7.	1	2	
A	8.	1	2	1

In Ex. 284 the introduction or *penyumu* and the first *palet* of *Saih Miring* are given in full orchestral form. The rest of the *gending* is reduced to *gangsa* and *saron* parts, which contain the melodic essence of the composition. Here the tonal changes can immediately be noted, sometimes occurring simultaneously in the two parts, sometimes anticipated in the *saron* part. Attention is called to the increasing syncopations in the *gangsa* melody as the *gending* progresses, which also occur in the *trompong* figuration. Note should also be made of little refrain motifs which recur in the *saron* part, notably:

Ex. 283.

Ex. 284. Tembang Saih Miring; jalan Panji chenik ♩ = 72

288

The complex melodic structure of *Saih Miring* is most clearly shown when the *pōkok* tones are expressed in cyphers as they occur in the *saih 7*.

	i	o	è	p	u	a	•
	1	2	3	4	5	6	•

By breaking up the *pōkok* continuity into small melodic units or tonal sequences of different lengths, we find the melody unfolding in an irregular though methodical way, progressing, returning to a previous tonal sequence, progressing further, returning to a still earlier sequence, until it reaches the final *palet*, a restatement of the first. In the dissection (Ex. 285) of the complete *gending* the component melodic units are indicated alphabetically. It will be seen that these units, when repeated, always recur in new relation to the *palet* scheme of thirty-two *pōkok* tones, until the restatement contained in the last *palet*.

Ex. 285. Tembang Saih Miring, tabuh 4; pōkok tones

palet scheme:

```
32 pōkok    • • • • • • • • • • • • • • • • • • • • • • • • • • • •
tones    G


                                                       (H)
palet                                      penyumu:  3 1 5 3 1 5 2 2


         A                B                C
A  1.    5 5 3 2 5 1 1 5  1 1 1 1 5 5 1 1  6 1 3 5 1 6 2 1 4 4 2 1 4 1 1 3

         D                C                              E
   2.    3 • 3 2 3 3 2 2  6 1 3 5 1 6 2 1 4 4 2 1 4 1 1 3 3 3 1 3 5 2 4 4

                          F                              B
   3.    2 • 4 4 2 4 2 1  4 4 2 1 4 2 4 4 2 2 2 2 3 6 3 3 1 1 1 1 5 5 1 1

         G                H                I
   4.    6 3 2 1 • 6 6 3  3 1 5 3 1 5 2 2  5 5 1 1 3 3 2 2 5 3 1 1 • 3 3 1

                                           H              C
B  5.    1 1 5 1 2 2 4 4 2 • 4 4 2 2 4 1  3 1 5 3 2 5 2 2 6 1 3 5 1 6 2 1

                          E                              I
   6.    4 • 2 1 4 1 1 3  3 3 1 1 5 2 4 4 2 • 4 4 2 1 2 3 5 5 1 1 3 3 2 2

                                                        H
   7.    6 3 1 1 • 3 3 1  1 1 5 1 2 2 4 4 2 2 4 4 2 4 4 1 3 1 5 3 1 5 2 2

         A                B                C
A  8.    5 5 3 2 5 1 1 5  1 1 1 1 5 5 1 1  6 1 3 5 1 6 2 1 4 4 2 1 4 1 1 3

         D
(2.)     3
```

The formation of the melody and its contrapuntal relation to the *palet* structure as defined by the *gong* accents can be summed up by the following chart. Here the melodic units are shown in terms of their relative length and given in their order of recurrence. An asymmetrical but balanced pattern is created that runs quite counter to the structural accents of the *gong* (●).

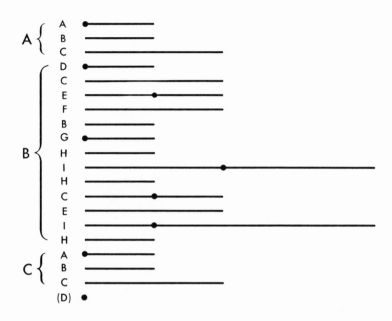

The general musical effect of *Saih Miring,* with its frequent tonal shifts and flowing melodic polyphony, is one of archaic beauty. Like the other *gending luang,* the piece is played without nuance, and with no change in tempo beyond a slight rallentando at the end of the first and the last *palets.*

The gamelan itself, because of its small size and unusual combination of instruments, has a distinctive and lovely sound. The contrasting movement and different timbres of the *gangsa, trompong,* and *saron,* sustained at intervals by the *jegogan* and *gong,* create an orchestral resonance unlike that of any other Balinese gamelan. The cymbals are used with discretion and do no more than add a rhythmic shimmer to the ensemble. When augmented by a second drum and additional small gongs to accompany ritual dances such as *baris* and *mèndèt,* the gamelan loses some of its distinction. But when the *gending luang* are performed, because of the long intervals between drum accents and the absence of secondary punctuating instruments, the effect is very different. An impression of utter serenity and timelessness is produced. The music seems suspended in mid air, supported only by the period reverberations of the *gong.* The word *luang* is said to mean universal space, void, emptiness. It may originally have suggested the special name for the gamelan. It might well refer to the actual *gendings* and the manner in which they are performed.

Chapter 17

The Gamelan Arja

A NIGHT performance of *arja*, the popular theater of Bali, never fails to draw a large audience, especially if the leading performers are well-known stars. Deriving from *gambuh* in style, but with a more sentimental repertory of plays, *arja* is the Balinese form of musical comedy, in which singing and spoken lines, stylized dance scenes, and amusing buffoonery are combined. Here is something for everyone—romance, melodrama, caricature, tender love songs, and ribald but hilarious puns.

The romantic scenes are played in the traditional formalized manner of the *gambuh* theater, half acted, half danced, but considerably speeded up in tempo. The songs, the *tembang arja*, of which Balinese never seem to tire, are sung by the leading characters and have *kawi* texts composed in classical Javanese meters of the late Majapahit period. They are given a line by line translation into colloquial Balinese by an attendant, which means that the singer must pause at the end of each line for the spoken clarification. The comic interludes are generally spoken in everyday Balinese. If the comedians are skilled, many of the lines and jokes are topical and improvised on the spur of the moment. This is especially so in *arja selusupan*, in which favorite actors and dancers from different companies are engaged to give an unrehearsed all-star performance.

The little instrumental ensemble used for the *arja* plays is ideal for vocal and dance accompaniment. The gamelan is composed of no more than one or two small *sulings*, two drums, a set of small cymbals or *rinchik*, and two bamboo *guntangs*, which will presently be described (Fig. 88). The ensemble is so soft in sound and light in timbre that every syllable of the songs can be heard. The musical repertory consists of three groups of compositions: *a*) the *pererèn*,[1] short instrumental pieces played before the performance begins which also serve as interludes between episodes or scenes, *b*) the pieces which accompany dance entrances, and *c*) the song accompaniments, which are also danced. In the songs the *sulings* become obligato instruments, weaving ornamental figuration around the voice in the octave above, and filling in the pauses for translation with melodic improvisation. Thus while the song is constantly interrupted by the rhythmically declaimed translation, the musical continuity remains unbroken from start to finish.

The special color of the *gamelan arja* derives largely from the *guntang*, a one-string bamboo zither which, when lightly struck, gives forth a soft but penetrating sound. The instrument is constructed from a section of bamboo, open at one end and closed by a nodal wall at the other. A thin strip is cut, but not detached, from the surface of the tube, and raised by bamboo pins wedged in at each end. A lengthwise opening is then cut into the tube below the raised strip. A wooden tongue is attached to the center of the strip which, through its added weight, prolongs the vibration of the strip.

---

[1] From *mererèn*, to pause or stop.

294

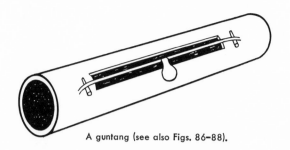

A guntang (see also Figs. 86–88).

Two *guntangs* are employed. A larger, so-called *kempur* supplies the main punctuation; the smaller, somewhat higher pitched *kempli* acts as time beater. The player sits with the *guntang* in his lap, the open end to his left, and holding the *panggul guntang*, a light stick, in his right hand. To imitate the pulsating tone of the bronze *kempur*, the player of the larger *guntang* holds his left hand across, but free of, the open end, with his thumb resting on the rim. As he strikes the instrument he rapidly flutters his palm over the opening. This increases the already throbbing tone of the *guntang*, almost ghostly in its softness. Most ensembles include a small gong, the *klènang* or *kelènang*, whose metallic ring adds a more precise note in the punctuation.

Ex. 286.

The instrumental combination described here is standard. Additional instruments, however, may be included for special effects. Occasionally one finds a pair of *lewanas*, the *gumanak* of the *gambuh* ensemble, augmenting the percussion group. Sometimes the Malayan *pantun*, a form of folk song based on a four-line stanza, is introduced among the songs. In this case, the Islamic *terbana* replaces the pair of drums. A toy form of *churing*, an antique two-octave *gangsa* formerly employed in the *gamelan Semar Pegulingan*, is sometimes added to the ensemble for exotic color (Fig. 89).

The *suling* used in the *gamelan arja* has a clear bright tone, slightly reedy but, if the bamboo is sufficiently aged, of remarkable sweetness. The average length is from ten to twelve inches, with a diameter of from three-quarters to one inch. The instrument is end-blown, and has an embouchure similar to that of the *suling gambuh*. Three types of *suling* are employed, with four, five, or six fingerholes. The four-hole *suling* produces a *sléndro*-type four-tone scale, popularly referred to as *saih angklung*. This *suling* does not properly belong to the *arja* ensemble, where it is used only for special effects. The five- and six-hole *sulings* are normally employed, and may be considered *pélog* instruments, since they are both used primarily to accompany *pélog* vocal melody. While the five-hole *suling* can produce a six-tone scale, from all closed to all open stops, it is generally restricted to a single five-tone scale. The six-hole *suling* can be used for both *pélog* and *sléndro* vocal melody.

The range of the *suling* extends to two octaves, but the highest tones, especially in the smaller *sulings*, are difficult to obtain and are seldom used. The pitch varies considerably, the

lowest tone of the scale ranging between and . It is usual for each of

the *suling* players to bring several instruments to a performance, in order to have a choice of pitches when accompanying the different singers.

Because of its convenient size, and the ease with which the tones are produced, the *suling arja* is a far more flexible instrument than the *suling gambuh*. The fingerholes are more closely spaced, and Balinese players delight in swift ornamental figuration—the *kōtèkan*—which they perform with lightness and grace. However these florid passages never cover up the voice. They serve mainly to fill in the vocal pauses between lines, when the translator is heard, and the longer melodic breaks between stanzas when the dancer moves about the stage. They are elaborately developed in the instrumental numbers. If two *sulings* are included in the ensemble, the *kōtèkan* is generally performed by a single player, while the other player pauses. In Ex. 287, an instrumental number, the *lagu* or melody is seen repeated several times in plain style, then followed by the improvised *kōtèkan* or variation.

Ex. 287. Pererèn arja; suling and guntangs ♩ = 144

The *arja* plays owe much of their popular appeal to the inclusion in the cast of young girls, as well as boys and older men. In many villages, the local *arja* society is primarily a recreational club for teenagers of both sexes. Unlike the boys, however, once married, a girl retires, her brief public career over.

There is complete disregard for sex, and sometimes even for age, in assigning roles. Both male and female parts may be played by girls, who, because of their higher pitched voices and more delicate physique are generally preferred for the high-born, *alus* heros. Similarly, perhaps because of some special grace or talent in acting and dancing, youths are frequently seen in female roles; while it is not unusual to find an elderly male star, famed for his singing and impersonations, continue to play the part of the maiden princess.

While the male singer may have a wider, though lower, vocal range, that of the girls lies generally between ♮ and ♮ . The general range of the tenor or high (*memen-yik*) voice, lies about a fourth lower. The general range of the baritone voice, *swara gedé* or *lauh*, begins about a fifth below the tenor range. Most *arja* songs lie within the octave, rarely extending beyond. Some male singers, however, have a two-octave range, and are noted for their ability to sing in both high and low registers.

The performers sing with a peculiar and penetrating intensity. Both the girls' voices and the men's, when singing in the upper register, have a strained and artificial quality that is hard to describe—bright, thin, vibrant, and somewhat wiry, and never relaxed. The baritone voice is darker, richer in color, with a more natural resonance. The *arja* songs are remarkable for their long drawn out phrases that are frequently adorned with graceful embellishments, and make no light demands on breath control. Yet after training all sing without effort, executing the rapid ornamental figures with lightness and elegance.[2]

While the *arja* songs are basically pentatonic in structure, they are sung with considerable freedom of intonation, so that it is sometimes impossible to determine whether the song properly belongs to the *pélog* or *sléndro* category. Two noticeably different forms of *pélog* may be distinguished, which may be approximately described:

Ex. 288.

Many *arja* songs make use of a four-tone scale similar to the *saih angklung*, but with more distinguishable major seconds, thirds, and perfect fifths. Occasionally a fifth tone is heard, extending the scale to a form of *sléndro*. This fifth tone, however, is never structural in the melody and is always heard as a secondary, ornamental tone. It is characteristic of songs having this scale form never to extend beyond the basic scale range.

---

[2] I was completely unprepared for the fine, natural resonance of Balinese male voices singing in unison on hearing my first performance of the *kèchak*, the male chorus still used to accompany certain old ritualistic trance dances known as *sanghyang*. Here ancient chants were sung by youths and older men alike in a rich, vibrant baritone that I would not have believed possible. But when the performance was over, and the chorus rose and dispersed into the night, the air was filled once more with high-pitched, nasal song as singers now and then burst into some favorite *tembang* as they left the temple.

Ex. 289.

The *tembang arja* are not formally composed melodies but freely performed chants sung to the rhythmic accompaniment of percussion and drums. Their melodic form depends on the words and stanza structure of the song. For a Balinese it is as impossible to sing or hum a *tembang* without its words as it is to read the written words instead of singing them. Thus by *tembang* is understood both verse and melody. *Tembang Sinom*, for example, has a stanza pattern and melodic structure that differentiates it from all other *tembangs*. *Sinom*, however, does not refer to the actual text, for new words can be written following the same stanza formula, while the general sentiment remains unchanged. No *arja* club is without its older scholars and youthful scholars who compose new verses with ease, accurately following the ancient established stanza patterns.

The *arja tembangs* belong to a special category of Javano-Balinese versification, lyrical rather than epic, which includes some sixty different varieties of stanza structure. Of these the average *arja* company has a repertory of songs which uses perhaps a dozen of the more widely known forms. The stanza pattern is distinguished by its number of lines, the number of syllables to each line, and the fixed sequence of vowel endings, open or closed. The stanza is a complete statement, while each line forms a separate, component phrase, punctuated by a pause in which the singer may take a breath and the line be given its translation.

A discussion of Balinese versification methods lies beyond the scope of the present study. Some idea, however, of the varied and the irregular but balanced form in *tembang* structure may be gained from the following chart. Here are shown the basic schemes for five stanza patterns used in the *arja* songs. When reduced to a graphic formula, each stanza shows its own harmonious design and individual symmetry.

Five arja stanza forms

tembang		syllables to a line	vowel endings
Durma	————————————————	12	a
	————————————	7	i
	———————————	6	a
	————————————	7	a
	—————————————	8	u
	—————————	5	a
7 lines	————————————	7	i

THE GAMELAN ARJA

Megatruh	12	u
	8	i
	8	u
	8	i
5 lines	8	o
Sinom	8	a
	8	i
	8	o
	8	i
	7	i
	7	u
	7	a
	8	i
	4	u
10 lines	8	a
Jinada	8	a
	8	i
	8	a
	8	u
	8	a
	4	i
7 lines	8	a
Kumambang	8	i
	8	a
	8	i
4 lines	8	a

The *gambuh* convention of accompanying different characters with identifying motifs and melodies continues in the *arja* play in the choice of *tembang*. Like the *gambuh* and *wayang* plays, the *arja* cast is divided into opposing ranks of the good and the evil. The plots, however, are no longer heroic, but romantic and highly sentimental, with banished prince or cruelly mistreated princess enduring endless trials. The cast is now augmented by two new types—the harsh stepmother (*limur*) and the ugly daughter (*liku*). Each leading character has his or her confidential attendant, who also translates or explains the songs. Occasionally the action takes place in some strange land, as in the popular play, *Sampik*, the tale of an unhappy

299

romance between a Chinese boy and girl. Whatever the plot or wherever the scene, the association of character type with appropriate *tembang* remains unchanged.

When it comes to singing the words, each line of the *tembang* is extended into a florid melodic phrase rhythmically supported by drums and percussion, but generally so prolonged that the meaning of the words is completely obscured. Even in lines filled with familiar words that need no translation the text is hard to follow, in spite of excellent diction and light orchestral accompaniment. Regardless of the sense, words are crowded together and syllables freely held to create a fluid melodic phrase. The words are of secondary importance, for there is always the clarification by the attendant at the end of each line.

Some idea of the way the text is treated vocally may be gained from the following example, which gives the first two lines of a *tembang Jinada*, the scheme of which is included in the preceding chart. This *tembang*, the first purpose of which is to impart information, may be sung by all leading characters, male and female. In this example a prince, making his entrance, addresses his attendant, Punta, whose customary role is that of comedian or *kartala*. As already shown, the *Jinada* stanza opens with an eight-syllable line, which is followed by a second of the same length. In the example given here, the first line lacks a syllable, though the vowel ending, *a*, is correct. The second line is broken in half by the translation, the first half having four syllables, the second actually five, but to be reckoned as four. The terminal vowel, *i*, also is correct. The text, with the *kartala's* clarifications, runs as follows:

line 1.   Pr.   *Kaka Punta kartala*
                 Brother Punta buffoon

          k.   *Ai enggèh patut tityang parrakan chōkor I Déwa!*
                 Ah yes indeed I'm the attendant at the feet of my Lord!

line 2.   Pr.   *Krana nira* ...
(a)   Because it ...

          k.   *Aing tityang uning chōkor I Déwa!*
                 Yes I understand my Lord!

line 2.   Pr.   ... *jani (me) tangi*
(b)   ... now grows light

          k.   *Ai enggèh dunian chōkor I Déwa menguwin sekadi semeng!*
                 Ah yes the world my Lord seems to change to day!

The melody itself is of the four-tone quasi *sléndro* type, with an ornamental fifth tone occurring in the word, *tangi*. The rhythmic notation in the following example is at best an approximation. The singer avoids the beat as much as possible. The tendency is to begin a phrase ahead of the beat and end it after a main beat. The rapidly recited words of the attendant are delivered in a kind of sprechstimme.

Ex. 290. Tembang Jinada* ♩ = 126

* As sung by a girl. Pitched around a fourth lower, the song would lie in the tenor range.

The two complete phrases given in Ex. 290 are sufficient to suggest the leisurely progress of the *arja* song. From them may be seen the melodic range of the song, or any other lying in this particular scale. Despite the narrow range, these songs have the lyric spaciousness characteristic of all *arja* songs. Their broad, graceful phrases, each sung with a single breath, float freely above the steady beat of the percussion instruments. The song is further supported and impelled by swift and continuous drumming, which imparts to the long drawn out phrases both tension and direction. From the above excerpt, which gives only two lines of a seven-line stanza, may be estimated the length of time needed to complete a stanza of from six to twelve lines. The song itself may have five or six stanzas. A lively continuity, however, is maintained through the drumming, which gives rhythmic support to the stylized gestures and danced progression of the singer.

Not all *tembangs* have so narrow a range. *Tembang Durma*, for example, a *pélog* song, has a widely extended compass, requiring both high and low registers of a baritone voice. The basic melodic contour of a complete *Durma* stanza, which has seven lines, is shown in Ex. 291.

Ex. 291. Tembang Durma

Many of the *tembang arja* supply the metric and melodic material for popular songs that are heard throughout Bali. With texts in colloquial Balinese, these songs are sung without accompaniment, but in the traditional artificial manner of the *arja* song. Even a small boy or girl will improvise melodic embellishments after the manner of a trained singer. The texts are sentimental, topical, and often most amusing. Here is the translation of a stanza composed in *Durma* meter by I Durus, a youth working in my house who played *kartala* in the *arja* company of Batuan.

> Were I rich I would take you to Den Pasar
> And we would go to the Bali Hotel[3]
> There the bedspreads are woven with gold
> The sheets are soft and green
> The pillows come from Java
> And when we had made love
> We'd leave in an Oakland sedan, proudly klaxoning.

As a musical composition, the *tembang* stands far apart from the *gending*. It is entirely dependent on text and stanza pattern for form and melodic contour. Unlike our popular songs, the *tembang* cannot be turned into an instrumental piece for orchestra. Similarly, to fit words to melody, as we so often do, is unheard of in Bali. As with *kidung* and other categories of Balinese sung texts, the *tembang* is completely involved with classical Javano-Balinese prosody, and forms the subject for a separate study from the present. One can only call attention to the survival of old and widely varied verse forms which still set the patterns in Bali for *arja* and other popular songs.

---

[3] The first-class tourist hotel in Den Pasar, where only a few high-cast Balinese had entrée.

Part Three: Modern Methods

Chapter 18

The Gamelan Pelègongan—New Devices

To examine the music composed in Bali in recent years is to enter a world of imagination and melodic charm. Here one may witness the breakdown of rigid classical forms and meters and the invention of new forms which, while based on the old, show great freedom and ingenuity. For the Balinese composer, music becomes more and more an individual form of expression, and while for ceremonial occasions the traditional repertories are preserved, at any festival new compositions may be heard whose form and content reflect the independent spirit of the composer.

In the thirties the main creative activities were found in the *gamelan pelègongan* and the modernized form of *gamelan gong* known as the *gong kebyar*. New compositions seemed to come into being overnight, filled with melodies of originality and grace. The traditional repertories were also drawn upon, and old melodies, both sacred and secular, were woven into the new music, given fresh life through abridgment and new orchestration. Much attention was given to the working out of intricate figuration patterns and colorful orchestral effects. Nightly practice was a necessity for those clubs wishing to learn the increasingly difficult compositions and play them with the technical perfection expected at any public performance.

The wider possibilities of the seven-tone scale system, however, were left unexplored; the resources of the five- and four-tone scale forms seemed inexhaustible to Balinese musicians. In 1952, during the appearance in New York of the Pliatan gamelan, conversations I had with the leading musicians revealed that the situation had not changed. I asked once again of my old friends why Balinese composers seeking new means of expression did not turn back to the gamelan with a seven-tone scale. I tried to point out some of the advantages—the melodic variety possible through the use of *penyorog* tones and, especially, the effect of change possible through modulation from one *saih* to another during the course of the composition. I was listened to with that serious assent I had long grown to expect in Bali when discussing a revival of formal methods, but I knew that once more I was speaking in vain. Composers, it seemed, were still content with the *saih lima*, in both *pélog* and *sléndro* forms. There also had been a great rise in popularity of the four-tone *gamelan angklung*.

Perhaps the most inventive and skillfully contrived music heard in Bali during the thirties was created for the *lègong* gamelan, to be played before the performance began and during the intervals between dances. Two forms of *gending* were generally known, the *penyelah*, or interlude, and the *pererèn*, compositions played either before the performance or during a pause while the dancers rested. While both terms have more or less the same meaning, the *penyelah* was more traditional in form, usually consisting of a single melodic period repeated several times. The more elaborately worked out *pererèn* showed a greater freedom of form, and enabled the composer to reveal his true creative ability. Each composition had its own unity, and its own melodic freshness resulting partly from new contours, partly from unusual phrase structure. While repetition of each melodic unit still played a basic part in formal organization, the longer *pererèns* were often extended fantasias consisting of a series of melodic episodes of contrasting mood and tempo. The *pererèns* not only showed great metric freedom and melodic invention but were characterized in particular by the development of rhythmic complexities unknown in the older music.

The present chapter is devoted to the methods of the composer, I Lotring, who was much admired by Balinese musicians during the thirties for his innovations and original music for the *lègong* gamelan. Many examples of his treatment of traditional music have already been cited in the *lègong* and *gendèr wayang* chapters of this book, wherever Kuta village has been given as source.

A gentle, friendly man with a ready smile, Lotring was born about 1900 and early trained as a dancer and musician at the now vanished court of Blahbatu. He later moved to Kuta, a small fishing village on the Badung coast, where he had family connections. Here he eventually became leader of both the *lègong* gamelan and the *gendèr wayang* ensemble. When not musically employed, he earned a scanty living as goldsmith, no longer a remunerative craft. The *lègong* gamelan and its dancers were famous in the twenties and even appeared in Java, but in 1929 the members of the club fell into a bitter disagreement over the division of club funds. The gamelan broke up and the instruments were stored away. Lotring now turned to training *lègong*, *jogèd*, and *gandrung* dancers for other village clubs, and occasionally created a new composition for some festive dance debut. When I knew him during the thirties he was without a gamelan of his own, which caused him much unhappiness, and although I succeeded in reviving for him the old Kuta gamelan, the club once more broke up when I left Bali for a year in the United States.

Other composers had been active since around 1915 in developing the new *kebyar* compositions for the modernized *gamelan gong*, and their stylistic methods undoubtedly had an influence on Lotring's music. His own methods and innovations, however, were so generally admired that many of his compositions were in turn taken over and adapted by *kebyar* composers. I frequently engaged Lotring to come for several weeks at a time to Sayan to teach the *Semar Pegulingan* gamelan some composition of his own. By omitting the *trompong* and employing a smaller set of cymbals, the gamelan was transformed into a typical *lègong* orchestra, instrumentally equipped to perform Lotring's music. In this way I was able to grow completely familiar with Lotring's special style, and note in full a number of his more intricate compositions.

Like most trainers of *lègong*, Lotring was expert both as a drummer and as a *gendèr* player. The delicate tone and difficult technique of the latter instrument seemed to hold some special appeal for him. It certainly colored all his music. He composed not only for the *lègong* gamelan but also for the *gendèr wayang*, in whose musical style he was equally expert. But what I found more remarkable was his transference of music originally composed for *gendèr wayang* into elaborately orchestrated pieces for the *lègong* gamelan, thus literally transposing from *sléndro* to *pélog*. He drew with equal ease from the *angklung* repertory, introducing four-tone *angklung* passages into his five-tone *pélog* compositions. These transferences always

308

seemed surprisingly natural, and gave continually new aspects to the original melodies and ornamental figuration.

How did Lotring actually compose, and communicate his composition to the musicians? He would lie awake nights, he once told me, thinking of new melodies and ornamental patterns. He never made any effort to record his compositions in notation, however. When a piece was set, or partly set, in his mind, he would teach it section by section, in the way already described on page 151. In longer compositions he sometimes created new sections as the piece was learned, for one passage would suggest another. "*Susah, karang!*" he would say, "It is hard, to compose!" His hair had grown thin from it!

A striking example of the way traditional material may be lifted from its original context and modified to create a completely new piece of music is found in Lotring's use of the *gambang* melody, *Pelugon*, in his tautly constructed composition bearing that name but more widely known as *Gambangan*—in *gambang* style. Melodically, the piece is based on two curtailed phrases from the original *Pelugon*, played by the *gendèrs* in the traditional syncopated style of the *saron gambang*, as shown in Ex. 272 and 273. An entirely new form of *kòtèkan*, inspired by the method of figuration used in the *gambang* ensemble, animates the composition throughout. Created in 1926 for the Kuta gamelan, this composition caused a sensation among Balinese musicians because of its originality, and *gambangan* compositions gradually became part of many gamelan repertories.[1]

Pelugon, which is given in full in Example 294, on pages 311-315, is beautifully condensed and balanced in form. It consists of a unison introduction for all instruments, a main polyphonic section, and a brief unison closing phrase. The main section is composed of two complementary melodic phrases (the *lagu* or tune), separated by purely rhythmic figuration (the *batèl*), which corresponds to the *gambang* passage-work that fills the melodic breaks in the *gending gambang* (Ex. 268). On the repeat of the main section, the second *batèl* passage is extended to form a coda. A slight break in the music separates the coda from the terminal unison phrase.

An unusual feature of the composition is the frequency of the *jegogan* tones, which occur with every other *pòkok* tone, here played in a continually syncopated manner by the *gendèrs*. The real technical difficulty of the piece, however, lies in the *kòtèkan* figuration and its coordination with the drumming. While the *mòlos* part follows the melodic line of the *gendèrs* in a simple rhythmic pattern of repeated tones, the *nyangsih* is highly syncopated throughout, sounding almost entirely off the beat, and falling on the beat from time to time merely to find a point of support.

---

[1] One *gambangan* composition was included in the program of the Pliatan gamelan during its 1952–53 tour. The original composition was recorded by Odeon in 1928. See Appendix 6, Recordings.

Ex. 292.

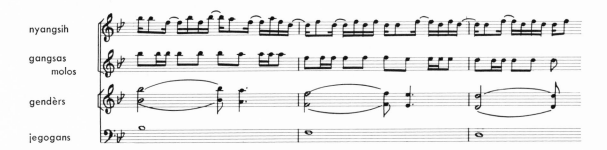

Further difficulties lie in the drumming, which, during the melodic sections, comes under no established classification. The basic pattern consists of rapid *tut-dag* interplay between *lanang* and *wadon* drums, continually off the beat, and closely coordinated with the *nyangsih* part in the figuration. The left hand of each drummer strikes lightly on the beat to give support. What actually is heard, however, is the resonant interplay of the interlocking right hand strokes.

Ex. 293.

The gamelan is held together primarily by the accents of the *kajar*, whose steady beat continues throughout the piece. While the *kempur* and *kemong* are silent during the *lagu* sections, they reinforce the *kajar* beats in the *batèl* passages, where they sound in regular alternation. It will be seen in the following example that the figuration of the *batèl* sections is based on a repeating pattern of eight 16th notes. This is continued until the seventh *kempur* stroke, when the repeating unit suddenly contracts to three 16th notes, racing ahead of the basic punctuation which remains unaffected. A tense rhythmic conflict between figuration and basic accentuation is thus set up. Balance, however, is restored with the thirteenth *kempur* stroke, on which the *lagu* is resumed.

In Ex. 294 *Pelugon* is given partly in full score, and partly condensed to *gendèr* and *nyangsih* parts. The drumming is reduced to *tut-dag* interplay between the two drums. Organic secondary strokes will be found in the introduction and in the signal accents immediately preceding the changes from *lagu* to *batèl* and back. The contrasting drumming in the *batèl* passages is filled with light *krèmpèng* interplay, and follows the standard pattern already shown in Ex. 103.

310

Ex. 294. Gending Pelugon (gambangan); Kuta village ♩ = 132

1. gangas and kantilans
2. gendèrs, gedé and barangan
3. jublags and jegogans

4. kajar
5. rinchik
6. kendangs, lanang and wadon

A introduction

B melody—first phrase

Ex. 294 (continued)

C interlude   M kemong   P kempur

312

Ex. 294 (continued)

D melody—second phrase   E interlude   M kemong   P kempur

Ex. 294 (continued)

Ex. 294 (concluded)

Both *lagu* sections of *Pelugon* are seen to be short one *pōkok* tone and two *kajar* beats, as indicated by the 2/4 time signature. Such contractions at important structural points in the composition were a favorite device of Lotring's, introduced to heighten structural tension. When summed up, *Pelugon* shows the following organization:

a) pengawit	introduction	
b) lagu	melody—first phrase	27 pōkok tones
c) batèl	interlude	12 kempur beats
d) lagu	melody—second phrase	17 pōkok tones
e) batèl	interlude	12 kempur beats
	repeat of sections b, c, d	
	extension of second batel, e	43 kempur beats
f) penyuwud	closing phrase	

In its original *gambang* form *Pelugon* belongs melodically to the second scale type in the Selat *lontar*. As may be seen in the table on page 268, the melody includes a secondary, sixth tone. Since the Kuta gamelan was a five-tone *Selisir* ensemble, to reproduce this tone would not have been possible. The two melodic phrases of Lotring's composition, however, do not extend to the point where a sixth tone is heard in the original. In the form examined here, *Pelugon* is no more than a creative evocation of the earlier *gambang* composition. Brilliant orchestration and constantly changing dynamics transform an ancient style to one of life and warmth.

A different kind of transformation takes place in the *pererèn*, *Sekar Ginotan*, by the same composer. This is a free adaptation of the *gending* by that name for *gendèr wayang*, in which *sléndro* melody and figuration are transferred to the five-tone *pélog* scale. The original composition is part of the standard repertory played before the beginning of the shadowplay. Every *gendèr wayang* ensemble has its own particular version; Lotring's version, as recorded by Odeon,[2] follows the traditional basic form, but shows various innovations in *kōtèkan* patterns. The piece is highly condensed in form, consisting of *a)* an introduction, *b)* first section, *c)* transitional passage, and *d)* finale. From this Lotring creates a composition for *lègong* gamelan that becomes an extended fantasia consisting of ten related but contrasting sections, some in unison for all instruments, others elaborately polyphonic. The main part of the composition derives directly from sections *b, c,* and *d* of the original; the rest is partly composed, partly adapted from other *sléndro* material.

Sekar Ginotan is too long for quotation in full. Its chief interest here is as a demonstration of how a Balinese composer can utilize *sléndro* material in a piece for *pélog* orchestra. Excerpts from four main passages, shown together with their source material, have been chosen as illustration. They are based on the systematic transposition of melody as found on the five tones of the *sléndro* scale, *ding, dong, dèng, dung, ding,* to the corresponding tonal series of the *pélog* scale.

Ex. 295.

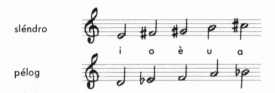

Our first quotation is from the introduction. The three-voiced *gendèr wayang* passage is reduced to a resonant unison passage for full orchestra, reinforced by simple drumming. The first phrase of the unison version derives from the lowest *gendèr wayang* part, and is a methodical transposition to corresponding tones in the *pélog* scale. The *pélog* phrase is seen to end on *dung,* while the *sléndro* phrase ends on *dèng.* The second phrase is a free parallel, but the last phrase is tone for tone again, this time deriving from the highest *gendèr wayang* part.

Ex. 296. Gending Sekar Ginotan; sléndro and pélog versions

_____
[2] See Appendix 6, Recordings.

1. gendèr wayang   2. gamelan pelègongan

The next example, Ex. 297, from the beginning of the first main section, is more complex. The melodic line of the *pélog* version derives from the basic melody on which the lowest voice of the *sléndro* version is based. The transposition to *pélog*, however, is not to corresponding scale tones. Instead it shifts the melodic line up two steps, from *dèng sléndro* to *dang pélog*, and continues this way throughout the passage. *Kempur* and *kemong* beats and time-beating *kajar* are added, while the figuration is quite independent of the original.

Ex. 297. Gending Sekar Ginotan; sléndro and pélog versions

In the transition leading to the finale, the *sléndro* ostinato-motif is transposed two tones higher when transferred to *pélog*, and shifted to a different beat, . The lower voice is changed, and *kempur* and *kemong* beats are added.

317

Ex. 298.

A more elaborate transformation occurs in the finale of the piece. The lowest voice of the *gendèr wayang* version is found transposed three tones higher and transferred to the *mōlos* part of the figuration. The *nyangsih* is seen to follow closely the original figuration, taking up first one voice then the other. A new melody for the *gendèrs* is introduced in the *pelègongan* version, while *kempur, kemong,* and *kajar* accents have been added.

Ex. 299. Gending Sekar Ginotan; sléndro and pélog versions ♩ = 120

It is hard to convey in words the novel effect of Lotring's *pélog* version of *Sekar Ginotan*, which lends fresh color to familiar patterns through change in scale, and transforms the delicate music of the *gendèr wayang* into a brilliant new composition for full orchestra.

This resourceful composer drew as well from the *angklung* repertory. In his composition, *Gending Angklung*, excerpts from well-known *angklung* pieces were combined, with the four-tone *angklung* scale now transferred to the *pélog* tones, *ding, dong, dang, dung:*

318

Ex. 300.

A single example will serve to illustrate the transformation occurring when *angklung* melody is transferred to the *lègong* gamelan. In the following passage from Lotring's composition (Ex. 301), the original four-tone melody is transposed note for note to the *pélog* scale, and varied in the third measure by the introduction of a fifth scale-tone* in the melody.

Ex. 301. Gending Angklung; saih angklung and pélog versions ♩ = 132

1. gamelan angklung   2. gamelan pelègongan; gangsas and gendèrs   3. jublags and jegogans

Balinese musicians still exclaim at the tricks (*akal*) in Lotring's music, and at how hard some of his pieces were to learn. This is largely due to the freedom of rhythm, the unusual drumming, and the constant modification of established metric forms. The standard melodic period based on a *palet* of sixteen *pōkok* tones is all but abandoned in favor of the shorter, irregular period containing, for example, twenty, twenty-eight, thirty, or even thirty-one *pōkok* tones. The period, however, is always repeated in performance, thus establishing a balance. The general practice followed not only by Lotring but other composers, especially in *kebyar* compositions, is to play the shorter melodic sections twice at the same speed, and a third time in more animated tempo. In Ex. 302, remarkable for its 7/4 phrase structure, the process is reversed. Here the complete melodic unit with which the composition opens is played twice in quick tempo, then at approximately half speed.

319

Ex. 302. Gending Sekar Ginotan; introduction, first part ♩ = 112

A characteristic procedure with Lotring was to drop a beat or half-beat somewhere in the middle of a passage, disturbing the rhythmic balance and throwing the rest of the passage into rhythmic dislocation. The missing beat is never forgotten, however, but is inevitably restored through the extension of some phrase, though often at so distant a point in the composition as to create a new element of surprise.

Ex. 303, a passage from the first section of *Sekar Ginotan*, is typical. It consists of a complete melodic period, played three times then followed by the transition, already referred to in Ex. 297, that leads to the second part of the composition. This transition serves later as a bridge to the final section of the piece. As given below, the full period is reduced to eight measures, some of which are seen to repeat. With the repeats, the period actually extends to thirteen measures, as numbered. The unusual feature of this passage lies in the occurrence at measure 7 of a 3½-beat unit, here indicated by the 7/8 time signature, actually a unit of 2/4 plus 3/8, as shown by the *kajar* beats and reinforcing drums. Since measures 6 and 7 are repeated, this robs the whole thirteen-measure period of one beat, reducing it to a period of fifty-one beats. As the section is played three times in all, three beats are thus lost. Two are immediately restored with the 2/4 link preceding the actual transition, which begins with the *kempur* accent. At the end of the transition, twenty beats later, the third beat is finally recovered and balance restored by a linking unit of three beats (3/4), which leads directly into the following section in 4/4.

320

Ex. 303. Gending Sekar Ginotan; end of first section and transition

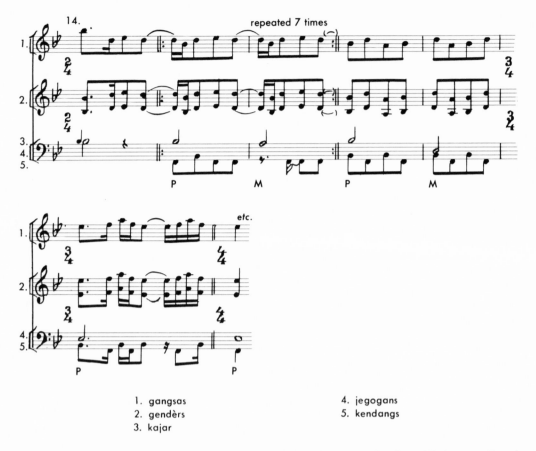

1. gangsas
2. gendèrs
3. kajar

4. jegogans
5. kendangs

One more passage—the final section of *Sekar Ginotan*—further illustrates Lotring's special gift for disturbing, then restoring rhythmic balance. The passage (Ex. 304) will be seen to consist of *a*) a short ostinato, repeated twelve times with changing dynamics, followed by *b*) a rhythmically complex bridge leading to *c*) the closing melodic section, played three times in all. Of special interest here is the syncopated bridge, where a whole beat is dropped in the 3/4 measure and recovered in the 5/4 measure near the end of the bridge, in preparation for the following closing section. Because of the speed at which the whole closing section is taken, coming immediately after the firmly established beat of the ostinato passage, the effect of this syncopated bridge is wild and exhilarating. The return to a regular beat at *c* restores a sense of order. But here, too, rhythmic disturbance is found in the abrupt break and syncopations at the end of melodic passage. Only with the final note of the second ending does the rhythmic tension of the long and elaborately constructed *Sekar Ginotan* find release.

Ex. 304. Gending Sekar Ginotan; closing section ♩ = 132

1. gangsas and gendèrs   2. kajar and kendangs

Typical instances of Lotring's rhythmic inventiveness may be found in his composition, *Gegènggongan*, *gènggong* music.[3] Immediately following the opening section, a rhythmically interesting unison passage is heard, as a rhythmic unit of 6/8 (indicated by *a* in the following example) is introduced and repeated three times until it resolves once more on a main beat (Ex. 305).

Ex. 305. Gegènggongan; excerpt ♩ = 136

[3] Included in the Odeon recordings. See Appendix 6.

1. gangsas, gendèrs   2. kajar, jegogans, kendangs

Perhaps the most engaging feature of all in this short piece is the twice repeated closing section, which ends in a syncopated passage hammered out by the orchestra in ringing unison (Ex. 306).

Ex. 306. Gegènggongan; closing section

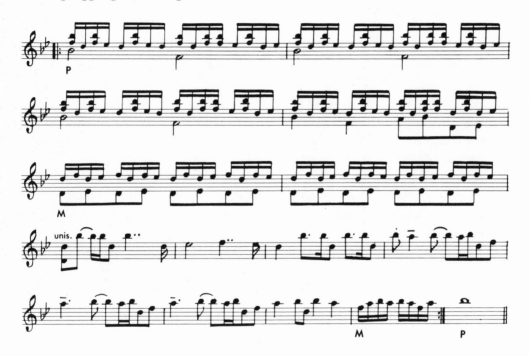

Unison passages, while not original with Lotring, are a favorite device of his, offering as they do strong contrast to the involved interplay of the polyphonic sections. When sounded in four octaves, from lowest *gendèr* to top *gangsa* tones, the unison passage can have great impact. When quietly played, an appealing and crystalline resonance results. Sometimes the passage takes the form of a free recitative, performed in a rubato, half-improvisational style. The fine precision with which such passages are played by a group of perhaps twelve *gangsas* and four *gendèrs* is a delight. Ex. 307 is a freely performed unison passage which serves as interlude between the opening and closing sections of *Gending Angklung*. Rhythmic notation is, of course, only approximate. During performance, great attention is paid to phrasing and shading, and to creating maximum contrast between the delicate, dry staccato of the muted repeating tones and the more expressive quality of the legato phrases.

Ex. 307. Gending Angklung, gendèrs and gangsas alone; excerpt*

Lotring was by no means the only composer of music for the *lègong* gamelan during the thirties. In attending performances of *lègong* and *Chalonarang* put on by the clubs of countless villages, one could continually hear bright new music composed for the occasion by local musicians. Some of these were older men, with long musical experience. Others were mere youths, with little if any technical knowledge of music beyond that acquired since joining the gamelan. A few, such as the Anak Agungs of Saba and Lukluk, princely amateurs of music, owned their own gamelans, trained their dancers themselves, and on occasion could rival Lotring in musical inventiveness. Musicians in search of new ideas traveled about considerably, hearing other gamelans at festival time, borrowing this, discarding that, and introducing new ideas into their own compositions. While few of these compositions approached Lotring's in craftsmanship, all showed in one way or another much creative imagination and a general liberation from the older established forms. It was the golden age of the *gamelan pelègongan.*

Ex. 308. Pengechèt Jagul*; Sayan village ♩ = 138

last time più animato

1. gangsas   3. jublags   5. jegogans
2. gendèrs   4. kajar   6. kendangs

327

Chapter 19

Kebyar—The Latest Style

It was probably in the early years of the present century that musicians in certain villages of north Bali, the territory of many innovations, began to transform the traditional *gamelan gong* into the modernized form known today as the *gamelan gong kebyar*. The *trompong* was dropped, except for the old ceremonial music; the *sarons* were abandoned in favor of the *gangsa gantung*, whose range was now extended to nine or ten tones, while the original *réong* of four gongs was expanded to include a series of twelve. The cymbal section was reduced to two or three players; the cymbals used were smaller and lighter in sound, and mounted to permit the technique employed by the *rinchik* in the *gamelan pelègongan*. For this streamlined orchestra an exuberant new form of music known as *kebyar* was developed by north Bali composers, with a percussive and exciting style which was to sweep the island.

According to the Regent of Bulelèng, Anak Agung Gedé Gusti Jelantik, who told me in 1937 that he noted the date in his diary at the time, the first *kebyar* music was publicly heard in December 1915, when several leading north Bali gamelans held a gamelan competition in Jagaraga, a village still celebrated in Bali for its superb gamelan and bold, dramatic music. Whereas today the *kebyar* composition is generally intended to accompany the dance by that name, originally the *kebyar* was a purely instrumental composition, a virtuoso piece created to show off the technical skill of the gamelan. Intended primarily as diverting festival music, it drew large crowds wherever it was performed, although older musicians lamented its loudness and restless lack of direction. It was some ten years after the date preserved in the Regent's diary that a Balinese audience witnessed the debut of I Mario of Tabanan, who is said to have created the new dance known as *kebyar*, in which the dancer, seated on a mat and surrounded on three sides by the facing musicians of the gamelan, interprets in movement the constantly changing moods of the music.

The word *kebyar* is hard to define. It applies to the new style and to the music itself, to the dance, and to the modernized *gamelan gong*. It refers in particular to the cymbals and their metallic clash, and to the explosive unison attack of the gamelan with which the music begins. It has been explained to me as meaning a sudden outburst, "like the bursting open of a flower," as one informant engagingly illustrated by opening a tightly closed hand. In the new freedom of form, the lavish and varied orchestral effects, and the bold syncopations and intricate passage-work, *kebyar* was indeed a new flowering, a theatrical release from the forms of the past. By the middle thirties, in the villages and in the *puris*, inherited gamelans, *gong*, *Semar Pegulingan*, and *pelègongan*, were being dismantled everywhere, the smaller gongs and the bronze keys melted down and recast in new alloys and forms more suitable for the popu-

328

lar new gamelan. Only the sacred ensembles were spared destruction, protected by the demands of religious ritual.

The *gamelan gong kebyar*, more popularly known as the *gong kebyar*,[1] is actually a combination of the *lègong* gamelan and the older *gamelan gong*, with certain modified instruments introduced to give the orchestra its special color. Today, even more than in the thirties, the *gong kebyar* is used both in the temple and for all other ceremonial and state occasions. In the temple it accompanies the ritual dances and performs the standard repertory of *gending gong* in modern style. In public performances it accompanies not only the *kebyar* dance but also *baris* and *tōpèng*, and supplants with increasing frequency the *gamelan pelègongan* for performances of *lègong*.

While giving a fuller orchestra effect because of the more elaborate instrumentation, the *gong kebyar* is considerably smaller than the ceremonial gamelan it has replaced. Some twenty-five performers are now sufficient for the average gamelan. The highly trained players and the scintillating music appeal to modern taste far more than the grandiose but simpler orchestral style of the past.

For the modern compositions the leading melodic instrument of the gamelan is now the *gangsa gantung*, commonly known, according to the number of keys, as the *gangsa siya* (nine), or *gangsa dasa* (ten). The *gangsa gantung* is actually a modified *gendèr* with a smaller range. It is not played with both hands in *gendèr* fashion, however, but in the easier *gangsa* manner, with the right hand holding the *gangsa* mallet while the left hand damps the keys in the usual way (Fig. 93). The delicate tone of the *gendèr* is thus lost, replaced by a more percussive, metallic sound. Two forms of *gangsa* are in use today. The form having its keys suspended over the resonators is generally favored throughout south Bali for its richer tone. In north Bali and in villages following north Bali methods the preference is for a harder tone, and the *gangsa* keys are mounted *gangsa jongkok* fashion, resting above the resonators on shock-absorbers of felt, cork, or rubber (Fig. 98).

The *gangsa* used in the gong *kebyar* is made in two sizes, the large *gangsa gedé* and the smaller *barangan*, pitched an octave higher. A group of ten or twelve *gangsas* forms the main section of the gamelan. To the large *gangsas* is assigned the leading melody, as developed from the *pōkok* tones; the *barangans* are given various forms of melodic paraphrase and ornamental passage-work. As in the *gamelan pelègongan*, the *pōkok* tones are sounded by two or four *jublags*, and stressed at intervals by a pair of *jegogans*.

The most striking feature of the gamelan, however, is the *réong*, here extended to a range of two and a half octaves. Similar to the *trompong* in appearance, it requires, instead of a soloist, a quartet of players to perform the *réongan*—an intricate figuration accompaniment composed of four interlocking parts, which gives continuous movement and sparkle to the music (Figs. 90, 91).

From *jegogan* to *gangsa barangan*, the scale of the gamelan extends to five octaves, the different instrumental ranges found in the order shown in Ex. 309.

---

[1] Today the word *kebyar* has been dropped, and the orchestra is called *gamelan gong*.

Ex. 309. Gamelan gong kebyar; instrumental ranges

gangsa barangan

gangsa gedé

réong

trompong

jublags

jegogans

kempur
gongs   lanang
         wadon

pitch variable

The instruments are set out to form a square (Figs. 90, 94). The metallophones line the two sides. At the back is placed the *réong*, behind which stand the *gongs* and *kempur*. In front, closing the square, is set the *trompong*, which is present only if the ceremonial *gending gong* are played. Facing the gamelan sit the two drummers. This arrangement ensures unity and the precision of ensemble which is so essential in *kebyar*. At the beginning of a composition the facing players catch each other's eyes, and wait in readiness for the up and down flash of the leading *gangsa's* mallet which brings them in on the opening unison accent.

Because of the instrumental range and the flexibility of the single-handed striking method, *gangsa* melody acquires here a new mobility and brightness, quite different from that of the *gendèr*. All tones have an incisive attack, and in even the softest passages ornamental tones ring with crystal clarity. Because of the playing method the instrument has a wide dynamic range. The mallet may strike from a point close to the keys, impelled by a light wrist motion; or it may be brought down full force with an energetic forearm stroke. Unison passages for the entire *gangsa* group can thus be executed with percussive intensity or with extreme delicacy. Such a passage as the following melodic episode (Ex. 310) for the *gangsas*, coming as it does after a long fortissimo passage for all the instruments, is refreshing in its serenity and lyric grace.

330

Ex. 310. Kebyar Ding, gamelan gong kebyar, Belaluan* ♩ = 88

* The above passage is from part two of Kebyar Ding, called Surapati. The whole composition was recorded by Odeon. See Appendix 6, Recordings.

Gangsa figuration is developed in endless ways. The basic method of dividing the passage-work into *mōlos* and *nyangsih* parts is retained, but with a wider scale-range to move in, the patterns attain great freedom and variety. North Bali, according to an article in *Bhawanagara*,[2] distinguishes four basic types of figuration—two in which *mōlos* and *nyangsih* parts alternate tone by tone, and two in which the parts interlock in syncopated patterns:

a) alternating: *chandetan*
tutugan

b) interlocking: *ōchètan*
stengah ōchètan (semi-*ōchètan*)

Any one type may be consistently employed throughout a passage, or all may be used in turn during the same passage. The following passage (Ex. 311) includes all four, along with the *lagu* or melody from which they derive. In the two alternating types, the melodic tones will be found in the *mōlos* part, sounding on the beat. In the *chandetan* patterns the *nyangsih* differs from the *mōlos* part melodically, while in the *tutugan* the *nyangsih* follows the *mōlos* with the same melodic tones, as shown below.[3] In the *ōchètan* the two parts interlock in such a way as to create two separate voices when the parts meet; in the semi-*ōchètan* the two parts always meet on a unison.

Ex. 311.

In south Bali the term, *chandetan*, generally covers all forms of figuration patterns, although *tutugan* patterns are distinguished by name.

Gangsa figuration now frequently occupies the foreground. The melodic line, as developed from the *pōkok* tones, is often dropped entirely and both large and small *gangsas* assigned the same patterns. These replace the melody, creating instead a form of melody figuration (Ex. 312).

---

2 "*Gong-Gedé (Kebijar), ōlèh Balyson*" (by *Balyson*), *Bhawanagara*, April–May–June 1934. The article was published in Malay.
3 The *tutugan* is also a technical device in *trompong* playing. See Ex. 11.

Ex. 312. Chandetan and pōkok tones, gamelan gong kebyar; Mengwi village ♩ = 144

It is hard to believe that such a passage, divided equally between eight or ten *gangsas*, can be smoothly performed, especially at the tempo given here. Yet in a well-rehearsed gamelan the passage will sound as though played by a single instrument. The *mōlos* part offers no difficulty since it is always on the beat, but the *nyangsih* is offbeat throughout. The even flow is maintained through the left hand, which damps the keys *on* the beat, thus giving continuous rhythmic support.

A more involved form of *chandetan*, or *tutugan*, as it is called in south Bali, is found in Ex. 313. Here the relationship of the two parts is less transparent. The *nyangsih* clashes periodically with the *mōlos*, creating seconds and thirds.

Ex. 313. Tutugan, gamelan gong kebyar; Pliatan village ♩ = 96

A fuller sounding form of *chandetan*, developed in north Bali in the late thirties, is shown in the following example. Here the *mōlos* and *nyangsih* no longer interlock. Instead, lying two scale-tones apart, they run parallel to each other. The two excerpts given in Ex. 314 are from the section named *gendèran* ("gendèr episode") from a new *kebyar* taught to the gamelan of Ubud, in south Bali, by the young *kebyar* composer, Gedé Manik, of Jagaraga village in north Bali (Figs. 95, 96). In the first excerpt the *chandetan* is played by the *barangan* group only, two octaves above the melody. In the second the *barangan* players are doubled an octave below by the large *gangsas*. Both passages, especially the second, bring an unusual tone color to the gamelan, and are typical of the Balinese search for new instrumental effects at that time.

333

Ex. 314. Chandetan, gamelan gong kebyar; Ubud village $\quad \downarrow = 80$

Much of the special color of the *gong kebyar* derives from the *réongan* or *réong* playing, which animates the music throughout with rippling figuration and sudden brassy accents. Modern *réong* technique is a virtuoso development of the archaic figuration performed by the four-tone *réong* of the traditional *gamelan gong*. The modern *réong* not only has a complete five-tone scale but a range of two and a half octaves. While the new figuration still consists of the interplay of two rhythmically interdependent parts, it is now possible not only to expand the patterns, because of the fifth tone, but to double them an octave higher. Four players are thus required instead of the original two. They sit side by side at the *réong*, with the twelve gongs evenly divided between them (Fig. 91). Taken in ascending order, players 1 and 2 perform *nyangsih* and *mōlos* parts, respectively, while players 3 and 4 double these parts an octave above. Since the figuration now moves freely about, as will later be shown, each player is not strictly limited to three gongs only, but may reach to an adjacent one, according to the movement of the patterns. Occasionally, when the figuration of the lower pair rises too far beyond their basic range, adjustments must be made in the doubling parts. Since the *réongan* as performed by the first two players is complete in itself, the two doubling parts are not included in the illustrations which follow.

The essence of modern *réong* technique can be found in Ex. 315, *tabuh talōh tōpèng*, the opening music to the *tōpèng* performance as played by the *gong kebyar* of Pliatan. Here is shown the full range of the *réongan* as played by the first two musicians, with no adjustments needed in the parts doubling an octave higher. In this example the *gangsas* function as a unison group, sounding the melody in repeated tones and leaving all figuration to the *réongs*. A glance back to the *réongan* of Ex. 3–5, 15–17, will show the change that has taken place in the *réong* style.

334

Ex. 315. Tabuh talōh tōpèng, gamelan gong kebyar; Pliatan village   ♩ = 116

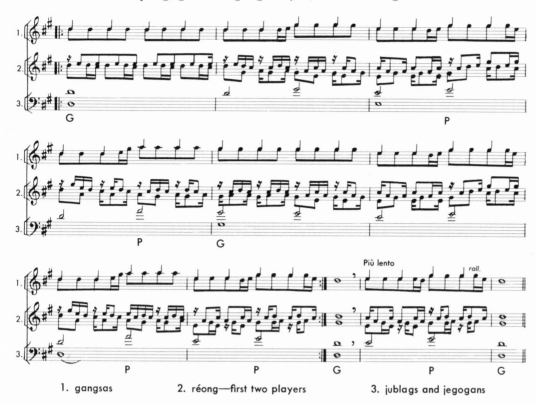

1. gangsas   2. réong—first two players   3. jublags and jegogans

When combined with the *gangsa* figuration the *réongan* shows close agreement, sometimes doubling with absolute precision but more often moving in free but related patterns. When examined together, the care with which these two quite differently produced patterns are integrated becomes evident. By way of illustration, four different examples of coordination between *réong* and *gangsas* are given here. In the first (Ex. 316) the *gangsa* figuration will be found reproduced almost note for note in the *réongan*, with the *gangsa* tones divided equally between upper and lower parts.

Ex. 316.

gangsas

réong

Ex. 317 shows greater freedom between *réongan* and *gangsa* figuration, as played by the smaller *gangsas*. Each follows in its own way the *lagu*, or melody, played by the large *gangsas*. Together they complement each other in creating an elaborate and varied form of polyphonic accompaniment.

Ex. 317.

Strict doubling between *réong* and *gangsa* parts may be employed when an effort of extreme clarity is wanted (Ex. 318).

Ex. 318.

In Ex. 319 the lower parts of *réongan* and *chandetan* are seen to double each other, while each upper part interlocks with the lower in a different way. Attention is called to the second measure, where *gangsa* and *réong* parts move in contrary motion to new pitch levels, creating a subtle change in tonal color.

Ex. 319.

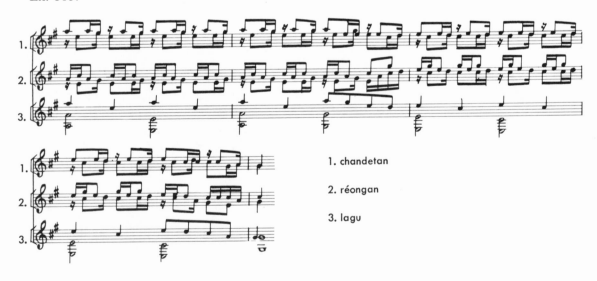

1. chandetan

2. réongan

3. lagu

When the *trompong* is included in the *gong kebyar* for the performance of the *gending gong*, it no longer stands out as solo instrument against an austere background of nuclear melody. Its fluid melodic line is now obscured by the complex accompaniment of *gangsas* and *réong*. The basic melodic idea, however, is not lost, but now emerges richly embellished with constantly moving figurations. The following passage (Ex. 320) from *tabuh talōh*,[4] opening music, offers a typical example of how *gangsas*, *réong*, and *trompong* meet in unison on the *pōkok* tones, each filling in between the tones in a different and characteristic way.

Ex. 320. Tabuh talōh, gamelan gong kebyar; Badung ♩ = 72

Ornate arrangements of the old *gending gong*, such as that shown here, had become standard in Bali by the thirties. Today, I am informed, the *trompong* is no longer employed in most gamelans performing the *gending gong*. The *pōkok* tones of the *gending* now form the melody, around which continuous figuration by *gangsas* and *réong* is woven. The *trompong* solo has become outmoded, to be heard only in remote mountain villages.

---

[4] Transcribed by the author for two pianos and published by G. Schirmer, New York. See Appendix 5.

The tone of the *réong* resembles that of the *trompong* used in the *gamelan Semar Pegulingan*, resonant and bell-like in the lower register, sweet and chiming in the upper. The tone of each gong is normally allowed to ring, the player raising the mallet immediately after striking. For special effect, however, it may be stopped by a second lighter stroke, in which the mallet rests momentarily on the boss, silencing the sound. The contrast between the two tones, one clear and ringing, the other almost a click, is particularly effective in rhythmic passages:

Ex. 321.

Another effect is obtained by striking the gong on the rim, thus producing a thin brassy sound resembling a cymbal clash. In slower tempos the player strikes the rim with both mallets at the same time; swiftly alternating strokes produce a clanging tremolo. These rim sounds are usually reinforced by cymbals, with which their metallic timbre blends.

Ex. 322. ♩ = 142

Another characteristic *réong* effect is obtained by striking four of the five scale tones simultaneously. Divided among the four players, these form widespread and ringing chords:

Ex. 323.

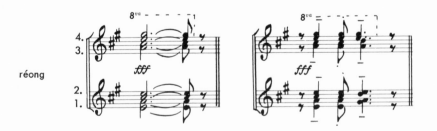

These chords are used primarily for rhythmic emphasis. They add fullness and dramatic impact to the sudden opening of a *kebyar* composition, sounded in crashing unison by the entire gamelan:

338

Ex. 324.

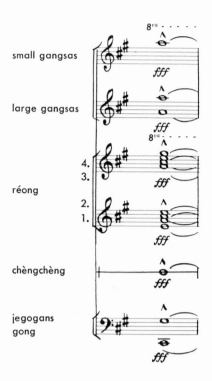

The *réong* chord plays an important part in *kebyar* music, and is employed in many ways to add brilliance and fresh color to the instrumentation. Like the single *réong* tone, the chord may be allowed to ring free or can be stopped; a remarkable difference in timbre exists between the resonant open chord and the percussive click of the one that is stopped.

An example of contrasting *réong* sounds will be found in Ex. 325, a passage from the *kebyar*, *Kapi Raja* (*Ape King*), composed for a *kebyar* choreography. The passage is from the opening episode, *bapang*,[5] which has been introduced by a short fortissimo passage sounded in unison by all instruments. The *bapang* motif is softly repeated six times by the large *gangsas*, with figuration accompaniment by the small *gangsas* alone. The cymbals lightly underline the passage. With the seventh repeat the dynamics suddenly change in preparation for the *angsel*, or phrase break, which occurs with the eighth. *Gangsas* and cymbals break into a sudden forte, while the *réong* players enter with brassy repeating tones produced on the rim of the gongs. On the eighth repeat they suddenly jump to chord formation, striking on the boss of each gong. In a rhythm underlined by the cymbals two muted chords are followed by an open one, which is allowed to ring briefly and then is silenced by a stopping chord. Thus in progressive stages the passage rises from the light clash of cymbals through the brassy rim tones of the *réong* and the two stopped *réong* chords to the resonant open chord which is the climax of the passage and on which the dancer pauses in a phrasing break.

---

[5] Compare with *bapang pelègongan*, Ex. 129.

339

Ex. 325. Kebyar Kapi Raja, gamelan gong kebyar; Pliatan village ♩ = 120

In Ex. 326, a passage from an extended melodic section in the same composition, the *réong* chord (here reduced to rhythmic notation) is used to reinforce the cymbal accents in a cross-rhythmic figure that periodically disturbs the basic beat.

Ex. 326. Kebyar Kapi Raja

1. large gangsas   2. réong—full chord   3. chèngchèng

In quiet lyrical passages the *réong*, if used at all, softly supports the *gangsa* melody at intervals, adding color and nuance. Delicate acoustic effects are obtained through the blending and contrasting of *gangsa* and *réong* timbres. Some idea of the subtle underlining of the *gangsa* melody may be gained from Ex. 327 and 328. In the first, the melody, played in soft unison by the *gangsas*, opens without accompaniment. With the entrance of the *réong*, the melody is lightly reinforced through doubling, passing back and forth between the lower and upper parts.

Ex. 327. Kebyar Ding, gamelan gong kebyar; Belaluan, Badung ♩ = 100

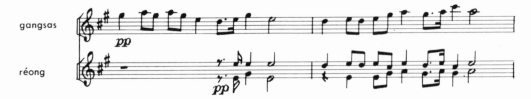

340

In Ex. 328 the *réongan* at first supplies a simple rhythmic background for the melody, but later develops into a melodic variation.

Ex. 328. Kebyar Ding ♩ = 100

While the two-voiced *réongan*, doubled in the octave above by the third and fourth players, is in general use everywhere, a more complex form of *réongan* was developed in north Bali in the late thirties, composed of four separate but interlocking parts. Too elaborate for passages taken at high speed, this type of *réong* figuration is occasionally employed in slower, more lyrical episodes, where it forms an intricate and lovely accompaniment for the *gangsa* melody (see Ex. 329).

Ex. 329. Gambangan episode, Kebyar Jagaraga; four-part réongan* ♩ = 58

* As taught in 1938 to the gamelan gong kebyar of Ubud by the young composer, Gedé Manik, of Jagaraga village, Bulelèng.

Supported only by sustained *jublag* and *jegogan* tones and by all but inaudible drumming, passages such as this sound extremely beautiful. They seem literally to float in the air. The *réongan* is worked out with the utmost care for harmonious integration of all four parts, so that through ingenious doubling and combining of tones the separate patterns merge in a figuration of remarkable transparency.

The *kebyar* compositions are completely free in form—lengthy fantasias of traditional and newly composed melodies linked together in a constantly changing orchestration. Some are skillfully put together, showing the composer's concern for contrast and condensation. Others are greatly overextended, their once striking effects transformed into clichés through constant recurrence. Many are marred by the excessive use of virtuoso cadenza-like passages which link together the main episodes and which aim primarily at display of skill. Lacking the classic calm, the broad melodic line, and the unity of mood of the older music, these tempestuous rhapsodies have great popular appeal because of their novelty and excitement.

Although musical notation is now extended to convey the main melodic line of two-octave instruments, through the substitution of cyphers for the original symbols, few composers bother to preserve even the basic tones of their compositions. Pieces are taught to groups who may either pass them on or stop playing them, so that many compositions are lost with that disregard which comes of knowing that new music will be created tomorrow.

While part of the musical material in the *kebyar* is newly composed, much is borrowed from traditional repertories, especially those of the *gambuh* and *lègong*. These are still rich melodic sources, especially if the *kebyar* is composed with a choreography in mind, in which case it serves not only as an instrumental show piece but can also be performed with the dance. Some dance teachers compose their own music, working out the composition as they develop the choreography. Some choreographies are created for an existing *kebyar*. The *kebyar* itself may have been bought by the gamelan club from some renowned composer who was engaged to create a new piece for them alone and expressly bound to teach it nowhere else. Clubs often learn or secretly steal desired compositions by sending a little group of musicians to attend some other club's rehearsals. One will devote his attention to the melody, a second to the figuration, a third to the drumming. Together they bring the music home piecemeal and relay it to their own club. Quite often the *kebyar* is the creation of the club itself, with different musicians contributing ideas and suggestions at nightly rehearsals. With a standard melodic repertory to draw from, and no set rules for formal structure, composite fantasias are evolved in which every key musician of the gamelan has a say.

Whatever its ultimate form, the *kebyar* is sure to begin with an explosive, strongly syncopated unison passage, the *kebyar* proper, from which this type of composition derives its name. This section sets the tone of the piece, representing the gamelan at its maximum percussive brilliance. Throughout the composition, similar fortissimo unison passages recur, alternating with the lyrical sections with almost mechanical regularity.

After the opening *kebyar* section the composition begins to take its own particular form. Any number of contrasting episodes, brief or extended, may follow, linked together with syncopated unison cadenzas. The termination of the piece with a more or less classical *pengawak* and *pengechèt*, adapted from the *gambuh* or *lègong* repertory, is fairly standard.

A typical example of the shorter *kebyar* is found in the composition, *Jerebu*, by I Regog of Belaluan, which was created for a dance and was recorded, though never released, by Odeon in 1928. It consists of four sections or movements joined together, and takes some fifteen minutes to perform.

1. kebyar	introduction
2. chondong	chondong music from lègong
3. pengechèt	allegretto section from
Playon	the gending lègong, Playon
4. pengawak and	slow movement and
pengechèt	concluding allegretto

But the *kebyar* can also be extended into a long entertainment that includes not only dance and instrumental interludes but the chanting and recitation of classical literature as well. The following synopsis was noted in 1938, during a gamelan performance at a popular night fair (*pasar malam*) at Singaraja, in north Bali. Admission was charged to enter the grounds, crowded with food stalls, naive freak shows, novelty booths, and little gambling tables. Around the large gamelan a silent audience sat enthralled for nearly two hours. Here the performance did not open with the usual crashing *kebyar*. Instead, a quiet prelude by the gamelan was followed by unaccompanied chanting by a finely trained male singer of a passage from the *Mahabharata*. A brief interlude by the gamelan introduced a recited passage, and only after this did the customary *kebyar* outburst take place.

1. kekawin	unaccompanied chanting of kawi text
2. palawakia	unaccompanied recitation in kawi, but with line by line translation into Balinese by a second performer
3. kebyar	gamelan introduction to the main composition
4. chondong	chondong episode from lègong, danced by two girls
5. gabor	melody from the ritual dance, gabor, danced by the same
6. bapang	music for a high official, same dancers
7. gilakan	baris music, same dancers
8. kebyar	percussive unison passage, same dancers
9. gilakan	similar to No. 7, different choreography
10. bapang	similar to No. 6, different choreography
11. pengechèt	allegretto in classical style, same dancers
12. pengisep	variation, conclusion of dance
13. pengalang	melodic interlude—gamelan
14. gambangan	gambang melody with kekawin singing
15. pengechèt	allegretto in classical style—gamelan
16. pengawak	slow movement in classical style—gamelan
17. pengechèt	concluding allegretto—gamelan

Here was *kebyar* in a new light, no mere show piece, but a rich and varied presentation, both diverting and serious, in which classical and even sacred elements were interwoven to create a new and popular form of entertainment.

The actual *kebyar* passages which characterize this form of compositions are marked by an intentionally bewildering metric freedom. While the classically derived episodes are based on solid and well-defined metric structure, the *kebyar* sections, by contrast, give the impression of complete and uncalculated improvisation. The long and rhythmically complex passages, performed in unison by all instruments and lacking all metric punctuation, take on the free character of the cadenza in a Western concerto. There is, however, the great difference that these passages are orchestral, never solo, performed in unison by some sixteen players.

These cadenzalike interludes are based on an unusual and characteristic rhythmic unit containing five fractional beats, $\frac{5}{8}$ ♩♪♩. Tense passages of great rhythmic drive are built up through the extended repetition of this unit.

Ex. 330.

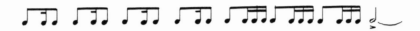

In a sense, such a passage could be metrically considered as an extended syncopation of a regular, though silent, beat, leading off in the following manner:

Ex. 331.

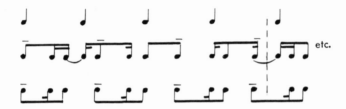

As such, its syncopation is closely related to that of the interlocking *mōlos* and *nyangsih* parts in *gangsa* and *réong* figuration.

But as the 5/8 unit is repeated, it emerges more and more as an independent and structural rhythmic unit. This is borne out by the way certain clubs, in order to increase the speed of the passage, shorten the 5/8 unit to 4/8, thus robbing the rhythm of its original tension.

Ex. 332.

When extended, the *kebyar* passages can be extremely complex. Ex. 333, the opening to *Kapi Raja*, is offered as a first illustration because of its brevity and because it contains all the elements of the typical *kebyar* introduction. The prolonged opening tone is amplified by a *réong* chord. A free unison passage leads directly to the metrically stable opening episode, played by the *gangsas* alone and taken at a restrained tempo. The contrast between introduction and opening episode is dramatic. The introduction is visually conducted by the leading *gangsa* player. He gives a clear, swift downbeat with his mallet at three places—on the

344

opening beat and at the start of the two following phrases that compose the introduction. With the entrance of the stabilized first episode the direction is given over to the drums.

Ex. 333. Kebyar Kapi Raja; introduction and opening section ♩ = 108

1. gangsas; leader and group   2. réong   3. chèngchèng   4. kempli   5. jegogans

In more extended *kebyar* episodes, passages are built up through a seemingly endless repetition of the 5/8 unit. Ex. 334 gives only the first two phrases of a long passage that forms the middle section of *Kapi Raja*. Like all such passages, it is performed fortissimo throughout, literally hammered out with tireless energy. Here the leading *gangsa* player becomes conductor once more, signaling the change in the patterns with sudden accents.

Ex. 334. Kapi Raja; kebyar passage ♩ ♪ = 120

The conclusion of the passage marks the culmination of the first part of this composition. Here the dancer, if included in the performance, pauses. A free orchestral interlude follows, taking the form of an instrumental dialogue. The *réong* is first heard alone in rapid passage-work, but is soon dramatically interrupted by the *gangsas* and cymbals in vigorous unison. The *réongan* is resumed, only to be interrupted once more by the *gangsas*.

Ex. 335. Kapi Raja; kebyar interlude, commencement

346

The mood of this orchestral dialogue gradually changes, growing light and vivacious. *Réong*, cymbals, and drums engage in playful colloquy. Finally the leading *gangsa* is heard in a quiet melodic phrase. The rest of the *gangsas* follow, accompanied by the *réong*, in an ornamental introductory passage that leads immediately to the concluding section of the composition (Ex. 336).

Ex. 336. Kapi Raja; kebyar interlude concluded ♩ = 160

The long, cadenzalike interlude is thus brought back to metric order with the entrance of the *gangsas*, followed by the time-beating *kempli*. With the resumption of a fixed tempo (M. 144) the dance is resumed, to be continued to the end of the composition.

Not all the modern compositions of the *gamelan gong kebyar* are in freely extended *kebyar* form. Every gamelan includes in its repertory a certain number of short, lyrical pieces, simple in form, in which the loud display passages characteristic of the *kebyar* are omitted altogether. The musical illustrations given in this chapter can do no more than suggest the invention and vigor of *kebyar* style in general, and perhaps indicate some of the bold orchestral effects and the variety of orchestral colors found in this newer music. If the longer compositions lack the unity of form and mood of the older music of Bali, they compensate for this in their imagination and exuberant life, and in the melodic grace of the quiet passages. Three concluding examples are offered here in illustration. Two are adaptations of *gambang* melody, the first a complete composition in itself, the second a passage from a longer *kebyar*. Each arrangement differs in its own way from the *Gambangan* by Lotring which was discussed in the previous chapter. Both versions interpret the melody in a quiet, lyrical manner, with none of the tension and excitement which characterized the Lotring composition.

While Ex. 337 is complete in itself, it may also be included as an episode in an extended *kebyar* composition, where it serves as a quiet interlude between danced episodes. The melody is given to the *gangsas*, sounding in octaves against *réong* figuration. The traditional *gambang* style of playing the melody in the rhythm, ♩ ♪♩. , is relinquished for a more relaxed ♩. ♩ . Attention is called to the carefully worked out *réongan*, with its constantly changing patterns and occasional clashes with the melodic tones. The complete piece is so short that it can be given here in full. After a free introduction, led off by the leading *gangsa*, the melodic period is played three times, twice at a moderate tempo, the last time suddenly faster, with a return to the original tempo at the close.

Ex. 337. Gambangan, gamelan gong kebyar; Pliatan village* ♩ = 76

* Transcribed for two pianos by the author, and published, with the title Gambangan, by G. Schirmer, New York. See Appendix 5.

1. gangsas
2. réong
kempur and gong ageng, actual pitch
3. jublags and jegogans

Quite different in style is the *gambangan* passage from a north Bali *kebyar* (Ex. 338). While the *réongan*—not given here—remains essentially the same as that of the previous example, the *gangsa* melody is delivered in the traditional syncopated manner. The large *gangsas* play the melody in its original form; the small *gangsas* double and embellish the melody in the octave above, anticipating the longer tones with ornamental preparatory tones.

349

Ex. 338. Gambangan episode, gamelan gong kebyar; Jagaraga village ♩ = 76

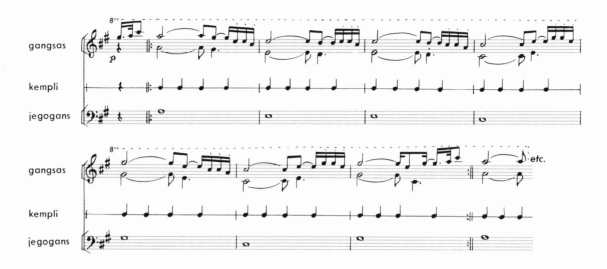

In a lyrical passage such as this, performed by ten or twelve *gangsas*, everything depends on absolute perfection of ensemble, especially if the ornamental tones are to have clarity and grace. The passage, however, is rhythmically stabilized by the *réongan* figuration and drumming, and by the regular beat of the *kempli*.

A quite different skill, similar to that required for the passage quoted in Ex. 306, is needed if the following passage (Ex. 339) for *gangsas* alone is to be played in unison. With no rhythmic support of any kind, the players must follow the leading *gangsa*, partly by watching, partly by ear. They must all feel in the same way the flexible, rubato nature of the passage. The charm of this episode, as played by the gamelan of Jagaraga in 1938, was irresistible. It lay partly in the melody itself, sounding in thinly chiming octaves and stressed at intervals by the vibrant tones of *jublags* and *jegogans*. But perhaps most enchanting of all was the lovely pliancy of the passage, and the perfect accord of all the players.

Ex. 339. Gangsa passage, gamelan gong kebyar; Jagaraga village ♩ = 66

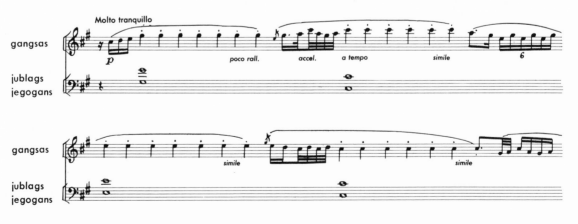

350

KEBYAR—THE LATEST STYLE

Appendices

Appendix 1. Notes to Chapters

Chapter 5

PRINCIPAL DANCE AND DRAMATIC FORMS

arja: a popular singing-play based on traditional Balinese theater, with romantic plots, comedy interludes, and songs with lyrics composed in classical Javanese meters. The average cast is made up largely of youths and young girls, although in more professional companies older men play leading and comedy roles. Examples of different verse forms used in *arja*, along with English translations, will be found in the chapter devoted to literature in Raffles' *History of Java.*

baris: a ceremonial dance in line formation performed by men. There are many variants. *Baris gedé,* great *baris,* a warriors' drill dance which was originally performed during temple ceremonies but is now incorporated into dance plays, is a dance of great tension—a controlled but dramatic display of physical vigor performed by young men after a prolonged and rigorous training. Less spectacular and ancient forms of *baris,* danced by older men, are still part of temple ritual in many mountain villages. These dances have not the tension and technical difficulty of *baris gedé;* they are more in the nature of simple folk dances, and consist chiefly of posturing with spears, shields, or krisses, or moving in stylized imitation of animals or birds. *Baris goak,* crow *baris,* is based on bird movement; *baris irengan* derives from the deliberate movements of the *irengan* or black ape. Among the more fantastic variations are *baris kupukupu,* butterfly *baris,* danced by young boys supplied with fans, and *baris china,* Chinese *baris.* *Baris pèndèt* is a ritual dance, offering burning incense, which is frequently performed. Walter Spies and R. Goris, in "Overzicht van Dans en Tooneel in Bali," *Djawa,* *17* (1937), list by name thirty variants of *baris.*

barong: a form of masked beast, operated by two dancers concealed within a framework covered with horsehair or feathers, and crowned with an elaborate headdress of gilded leather. The mask, with movable lower jaw, is baroquely carved in the form of a mythological lion, tiger, or boar. Most frequently met with is the lion form of *barong,* magically protective patron of the village. When not in use, this *barong* is kept in the temple. During the *galungan* holidays, when the spirits of the dead are said to revisit the world, the *barong* plays a role similar to that of the Chinese New Year dragon, passing through the village and stopping at each doorway to rout all imps and demons. In plays the *barong* is frequently introduced to represent the magic transformation of king or holy man. The *barong* dance is a capricious blend of moods; in turn the creature is represented as proud, playful, shy, and threatening. There is fine coordination between the two dancers, whose ankles and feet alone are visible, to create the illusion of a living, supple animal.

gabor: a women's ritual dance with offerings, performed in the temple.

gambuh: a classical and highly formalized dance drama with a large cast composed entirely of male actors. Formerly seen chiefly at court celebrations, these slow-moving plays are rarely presented today, but are still considered a main source for present-day dance, theatrical, and musical creation.

gandrung: the *jogèd* dance performed by a boy wearing *jogèd* costume.

jogèd: a popular street dance performed by a girl who solicits dancing partners from the onlookers. Villages specialize in either *gandrung* or *jogèd* performances, which are usually given at night and are always surrounded by a lively and somewhat rowdy audience. The performers may remain in the same spot all evening, in celebration of some holiday or village feast, or else travel from door to door (*melawan*), followed by the crowd, to give a short performance in return for a small sum of money.

kebyar: the brilliant exhibition dance, performed by a youth or small boy. Seated in a square enclosed by the instruments of the gamelan, the dancer translates into movement the constantly changing moods of the music. Half kneeling, half sitting, he dances from the waist only, moving now and then from one part of the square to another in a sudden gliding hop. The dance is a synthesis of male and female dance styles, combining both *baris* and *lègong* techniques. Both dance and music are a display of fireworks, showing off the technical skill of all performers.

lègong: the most highly perfected Balinese dance form, performed by a trio of small girls who are withdrawn at the approach of adolescence. Two of the dancers play leading roles. The third plays the part of *chondong* or maid-attendant, and also takes subordinate roles. The long and elaborately devised choreographies are partly abstract, partly storied.

nandir: a dance of former times, performed by a trio of boys, from which the *lègong* dance was developed. Maintained by the court, the dancers received the finest technical training. The Balinese composer, I Lotring (see p. 308), celebrated also as a dance teacher, was first trained in *nandir* at the court of Blahbatu, about 1906. The dance formed a link between *gambuh* and *lègong*. According to Lotring and other informants, the accompanying gamelan consisted of four *gendèr wayang*, two *sléndro* tuned *jegogans*, two drums, and a small percussion group.

(ng)ibing: a male dancing partner in the performances of *gandrung* and *jogèd*. Unlike the trained dancer, the *ngibing* dancer rarely receives any technical training, but he often shows considerable imagination in improvising lively accompanying dances.

rèjang: a ceremonial processional dance performed in the temple by unmarried girls.

sanghyang: the pantomimic performance of a dancer brought into trance with incense and chanting, and now possessed by a *sanghyang*, a divinity or spirit. Many forms of *sanghyang* are known, named after the spirit pantomimed. *Sanghyang dedari* is performed by two small girls who, dressed in *lègong* costume, "have become" (*jadi*) heavenly nymphs (*dedari*). *Sanghyang dèling* is also performed by two small girls who have become dolls. In certain parts of Bali, notably the Karangasem district, *sanghyang* performances are given in which youths or men become deer (*s. kidang*), monkeys (*s. bōjog*), serpents (*s. lilipi*), or swine (*s. chèlèng*). *Sanghyang jaran*, horse spirit, is performed by men astride sticks with carved horse heads. The performance usually takes place to the singing of special chants, in which the divinity or spirit is invoked.

tōpèng: a classical formalized pantomime with masked actors. The plots derive from Balinese historical chronicles (*babad*) dealing with former kings and princes, local wars, and the conquest of Lombok, the small island to the east of Bali. *Tōpèng* may take the form of a play with spoken dialogue, but in its most ceremonial form it is a silent performance given by a single dancer, and known as *tōpèng pajegan*. The dancer presents one character after another in turn. At the end of each representation the dancer goes to one end of the stage, turns his back to the audience and changes masks beneath a cloth thrown over his head. The cloth is quickly removed and the dancer suddenly turns round, transformed into a new personality. Each dance is different, stylistically interpreting the character expressed by the mask.

wayang kulit: the shadowplay. The word, *wayang*, is old Javanese for shadow or shade. *Wayang kulit* means literally leather shadows; *kulit* refers to the buffalo hide from which the shadow puppets are made. For a description of the performance see Chapter 14.

wayang wong: a dramatic performance performed by living actors or "mortal shades." It is limited to the *Ramayana* repertory, and requires a large cast of actors, both masked and unmasked. Rarely seen, it resembles the *gambuh* drama in its slow pace and archaic formalities. The same music as that played for the shadowplay performances of the *Ramayana* is used, with an accompanying ensemble consisting of a quartet of *gendèr wayang*, augmented by two drums and a percussion group.

THE CHUPAK STORY

Any Balinese child can give an outline of the moralistic story of braggardly Chupak and his gentle but courageous younger brother, Grantang, or draw their pictures on village walls as they appear on the stage or in the shadowplay. The contrast between stupidity and intelligence, coarse and fine, dark and light, is nowhere more plainly revealed in the Balinese theater than in this tale of two brothers so essentially different in character. The following synopsis is condensed from a palmleaf manuscript (*lontar*) belonging to Déwa Nyoman Rai of Pliatan, who translated it for me from the original *kawi* into Malay.

It is said that the demon Kala entered the child Chupak at birth, making him a blusterous, lazy, gluttonous, and boastful coward. Through a trick, Chupak turns his parents against his gently mannered and beautiful younger brother so that they turn him out of the house. Grantang is forced to wander afar through wilderness and forest. Nevertheless, Chupak accompanies him. He brings along a great supply of food, which is carried by Grantang but eaten by Chupak. They meet with various adventures, in which Chupak takes all the credit, although it is Grantang who acts. Finally they reach the court of Daha (a principality of East Java during Majapahit). The king, hearing of Chupak's heroism, asks him to recover his daughter, abducted by the giant, Limandaru. Chupak boasts he will slay the giant, no matter what his size. Grantang says he will also try, but can promise nothing beforehand. They set out, Chupak boldly in front, but at the first sight of the giant's footprints he trembles and orders Grantang to go ahead. When they find the giant, Grantang does the fighting, while Chupak takes refuge behind a tree. Grantang eludes the giant "like a butterfly," kills him and rescues the princess. They fall in love.

On the way back they pass through a deep forest. Chupak promises to keep watch while the two sleep. A demon appears in the night and carries off the princess. Chupak is too frightened to cry out. Grantang wakes and starts in pursuit. The demon is found in its den at the bottom of a deep well. When the demon is asleep Grantang descends by means of a rope and rescues the princess. Chupak pulls her up, but cuts the rope before Grantang reaches the top. He returns to the court with the princess. They are betrothed. Chupak passes the days in feasting, drunkenness, and debauch.

Meanwhile Grantang has killed the demon. He makes a ladder with the demon's bones and climbs out. He is so emaciated from hunger that people take him for an evil spirit. No one will help him. When he reaches the court Chupak denounces him as an impostor and orders him cast in the sea.

Grantang is picked up by a poor fishermen whose nets are always empty. The rescue brings him luck, for now each day he finds his nets immediately filled. He and his wife gratefully nurse Grantang back to health. His beauty returns. One day he is discovered by the princess, who has managed to delay her marriage to Chupak. She begs her father to let her be married to the bravest warrior in the land. She urges Grantang to challenge his brother, and sends him fine clothing. In the fight that follows Chupak is beaten, disgraced, and banished. Grantang marries the princess and inherits the kingdom.

THE CHALONARANG STORY

The scene of the play known as *Chalonarang* is eleventh century East Java. The literary sources of the play can be found in various Balinese manuscripts bearing that name, often differing in detail, but all dealing with certain legendary-historical events happening in East Java during the rule of Erlangga, A.D. 1010—42. Unknown in Java, the account has special reality for the Balinese, since Erlangga was born in Bali of a Balinese mother of royal lineage. After an adventurous youth he became one of the great kings of Java, but later retired to a hermitage. Many different versions of the Chalonarang story are given in play form, but all follow the same basic pattern. The following outline is condensed from a Balinese *kawi* manuscript of unknown date, translated into Dutch by R. Ng. Pubacharaka.

During the reign of Erlangga there lived in the province of Dirah a great sorceress named Chalonarang, also known as Rangda, the Widow. She had a beautiful daughter named Ratna Mangalli, but no man dared ask for her in marriage, for her mother was too greatly feared. In growing anger the sorceress seeks the aid of Durga, goddess of Death. She makes offerings and asks to be allowed to spread plague and death throughout the land. Permission is given, and she calls together her pupils in witchcraft, lovely young girls until transformed through magic formulas into monsters. They meet at night in the graveyard, where, after a wild dance, they form a plan of destruction. They disperse in all directions to commence their evil project. In villages everywhere people begin to sicken and die. As the plague increases the roads grow filled with those still able to flee to far-off parts.

On the advice of the great saint, Mpu Bharada, Erlangga sends his first minister, attended by soldiers, to kill the witch. They proceed to her house and attack her at midnight while she sleeps. But Chalonarang springs up. "And from her eyes, ears, nostrils and mouth issued fire which, flaming and curling, consumed the minister." The soldiers flee to notify the king, while Chalonarang and her pupils continue their destructive work with even greater ferocity. Transformed into hideous shapes they dance at crossroads and in graveyards. The dead are revived so the dancers may drink warm blood. Bodies are disembowelled and the entrails used for necklaces by the dancers. Soon the whole land is deserted and nothing may be heard but the cry of ravens.

Once more Erlangga appeals to the saint, who now sends his chief acolyte, Bahula, to marry the daughter and thus appease the witch. After the wedding, Ratna Mangalli steals her mother's book of magic formulas, hoping to weaken her. Even so Chalonarang's power remains undiminished. Still unappeased, she continues on her course of destruction.

Finally the saint himself sets out to confront her. Reaching Dirah, he encounters the pupils in the graveyard. He converts them to the Way and dismisses them. He soon finds himself before the witch herself, and now the great test of magic strength between the two begins. With sweet, deceitful words the Rangda asks to be shown the "Right Path." She is told this may be achieved only through death. In sudden rage she replies that she will kill the saint and expiate in hell. To show her magic strength she causes a great banyan tree to burst into flames and burn to ashes. With a *mantra* the saint calmly restores the tree. The witch sends streams of fire from her body that envelop the saint. He remains unharmed. With a sacred gesture he destroys her, then immediately brings her back to life. With bitter words the witch reproaches him for reviving her. He answers this was done in order that she might see the Way. Calmed at last, Chalonarang finds peace and is put to death once more, absolved.

No performance, however, ever ends with the witch's death, or even on a note of redemption. In fact, most performances have no conclusion at all, but end with the actor who played the witch and the two men who animate the *barong*, which now represents the transformed saint, falling into a violent trance. As the audience apprehensively breaks up, the two opponent figures leave the stage, accompanied by attendants, to be brought back to consciousness by the smoke of incense and the calming words of the village priest.

Chapter 6

RICE-POUNDING MUSIC

Pounding unhusked rice (*nebuk padi*) to remove the hulls is a daily task in the Balinese household. The work is normally done by women, although in wealthy families it is sometimes done by male servants. For the small amounts of rice needed for immediate consumption, the grain is generally pounded on the ground. Two, three, or four women stand around the little heap, pounding with heavy, eight-foot poles. The pole is raised with one hand and dropped by the other with a downward thrust. As it bounces back the first hand catches it on the rebound and raises it. The poles are dropped in regular alternation. Since no two poles are exactly the same length or thickness there is a recognizable difference in the sound and pitch of the different poles. A variety of sound patterns can thus be created, from the simple alternating strokes of two workers to the more varied interplay produced by three or four poles. The normal speed at which each pole is dropped is around a stroke per second, and women will pound for hours with no apparent fatigue, taking pleasure in the different patterns they create.

Ex. 340.

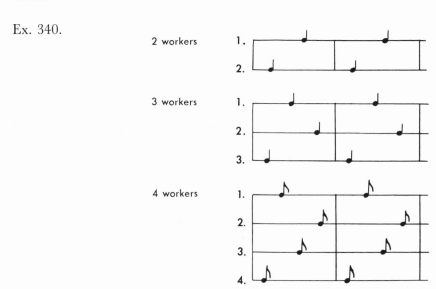

While in the average small household rice is usually pounded on the ground, large households and most temples may possess a long wooden trough, the *lesung*, in which large amounts of grain may be threshed at one time. The trough is free of the ground, resting at each end on a log set crosswise, and is resonant as a drum when struck. While the sound of the poles pounding rice on the ground is a dull thud, when dropped in the *lesung* the poles produce clear musical sounds of distinguishably contrasting pitch. In spite of the grain in the trough, which acts as shock absorber, the tones can be heard a mile away. The women, now invariably four, stand in a row or in facing pairs (Fig. 101–103). From time to time the patterns change as a worker drops out for a while or a new pole sequence begins. A tone in the pattern may also take on a certain emphasis as one worker or another drops her pole with a more energetic thrust.

Ex. 341.

Continued indefinitely, sound patterns such as these provide stimulating work music. In certain parts of Bali, however, when there is much rice to be threshed, it is still the custom for boys and men to gather around the women and turn work into play by beating out lively polyrhythmic accompaniment on the sides of the *lesung*. Husking great amounts of rice for a coming feast becomes a gay party, continuing from one moonlit night to the next. While the women maintain a steady beat as they pound the grain, a lively accompaniment, the *chandetan*, is beaten out with sticks and short poles in polyrhythmic interplay similar to that of the cymbals in the *gamelan gong*, as shown in Ex. 39 and 40. Different resonant spots of the *lesung* are sought, each with its characteristic sound. Each man performs his particular rhythmic pattern where it can be heard to best advantage, so that the wooden trough becomes a vibrant, many-voiced drum. As a resonant object the *lesung* is now generally referred to as the *ketungan*, from "*tung*," the sound of the *lesung* when struck with a wooden pole or stick.

When performed with *chandetan*, the women's part in the ensemble is known by the differentiating term, *ngijengin*, the stationary, unchanging part (from *ngijeng*, stay, or remain in the same place). The *chandetan* (from *nyandet*, make syncopated accompaniment) can be performed by two men alone beating out interlocking rhythmic patterns. Six at least are considered essential to create a full and satisfying *kilitan* or "binding together" of different sounds. In the following diagram, which represents the *lesung* or *ketungan* in cross-section, characteristic *chandetan* strokes are shown.

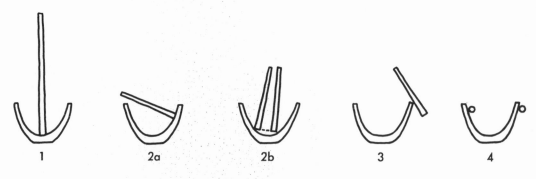

1   2a   2b   3   4

APPENDIX 1. NOTES TO CHAPTERS

No. 1 shows the *ngijengin* stroke of the rice-pounders, who stand near the middle of the *lesung* (Fig. 101). The remaining strokes are made near the ends (Figs. 102 and 103). While these are all classified as *chandetan* strokes, No. 2 represents the actual *nyandet* stroke, produced a) by knocking the stick against the inner side of the trough, or b) by dropping it on the bottom, then knocking it against the side. This latter stroke is similar to the quick double knock of the *angklung*. No. 3 represents the *ngōtèk* stroke, used in the rapid *kōtèkan* parts (Ex. 344), beaten lightly on the outer edge of the trough. No. 4, the *ngōplak* or *ngōplek* stroke, is produced by holding the stick with both hands and knocking it sideways against the inner or outer edge. Additional strokes are the *nachalin* (*salin*, changed; contrasting rhythm), struck on the end of the *ketungan*, and the *ngeteg*, beaten on the edge. A heavy wooden mallet is generally used for these latter strokes (Fig. 103).

Since the *chandetan* performers number anywhere from two to six or seven, the rhythmic combinations are endless. Three or four examples will suffice to illustrate the characteristic interplay. Typical three-part accompaniment of the *ngijengin* pounders consists of two *nyandet* beaters and one *ngōplak*.

Ex. 342.

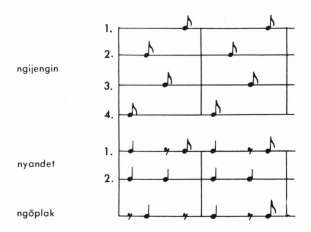

While the *nyandet* parts tend to remain fixed in short repeating patterns, the *ngōplak*, heavier in sound, may extend into an independent "solo."

Ex. 343.

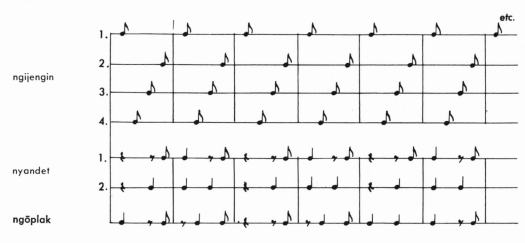

Although a second *nyandet* part is optional, the *ngōtèk* or *kōtèkan* is essentially two-voiced. The two parts interlock to produce an interplay at double the speed of the *nyandet-ngōplak* interplay.

Ex. 344.

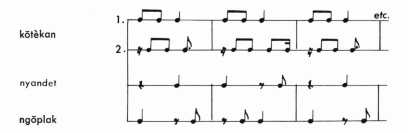

Various forms of *kōtèkan*, based on different rhythmic units, are in use. To indicate any unit the word *chat* or *chah* (*chahchah*—number, total, something chopped fine) is employed. *Chat* 3 is thus a unit having three strokes in each part. Four different units are generally known.

Ex. 345.

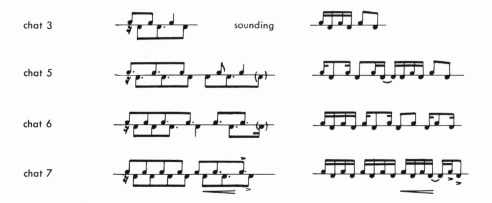

The sound of this little percussion group is lively and exhilarating. Above the deep, resonant tones produced by the rice-pounding poles, the animated polyrhythmic accompaniment clatters with tireless energy. Pounding rice in this way is known in some parts as *ngebuk onchang*, pounding accompanied by *onchang* (or *onchang-onchangan*), any form of organized polyrhythmic sounds. The performance is constantly varied by changing suddenly from loud to soft, creating *ombakan* or "waves."

Various forms of rice-trough music are known in different parts of Indonesia. In the small island of Lombok, off the east coast of Bali, I witnessed festive performances by unmarried girls and youths which took place at the time of the full moon. The girls stood in line on one side of the trough while the boys faced them on the other. A single pole was shared by each couple, boy and girl passing it back and forth in alternate strokes. Free, antiphonal songs were sung in unison, the girls singing one line or couplet, the boys the next.

362

APPENDIX 1. NOTES TO CHAPTERS

Chapter 13

JOGÈD BUMBUNG

It is but a step to transform the various patterns produced by the rice-pounders into simple rhythmic accompaniment for the *jogèd bumbung*, a dance occasionally performed by women or girls at harvest festivals (*usaba*). Instead of poles, the *bumbung* or *bungbung*, short bamboo tubes of different lengths which are open at the top and closed at the bottom, are held in upright position and pounded on a raised plank that acts as resonator. Like the rice-pounding poles, a complete *bumbung* set consists of four tubes, each with its individual and recognizably different pitch. Here, for once, the musical performers are women. They stand in a row behind the plank that extends before them at waist level, each holding a single tube and pounding (or dropping) it in turn against the plank (Fig. 104). As in rice-pounding, various sound patterns are created through changing the sequence of the striking tubes. Although, according to informants, *bumbung* music can be performed with *chandetan* accompaniment, I found no instance of this during my stay in Bali.

Unlike the popular street dance with trained *jogèd* dancer, no partners participate in this performance. The dance itself is extremely simple, similar to that of the ceremonial *rèjang* and *gabor* dances performed in the temple. Two, four, or six women may take part, wearing traditional ceremonial clothes and elaborate floral headdresses, and each holding in the right hand an open fan. On one rare occasion, during a festival held in a small village in Tabanan in 1938, the dance took the form of a slow processional of some fifty dancers, all young unmarried girls. Along the side of the road where the dance took place a wooden rail extended one hundred yards or more, behind which stood a long row of women to perform the *bumbung* accompaniment. The rhythmic patterns now lost all clarity of pitch, giving way to a steady tapping as countless bamboos were dropped, in arranged turn, up and down the plank. Girls from twenty villages gathered that day, and before nightfall some three hundred were said to have danced. Great congregations such as this are most unusual. That witnessed in 1938 was said to be the first revival of an old custom in forty years.

KŌPRAK AND KULKULAN

Occasionally heard at harvest festivals is the *kōprak* or *kōpiak*, a form of bamboo slit drum used chiefly as a noise maker. It consists of a septum of bamboo, closed at each end and having a longitudinal slit, and is actually a form of bamboo *kulkul* which can be carried in the hand. A number are sometimes carried in festive processions by a group of boys and men, who beat out lively polyrhythmic music called the *onchang-onchangan*, which is essentially the same as the *chandetan* accompaniment to rice-pounding. When the rice fields become infested with rats, *kōprak* parties are often organized to drive them out with a din of many clattering instruments. The *kōprak* may also consist of a bamboo pole of six or more septums, each sealed from the next by a nodal wall. Each septum has a slit, thus creating a series of adjoining drums. In this form the *kōprak* is mounted horizontally at a convenient height, fastened at the ends to posts driven into the ground. Two bamboos are generally used, forming a double instrument. Men stand on both sides facing each other, each with his own septum before him (Fig. 106). The group performs energetic *onchangan* patterns or beats out rhythmic passages in simple unison.

The *kōprak* may also be heard in festive "*kulkulan*" parties. In some districts these may continue for weeks after the rice has been harvested. A wooden slit drum of enormous size and corresponding resonance, modeled after the familiar *kulkul* that hangs in every marketplace, is mounted in horizontal position. Raised high in the air for all to see, and set in a bamboo scaffold, the *kulkul* is beaten by two men who sit on planks running along each side of the drum (Fig. 107). Holding heavy wooden mallets, they strike alternately on opposite sides of the drum's slit; the deep booming tones carry for miles. Two tones of recognizably different pitch are produced, a female or *wadon* tone, and a male or *lanang*, sounding a third or fourth higher in pitch. By means of syncopated interplay between the two performers, *kulkul* solos, or *kulkulan*, are improvised against a steady background of repeated strokes beaten in unison by the *kōprak* group. These *kulkulan* compositions generally consist of short passages or rhythmic motifs separated by silences, in which the *kōprak* players continue alone. A *kulkulan* performance can go on for hours without a break as one pair of *kulkul* beaters is replaced by another, and as one by one new performers take their place at the *kōprak*.

Ex. 346. Kulkul rhythms ♩ = 60

Dances are occasionally improvised by the *kulkulan* performers. Instead of sitting, a pair of youths stand facing each other on opposite sides of the drum. Alternately, they crouch low over the *kulkul* to beat a brief rhythmic passage, then stand, to perform an equally brief dance passage to the *kōprak* accompaniment. The dancers remain stationary, moving rhythmically with their bodies and gesturing with their arms. The performance is similar to the *gandrung* or *jogèd* dance, one youth taking the female role, the other the male role of partner.

Ex. 347. Kulkul dance rhythms ♩ = 60

364

APPENDIX 1. NOTES TO CHAPTERS

Kulkulan as a form of festive entertainment may not be seen for years at a time. In 1938, the same year as the great convention of *jogèd bumbung* dancers, it suddenly became popular in several neighboring villages of Tabanan. Youths of each village tried to outdo the others in making a more enormous drum. For a month or two *kulkulan* performances took place every day and night. When the *kulkul* was not in use it was covered with a richly brocaded cloth and laid out in state in a small pavilion decked with streamers and paper fringe that stood in the center of the village. Suddenly enthusiasm died and the parties ended. In each village the drum was removed from its ceremonial pavilion and stored in the village clubhouse or the temple.

Chapter 16

THE GENDING LUANG

Since my information concerning the musical repertory of the *gamelan gong luang* is contradictory to that given by Jaap Kunst in his book, *De Toonkunst van Bali* (*1*, 35s), I feel that his statement should be included here for comparison.

> Its music falls into three modal groups, named: *Lilit, Tjenada,* and *Saih Miring.* In addition, six different *gendings* are known by this ensemble, each of which can be performed in the three named ways. These consist of the *gendings:*
>
> > *Saih pandji*
> > *Saih pandji ngiring*
> > *Saih njoera*
> > *Saih njoera ngiring*
> > *Saih wargasari*
> > *Saih pandji gedénan*
>
> To indicate the manner of playing a *gending,* one of the six above names is combined with one of the three modes, as for example, *Saih pandji ngiring lilit,* or *Saih pandi gedénan Saih miring.*

In my own experience, actual practice proved to be quite the reverse. The musicians of both Sèséh and Ampuan, the two *banjars* of Singapadu village each owning a *gamelan luang*, agreed in general regarding the musical repertory which they shared in common, and referred to *Lilit, Chenada,* and *Saih Miring* as *tembang* or *gending.* When the *pòkok* tones to these *gendings* were obtained, each was found to differ both in melodic line and in metric structure, one being in the *tabuh 4* category, the other two classified as *tabuh 8.* As described in Chapter 16, each *gending,* when transposed from one to another of the six scales or *jalans*, listed above as *gendings*, retained its own basic melodic outline. In his book, Kunst refers to a *gamelan luang* in Singapadu, but does not mention from which *banjar.*

365

Appendix 2. Glossary

abhōgari, tabuh gari closing music, played at the end of a performance

ageng large; deep or relatively low in pitch

alit small; relatively high in pitch

alus fine, gentle, refined, soft

ambah, ampah to play in a particular mode or scale

angkat-angkatan a group of compositions which are played in *wayang kulit* and *wayang wong* performances during active scenes

angklung archaic form of tuned bamboo rattle

angsel rhythmic phrasing break in both music and dance movement

apada stanza, strophe; a complete musical period

arja popular singing play; see p. 355

arum-aruman a group of quiet pieces in the *gendèr wayang* repertory, said to derive from *kekawin* chants, and often played on more solemn religious occasions

awi, awi-awi to compose, create—music, text, dance; *kawitan*, something composed

babad parchment of *kerbau* intestine which closes the body of the *rebab*

balung gending the Javanese term for the nuclear tones of a *gending*, occasionally heard in Bali

banchih bisexual; *kendang bebanchian*, a form of drumming performed by a single drum, in which the main accents of the male and female drums are combined, and used mainly for *jogèd* and *gandrung* performances; *suling banchih*, a type of flute used in the *arja* play to accompany both male and female performers

bangkiwa of mixed racial descent; *kendang bangkiwa*, a type of drumming which can accompany both male and female dancers

banjar district or ward of a town or village

bapang group of ostinato motifs used to accompany the entrance dance of court official or herald; the middle section in the *baris gedé* dance

barangan follower; the smaller *trompong* or pair of *gendèrs*, pitched an octave above the leading instruments

baris a large group of ceremonial dances for men; see p. 355

Baro one of the five scales in the *saih 7 pegambuhan* system

barong a mythological masked beast, operated by two dancers; see p. 355

basa, bahasa language, speech, as opposed to singing; see *juru basa*

batèl ensemble of purely rhythmic percussion instruments; rhythmic percussion accompaniment to stage scenes of violent action; march music

batèl maya loud percussive passage for entire gamelan, based on the prolonged reiteration of a single tone, which signals the beginning of the actual story in the *lègong* dance and can also indicate a change of scene

batok the half-shell of coconut which usually forms the body of the *rebab*

bebendé, bendé a special type of large gong with sunken boss, used only in the *gamelan gong* and the *bōnang* ensemble

366

bechat   quick, lively; *gending bechat*, short compositions in quick tempo for the *gamelan gong*. *Mechatan!* Faster!

bèro   off-pitch, out of tune

bhèri   older name for *bendé*

bibih   lip; the rim of gong or drumhead

bisah   name of a symbol in musical notation

bōnang   a type of small gong struck in horizontal position; a set of such gongs arranged in a horizontal row or rows

bōnangan   that section of the music played on the *bōnang*

bruk   Abang term for coconut shell resonator in the special form of xylophone known there as the *trompong bruk*

bumbung, bungbung   septum of bamboo, open at one end, used as a musical instrument to accompany the *jogèd bumbung* dance

bung   bamboo resonator of an instrument

çangka   see *sangkah*

chagat   the poles supporting the large gongs

chak, kèchak   the chorus of men providing vocal accompaniment for the various forms of *sanghyang* dances

chakep(an)   pair, as of cymbals; set, as of *réongs*

chalung   another name for *jublag*

chandetan   polyrhythmic percussion accompaniment in rice-pounding music; two-voiced figuration in modern gamelan practice

chang kendang   muted drum stroke

changah   the upright poles supporting the *chagat*

changkriman   a popular verse form of Javanese origin, with its special melodic pattern, in which songs sung to small children are composed

chanteng   the bridge of the *rebab*

chantik   the tongue of the *gènggong*

charik   punctuating sign, corresponding in literature to a comma; in musical notation used to indicate the end of a melodic section

charik kalih   double *charik*, corresponding to a period; in musical notation used to indicate the end of a composition

charuk   Karangasem name for an antique form of xylophone, known elsewhere by the misleading name, *saron*

chat, chah   a complete rhythmic unit in polyrhythmic cymbal playing or rice-pounding music

chat lima   a rhythmic unit composed of five beats

chat nem   a rhythmic unit composed of six beats

chat pitu   a rhythmic unit composed of seven beats

chāt telu   a rhythmic unit composed of three beats

chegir   name for the sound produced by the *gong lanang*

chegur   name for the sound produced by the *gong wadon*

cheluluk   another name for the *kajar;* tones produced on the boss of the *kajar*

cheluring, churing   an obsolete musical instrument consisting of a series of tuned bronze cups fastened to an underframe and struck with a metal rod

chempala   the *dalang*'s signal block, held between the first and second toes of the left foot

chèngchèng   large cymbal, cymbal pair, or group of cymbals, used in the traditional *gamelan gong*

chenik   small; relatively higher in pitch

chiblon   water music; rhythms beaten by the hand, cupped or flat, on the surface of the water

chondong   lady-in-waiting or maid-attendant in stage productions

chongé-chongé   Karangasem name for medium size *chèngchèng*, and their particular rhythmic pattern in the interplay of cymbals

chungklik   a form of xylophone with keys resting over a deep resonance box, used mainly in the home as a recreational instrument

churing   a form of metallophone rarely seen today, having a two-octave range and keys resting over a shallow resonance box

dag   the basic, open sound of the *kendang wadon*, produced by the palm of the right hand

dalang   the operator of the puppets and reciter of the dialogue in the shadowplay

dang   the fifth tone of the *saih 5*

dang ageng   the third tone of the *saih 7*, *gambang* system

dang alit   the sixth tone of the *saih 7*, *gambang* system

deng   the third tone of the *saih 5;* the fourth tone of the *saih 7*, *gambang* system

ding   the first tone of both the *saih 5* and the *saih 7*, *gambang* system

don, daun   leaf; the key or keys of a metallophone or xylophone

dong   the second tone of the *saih 5;* the fourth tone of the *saih 5*, *gambang* system

dong ageng   the second tone of the *saih 7*, *gambang* system

dong alit   the seventh tone of the *saih 7*, *gambang* system

dung   the fourth tone of the *saih 5;* the fifth tone of the *saih 7*, *gambang* system

ékara   name for a symbol in musical notation

embat   to stretch out or span; *embat-embatan*, to dance with arms outstretched, as in *rejang;* to play an instrument, such as the *trompong*, requiring outstretched arms; *gending embatan*, those compositions in the traditional *gamelan gong* repertory in which the leading melody is played by the *trompong*

gabor   a ceremonial dance for women; see p. 355

galungan   the most important Balinese religious holiday, occurring every 210 days and lasting ten days; a festival spirit prevails, when dances and popular plays take place throughout the island

gambang   a special form of bamboo xylophone retained from the past for the performance of sacred music during cremation rites

gambangan   a recently developed form of composition making use of traditional *gambang* melodies

gambuh   the classical theater of Bali; see p. 355

gamelan   any ensemble composed primarily of percussion instruments

gandrung   popular form of dance performed by a boy; see p. 356

gangsa   bronze; a name interchangeable with *saron* in indicating any one-octave metallophone with keys resting over a sound-box and struck with a single mallet

gangsa gantung   *gangsa* with keys suspended *gendèr* fashion

gangsa jongkok   the usual *gangsa* or *saron*

gangsa siya   the nine-keyed *gangsa gantung*, employed in the modern *gamelan gong kebyar*

gangsar   quick; *gangsaran!* increase the tempo!

gebug   to strike, beat (pop.); *gebug maya*, to play with rhythmic freedom, as in the syncopated style often employed in *trompong* playing

gedé   large; deep in pitch

gendèr   metallophone having a two-octave or wider range, with keys suspended over tubular resonators, and played with two mallets; *gendèr dasa*, ten-keyed *gendèr; gendèr telulas*, thirteen-keyed *gendèr; gendèr limolas*, fifteen-keyed *gendèr*

gender wayang   or *gendèr dasa;* the special, *sléndro*-tuned *gendèr* used in the shadowplay and *wayang wong* ensembles

gending   instrumental composition

gending ageng   composition in large form; a group of ceremonial compositions notable for melodic breadth which forms the major part of the repertory of the traditional *gamelan gong*

gending angklung   repertory of compositions for the *gamelan angklung*, characterized by their metric variety

gending gambang   compositions performed during cremation rites by the *gambang* ensemble

gending gangsaran   compositions in relatively fast tempo; a group of short compositions in the *gamelan gong* repertory

gending gong, pegongan   the large repertory of compositions performed by the *gamelan gong*

gending lambat   compositions in slow tempo; another name for the *gending ageng*

gending lawas   old compositions; a classical *gending*

gending longgor   a group of compositions of the *gangsaran* category, often used as finale in the *gending ageng*

gending luang   small group of *gendings* played by the *gamelan luang*

gending pegambuhan   repertory of compositions performed for the *gambuh* plays, and forming the basis for the repertory of the *gamelan Semar Pegulingan*

gending pelègongan   compositions deriving for the most part from the *gambuh* repertory and arranged to accompany the *lègong* dance

gènggong   Balinese form of jews harp, made from sugarpalm wood

genta, ghanta   priest's handbell

gentorak   rack of small bells

gihing, giying   backbone; Karangasem term for *gangsa* solo introducing the *gending angklung*

gineman   see *guneman*

gita   chants sung in the temple

gong   name for the largest metallophone in the *gamelan selundèng*

gong, gong ageng   the largest form of gong, found in the *gamelan gong*

gong lanang   the male *gong*, smaller of the pair employed in the *gamelan gong*

gong wadon   the female *gong*, larger in size and lower in pitch

gongan   a complete melodic period, terminating with a *gong* stroke

gongsèng   form of pellet bell

grantang   the symbols used in musical notation; an old form of xylophone, having bamboo tubes for keys

grubungan   wooden cowbell, made in many sizes

gumanak   small cylindrical percussion instrument of bronze or iron, used in the *gamelan gambuh*

guneman   improvisatory solo introduction preceding the *pengawit* to a composition

guntang   one-stringed bamboo zither, used as a percussion instrument

gupek   name for drum beaten with hands only

gupekan   drumming produced by the hands and fingers

igèl   dance; *menigèl*, to dance

inting   the second largest metallophone of the *gamelan selundèng*

jangat   the tuning strings of a drum

jegogan   the largest of the one-octave metallophones of the *gendèr* family

jogèd   popular form of dance performed by a girl; see p. 356

jublag   the second largest of the one-octave metallophones of the *gendèr* family

juru basa   the speaker who gives a line by line translation into Balinese of the *kawi* text sung by the *juru memacha* in a performance of *kekawin*

juru gamelan   member of the gamelan

juru gendèr   *gendèr* player

juru memacha   the reader, who sings or recites the *kawi* texts in a *kekawin* performance

juru tandak   the singer, occasionally included in the *gamelan pelègongan*, whose lines clarify or comment on the dramatic action of the dance

kajar   small gong with sunken boss, similar to the *bendé* in form, included in the *gambuh, Semar Pegulingan*, and *pelègongan* orchestras

kala   *kawi* word for cymbals

kaling   earthen jar forming the resonator of the *kempur kōmōdong*

kangsi   small cup-shaped cymbals mounted in pairs at the ends of sticks and struck against the ground, used only in the *gambuh* orchestra

kantilan   the smallest of the one-octave metallophones of the *gendèr* family; another word for *kotèkan*

karang   to compose—music, poetry, a painting; *karangan*, a composition; *dikarang olèh* X, composed by X; *karang sendiri*, I composed it myself

katik   stick; *katik réong*, the wooden body of the *réong angklung; katik rebab*, the *rebab* bow

kawat   wire; the *rebab* strings

kawi   formal literary language, composed mainly of old Javanese and Sanskrit

kayon   the stylized "tree" of the shadowplay, set up before the performance begins, whose later appearances represent wind, rain, or fire, and also indicate a change of scene and the end of the play

kebyar   a modern dance, performed by a boy or youth to the accompaniment of the *gamelan gong kebyar;* the music which accompanies the dance; see p. 356

kèchak   see *chak*

kekawin   epic poetry in classical Hindu meter; the chanting of such texts, along with line by line translation from *kawi* into colloquial Balinese

kèmanak   see *gumanak*

kembang   flower (Mal.); *kembangan*, ornamental passages in music, painting, and carving (pop.)

kembang kirang   lacking a flower—an old name for the *gamelan angklung*

kemong, ken(t)ong   small perpendicular gong of fine resonance used in the *gamelan pelègongan*

kempli   small horizontal gong supplying secondary punctuation

kempur   large perpendicular gong supplying secondary punctuation in the *gamelan gong*, and replacing the *gong ageng* in other ensembles

kempur kōmōdong   a substitute instrument used in the *gamelan pejogèdan*, consisting of a large bamboo key suspended over an earthen jar

kempyang, kōmpyang   the higher pitched of the two gongs that compose the *pōnggang*

kempyong, kōmpyong   the lower pitched of the two *pōnggang* gongs

APPENDIX 2. GLOSSARY

ke(n)chek   medium sized cymbals used in *kebyar*

kendang   drum, especially a drum beaten with drumstick

kendang lanang   male drum; the smaller, higher pitched of the drum pair

kendang wadon   female drum; the larger, lower pitched of the drum pair

kendangan   drumming

kenyir   small *gangsa* having three keys of the same pitch, which are struck with a triple-headed hammer; used in the *gambuh* orchestra only

keplakan   a form of bamboo rattle used to frighten birds

kepuakan   another name for the *keplakan;* the largest pair of cymbals and their rhythmic patterns, as found in certain *angklung* ensembles of Karangasem

ketungan   rice-pounding music

kichak   the smallest cymbals and their rhythmic patterns, as found in certain Karangasem *angklung* ensembles

kidung   classical poetry in old Javanese meters; *mekidung*, the singing of *kidung*

kilit   bound together; *kilitan*, the interlocking patterns of a pair of drums; a third part in *kōtèkan* figuration, binding together the two main parts; see *lilit*

kiwa   left side; *gending pengiwa*, compositions played for puppets belonging to the left side of the *dalang; suling pengiwa*, flute that can accompany both male and female voices; see *pengiwa*

klènang, kelènang   a small, high pitched gong sounded on the offbeats

klèntèng   old word for *réong* as found in the *gamelan angklung*

klèntèngan   the part played by the *réongs* in the *gamelan angklung; kajar* passages performed on the surface instead of the boss of the gong

klènti   old word for *kempli*

kōpiak, kōprak   a form of bamboo slit drum

kōtèkan   in Java, the name for rice-pounding music; in Bali, the polyrhythmic accompaniment beaten on the side of the rice trough as the rice is pounded; general term for two-part *gangsa* figuration, but interchangeable with *kantilan*

kras   vigorous, strong, rough, as opposed to *alus*, fine, restrained

krawang   bronze; *gamelan krawang*, an ensemble composed of bronze instruments

krèmpèng(an)   high-pitched drum tones produced by striking the fingertips near the rim of the drumhead

krinching(an)   shell jingle consisting of snail shells with or without clappers which are hung in a frame, where they can be set in motion by the wind

krumpung(an)   drum tones deeper in pitch than the *krèmpèng*, produced by striking nearer the center of the drumhead

kulkul   slit drum of wood or bamboo used for signaling and summoning, found alike in temple, palace, marketplace, and household

kulkulan   sounding of the *kulkul;* also a form of diversion in which rhythmic patterns are beaten on the *kulkul* to polyrhythmic *kōprak* accompaniment

lagu   melody, tune; name of a symbol in musical notation

lambat   slow; see *gending lambat*

lampahan   play, drama; *baris melampahan, baris* performance with dramatic plot

lanang   male; the smaller, higher pitched of two drums or gongs

laras   scale, tone series—a term interchangeable with *saih*

laras tuju   colloquial for *saih pitu*

lawas   old; *gending (le)lawasan*, old compositions performed in classical or ancient style

Lebeng   one of the five scales in the *saih 7 pegambuhan* system

lègong   a form of dance performed by three small girls; see p. 170

lilit   vine; *mekilit*, to interlock, as in the interdependent rhythms of the two drums; to bind together, as when a third part is added to the *kōtèkan;* see *kilit*

longgor   a type of heavy, rapid drumming produced with drumsticks; a group of compositions in the *gamelan gong* repertory; see *gending longgor*

lontar   manuscript or book composed of leaves of the *tal* palm

lupita, chelupita   a form of wooden clapper formerly used in the *gambuh* orchestra

manis   sweet, soft

mantra   prayer formula

marga   road; occasionally used to indicate a particular scale

mata titiran   wood dove's eye; a symbol in musical notation in the form of a circle, indicating the gong stroke at the end of a melodic period

mechandet   to perform *chandetan* figuration

medet   down-bow in *rebab* playing

megambel   to play in the gamelan

mekilit   see *lilit*

melawan   *lawan*, doorway; to perform from door to door

menabuh   to strike, perform music; see *tabuh*

mepadu   to compete; *mepadu gong*, festival competition of outstanding *gamelan gong kebyar* orchestras

metanguan   to echo, as a tone continuing to vibrate within a resonator

mipil   the suddenly faster closing section of a movement, leading to the closing phrase which is taken at the opening tempo

mōlos   *pōlos*, simple, direct; the upper of two parts in interlocking figuration, which follows more closely the basic melodic line

monchol   the boss of a gong

mudra   ritualistic hand gestures of the priest that accompany the recitation of *mantras*

murid   pupil

nakah   to repeat a melodic period; to return to the beginning of a movement

nandir   a former dance, performed by three boys, from which *lègong* is said to derive; see p. 356

narik (narèk) kendang   *tarik*, pull, draw tight; suddenly animated and stringendo drumming during the *mipil;* see *penarik*

neteg   a rhythmic unit in *chèngchèng* playing similar to the *nyachah*

ngandap   low register of an instrument

ngarèn   to play offbeat; syncopated *trompong* passages in which the soloist sometimes anticipates, more often delays, the structural melodic tones

ngateh   unison, as opposed to the octave

ngebug   to strike; *ngebug gamelan*, to sound the gamelan; *ngebug gendèr*, play *gendèr* (pop.)

ngedig   to perform, play; *Kèn-kèn ngedig?* How is it played? How do you play it? (pop.)

ngelik   to play in the high register of an instrument; see *pengelik*

n(g)embat   *embat*, extend; *trompong* passages performed in octaves

ngetetang   *rebab* bowing term; a single bowing of unequal speed and pressure, producing an alternately heavy and light tone

APPENDIX 2. GLOSSARY

n(g)ibing   male partner in the *gandrung* or *jogèd* dance; see p. 356

ngisep kendang   light passage for the two drums in the *gending ageng*, in which main accentuation is supplied by one drum only, while the cymbals are silent

ngiwa   see *pengiwa*

ngōbak   a rhythmic unit in *chèngchèng* playing

ngorèt   short glissando within the octave

nguchekan   a term for syncopated *trompong* passages (pop.)

ngumbang   *kumbang*, mason bee; the rapid stride of actor or dancer covering the whole stage "like a *kumbang* flying around," forming a contrasting animated episode between more stationary dance passages; see *pengumbang*

niba   see *pengiwa, peniba*

nichak   a rhythmic unit in polyrhythmic cymbal playing

nichik   the smallest of the *chèngchèngs;* their particular rhythmic pattern

nongsok   up-bow in *rebab* playing

numpuk   a form of embellishment in *trompong* playing

nyachah   a rhythmic unit in polyrhythmic *chèngchèng* playing

nyading   a term for *gambang* figuration

nyakadin   Karangasem term for *nyangsih*

nyalit   to play in the high register of an instrument; see *penyalit*

nyandet   a syncopated rhythmic unit in both polyrhythmic *chèngchèng* playing and rice-pounding music

nyangsih   *sangsih*, differing; the second, filling-in part in two-part figuration

nyaring   shrill, ringing

nyerodin   Karangasem term for two-part figuration

ochèt-ochètan   a form of figuration in *kebyar* music

ōdalan   semi-annual temple feast

ombak-ombakan   waves; vocal embellishments; alternately loud and soft passages in *kebyar*

onchang-onchangan   Karangasem term for *trompong* playing; polyrhythmic accompaniment in rice-pounding music

pada   see *apada*

pakahad   *mekahad*, withdraw; closing section in the *lègong* dance and accompanying music; see *penyuwud*

pakètan   Karangasem term for *kōtèkan*

palawakiya   epic prose recited in formal declamatory style, the text consisting of a *kawi* version of the *Mahabharata;* today a public performance often includes instrumental interludes by the *gamelan gong kebyar*

palet, paletan   a unit or set; *réong apalet*, a complete set of *réongs;* a metric unit of the *gongan;* an entire movement of a *gending* (rarely used); in *kekawin* texts a complete section composed of stanzas having the same meter

palu   hammer; the special hammer-headed mallet used to strike the *saron* and *gangsa*

pandé krawang   a metal smith specializing in casting gongs and metallophones, and in retuning gamelan instruments

panggul   the inclusive word for hammer, mallet, or stick used in striking gongs, drums, metallophones, and all other percussive instruments

pantun   Malayan four-line verse form sometimes sung in *arja*

parikan   version, adaptation; *ditarik ring gending gambang*, drawn from the *gending gambang*

patutan   *patut*, right, correct; tuning, the tuning of the gamelan; *patutan Segara Wira, Pudak Setegal, Chelagi Menyan, Sekar Kemuning, Selisir Gong*, names of different tunings, of which the final standards cannot be determined

pegineman   improvisatory solo preluding by *gendèr*

pelawah, plawah   the stand or wooden base of an instrument, on which gongs or keys are mounted

pelayah   the wooden "tongue" on the *guntang* string

pélog   the seven-tone scale system allowing for various forms of pentatonic scales

pemèro   one of the two secondary tones in the Balinese *saih 7 pegambuhan* scale system

pemetit   a name for the smallest *gambang* in the *gamelan gambang*

pemungkah   *bungkah*, to open up; the opening music to the shadowplay, played while the puppets are set up at the sides of the screen

penangkep   term for octave; passages performed in octaves on the *trompong*

penarik, penarèk   another term for *batèl maya;* a Buleleng name for the two smallest *gambangs* of the *gamelan gambang*

penchu   the boss of the gong

penem   one of the two medium sized metallophones in the *gamelan selundèng*

pengalian   *ngalih*, seek; freely performed introduction to a movement by the two leading *gendèrs* in the *gamelan pelègongan*

pengaras   introductory section to the second movement of the *gending ageng*

pengawak   *awak*, body; the first movement of the *gending ageng, gending pegambuhan*, and other two-movement compositions

pengawit   *kawit*, begin; the thematic solo introduction which indicates the melody to the musicians; see *gihing*

pengechèt   the second movement in a two-movement composition; the *pengechèt* usually follows immediately after the *pengawak*, although some *gendings* both open and close with the *pengechèt*

pengedé   the largest form of *rindik* in the *gamelan pejogèdan*

pengelik   a secondary melodic section in the high register following the main melodic section in the low or middle register; see *penyalit*

pengèntèr   a name for the largest *gambang* in the *gamelan gambang*

pengetog, pengōtog   linking passage between sections in a *lègong* composition, starting in slow tempo and leading with a gradual accelerando to the following section, which is taken at double speed

pengipik   Badung term for *mipil*

pengipuk   the movement in a dance suite which accompanies a love scene

pengisep   the slightly higher pitched of an instrumental pair, so tuned to create beats when the instruments are played in unison

pengitil   Badung term for animated drumming occurring during the *pengipik* or *mipil*

pengiwa(n), peniba(n)   the final repetition of the *pengawak* in the *gending ageng*, now melodically altered, and with different drum patterns; thus a transformation or variation of the main melody

pengōpak   drum passages in which loud slapping sounds (*ngōpak*) predominate

pengorot   another Badung term for *mipil*

pengumbang   the lower pitched of an instrumental pair (see *pengisep*); a secondary and contrasting melodic section in quick tempo played when the dancer suddenly moves animatedly about the stage; see *ngumbang*

penyachah   one-octave metallophone of the *gendèr* family pitched an octave above the *jublag*

penyalit *salin*, to change; a contrasting melodic section in a composition, lying in the high register

penyelag solo interlude between movements in the *gending ageng* played by the *trompong*

penyelah short compositions played before or during an interlude in a performance

penyelat one of the middle sized *gambangs* in the *gamelan gambang*

penyorog one of the two secondary tones in the *saih 7 pegambuhan* system

penyumu a name for the solo introduction to a *gending*

penyuwud closing section to a *gending*, especially in a *lègong* dance suite

pepet name of a symbol in musical notation

peregina actor or dancer with a speaking part

pererèn *mererèn*, to pause; compositions, often elaborate in form, played at the beginning or during a pause in a performance

pererèt improvised shawm; name for the now obsolete *seruni*

petuduh one of the two medium-sized metallophones in the *gamelan selundèng*

pinchakan form of bamboo rattle operated by the wind

plak kendang loud slapping drum stroke signaling the closing phrase of a melodic period

pōh name of a symbol in musical notation

pōkok, pōkok gending the basic or nuclear tones of a composition

pōlos see *mōlos*

pōnggang a pair of small horizontally mounted gongs formerly used in the old *gamelan gong* and *gamelan Semar Pegulingan*

prapèn another name for *pandé krawang*

pugpug the rib of the sugarpalm leaf from which the *gènggong* is made

puh, pupuh tune, melody, instrumental or vocal; verse form and melody; notation of a melody rather than its *pōkok* tones

rangda widow; the sorceress Chalonarang in the dance play by that name

rangkep double; double speed; passages performed with both drums, together with cymbals; *penangkep*, octave

rebab two-stringed bowed lute of Bali and Java

rèjang processional dance for girls; see p. 356

réong one or a set of small gongs, mounted in various ways, requiring two or four players

réong angklung as found in the *gamelan angklung*, the *réong* consists of a slender wooden crosspiece with a small gong mounted perpendicularly at each end. Two such instruments are needed to produce the complete four-tone scale of the gamelan. Two players are required

réong gong as found in the traditional *gamelan gong*, the four gongs composing the *réong* are mounted horizontally in a row. Two players are required

réong kebyar the modern form of *réong* used in the *gamelan gong kebyar*. The horizontal row of four gongs has been extended to twelve, requiring four players

réongan the part performed by the *réongs*

rinchik small, lightly sounding cymbals used in dance and theater music

rindik xylophone used in the *gamelan pejogèdan*, having a range similar to that of the *gendèr*

riong another pronunciation of *réong*

saih series, row; scale, scale system

saih angklung the four-tone scale of the *gamelan angklung*

saih gendèr wayang general Balinese name for the *sléndro* scale as found in the *gendèr wayang*

saih lima   five-tone scale, *pélog* or *sléndro*

saih pitu   the seven-tone *pélog* scale

sampang   a kind of resin used on the *rebab* bow

sanan   bamboo pole used to carry a gamelan instrument

sanghyang   various forms of dances performed in trance

sangkah   priest's shell trumpet

sarad   the *rebab* bow

saron   one-octave metallophone with keys resting over a sound box and struck with a single mallet; name for type of xylophone similar to the *charuk* found in the *gamelan luang*

sawangan   small whistle attached to neck or tail of domestic pigeon

seh   gesture, sign, in dance; sign for action; accent on drum to indicate a change in speed; upbeat given by leading *gangsa* player in modern *kebyar* compositions which have no solo introduction

seka, sekaha   club, society

sekati, sekatèn   old word for *bōnang;* the modern *réong; gamelan gong sekati*, the *gamelan gong* with modern *réong*

sekatian   *réong* passage-work, *réongan*

Selisir   one of the five scales in the *saih 7 pegambuhan* system

Selisir gong   the name for the scale of the *gamelan gong*, of which there are said to be five tunings or pitches, named, in respective order of rise in pitch, *Selisir ageng, madé, nyōman, ketut*, and *chenik*

selundèng   general name for the special iron-keyed metallophones of the *gamelan selundèng*

seruni, serunai   a double-reed wind instrument with flaring wooden bell, now obsolete

sesèndon, sèndon   preliminary improvisational solo playing by the *trompong* in the *gamelan gong*. There are said to be two varieties—*Selisir*, lying in the high register, and *Tembung*, lying mainly in the lower octave. Unison singing by the actors in *wayang wong;* songs sung by the *dalang* during the shadowplay

Silir, gending Silir   a group of short compositions of the *gangsaran* type for the *gamelan gong*

singlatan   a special type of drumming used in the *pengisep* section of *tabuh 1* in the *gamelan gong* repertory

sisya   *sisya*, pupil; the pupils of the sorceress Chalonarang; *sisyan*, compositions based on the ostinato form which accompany their entrances on the stage

sléndro   the five-tone scale system having no semitones

suku   name of a symbol in musical notation

suling   endblown bamboo flute, of which there are various forms, having four, five, or six fingerholes; *suling gambuh*, the large flute used in the *gambuh* ensemble

Sunarèn   one of the five scales in the *saih 7 pegambuhan* system

sundari   a form of Aeolian flute set up in the fields

surang   name of a symbol in musical notation

swara   voice, tone

tabèh-tabehan   an old name for gamelan, meaning a group of instruments which are struck (*tabèh*) with some form of stick or mallet

tabuh   stroke; the hammer or stick with which an instrument is struck; a gamelan composition; *tabuh gong*, composition(s) for the *gamelan gong; tabuh-tabuhan*, all kinds of gamelan compositions. *Tabuhin!* Strike up! Begin playing! *Menabuh gamelan*, the gamelan plays; playing by the gamelan

tabuh gari   see *abhōgari*

tabuh gong   compositions for the *gamelan gong*, including both *gendings ageng* and *gangsaran*. The *gendings ageng* are classified according to the number of *palets* to the *gongan*, or melodic period, forming the first movement, of which there are nine varieties. *Tabuh besik* (*tabuh 1*), an irregular form, is based on a single, repeating *palet*. *Tabuh rō* (2) has two *palets* to the *gongan*. The remaining species are:

tabuh telu	(3)	with 3 *palets*
pat	(4)	4
lima	(5)	5
nem	(6)	6
pitu	(7)	7
kutus	(8)	8
rōhras	(12)	12

tabuh talōh   commencement music; a small group of pieces in the *gamelan gong* repertory based on a five- or sometimes four-*palet gongan*, and of which one is customarily played at the beginning of any program

talèng   name of a symbol in musical notation

talin rebab   *rebab* string

tambur   a rare form of gong with an unusually deep rim, not included in the gamelan but used as a signaling instrument

tampak dara   dove's footprint; a symbol in the form of a cross used in musical notation to indicate the *kempli* accent

tanda ngorot   a symbol in musical notation indicating a short glissando or melodic embellishment

tandak   the singer whose lines relate the action in *gambuh* and *lègong* performances

tari   dance; *menari*, to dance

taring   stage clearing or theater pavilion

tedung   name of a symbol in musical notation

tekep   to close or cover; to finger the *suling* or *rebab;* to play in one scale or another, e.g., *tekep Selisir*, play in the scale, *Selisir*

tembang   poetry, poem, song; verse form and melody

Tembung   one of the five scales in the *saih 7 pegambuhan* system; a group of compositions of the *gangsaran* type in the *gamelan gong* repertory

terbana   bowl-shaped drum of coconut fiber, used only in the *jangèr* performance

tingklik   another name for *chungklik*

tōpèng   performance with masked actor(s)

trompong   row of small, horizontally mounted gongs used as solo instrument in the *gamelan gong* and *Semar Pegulingan*

trompong barangan   the following *trompong*, pitched an octave higher

trompong pengarep   the larger and leading *trompong* when two instruments are employed

tukud, blus tukud   rapid beating of the *kulkul*, broadcasting robbery, fire, etc.

tut   the main, open tone of the *kendang lanang*

tutugan   ornamental passages in *trompong* playing, in which each tone is repeated

tutug-tutugan   a form of *gangsa* figuration in the modern *gamelan gong*, based on the repetition of melodic tones

ukara   name of a symbol in musical notation

ulu   name of a symbol in musical notation

ulung   to fall; to repeat a motif or musical period without a break; *berulung-ulung*, continuous repetition, as in the ostinato compositions

wadon   female; the larger, deeper pitched of two drums or great *gongs*

wayang   *wayang kulit*, the shadowplay; *wayang wong*, a special form of play with living actors

wirama   meter; method of singing texts in Hindu meter, employed chiefly in the *Ramayana* readings

Appendix 3. Musical examples

Ex. 348. Trompong introduction to Tabuh Talōh; gineman and pengawit*

gineman; played freely

pengawit

---

* *Tabuh Talōh* is included in the two-piano transcriptions made by the author and published under the title, *Balinese Ceremonial Music* (see Appendix 5). The gending, with the above introduction, is among the recordings made by Odeon of the gamelan gong of Belaluan.

Ex. 349. Gong interplay; gamelan bebōnangan, Gending gilakan* ♩ = 100

* Traditional processional music.

1. réongs   4. bebendé
2. pōnggang   5. kempur
3. kempli   6. gong ageng

APPENDIX 3. MUSICAL EXAMPLES

Ex. 350. Réongan, old style; gamelan gong; Bangli district   ♩ = 84

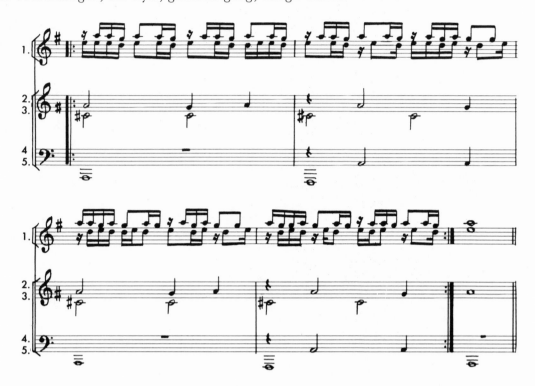

1. réongs
2. pŏnggang
3. kempli
4. kempur
5. gong ageng

Ex. 351. Réongan; gamelan gong kebyar; Jagaraga village ♩ = 112

The passage is played three times, twice *piano*, once *forte*, and is then followed by a new section.

APPENDIX 3. MUSICAL EXAMPLES

Ex. 352. Gendèr wayang; angakat-angkatan, excerpt; Kuta village ♩ = 132

1 and 2; gendèr barangan   3 and 4; gendèr gedé

Ex. 353. Gamelan angklung; old style. Gending Guak Maling Talōh;
 Chulik village ♩ = 100

1. gendèrs chenik and gedé
2. grantang
3. chungklik
4. angklungs
5. réongs
6. 4 medium chèngchèngs
7. chongé-chongé
8. kendangs
9. jegogans
10. kempur

Ex. 353, continued

1. gendèrs chenik and gedé
2. grantang
3. chungklik
4. angklungs
5. réongs

6. 4 medium chèngchèngs
7. chongé-chongé
8. kendangs
9. jegogans
10. kempur

Ex. 354. Gamelan angklung; modern style. Pengechèt Bèrong, closing phrase;
Mōgan village ♩ = 108

1. suling
2., 3., 4. gendèr chenik
5., 6., 7. gendèr gedé
8. réongs
9. jegogans

10. kelenang
11. kempli
12. kempur
13. kendangs
14. rinchik

APPENDIX 3. MUSICAL EXAMPLES

Ex. 355. Gamelan angklung; gending Sekar Uled; Sayan village ♩ = 126

1. gendèrs   2. jegogans   3. kempur

All sections repeat once, with the exception of the section marked *più animato* which is repeated ten times, with changing dynamics. If the piece is played in a procession the tempo remains steady throughout.

Ex. 356. Two different realizations of the same pōkok tones by trompong Semar Pegulingan and gendèr pelègongan, as played by I Lotring of Kuta village. The passage is from gending Pengegèr.

APPENDIX 3. MUSICAL EXAMPLES

Ex. 357. Pengechèt Brahmara; suling gambuh, tekep Selisir ♩ = 100

When this example is compared with the *trompong* version given in Ex. 114, the general melodic line will be found to remain basically the same. Both versions take as point of departure the tone *ding*, although the *suling* version uses the Selisir scale, while the *trompong* version was played in *Tembung*. In the second strophe of this example the first two *penyorog* tones (indicated by *a*) will be seen to occur in the same place in the *trompong* version, which, however, omits them further. The repeat in the first strophe of this version is optional. Attention is also called to the abbreviated second strophe, noted as played by the Tabanan musicians.

Ex. 358. Pengechèt Sekar Gadung; suling gambuh, tekep Selisir ♩ = 100

Appendix 4. Nuclear tones to gamelan compositions

I. Gending Gong

A. GENDING AGENG*

1. Tabuh 1, gending Sekar Jepun; Payangan village

1	2	3	4	5	6	7	8	9	10	11	12	13	14	15	16	Label
2	3	1	3	2	3	1	2	5	3	3	3	3	5	4	3	pengechèt
G		P		k		P		G		P		k		P		
2	·	3	3	1	2	5	1	2	2	3	5	3	5	4	3	pengawak
G				P				k				P				
3	3	4	1	3	5	1	1	5	1	5	4	3	5	4	3	
G				P				k				P				
2	2	3	3	1	2	5	1	5	1	5	4	3	5	5	4	
G				P				k				P				
3	3	4	2	3	5	4	1	5	1	5	4	3	5	5	4	
G				P				k				P				
5	5	5	5	1	2	2	3	2	2	3	1	4	4	4	4	pengiwan(g)
G				P				k				P				
2	2	3	2	4	4	4	2	3	3	3	2	3	5	5	1	
G				P				k				P				
5	5	5	5	1	2	2	3	2	2	3	1	4	4	4	4	
G				P				k				P				
2	2	3	3	1	2	3	1	2	2	3	5	1	3	4	2	
G				P				k				P				
3	3	4	2	3	5	5	1	1	1	5	4	3	5	4	3	
G				P				k				P				
2	3	1	3	2	3	1	2	5	3	3	3	3	5	4	3	pengechèt
G		P		k		P		G		P		k		P		
2																
G																

* Unless otherwise indicated, only the pengawak, along with its concluding variation, the pengiwan, is given, since in many gendings there is considerable freedom in the choice of pengechèt.

390

2. Tabuh 1, gending Kumambang; Payangan village

	1	2	3	4	5	6	7	8	9	10	11	12	13	14	15	16	part
‖:	4	2	4	2	4	4	3	4	2	5	5	5	5	2	1	5 :‖	pengechèt
	G		P		k			P	G		P		k		P		
‖:	4	•	4	5	3	4	2	3	4	4	3	2	3	5	5	4	pengawak
	G				P				k				P				
	5	5	1	5	2	1	5	2	1	1	4	5	3	4	2	3 :‖	
	G				P				k				P				
	4	•	4	4	4	4	4	4	4	5	5	4	3	3	2	2	pengiwan(g)
	G								P								
	3	3	4	4	4	3	2	4	3	3	1	2	1	3	3	2	
	k								P								
	4	•	4	4	3	5	4	3	4	4	3	2	3	5	5	4	
	G								P								
	5	5	5	5	5	1	5	4	5	4	3	2	5	2	1	5	
	k								P								
	2	1	5	4	3	3	2	2	2	2	2	2	3	4	4	3	
	k								P								
‖:	4	4	4	5	3	5	5	3	4	4	3	2	3	5	5	4	pengawak
	G				P				k				P				
	5	5	1	5	2	1	5	2	1	1	4	5	3	4	2	3 :‖	
	G				P				k				P				
‖:	4	2	4	2	4	4	3	4	2	5	5	5	5	2	1	5 :‖	pengechèt
	G		P		k			P	G		P		k		P		
	4																
	G																

3. Tabuh 2, gending Kalang-ōlang; Payangan village

	1	2	3	4	5	6	7	8	9	10	11	12	13	14	15	16	part
‖:	4	•	4	4	4	5	1	4	5	5	5	4	5	1	4	2	pengawak
	G								P								
	1	1	1	5	4	4	5	1	5	˙5	2	2	1	4	4	3 :‖	
	k								P								
	4	•	4	4	4	1	5	4	3	3	2	1	5	3	3	2	pengiwan(g)
	G								P								
	3	3	3	2	4	4	2	1	5	5	3	4	2	4	4	3	
	k								P								
	4	•															
	G																

4. Tabuh 2, gending Kerangian; Payangan village

	1	2	3	4	5	6	7	8	9	10	11	12	13	14	15	16	part
‖:	2	•	2	2	2	3	3	2	3	3	3	4	4	2	3	4	pengawak
	G								P								
	3	3	3	2	4	4	5	4	3	3	2	2	5	2	2	3 :‖	
	k								P								
	5	•	5	5	5	1	5	4	5	5	5	3	2	2	5	4	pengiwan(g)
	G								P								
	5	5	5	3	2	2	5	4	5	5	4	3	2	5	5	4	
	k								P								
	5	•															
	G																

5. Tabuh 2, gending Mayat; Payangan village

```
5  .  5  5  5  1  5  4  5  5  2  3  4  3  2  1    pengawak
G                          P
5  5  2  3  4  3  2  1  5  3  5  4  3  5  4  3
k                          P
5  .  5  5  5  2  2  3  2  2  2  3  4  4  3  4    pengiwan(g)
G                          P
3  3  3  2  4  3  2  1  5  3  5  4  3  5  4  3
k                          P
5  .
G
```

6. Tabuh 2, no name; Payangan village*

```
2  .  .  .  .  .  .  .  5  5  5  5  4  3  3  3    pengawak
G                          P
4  4  3  4  5  3  4  2  3  3  2  3  4  3  4  3
k                          P
2  2  5  2  5  2  3  4  5  4  5  3  4  3  3  3    pengiwan(g)
G                          P
4  4  3  4  5  3  4  2  3  3  2  3  4  3  4  3
k                          P
2  5  5  3  5  2  3  4                            pengechèt Longgor
G        k  P     P
2
G
```

---

* As played, no break between the pengawak and pengechèt

392

APPENDIX 4. NUCLEAR TONES TO GAMELAN COMPOSITIONS

7. Tabuh 3, gending Sekarini; Payangan village

```
||: 1   .   .   .   .   .   .   .    1   1   1   1   2   4   4   5        pengawak
    G                                P
    4   4   5   4   3   1   1   2    1   1   4   4   1   1   4   3
    k                                P
    4   4   2   2   2   3   1   2    5   5   2   3   4   2   2   5  :||
    k                                P

    1   .   .   .   .   .   .   .    1   1   2   3   2   2   1   5        pengiwan(g)
    G                                P
    1   1   2   3   2   2   1   5    1   1   4   4   1   1   4   3
    k                                P
    4   4   2   2   2   3   2   1    5   5   2   3   4   1   1   5
    k                                P
    1   .
    G


    1   1   1   1   1   1   2   2    1   1   2   3   4   4   2   3        pengechèt*
    G               P                k               P
    1   1   1   1   1   1   2   2    2   2   3   3   3   1   1   5
    G               P                k               P
    1   1   1   1   4   4   5   2    2   3   3   4   3   1   1   5
    G               P                k               P
    1   3   2   1   5   1   3   4
    G               k   P       P
    1   1   1   1   4   4   5   3
    G               k   P       P
    1   1   1   1   4   3   3   2
    G               k   P       P
    1   1   1   1   2   3   3   2
    G               k   P       P
    1   1   2   3   4   4   5   3
    G               k   P       P
    1   1   1   1   2   3   3   2
    G               k   P       P
    1   1   1   1   2   3   3   2
    G               k   P       P
    1   3   2   1   5   3   4   5
    G               k   P       P
    1
    G
```

────────────

* All lines repeat once.

8. Tabuh 4, gending Mayang; Payangan village

‖: 1 (G)	•	1	1	1	2	1	5	1 (P)	1	3	1	2	3	1	2	pengawak
3 (k)	3	3	3	3	4	3	2	3 (P)	4	3	2	1	1	1	2	
3 (k)	4	3	2	1	1	2	3	4 (P)	5	4	3	5	4	3	2	
1 (k)	1	4	4	4	3	5	4	3 (P)	4	5	3	1	1	5	2 :‖	
1 (G)	•	1	1	1	2	1	5	1 (P)	1	2	2	5	1	4	5	pengiwan(g)
1 (k)	1	2	2	5	1	4	5	1 (P)	1	5	4	1	1	4	3	
4 (k)	5	1	2	5	1	4	5	1 (P)	1	5	4	1	5	4	1	
2 (k)	2	2	2	2	3	3	4	3 (P)	4	4	3	1	1	5	2	
1 (G)	•															

9. Tabuh 4, gending Kenyung Manis; Payangan village

‖: 5 (G)	•	5	5	5	3	3	2	3 (P)	3	4	5	4	4	3	2	pengawak
3 (k)	3	4	5	4	4	3	1	1 (P)	2	1	1	5	5	3	2	
3 (k)	3	4	5	4	4	3	1	1 (P)	2	1	1	5	5	3	2	
3 (k)	3	4	5	4	3	4	3	2 (P)	2	5	5	2	1	2	1 :‖	
5 (G)	•	5	5	5	2	2	3	2 (P)	2	2	1	5	2	2	3	pengiwan(g)
2 (k)	2	2	1	5	3	3	2	3 (P)	3	3	4	5	4	4	5	
4 (k)	4	4	3	2	2	1	3	2 (P)	2	2	2	1	1	5	2	
3 (k)	3	4	5	4	3	4	3	2 (P)	2	5	5	2	1	2	1	
5 (G)	•															

394

APPENDIX 4. NUCLEAR TONES TO GAMELAN COMPOSITIONS

10. Tabuh 4, gending Sekar Gendis

‖: 4 (G)	•	4	4	5	5	3	2	2 (P)	5	2	2	2	3	3	4	pengawak
3 (k)	3	4	4	2	4	4	5	4 (P)	4	4	4	4	1	5	4	
5 (k)	5	4	4	3	4	4	5	4 (P)	4	3	3	2	2	3	4	
3 (k)	3	4	4	5	5	2	1	5 (P)	5	4	4	3	2	3	4 :‖	
3 (G)	•	3	2	4	5	1	1	4 (P)	4	2	2	4	4	2	3	pengiwan(g)
1 (k)	1	5	5	5	1	4	5	5 (P)	1	4	5	1	1	3	5	
1 (k)	1	5	5	2	3	1	2	5 (P)	1	4	5	3	4	5	3	
1 (k)	5	1	2	3	4	2	3	3 (P)	4	5	3	1	5	1	2	
3 (G)	•															

11. Tabuh 4, gending Kunyur

‖: 2 (G)	•	2	2	2	5	2	3	2 (P)	2	4	5	3	5	4	3	pengawak
2 (k)	2	4	3	2	2	4	5	4 (P)	4	4	4	4	1	5	4	
3 (k)	2	5	4	3	2	5	1	4 (P)	4	5	5	3	3	4	3	
2 (k)	2	5	5	5	1	4	5	5 (P)	5	2	3	2	4	4	3 :‖	
2 (G)	•	2	2	2	2	4	4	2 (P)	2	4	4	2	4	3	1	pengiwan(g)
5 (k)	5	5	5	5	2	2	3	2 (P)	2	2	1	5	3	3	2	
3 (k)	3	3	4	5	4	4	5	4 (P)	4	4	4	2	2	1	3	
2 (k)	2	2	2	1	1	5	2	3 (P)	4	5	3	4	2	2	1	
2 (G)	•															

395

12. Tabuh 4, gending Kembang Jinar; Payangan village

‖: G	4	·	4	4	4	2	4	5	4 (P)	4	5	1	5	5	4	3	pengawak
k	2	2	4	4	3	1	1	5	1 (P)	1	4	4	1	1	5	4	
k	4	4	1	4	5	1	4	5	3 (P)	3	5	5	3	1	1	2	
k	1	1	3	3	2	2	2	3	2 (P)	2	3	1	4	4	3	5 :‖	
G	4	·	4	4	4	5	4	3	4 (P)	4	4	5	1	1	2	1	pengiwan(g)
k	5	5	5	5	4	4	3	5	4 (P)	4	4	5	1	1	2	1	
k	5	5	5	5	4	4	3	5	4 (P)	4	4	5	3	1	1	2	
k	1	1	3	3	2	2	3	1	4 (P)	4	3	4	2	2	4	3	
G	4	·															

13. Tabuh 4, gending Subandar; Payangan village

‖: G	3	·	3	3	3	4	3	2	3 (P)	3	4	4	2	2	4	5	pengawak
k	3	3	4	4	2	2	4	5	3 (P)	3	5	1	4	4	2	1	
k	2	2	2	4	3	3	5	4	3 (P)	3	3	4	5	5	3	4	
k	5	5	5	4	2	2	4	3	5 (P)	5	5	5	2	3	3	4 :‖	
G	3	·	·	·	·	·	·	·	3 (P)	3	3	2	5	5	2	1	pengiwan(g)
k	2	2	2	3	2	1	5	2	3 (P)	3	3	2	5	5	2	1	
k	2	2	2	2	1	1	5	2	3 (P)	3	3	4	5	5	3	4	
k	5	5	5	4	2	2	4	3	5 (P)	5	5	5	2	3	3	4	
G	3	·															

14. Tabuh 4, gending Semuradas; Payangan village

‖: G	3	·	3	3	2	2	1	5	4 (P)	1	1	1	1	5	3	5	pengawak; misi gongan tigang (containing three gongan)
k	1	1	2	3	2	2	1	4	4 (P)	1	4	4	4	1	3	3	
k	3	3	4	3	2	2	1	4	4 (P)	4	1	1	2	2	5	4	
k	3	3	4	4	3	3	1	4	4 (P)	1	4	4	4	1	2	5	

(14. gending Semuradas, *continued*.)

4 G	•	4	4	3	5	4	3	4 P	4	1	2	3	3	2	5	
4 k	4	3	3	3	2	2	3	2 P	2	3	4	3	3	2	1	
1 k	1	3	2	1	1	4	5	3 P	3	4	4	2	2	3	1	
1 k	1	4	4	4	1	2	5	3 P	3	2	3	1	1	3	2	
3 G	•	2	2	4	4	2	3	1 P	1	1	1	1	• 1 •		2	
4 k	4	2	3	5	1	4	5	3 P	3	2	3	1	1	3	2	
3 k	3	2	2	4	4	3	2	1 P	1	1	1	1	• 1 •		1	
2 k	2	3	3	2	2	1	4	4 P	1	4	4	2	3	3	2 :‖	
3 G	•	3	3	2	2	1	4	4 P	4	1	1	1	5	3	5	ngalih pengiwan(g)
1 k	1	2	3	2	2	1	4	4 P	1	4	4	1	3	3	2	(seek, proceed to the pengiwan); transition
3 k	3	4	3	2	2	1	4	4 P	4	1	1	2	2	5	4	
3 k	3	4	4	3	3	1	4	4 P	1	4	4	4	1	2	5	
4 G	•	4	4	3	5	4	3	4 P	4	1	2	3	3	1	5	
4 k	4	3	3	3	2	2	3	2 P	2	3	4	3	3	2	1	
1 k	1	3	2	1	1	4	5	3 P	3	4	4	2	2	3	1	
1 k	1	4	4	4	1	2	5	3 P	3	3	3	2	3	1	2	
3 G	•	3	4	4	3	5	4	3 P	3	5	4	3	3	2	1	pengiwan(g)
1 k	4	1	1	4	1	4	5	4 P	4	3	3	3	2	3	4	(ends with the last palet in the second gongan of pengawak)
3 k	3	3	4	4	3	5	4	3 P	3	5	4	3	3	2	1	
1 k	4	1	1	4	4	1	1	4 P	4	1	1	3	3	1	4	
4 G	•	1	1	3	3	1	1	3 P	3	1	1	3	3	1	1	
4 k	4	1	1	3	3	1	1	3 P	3	1	3	1	3	2	1	
2 k	2	5	4	4	4	2	4	5 P	5	2	4	5	5	3	3	
1 k	1	4	4	4	1	2	5	3 P	3	2	3	1	1	3	2	
3 G	•															

15. Tabuh 4, gending Semarandana; Payangan village

```
||: 1  .  1  1  1  4  1  2  1  1  1  1  2  4  4  5    pengawak
    G                    P
    4  3  5  4  3  1  1  2  1  1  3  3  4  2  2  3
    k                    P
    2  2  2  5  1  4  1  5  4  4  4  5  1  1  3  2
    k                    P
    1  1  2  2  5  2  2  3  2  2  3  4  3  1  1  2 :||
    k                    P

    1  .  1  1  1  2  1  5  1  1  3  3  1  1  3  5    pengiwan(g)
    G                    P
    1  1  3  3  1  1  3  2  3  3  2  1  3  3  1  5
    k                    P
    1  1  3  1  1  3  1  2  3  3  2  1  3  3  1  5
    k                    P
    1  1  1  1  5  4  2  1  5  5  2  2  3  1  1  5
    k                    P
    1  .
    G

    1  .  1  1  1  1  2  2  1  1  2  3  4  4  2  3    pengaras
    G     P     k     P     k     P     k     P
    1  1  1  1  1  1  2  2  1  1  2  3  4  4  2  3
    G     P     k     P     k     P     k     P
    1  4  4  4  4  4  5  4  3  2  2  3  2  2  5  1
    G           P           k           P
    4  4  4  3  4  1  5  2  2  3  3  4  3  1  1  5
    G           P           k           P
    1  1  2  4  4  4  5  3  3  2  2  3  2  2  5  1
    G           P           k           P
    4  4  4  3  4  1  5  2  2  3  3  4  3  1  1  5
    G           P           k           P

||: 1  3  2  1  5  1  4  5    pengechèt Longgor
    G           k  P     P
    1  3  2  1  5  1  4  5
    G           k  P     P
    1  1  1  1  1  3  3  3
    G           k  P     P
    1  1  1  1  1  3  3  3
    G           k  P     P
    3  3  3  3  3  1  1  2
    G           k  P     P
    1  1  1  1  1  4  4  3
    G           k  P     P
    4  4  4  4  4  2  2  3
    G           k  P     P
    2  2  2  2  2  3  3  4
    G           k  P     P
    3  3  3  3  3  1  1  2 :||
    G           k  P     P
    1  2  1  2  1  2  1  3
    G           k  P     P
    2  3  2  3  2  5  4  5
    G           k  P     P
```

sampun di ding
malih melipet
(when you reach ding
repeat again)

(15. gending Semarandana, *continued.*)

```
 1  2  1  2  1  2  1  3                    naglih pengabisan
 G           k  P     P                    (go on to ending)
‖:2  3  2  3  2  5  4  5:‖
 G           k  P     P
 1
 G
```

16. Tabuh 4, gending Blandongan; Payangan village

```
‖:5  •  5  4  1  1  1  3  3  3  1  3  1  3  2  1    pengawak
 G                       P
 2  2  2  1  4  4  1  5  1  1  1  5  1  1  4  4
 k                       P
 2  2  2  2  4  3  2  4  5  5  3  5  3  5  4  3
 k                       P
 2  2  2  2  4  4  3  5  5  5  2  3  2  2  4  3:‖
 k                       P
 5  •  5  5  5  1  5  4  5  5  2  3  1  1  4  3    pengiwan(g)
 G                       P
 5  5  3  3  4  2  2  3  2  2  2  3  4  4  5  4
 k                       P
 3  3  3  2  1  1  5  1  5  5  2  1  5  2  2  3
 k                       P
 2  2  2  1  4  4  3  5  5  5  2  3  2  2  4  3
 k                       P
 5  •
 G
```

```
 5  •  5  5  2  2  3  3  2  2  3  3  2  5  5  4    pengaras Selisir
 G     P     k     P     k     P     k     P
 5  5  5  5  2  2  3  3  2  2  3  3  2  5  5  4
 G     P     k     P     k     P     k     P
 5  5  5  5  2  2  3  3  2  2  3  3  2  4  4  3
 G     P     k     P     k     P     k     P
 4  4  5  3  4  4  5  3  4  4  5  3  4  2  2  3    pengisep
 G           P              k              P
 2  3  3  1  2  3  3  1  2  3  3  1  2  4  4  3
 G           P              k              P
 4  5  5  3  4  5  5  3  4  5  5  3  4  2  2  3
 G           P              k              P
 2  3  3  1  2  3  3  1  2  3  3  1  2  5  2  1
 G           P              k              P
‖:5  5  2  3  2  3  2  2                            pengechèt
 G        k  P     P
 5  5  2  3  2  3  2  1
 G        k  P     P
 3  3  3  4  3  4  3  2
 G        k  P     P
 4  4  4  5  4  5  4  3
 G        k  P     P
 2  2  2  3  2  3  2  1
 G        k  P     P
```

(16. gending Blandongan, *continued*.)

```
  5   5   2   3   2   3   2   1
  G               k   P       P
  3   3   3   4   3   4   3   2
  G               k   P       P
  4   4   4   5   4   5   4   3. ||
  G               k   P       P
||:2   4   4   5   3   5   4   3
  G               k   P       P
  2   1   3   1   5   1   3   1. ||
  G               k   P       P
||:2   4   4   5   3   5   4   3
  G               k   P       P
  2   1   3   1   5   1   3   1. ||
  G               k   P       P
  2
  G
```

17. Tabuh 5, gending Batu Rubuh; Payangan village

```
||:4   .   4   4   4   5   4   3    4   4   5   3   4   3   2   4     pengawak;
  G                                P                                 misi gongan duang
  5   5   2   2   5   2   1   5    4   5   4   4   3   3   2   4      (containing  two
  k                                P                                 gongan)
  5   5   2   2   5   2   1   5    4   3   3   5   5   3   4
  k                                P
  2   2   2   2   2   5   2   3    2   3   3   2   2   1   3
  k                                P
  2   2   4   4   4   3   3   2    1   1   3   2   5   3   3   2
  k                                P
  3   .   3   3   3   2   2   3    2   2   4   5   4   4   3   2
  G                                P
  3   3   4   5   4   4   3   1    1   2   1   1   5   5   3   2
  k                                P
  3   3   4   5   4   4   3   1    1   2   1   1   5   5   3   2
  k                                P
  3   3   4   3   2   2   1   3    2   2   1   2   4   1   4   5
  k                                P
  4   4   3   5   4   4   2   3    1   1   2   5   1   4   4   3. ||
  k                                P
  4   .   4   4   4   5   4   3    4   4   5   3   4   3   2   4
  G                                P
  5   5   2   2   5   2   3   1    4   5   4   4   3   3   2   4
  k                                P
  5   5   2   2   5   2   3   1    4   4   2   4   5   5   3   3
  k                                P
  2   2   2   2   2   3   2   2    1   2   2   2   1   1   5   1      ngalih pengiwan(g)
  k                                P
  3   3   5   5   3   5   4   4    2   2   4   3   2   4   5   3
  k                                P
```

(17. gending Batu Rubuh, *continued*.)

```
4  ·  4  4  4  5  4  4  3  4  4  4  3  3  2  4     pengiwan(g)
G                          P
5  5  2  2  5  2  3  1  4  5  4  4  3  3  2  4
k                          P
5  5  2  2  5  2  3  1  4  4  2  4  5  5  3  3
k                          P
2  2  2  2  2  3  2  2  1  1  2  2  1  1  5  2
k                          P
3  3  5  5  3  5  4  4  2  2  4  3  2  4  5  3
k                          P
4  ·
G
```

18. Tabuh 5, gending Lasem; Sulaan village

```
‖: 3  ·  ·  ·  ·  ·  ·  ·  3  3  5  4  1  1  3  2     pengawak
   G                          P
   3  3  3  5  4  4  2  3  1  1  2  5  1  3  4  2
   k                          P
   3  3  3  5  4  5  3  5  4  4  3  5  1  2  1  5
   k                          P
   4  4  1  5  5  1  4  1  1  5  4  1  1  5  4  1
   k                          P
   2  2  2  2  2  3  2  1  1  1  3  3  4  4  1  2 :‖
   k                          P
   3  ·  ·  ·  ·  ·  ·  ·  3  3  1  2  1  1  4  3     peniban
   G                          P
   4  4  4  4  3  3  1  2  1  4  1  2  1  1  4  3
   k                          P
   5  4  1  5  5  1  4  1  1  5  4  1  1  5  4  1
   k                          P
   2  2  1  2  3  3  2  3  1  1  5  2  2  2  5  4
   k                          P
   5  5  2  3  2  3  2  1  5  5  3  2  4  4  1  2
   k                          P
   3  ·
   G
```

```
   3  ·  3  ·  3  ·  5  ·  3  ·  5  ·  2  ·  5  ·     pengechèt Selisir
   G        k     P     k     P     k     P
   3  3  3  3  3  3  5  5  3  3  5  5  2  2  5  5
   G        k     P     k     P     k     P
‖: 3  3  3  3  3  3  5  5  3  3  5  2  2  2  5  5 :‖
   G        k     P     k     P     k     P
   3  4  5  3  1  1  3  2  4  4  1  5  2  2  5  3
   G        k     P     k     P     k     P
   3  3  3  3  3  3  4  4  2  2  5  3  2  2  5  3
   G        k     P     k     P     k     P
   3  4  5  1  1  1  3  2  4  4  1  1  2  2  5  3
   G        k     P     k     P     k     P
```

(18. gending Lasem, *continued.*)

```
    3   3   3   3   3   3   1   1   3   3   1   1   3   5   1   2
    G               k       P       k       P       k       P

    3   3   3   3   2   4   1   1   3   3   1   1   3   5   1   2
    G               k       P       k       P       k       P

    3   3   3   2   4   4   4   2   5   5   3   3   5   3   3   2
    G               k       P       k       P       k       P

    3   3   3   2   3   3   1   1   3   3   1   1   3   5   1   2
    G               k       P       k       P       k       P

    3   3   3   2   4   4   4   2   4   4   5   3   5   3   3   2     chepetan
    G               k       P       k       P       k       P        (faster)

||: 3   3   3   2   3   3   1   1   3   3   1   1   3   5   1   2 :||
    G               k       P       k       P       k       P

    3   3   4   2   4   4   4   2   4   4   4   3   5   3   3   2
    G               k       P       k       P       k       P

    3   3   3   2   3   3   1   1   3   3   1   1   3   5   3   5
    G               k       P       k       P       k       P

||: 3   5   4   3   2   3   1   2 :||
    G               k   P       P

    3
    G
```

19. Tabuh 6, gending Galang Kangin

```
||: 4   .   4   4   4   5   4   3   4   4   4   3   2   4   3  .5     pengawak
    G                               P

    4   4   4   3   2   5   5   4   5   5   5   3   4   5   3   4
    k                               P

    5   5   5   3   4   2   4   3   2   2   2   3   4   2   4   3
    k                               P

    2   2   2   3   4   3   5   4   3   3   3   2   3   4   2   4
    k                               P

    3   3   5   5   5   2   2   3   4   4   4   5   4   2   2   1
    k                               P

    5   5   5   3   4   4   3   5   3   3   4   3   2   4   4   3 :||
    k                               P

    4   .   4   4   4   5   4   3   4   4   4   5   5   2   2   3     pengiwan(g)
    G                               P

    2   2   2   1   4   4   3   1   4   4   4   5   5   2   2   3
    k                               P

    2   2   2   1   4   4   3   5   4   4   4   5   3   5   4   3
    k                               P

    2   2   5   5   2   4   4   3   4   4   3   3   5   5   3   4
    k                               P

    2   2   5   5   5   2   2   3   4   4   4   5   4   2   2   1
    k                               P

    5   5   5   3   4   4   3   5   3   3   4   3   2   4   4   3
    k                               P

    4   .
    G
```

(19. gending Galang Kangin, *continued.*)

```
4   •   4   4   4   4   1   1   4   4   1   1   4   4   3   2      pengaras
G               k       P       k       P       k       P

4   4   4   4   4   4   1   1   4   4   1   1   4   4   3   2
G               k       P       k       P       k       P

‖: 4  4   4   3   5   5   3   4   2   2   3   3   5   4   3   5    (repeat once)
G               P               k               P

4   4   2   2   2   4   3   2   3   3   4   3   2   2   5   2      (repeat once)
G               P               k               P

4   4   4   3   5   5   3   4   2   2   4   3   5   4   3   5 :‖
G               P               k               P

4   •   4   1   4   1   4   1                                     pengechèt Tembung
G               k   P       P

‖: 4   1   1   5   3   3   1   2 :‖                               (twice or more)
G               k   P       P

‖: 4   4   5   3   1   1   3   2 :‖                               (twice or more)
G               k   P       P

4   4   4   4   4   1   1   3
G               k   P       P

3   3   3   3   3   4   3   1
G               k   P       P

1   1   3   1   2   4   3   1                                     (repeat once)
G               k   P       P

1   1   2   4   2   4   2   5
G               k   P       P

4   5   2   4   2   4   3   5
G               k   P       P                                    pengechèt dados
                                                                 melipet
4   4   1   1   4   1   4   1                                     (the pengechèt can
G               k   P       P                                    be repeated)

4
G
```

20. Pengaras Galang Kangin, another version; Payangan village

•	•	4	4	4	4	1	1	4	4	1	1	4	4	3	2
				k		P		k		P		k		P	
4	4	4	4	4	4	1	1	4	4	1	1	4	4	3	2
G		P		k		P		k		P		k		P	
4	4	4	3	5	5	3	4	2	2	4	3	5	4	3	5
G				P				k				P			
4	4	2	2	2	4	3	2	3	3	4	3	2	2	5	1
G				P				k				P			
4	4	4	3	5	5	3	4	2	2	4	3	5	4	3	5
G				P				k				P			
4	4	4	1	4	1	4	1	4	1	1	5	3	3	5	1
G					P		P	G					P		P
4	1	1	5	3	3	5	1	4	1	1	5	3	3	5	1
G					P		P	G					P		P
4	4	5	3	1	1	3	2	4	4	5	3	1	1	3	2
G					P		P	G					P		P
4	4	4	4	4	1	1	3	3	3	3	3	3	4	3	1
G					P		P	G					P		P
1	1	3	1	2	4	3	1	1	1	3	1	2	4	3	1
G					P		P	G					P		P
1	1	2	4	2	4	5	4	4	5	2	4	2	4	2	4
G					P		P	G					P		P
‖: 4	4	4	1	4	1	4	1 :‖								
G					P		P								
4	•														
G															

dados melipet
(can repeat)

pengechèt Tembung
disambung
(join with pengechèt
Tembung)

APPENDIX 4. NUCLEAR TONES TO GAMELAN COMPOSITIONS

21. Tabuh 6, gending Penginyan; Alis Bintang village

4	.	.	.	.	.	.	.	4	4	1	2	1	1	4	3	pengawak
G								P								
4	4	1	2	1	1	4	3	4	5	4	4	3	3	1	1	
k								P								
1	1	1	1	2	4	4	3	4	4	3	4	3	1	1	2	
k								P								
1	1	3	3	2	2	5	4	5	5	5	4	1	1	4	1	
k								P								
2	2	3	3	2	2	2	3	4	4	4	5	4	1	1	2	
k								P								
1	1	4	4	1	1	4	4	2	3	2	2	1	4	4	1 :‖	
k								P								

4	.	.	.	.	.	.	.	4	4	1	2	1	1	4	3	pengiwan
G								P								
4	4	1	2	1	1	4	3	4	5	4	4	2	3	2	1	
k								P								
1	4	3	3	3	4	3	2	3	3	3	2	3	2	1	3	
k								P								
2	4	3	4	4	3	4	4	2	2	4	4	3	2	1	3	
k								P								
3	3	4	4	2	3	2	3	1	1	4	4	4	1	4	5	
k								P								
3	3	3	2	4	4	2	3	1	1	2	2	1	4	4	1	
k								P								
4	.															

4	.	4	.	4	.	1	.	4	.	1	.	4	.	2	.	pengechèt Selisir
G				k		P		k		P		k		P		

‖:

4	4	4	4	4	4	1	1	4	4	1	1	4	4	2	2 :‖
G				k		P		k		P		k		P	

‖:

4	4	4	3	4	4	1	1
G		k		P		P	
4	4	1	1	4	1	2	3 :‖
G		k		P		P	

‖:

4	4	4	1	4	1	4	3	chèngchèng diam (cymbals pause)
G		k		P		P		
3	4	4	3	4	1	1	3	
G		k		P		P		
2	4	1	3	2	4	1	3	
G		k		P		P		
1	3	4	2	5	2	2	5 :‖	
G		k		P		P		

‖:

4	4	4	1	4	1	4	3	tambah chèngchèng (add cymbals)
G		k		P		P		
3	4	4	3	4	1	1	3	
G		k		P		P		
2	4	1	3	2	4	1	3	
G		k		P		P		
1	3	4	2	5	2	2	5	
G		k		P		P		
2					:‖			
G								

22. Tabuh 7, gending Ginanti; Payangan village

```
‖: 2  •  2  2  2  5  2  3   2  2  2  3  2  5  5  4    pengawak
   G                        P
   5  5  5  5  4  2  2  3   2  2  2  1  5  3  3  2
   k                        P
   3  3  3  3  5  4  3  5   4  4  2  1  3  5  5  4
   k                        P
   5  5  5  5  5  1  5  4   5  5  3  2  1  3  3  4
   k                        P
   3  3  3  4  5  4  4  5   4  4  4  2  3  1  1  5
   k                        P
   1  1  1  2  3  2  1  3   2  2  2  1  2  5  5  4
   k                        P
   5  5  3  3  3  4  4  5   4  4  2  2  5  2  1  3 :‖
   k                        P
   5  •  5  5  5  1  5  4   5  5  2  3  2  2  5  4    pengiwan(g)
   G                        P
   5  5  3  2  4  3  2  4   5  5  3  3  3  4  3  2
   k                        P
   3  3  4  4  3  5  4  3   2  2  3  3  2  3  2  1
   k                        P
   5  5  2  2  1  2  1  5   5  5  3  3  1  3  3  4
   k                        P
   3  3  3  4  5  4  4  5   4  4  4  2  3  1  1  5
   k                        P
   1  1  1  1  3  2  1  3   2  2  2  1  2  5  5  4
   k                        P
   5  5  3  3  3  4  4  3   2  2  5  5  2  1  2  4
   k                        P
   5  •
   G
```

APPENDIX 4. NUCLEAR TONES TO GAMELAN COMPOSITIONS

23. Tabuh 7, gending Penginyan; Batuan village

```
‖: 2  .  .  .  .  .  .  .   2  2  2  1  4  4  2  1      pengawak
   G                        P
   2  2  2  3  4  4  4  3   2  2  2  1  4  4  2  1
   k                        P
   2  2  1  2  3  3  3  2   1  1  3  3  2  2  5  4
   k                        P
   5  5  2  2  1  3  2  1   5  5  2  1  2  4  4  5
   k                        P
   4  4  4  4  4  1  5  4   3  3  2  1  5  3  3  4
   k                        P
   3  3  3  4  5  3  4  5   4  4  4  3  5  4  3  2
   k                        P
   5  5  5  5  2  1  5  2   3  3  5  5  4  2  2  3 :‖
   k                        P

   2  .  .  .  .  .  .  .   5  5  5  5  2  2  5  4      pengisep
   G                        P                          (pengiwan)
   3  3  3  2  4  3  2  4   5  5  5  4  2  2  5  4
   k                        P
   3  3  3  2  4  3  2  4   5  5  5  4  2  2  5  4
   k                        P
   5  5  2  2  1  3  2  1   5  5  2  1  2  4  4  5
   k                        P
   4  4  4  4  4  1  5  4   3  3  2  1  5  3  3  4
   k                        P
   3  3  3  4  5  3  4  5   4  4  4  3  5  5  3  2
   k                        P
   5  5  5  5  2  1  5  4   3  3  5  3  5  .  2  3
   k                        P
   2
   G


   2  .  2  .  2  .  3  .   2  .  3  .  5  .  4  .      pengaras
   G        P        k        P
   2  2  2  2  2  2  3  3   2  2  3  3  5  5  4  4
   G        P        k        P
   2  5  5  4  5  5  3  4   2  5  5  4  5  2  2  3
   G        P        k        P
   3  4  3  2  3  3  3  1   4  4  4  3  5  5  3  4
   G        P        k        P
   2  5  5  4  5  5  3  4   2  5  5  4  5  2  2  3
   G        P        k        P
   2  3  2  3  4  5  4  3   2  3  2  1  5  4  3  5
   G        P        k        P
‖: 4  5  4  3  2  4  3  5 :‖                            pengechèt
   G           k  P     P
   4
   G
```

24. Tabuh 8, gending Ludira; Bangli

4(G)	•	•	•	•	•	•	•	5(P)	5	5	4	3	2	4	3	pengawak
2(k)	2	2	4	3	4	2	3	4(P)	4	4	5	2	5	4	3	
2(k)	2	2	2	2	3	2	1	2(P)	2	5	1	2	2	1	2	
4(k)	4	4	3	2	1	2	3	4(P)	4	4	3	2	3	1	2	
3(k)	3	3	3	3	4	3	2	3(P)	3	2	2	5	2	2	3	
2(k)	2	2	2	2	3	2	1	2(P)	2	5	1	2	2	1	2	
4(k)	4	4	3	2	1	2	3	4(P)	4	4	3	2	3	1	2	
3(k)	3	3	3	3	3	1	5	2(P)	4	2	3	4	5	3	5:	
4(G)	•	•	•	•	•	•	•	4(P)	4	3	2	4	2	4	3	pengisep (pengiwan)
4(k)	4	3	2	5	5	4	3	4(P)	4	3	2	4	2	4	3	
2(k)	2	2	2	2	3	2	1	2(P)	2	5	5	5	4	3	5	
4(k)	5	3	5	4	5	3	5	4(P)	5	4	4	3	3	4	3	
2(k)	2	2	4	3	4	2	3	4(P)	4	4	5	3	5	4	3	
2(k)	2	2	2	2	3	2	1	2(P)	2	5	5	2	2	1	2	
4(k)	4	4	3	2	4	2	3	4(P)	4	4	3	2	3	1	2	
3(k)	3	2	1	3	3	1	5	2(P)	4	2	3	4	5	3	5	
4(G)	•															
4(G)	•	4	•	4	•	5	•	4(k)	•	5(P)	•	2	•	5(P)	•	pengaras
4(G)	4	4	4	4(k)	4	5(P)	5	4(k)	4	5(P)	5	2(k)	2	5(P)	5	
5(G)	2	2	1	2(P)	2	5	1	4(k)	2	2(P)	1	2(P)	4	4(P)	3	
4(G)	4	4	5	3	3	1	5	1(k)	1	5(P)	2	2	2	1(P)	5	
4(G)	4	5	4	3	3	3	1	1(k)	1	5(P)	2	2	5	5(P)	4	
5(G)	5	1	5	1	1	5	2	2(k)	2	5(P)	2	2	4	4(P)	3	
4(G)	4	4	5	3	3	1	5	1(k)	1	5(P)	2	2	4	4(P)	3	
4(G)	4	4	5	3	3	1	5	1(k)	1	5(P)	2	2	1	5(P)	2	

APPENDIX 4. NUCLEAR TONES TO GAMELAN COMPOSITIONS

(24. gending Ludira, *continued.*)

```
4   .   4   2   4   2   4   3              pengechèt
G           k   P       P
3   4   4   5   3   1   1   5
G           k   P       P
3   4   4   1   3   1   1   4
G           k   P       P
3   3   5   5   3   3   5   2
G           k   P       P
1   1   3   3   1   1   3   1
G           k   P       P
4   4   4   1   4   1   4   3
G           k   P       P
4
G
```

25. Pengaras and pengechèt, gending Mèrong; Payangan village

```
2   .   2   2   2   2   3   3   2   2   3   5   5   5   3   4    pengaras
G           k       P       k       P       k       P
2   2   2   2   2   2   3   3   2   2   3   5   5   2   2   3
G       P   k       P       k       P       k       P
2   2   3   5   3   3   2   2   2   3   2   2   2   3   3   5
G               P               k               P
3   3   3   3   3   3   2   2   2   3   2   2   2   3   2   4
G               P               k               P
5   5   5   4   5   3   3   5   3   3   2   2   2   2   5   1
G               P               k               P
4   4   4   3   4   4   4   3   1   1   3   1   1   1   4   4    pengechèt Selisir
G               P               k               P
```

```
‖: 2   2   2   4   2   4   2   2
   G           k   P       P
   2   2   2   2   5   1   3   1
   G           k   P       P
   5   1   3   1   5   3   2   1
   G           k   P       P
   3   5   4   5   3   2   4   4
   G           k   P       P
   1   1   1   4   1   4   1   2
   G           k   P       P
   2   2   2   2   5   1   3   1
   G           k   P       P
   5   1   3   1   5   4   2   1
   G           k   P       P
   3   5   4   5   3   2   5   5 :‖     lipet-lipetan malih
   G           k   P       P           (repeat several times)
   1
   G
```

409

B. GENDING GANGSARAN

1. Tabuh Talōh; Payangan village

4	.	4	1	4	1	5	2	4	4	3	1	5	2	1	3
G				k		P		k		P		k		P	
2	2	2	4	3	2	4	3	1	1	4	3	2	4	3	5
G				k		P		k		P		k		P	

4	4	4	5	3	1	1	2
G				k	P		P
4	4	2	2	5	2	1	3
G				k	P		P
2	2	2	4	3	2	4	3
G				k	P		P
1	1	4	3	2	4	3	5
G				k	P		P
4	4	4	5	3	1	1	2
G				k	P		P
4	4	2	1	5	2	1	3
G				k	P		P
2	2	2	4	3	2	4	2
G				k	P		P
1	1	4	3	2	4	2	3
G				k	P		P
4	4	4	5	3	1	1	2
G				k	P		P
4	4	2	1	5	2	1	3
G				k	P		P
2							
G							

2. Tabuh Talōh; Payangan village

2	.	2	4	2	4	2	2
G				k	P		P
2	2	2	1	2	4	4	1
G				k	P		P
5	5	1	3	1	2	5	1
G				k	P		P
4	4	1	2	5	1	4	3
G				k	P		P
2	2	2	4	2	4	2	2
G				k	P		P
2	2	2	1	2	4	4	1
G				k	P		P
5	5	2	3	1	2	5	1
G				k	P		P
4	4	1	2	5	1	4	3
G				k	P		P
2							
G							

3. Gending Silir; Batuan village

‖: 3	3	3	4	2	5	3	4
G					P		P
2	4	2	4	2	4	2	3
G					P		P
1	1	1	2	1	5	2	5
G					P		P
4	3	2	5	4	3	2	1 :‖
G					P		P
3	3	3	4	2	5	3	4
G					P		P
2	4	2	4	2	4	2	3
G					P		P
1	1	1	2	1	5	2	5
G					P		P
4							
G							

4. Gending Silir; Batuan village

‖: 2	3	3	2	1	4	4	1
G					P		P
2	3	3	2	1	4	4	2
G					P		P
4	4	1	1	4	4	1	4
G					P		P
2	4	4	2	2	4	2	1 :‖
G					P		P
2	3	3	2	1	4	4	1
G					P		P
2	3	3	2	1	4	4	2
G					P		P
4	4	1	1	4	4	1	4
G					P		P
2							
G							

5. Gending Silir; Batuan village

```
‖: 2   2   2   2   5   1   3   1
 ·                     P       P
   G

   5   1   3   1   5   5   2   1
   G               P       P

   3   5   2   5   3   2   4   3
   G               P       P

   1   4   4   1   1   4   1   2 :‖
   G               P       P

   2   2   2   2   5   1   3   1
   G               P       P

   5   1   3   1   5   5   2   1
   G               P       P

   3   5   2   5   3   2   4   3
   G               P       P

   1
   G
```

6. Gending Tembung; Batuan village

```
   1   ·   2   4   2   4   2   5
   G                   P       P

‖: 1   5   2   4   2   4   1   5 :‖   pengawak
 ·                     P       P
   G

   1   5   2   2   2   2   3   1       pengelik,
   G               P       P          (high register
                                      of trompong)
   5   5   5   1   2   2   3   1
   G               P       P

   5   5   5   1   5   1   5   1
   G               P       P

   3   4   4   3   2   5   5   2
   G               P       P

   4   4   4   5   4   5   5   1
   G               P       P

   3   1   1   3   2   5   1   4
   G               P       P

   3   4   4   3   2   5   5   2
   G               P       P

   4   5   2   5   3   3   3   4
   G               P       P

‖: 1   5   2   4   2   4   2   5 :‖   pengawak
 ·                     P       P
   G

   1
   G
```

412

APPENDIX 4. NUCLEAR TONES TO GAMELAN COMPOSITIONS

7. Gending Tembung; Batuan village

2	•	4	2	5	2	5	4	
G					P		P	
‖: 2	3	4	3	5	2	5	4 :‖	pengawak
G					P		P	
‖: 2	2	2	3	2	3	2	1	pengelik
G					P		P	
5	5	5	2	5	2	5	1	
G					P		P	
2	2	2	3	2	3	2	1	
G					P		P	
5	3	3	3	3	4	5	1	
G					P		P	
5	5	5	2	5	2	5	4 :‖	
G					P		P	
‖: 2	3	4	3	5	2	5	4 :‖	pengawak
G					P		P	
2								
G								

8. Gending Tembung; Batuan village

1	2	3	2	4	1	4	1	
G					P		P	
‖: 1	2	3	1	4	1	4	2 :‖	pengawak
G					P		P	
‖: 1	1	1	2	1	2	1	1	pengelik
G					P		P	
4	4	4	1	4	1	4	2	
G					P		P	
1	1	1	2	1	2	1	1	
G					P		P	
4	2	2	2	2	3	3	2 :‖	
G					P		P	
4	•	4	1	4	1	4	2	
G					P		P	
‖: 1	2	3	1	4	1	4	2 :‖	pengawak
G					P		P	
1								
G								

C. DANCE *OSTINATOS*

1. Baris (Each *ostinato* is repeated indefinitely.)

a) gilakan

1. 5	2	1	3	2	5	3	4
G				G	P		P
5							
G							

2. 5	3	4	3	2	5	3	4
G				G	P		P
5							
G							

b) bapang

1. 1	4	3	4	5	4	3	2
G				P			
1							
G							

2. 4	5	1	5	4	3	2	5
G				P			
4							
G							

3. 2	5	4	3	2	3	1	3
G				P			
2							
G							

4. 2	4	5	4	3	2	1	4
G				P			
2							
G							

5. 2	3	5	4	3	2	4	3
G				P			
2							
G							

6. 5	2	4	5	2	1	3	2
G				P			
5							
G							

APPENDIX 4. NUCLEAR TONES TO GAMELAN COMPOSITIONS

2. Tōpèng (Each *ostinato* is repeated indefinitely.)

gilakan

```
1. 4   2   4   2   4   2   3   4     5   3   5   4   3   4   2   3
   G                                 G               P       P
   4
   G

2. 1   4   1   4   1   4   5   1     2   3   2   4   3   1   4   5
   G                                 G               P       P
   1
   G

3. 5   4   3   5   4   3   5   1     2   4   2   4   2   4   2   4
   G                                 G               P       P
   5
   G

4. 3   4   3   4   5   4   5   1     2   3   2   1   5   3   5   4
   G                                 G               P       P
   3
   G

5. 5   1   2   3   2   4   3   1
   G           G   P       P
   5
   G

6. 5   1   2   1   5   1   4   1
   G           G   P       P
   5
   G

7. 3   4   5   4   3   2   1   4
   G           G   P       P
   3
   G
```

II. Gending Semar Pegulingan.

1. Lagu Petanuan, tabuh 3 pegambuhan; Payangan village

pengawak

```
‖: 3 · 3 3 3 4 3 2 3 3 4 3 4 1 1 2 1 1 1 1 2 2 5 4 5 5 5 4 3 3 3 4
  P
   3 3 3 3 3 3 2 3 4 4 4 3 5 5 3 2 1 1 3 3 1 3 3 2 3 3 3 2 3 3 1 5
   k
   4 4 4 4 5 5 2 1 5 1 4 5 1 2 5 1 3 3 3 3 3 3 3 4 3 3 2 1 3 3 1 5
   k
   4 4 1 2 3 3 3 3 4 4 4 4 4 4 4 3 1 1 1 3 3 5 5 4 5 5 5 4 3 1 3 3 2 :‖
   k
   3
   P
```

pengechèt

```
‖: 3 3 3 4 1 2 5 4 3 2 4 5 1 3 3 3
  P                     k
   3 5 5 4 3 2 3 3 4 1 4 4 1 3 5 4 :‖
   k                 k
   3
   P
```

2. Lagu Lasem, tabuh 3 pegambuhan; Payangan village

pengawak

```
‖: 1 · 1 1 1 2 1 5 1 1 3 4 2 2 3 1 1 1 3 4 2 2 3 1 4 4 5 3 4 1 1 5
  P
   1 1 1 2 3 3 2 5 5 5 2 2 5 2 2 1 2 2 2 3 1 1 3 4 2 2 2 3 1 1 3 4
   k
   2 2 2 3 1 1 3 4 2 2 5 4 1 3 2 5 5 5 5 4 1 1 4 3 3 3 5 3 5 1 1 5
   k
   1 2 5 4 2 2 2 5 5 5 3 4 4 3 1 2 1 1 1 2 3 3 2 5 5 2 2 3 3 1 3 2
   k
   1 · 3 3 3 3 3 4 3 3 5 3 4 4 5 3 4 4 5 3 4 4 5 3 1 1 2 5 1 3 4 2
   P
   3 3 5 3 4 4 5 3 1 1 2 5 1 2 4 2 3 3 5 3 4 5 3 4 5 5 3 3 4 2 2 5
   k
   1 1 1 1 1 1 1 5 1 1 2 2 1 2 5 4 2 2 2 2 2 2 2 3 2 2 5 4 1 3 4 2
   k
   3 3 3 3 3 4 2 3 4 4 4 2 3 2 4 3 2 2 2 2 4 4 5 4 2 2 5 5 4 1 1 2 :‖
   k
   1
   P
```

pengechèt

```
‖:3 4 3 4 3 4 1 3 3 4 1 3 3 3 5 1
  P                 M
  1 1 1 5 2 3 2 1 3 3 4 4 2 4 5 1
  k               k (mipil)
  1 3 1 3 1 3 4 5 1 3 4 5 1 2 3 5
  P                 M
  2 1 2 1 2 1 2 1 5 1 4 4 1 3 5 4.:‖
  k               k (mipil)
  3
  P
```

3. Lagu Sumbambang Java, tabuh 3 pegambuhan; Payangan village

pengawak

```
‖:2 • • • • • • • 1 • 5 3 1 1 4 2 4 4 4 4 5 5 5 3 4 4 3 3 2 2 1 2
  P
  3 3 3 3 3 3 3 4 5 5 4 4 5 4 3 2 3 2 1 5 5 1 4 1 1 1 3 3 4 4 3 4
  k
  5 5 5 5 5 5 5 4 5 5 5 5 5 5 5 4 5 5 5 5 5 5 5 5 4 5 5 4 4 5 5 3 2
  k
  3 3 3 2 5 5 3 2 4 4 4 3 5 5 3 2 1 2 3 3 4 4 5 4 4 4 5 5 3 4 5 4
  k
  5 • • • • • • • 2 2 2 2 3 3 3 4 5 5 5 5 1 1 4 3 4 4 1 2 3 1 4 3
  P
  2 2 2 2 3 3 3 4 5 5 5 4 3 2 3 4 5 5 5 4 3 2 3 4 5 5 5 4 3 2 3 4
  k
  3 3 4 2 1 1 1 2 3 3 2 1 3 2 1 5 1 1 5 2 1 1 4 5 4 4 3 3 2 2 3.4
  k
  3 3 3 2 3 3 3 4 5 5 4 4 5 4 3 2 3 2 1 5 1 1 4 1 1 1 3 3 4 4 3 3.:‖
  k
  2
  P
```

pengechèt

```
‖:2 3 1 1 4 5 3 2 3 3 5 3 3 1 1 1
  P               k
  2 1 2 1 2 1 1 1 4 4 4 3 2 4 4 5
  k               k
  5 3 5 3 5 3 5 3 5 4 5 3 5 3 5 5
  P               k
  3 1 3 3 1 1 4 2 3 3 5 3 3 1 1 1.:‖
  k               k (mipil)
  2
  P
```

417

4. Lagu Tabuh Gari, tabuh 3 rangkep; Payangan village

penyumu

```
4  1  3  5  3  1  3  1  4  2  4  2  5  3  5  3  5  4  5  3  3  4  2  3  4  4  4  3  2  4  3  2
P                          M                                            M
```

pengawak

```
5  .  .  .  2  3  2  4  5  1  5  1  2  4  2  3  4  4  4  4  2  2  4  5  1  5  3  4  3  5  4
P                                            k                 M
3  2  2  3  2  1  5  4  3  4  3  4  5  1  5  3  4  4  3  5  4  3  1  2  5  1  4  3  2  5  2
k                 M                          k  (mipil)
2  .  .  .  .  .  .  3  4  3  2  3  5  5  4  5  .  5  3  3  2  5  1  2  3  2  4  3  2  1  5
P                                            k                 M
2  .  2  5  3  2  1  5  2  1  5  5  2  4  5  4  3  4  3  2  4  .  5  4  3  2  2  5  5  2  5  1
k                 M                          k  (mipil)
2  .  .  .  .  .  .  3  4  3  2  4  4  5  4  3  2  2  2  2  5  1  4  3  .  3  2  2  1  5  4
P                                            k                 M
3  4  3  4  5  1  5  3  4  2  5  1  2  4  2  3  4  4  4  4  4  3  3  2  .  3  .  3  .  2  .
k                 M                          k  (mipil)
```

pengechèt

```
5  5  2  2  5  5  2  3  4  3  4  3  5  4  3  2
P                 k           M
3  2  3  1  3  2  3  1  3  4  5  5  4  2  2  3
k           M     k           M
5  1  3  3  5  .  3  1  2
k           M     P
```

Appendix 5. Selected bibliography

Extensive bibliographies pertaining to Indonesian music are available in Mantle Hood's *Patet in Javanese Music*, and Jaap Kunst's *Music in Java*. Titles included here have been selected for their more direct bearing on Bali, both in regard to music and to general culture.

Bali, Studies in Life, Thought, and Ritual, by Dutch Scholars of the Twentieth Century; Vol. 5 of the series, *Studies on Indonesia*, The Hague and Bandung, W. van Hoeve, 1960.

Belo, Jane. *Bali: Temple Festival*, New York, J. J. Augustin, 1953.

——— . *The Balinese Barong*, New York, J. J. Augustin, 1950.

Bhawanagara, Singaraja, Bali, Kirtya Liefrinck- v. d. Tuuk. A monthly periodical published in Malay and Balinese, with articles pertaining to different aspects of Balinese culture written by a small group of young Balinese intellectuals. It ran from 1931 to 1937.

Covarrubias, Miguel. *Island of Bali*, with an album of photographs by Rose Covarrubias, New York, Alfred A. Knopf, 1942.

Crawfurd, John. *History of the Indian Archipelago*, 3 vols. Edinburgh, Archibald Constable, 1820.

Goris, R. *Bali*, published by the Government of the Republic of Indonesia. New English edition in press.

Handbook of Indonesia, Cornell University, 1961.

Hiss, Philip Hanson. *Bali*, New York, Duell, Sloan, and Pearce, 1941.

Hood, Mantle. *The Nuclear Theme as a Determinant of Patet in Javanese Music*, Groningen, Djakarta, J. B. Wolters, 1954.

Kennedy, Raymond. *The Ageless Indies*, New York, The John Day Co., 1942.

Kunst, Jaap. *Around von Hornbostel's Theory of the Cycle of Blown Fifths*, Amsterdam, Indisch Instituut, 1949.

——— . *The Cultural Background of Indonesian Music*, Amsterdam, Indisch Instituut, 1949.

——— . *Ethnomusicology*, 3d ed. The Hague, Martinus Nijhoff, 1959.

——— . *Music in Java*, trans. by Emile van Loo, 2d ed. 2 vols. The Hague, Martinus Nijhoff, 1949.

——— . *Supplement to the 3rd Edition of Ethnomusicology*, The Hague, Martinus Nijhoff, 1960.

——— , and Kunst-van Wely, C. J. A. *De Toonkunst van Bali, Deel 1*, Weltevreden, Koninklijk Bataviaasch Genootschap en G. Kolf, 1925; *Deel 2*, Weltevreden, Koninklijk Bataviaasch Genootschap en Albrecht, 1925.

McPhee, Colin. "The 'Absolute' Music of Bali," *Modern Music*, 12 (1936), 163–9.

——— . *Balinese Ceremonial Music, transcribed for two pianos; Pemoengkah, Gambangan, Tabuh Teloe*, New York, G. Schirmer, 1940.

——— . "The Balinese *Wajang Koelit* and its Music," *Djawa*, 16 (1936), 322–66.

——— . "Children and Music in Bali" in *Childhood in Contemporary Cultures*, Margaret Mead and Martha Wolfenstein, eds., Chicago, Chicago University Press, 1955.

——— . *A Club of Small Men*, New York, The John Day Co., 1948.

——— . "Dance in Bali," *Dance Index*, 7, Nos. 7, 8 (1948), New York, 1949.

——— . "The Five-Tone Gamelan Music of Bali," *Musical Quarterly*, 36 (1949), 250–81.

——— . *A House in Bali*, New York, The John Day Co., 1946.

Mead, Margaret, and Bateson, Gregory. *Balinese Character*, New York, New York Academy of Arts and Sciences, 1942.

———, and Wolfenstein, Martha. *Childhood in Contemporary Cultures*, Chicago, Chicago University Press, 1955.

Raffles, Thomas Stamford. *The History of Java*, 2 vols., London, Black, Parbury, and Allen, 1817.

Sachs, Curt. *The History of Musical Instruments*, New York, W. W. Norton, 1940.

———. *The Rise of Music in the Ancient World East and West*, New York, W. W. Norton, 1943.

Schlager, Ernst. "Bali," *Die Musik in Geschichte und Gegenwart*, *1* (1949–51), 1110–15.

Spies, Walter. "Bericht uber den Zustand von Tanz und Musik in de Negara Gianjar," *Djawa*, *16* (1936), 51–9.

———. "De Gamelan-wedstrijd te Gianjar . . . December 1938," *Djawa*, *19* (1939), 197 5207.

———, and Goris, R. "Overzicht van Dans en Tooneel in Bali," *Djawa*, *17* (1937), 205–27.

Stutterheim, Willem F. *Indian Influences in Old-Javanese Art*, London, The India Society, 1935.

Van der Tuuk, H. N. *Kawi-Balineesch-Nederlandsch Woordenboek*, 4 vols., Batavia, Landsdrukerij, 1912.

Vlekke, Bernard H. M. *Nusantara, A History of Indonesia*, The Hague and Bandung, W. van Hoeve, 1959.

Zoete, Beryl de, and Spies, Walter. *Dance and Drama in Bali*, with a Preface by Arthur Waley, New York, Thomas Yoseloff, 1958.

Appendix 6. Recordings

Dancers of Bali. Gamelan orchestra from the village of Pliatan, Bali, under the direction of Anak Agung Gede Mandera, Columbia LP, ML 4618. Side 1: Overture Kapi-Radja, Angklungan, Tumulilingan, Baris. Side 2: Gambangan, Kebyar, Gender Wayang-Angkat-angkatan, Legong, a) Lagu Chondong, b) Pengipuk, c) Garuda.

Music of Bali. Recorded in Bali in 1953 by the Pierre Ivanoff Expedition, Period LP, SPL 1913. Side 1: 1. Kebyar, 2. Baris, 3. Legong (Tobatelou), 4. Legong (Garouda), 5. Polayalol (Dancing Lesson). Side 2: 1. Song, 2. Gengong (Jew's Harp), 3. Wayang Koulit (Shadow drama). Good material, poor recording, ridiculous jacket notes.

Music of Bali. Gamelan orchestra from Pliatan, Indonesia, directed by Anak Agung Gede Mandera, Westminster LP, XWN 2209. Side 1: 1. Overture Kapi Raja, 2. Tumulilingan, 3. Kechak (male chorus). Side 2: 1. Lègong. Side 3: 1. Gambangan and Kebyar, 2. Olèg, 3. Barong. Side 4: 1. Jangèr, Endé, Baris.

Music of Java and Bali. Recorded by students of the Institute of Ethnomusicology at University of California, Los Angeles, under the direction of Mantle Hood. Columbia LP.

The following recordings, some of which have been discussed in the present book, are among the Balinese titles in the Record Archives of the Institute of Ethnomusicology at University of California, Los Angeles. The recordings given below were made in Bali by Odeon and Beka in 1928. Any of these titles are available on tape for study purposes for a nominal sum. They may not be used commercially.

Gamelan Angklung, Mōgan village
   Bèrong pengawak
   Bèrong pengechèt
   Pis Satus Selaka Loyang
   Sekar Jepun
Gamelan gong kebyar, Gamelan gong Belaluan, Badung
   Kebyar Ding; 1 Kebyar
             2 Surapati
             3 Onchang-onchangan
             4 Batèl
             5 Pengrang-rangan
             6 Pengawak dan pengechèt
   Churik Ngaras
   Kembang Langkuas
   Lagu Kebyar
Gamelan pelègongan, Kuta village
   Chalonarang; Ngalap Basé
             Sisiya
             Tundjang
   Gegènggongan
   Gontèng

Pelugon (gambangan)

Gamelan Semar Pegulingan, banjar Titih, Badung

    Lagu Ginanti

    Lagu Lasem

    Lagu Tabuhgari

Gambuh, Sesétan village

    Bapang Selisir

    Biakalang Perabangsa

    Peperangan sira Panji dengan Perebangsa

Gendèr Wayang, Kuta village

    Alas Harum

    Angkat-angkatan

    Merak Ngilo

    Sekar Ginotan

    Seléndro

    Pemungkah

Kekawin; singer and translator from Griya Pidada, Klungkung

    Kekawin Ramayana

    Kekawin Bharata-Yuddha

Kekawin with gamelan interludes; singer and translators with the gamelan gong of Belaluan

    Matinya Sang Abimanyu (Bharata-Yuddha)

    Menangis Perabu Judistira (Bharata-Yuddha)

    Sang Rama Déwa (Ramayana)

ILLUSTRATIONS

1. Village kulkul tower

2. Bebendé, gong lanang, and gong wadon

3. *Gamelan bebōnangan*, showing the kendang wadon and kendang lanang

4. Réong players in the *gamelan bebōnangan*

5. Bōnang players in the *gamelan bebōnangan*

6. Chèngchèng players in the *gamelan bebōnangan*

7. Gong wadon and gong lanang in the *gamelan bebōnangan*

8. *Gamelan gong gedé* of Sulaan village, formerly belonging to the court of Klungkung

9. Jegogan, jublag, and penyachah in the *gamelan gong gedé*

10. Jegogan, jublag, and penyachah in the *gamelan gong gedé*

11. Saron or gangsa jongkok in the *gamelan gong gedé*

12. Trompong in the *gamelan gong gedé*

13. Saron or gangsa jongkok in the *gamelan gong gedé*

14. Sarons, trompong, bendé, and gongs, in the *gamelan gong gedé*

15. Réong in the *gamelan gong gedé*

16. Pōnggang in the *gamelan gong gedé*

17. Kempli in the *gamelan gong gedé*

18. Kendang lanang and kendang wadon in the *gamelan gong gedé*

19. Kendang wadon and kendang lanang in the *gamelan gong gedé*

20. Chèngchèng group in the *gamelan gong gedé*

21. Bendé, gong wadon, gong lanang, and kempur in the *gamelan gong gedé*

22. Trompong player, as shown in a modern temple relief in north Bali

23 and 24. Trompong player

25. Suling gambuh

26. Suling gambuh

27. Suling gambuh, as shown in a stone figure at Sukawati village

28. Suling players in the *gamelan gambuh* at the court of Tabanan

29. Rinchik, kelenang, and kenyir in the *gamelan gambuh*

30. Rebab in the *gamelan gambuh*

31. Kelenang and kenyir in the *gamelan gambuh*

32. Gumanak and kangsi in the
    gamelan gambuh

33. Gumanak   34. Kangsi

35. *Gamelan pelègongan* of Kapal village

36. Gendèr limolas in the *gamelan pelègongan*

37. Jegogan in the *gamelan pelègongan*

38. Jublag or chalung in the *gamelan pelègongan*

39. Penyachah in the *gamelan pelègongan*

40. Saron or gangsa jongkok in the *gamelan pelègongan*

41. Kelenang in the *gamelan pelègongan*

42. Kajar in the *gamelan pelègongan*

43. Kajar and suling gambuh, as shown in stone figures at Sukawati village

44. Kemong and kempur in the *gamelan pelègongan*

45. Kendangs, wadon and lanang, in the *gamelan pelègongan*

46. Rinchik and kempur in the *gamelan pelègongan*

47. Kajar, kempli, rinchik, kempur, and gentorak in the *gamelan pelègongan*

48. Gentorak and rinchik

49. Paired drums, as shown in the reliefs at Borobudur

50 and 51. Kendangs lanang and wadon in the *gamelan pelègongan*

52. Preparation for dag stroke

53. Dag accent

54. Krèmpèng stroke

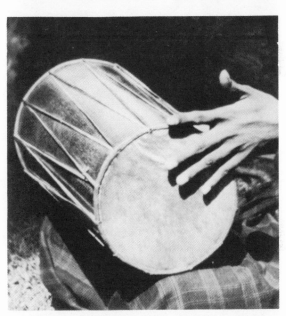

55. Krumpung stroke

56. Pek stroke

57. Gendèr and leading drum

58. Kendangs wadon and lanang

59. *Gamelan pelègongan*

60. Metallophone section of the *gamelan pelègongan* in Kuta village

61. Gendèr wayang ensemble

62. Three-tubed angklung

63. Four-tubed angklung

64. *Gamelan angklung* at Chulik village

65. Gendèrs in the *gamelan angklung*, Chulik

66. *Gamelan angklung* playing along the road

67. *Gamelan angklung*

68. The children's *gamelan angklung* in Sayan

69. Gendèrs in the *gamelan angklung*, Sayan village

70 and 71. Antique réong in the *gamelan angklung*

72. Horizontal réong in the *gamelan angklung*

73. Grantang

74. Chungklik and réong

75. Trompong misi bruk at Abang village

76. Charuk ensemble, with saron and charuk, at Selat village

77. Gambang ensemble at Tabanan village

78. Gambang

79. Saron or gangsa gambang

80. Saron and "trompong" in the *gamelan luang* at Singapadu village

81. Saron or gangsa in the *gamelan luang*

82. *Gamelan selundèng* at Tenganan village

83. Nyonyong in the *gamelan selundèng*

84. Petuduh in the *gamelan selundèng*

85. Petuduh keys

86. Guntang, kendangs, and suling in the *gamelan arja* at Pliatan village

87. *Gamelan arja*

88. Guntangs, "kempli" and "kempur"

89. Churing and kendangs in the *gamelan arja* at Singapadu village

90. Trompong and modern réong in the *gamelan gong kebyar* at Bulelèng

91. Modern réong

92. Trompong

93. Gangsa gantung in the *gamelan gong kebyar*

94. Chèngchèng in the *gamelan gong kebyar*

95 and 96. Kendang in the *game-lan gong kebyar*

97. Gendèr method of silencing the keys

98. Gangsa method of silencing the keys

99. Terbana

100. Gènggong

101. Rice pounders

102. Ngijengin and ngōtek

103. Ngijengin and ngeteg

104. Jogèd bumbung

105. Kulkul

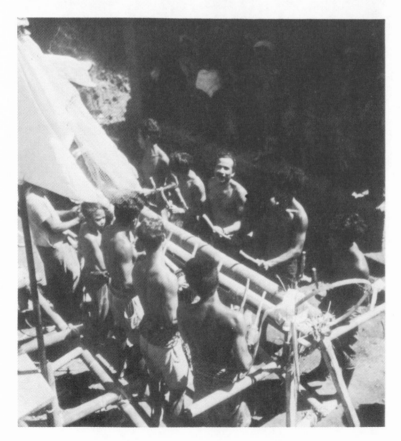

106. Kōprak

107. Kulkulan

108 and 109. Kebyar dance

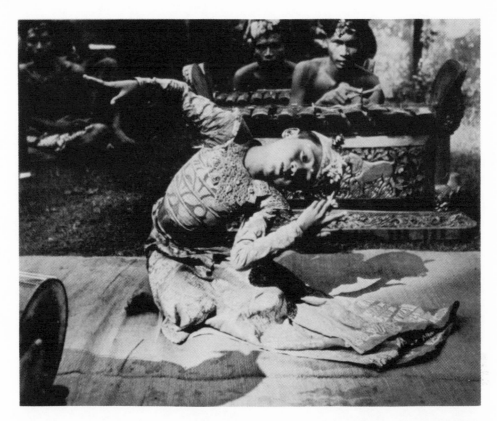

110 and 111. Kebyar dance

112. Gambuh players

113. Rangda

114. The barong

115. The raven in the lègong dance, at Lasem

116. Lègong dancers

117. Ceremonial baris

118. Rèjang dancers

119. Rèjang dancer

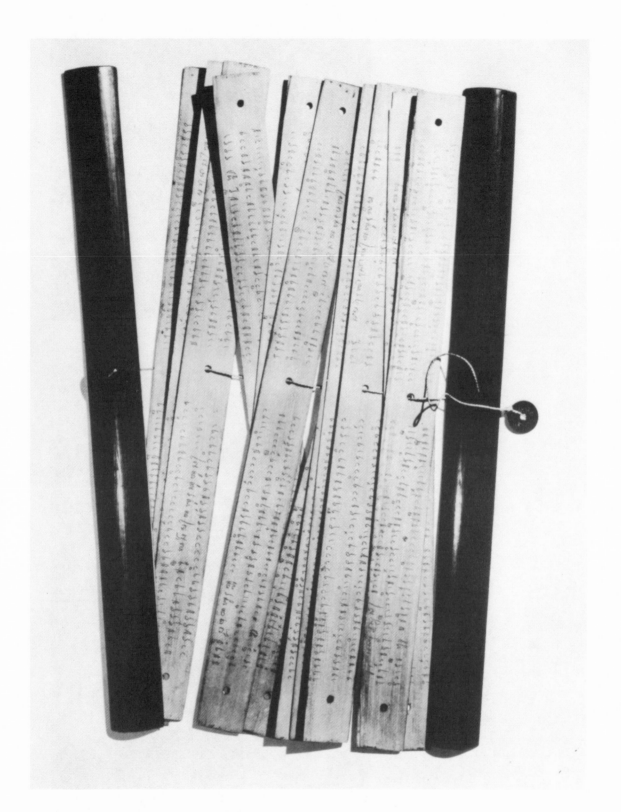

120. Lontar

Index

INDEX

Grove's *Dictionary of Music and Musicians*, cited, xv n.
Guderug, dance, 13
Gumanak, idiophone, 33, 121
Guntang, zither, 24, 34; described, 294–95

Harmony: chords in *gambang* figuration, 276; *réong* chords, 338–40
Harp, kite, 35
Hinduism, 3–4. *See also* India, Hindu
Hindu-Javanese empire, 3, 256
Holland, Dutch, 25; effect of rule in Bali, 4–5
Hornbostel, Erich Maria von, xiv, xv n., 27 n.
Houtman, Cornelius de, 25

I Lotring, composer, xvii, 62, 152, 165, 197, 204, 227, 348; biographical sketch of, 308; compositional method of, 308–09; music described, 309–27
I Lunyah, musician, xvii, 59, 73 n., 92, 124, 146, 148
I Sampih, dancer, xvi
Idiophones, 27. *See* Bells; Cymbals; Gong chimes; Gongs; Metallophones; Rattles; Slit drums; Stamping tubes
Improvisation, xvii, 66–68
India, Hindu: trade with Indonesia, 3–4; influence in Bali, 11, 13, 16, 62, 113; epics, 11, 14; music, 73. *See also* Hinduism; Hindu-Javanese empire
Instruments: materials of manufacture, 23–24, 26 (*see* Bamboo; Brass; Bronze; Coconut shells; Iron; *Nangka;* wood); main categories of, 27
Inversion, techniques of, 141
Iron, use in instruments, 258
Islam, 3, 4

Jaba, social class, 13
Jangèr, dance, xviii, 34
Java, Javanese, 3, 23, 24, 25, 26, 113, 235; music, xiv, xv, 4, 25, 75, scales, 37, notation of, 61, instruments of, 121, 155 n., 285; drama, 11; language (*kawi*), 14, 16, 24, 113, 225, 265, 280, 294; literature, 14, 256, 265; cultural influence on Bali, 113. *See also* Hindu-Javanese empire
Jegogan, metallophone, 31, 191–99 passim, 234, 239, 240, 244–53 passim, 282–87 passim, 293, 309, 342, 350
Jembrana, district, 5
Jews harp (*gènggong*), 255
Jogèd, dance, 7, 23, 32; described, 191; music of, 191–200. See also *Gamelan Pejogèdan*
Jublag, metallophone, 31, 329, 342, 350

Kali Durga, goddess, 10
Kajar, gong, 29, 118–19, 166–69, 201
Kangsi, cymbals, 33, 114, 121
Kantilan, metallophone, 31, 244
Karangasem, district, 5, 14, 32, 55, 234, 237, 239, 243 n., 244, 257, 265
Kaudern, W., *Musical Instruments of Celebes,* 23 n.
Kaula, social class, 13
Kawi, language, 14, 16, 24, 113, 225, 265, 280, 294
Kebyar, dance, 329. See also *Gamelan gong kebyar*
Kelènang (Klènang), gong, 29, 119–20, 151, 166, 295
Kemanak, Javanese instrument, 121
Kemong, gong, 29, 60 n., 152, 166, 310
Kempli, gong, 29, 191–201 passim, 234, 244; as name for *guntang,* 295
Kempur, gong, 28, 60 n., 118, 120, 191–201 passim, 234–47 passim, 248 n., 251, 252, 253, 310, 318; as name for *guntang,* 295
Kendang, drum, 33–34, 282. *See also* Drums (membranophones)
Kenyir, metallophone, 33, 114, 119–20
Kesatrya, aristocratic class, 13
Ketipluk, clapper drum, 35
Kichak, cymbals, 239
Kidung, chant, 265, 303. *See also* Index of Compositions
Kite-Flyers' Club, 6
Klungkung, district, 257
Kolenang, Javanese gong chime, 75
Kōprak, slit drum, 35
Korn, V. E., 243 n.
Kōtèkan figuration, 151, 152, 162–66, 175, 189, 192, 194, 203–13 passim, 255, 267 n., 282, 296, 309
Kulkul, slit drum, 24, 34–35
Kulungkung, district, 5
Kunst, Jaap, 23 n.; *De Toonkunst van Bali,* xiv, 269, 283; *Ethnomusicology,* xv; quoted, 24 n., 37; *Music in Java,* 27

Lagu, melody, 62. *See also* Index of Compositions
Lebeng, scale, 38–43 passim, 115, 137–43 passim
Lègong, dance play, 6, 7, 10, 19, 33, 113, 114, 140, 149; origin of, 13; choreography of, 150–51, 181–82; story basis of, 182; music of, 169, 182–89, 307–27 (see also *Gamelan pelègongan*); relation to *jogèd* dance, 191
Léko, dance, 13
Lewanas (gumanak), idiophone, 295
Liefrinck-v.d. Tuuk, Kirtya, 36 n.
Lintgensz, Aernoudt, quoted, 25

Index of Compositions

INDEX OF COMPOSITIONS